W9-AGC-975

JOE BROOKS

ON FISHING

JOE BROOKS
ON FISHING

Edited by
DON SEDGWICK

Foreword by
LEFTY KREH

THE LYONS PRESS

Guilford, Connecticut

An imprint of The Globe Pequot Press

The Lyons Press is an imprint of The Globe Pequot Press.

10 9 8 7 6 5 4 3 2 1

Printed in the United States of America

ISBN 1-59228-451-5

Library of Congress Cataloging-in-Publication Data is available on file.

Contents

Contents

II

Saltwater Fishing

Foreword

If you are an avid fly fisherman and under the age of fifty, chances are you have never heard of Joe Brooks, but you owe him a huge debt of gratitude. Until Joe Brooks arrived on the scene, most fly fishing was concentrated on freshwater trout in the streams of the eastern United States. Only a handful of fly fishermen were seeking bass or catching saltwater species. Travel to a foreign fishing destination meant a trip to Canada by car. Joe changed all of that! He was a true pioneer.

This book is a compendium of Joe's work. It is filled with the history of modern fly fishing, but the techniques that Joe so eloquently described are as valid today for catching the various species as they were when he wrote about them.

Above all else, Joe was a true gentleman. Talk to the many people who knew him well, and invariably they describe him as such. Joe was a tall and imposing man with broad shoulders, a flat belly, and the erect walk of a top sergeant. When he entered a room or you were in his presence, he exuded an almost regal air—which was totally unintentional. Despite his prodigious accomplishments in fly fishing, Joe was a humble man. He was also a superb athlete who, as a golfer at an early age, had a 4 handicap. He once bowled a perfect score of 300, and was even drafted by the Baltimore Orioles baseball team.

In 1945, Joe started writing an outdoors column for a small paper in Towson, Maryland. Joe then moved to Florida to become the executive director of the Metropolitan Miami South Florida Fishing Tournament, known nationally as The MET. At the time it was the largest fishing tournament in the world—and was one of the first tourneys to seriously promote the release of caught fish.

Soon after World War II, the government of Ontario, Canada recognized the economic value of bringing United States fishermen to their province. Mary Ainslie was director of travel and publicity for the Province of Ontario. She was also an excellent angler and writer. She set up some fishing trips for American outdoor writers, and Joe was one of those invited. It was love at first sight for Joe and Mary, and after a brief engagement they were married in Islamorada, Florida, with many well-known fishermen in attendance. It was a wonderful partnership. Joe helped Mary perfect her fishing techniques, and Mary, a talented businesswoman and writer, was able to help Joe. Together they would fish around the world. Later, Joe left The MET tournament to become the fishing editor for *Outdoor Life* magazine.

In the mid-1940s, most fly fishermen fished only the waters near home. A hundred-mile trip was a real expedition. Joe changed our fly-fishing world as no one else has. In 1939, Florida Keys Captain Bill Smith had caught a bonefish on a fly, but many considered it an accidental catch. In 1947, Joe announced through Allen Corison's outdoors column in the *Miami Herald* that he would intentionally catch a bonefish with a fly. He was guided by Captain Jimmie Albright, who was to become a legend among guides in the Keys. Joe caught two fish that day. One weighed eight pounds, and the other was a half pound heavier. The fly was tied by Red Greb, a well-known Miami fly fisherman.

For the next two decades, Joe fished for bonefish, tarpon, mutton snapper, and a host of other salt- and freshwater species. He wrote about his adventures in his outdoors column, and many sportsmen began to seek the same gamefish. In 1957, while fishing the Isle of Pines flats in Cuba, Joe caught the first permit taken on a fly. Not long after that, he caught a huge one in the Bahamas on a fly. At the time this was considered an impossibility.

Before the mid-1960s, there were no established standards for fly fishing. Three major organizations were formed at about the same time—each independent of the others—that were to change that. They were Trout Unlimited, the Federation of Fly Fishermen, and the Saltwater Flyrodders of America. At a meeting in the spring of 1965, Fred Schrier and a few local saltwater fly fishermen from Toms River, New Jersey invited Joe (regarded as the most important and influential person there), Charley Waterman, Harold Gibbs, Frank Woolner, Jim Green, Mark Sosin, Stu Apte, and me. The Saltwater Fly Rodders of America established the rules by which saltwater fly fishermen around the world now abide. Several of the senior advisors wrote glowingly about the organization and the rules, and chapters were formed as far away as California. But it was Joe's status that really got the ball rolling.

Joe and Mary began fishing the western United States for trout, and Joe wrote much about the fishing techniques, the people, and the West, which had streams filled with trout that few people were after. His influence was so great that the governor of Montana issued a proclamation indicating that Joe Brooks was to be known as Mister Montana.

Not content with opening up new fly-fishing waters only in North America, Joe and Mary journeyed to Africa, Central and South America, the South Pacific, and elsewhere in search of many different species in both fresh and salt water. Joe caught a monster brown trout on a popping bug at the southern tip of Argentina. He caught tiger fish in Africa—and it was decades later before fly fishermen began to seriously seek this species. Joe would cast his flies wherever on the planet he heard there were fish to be caught, whether it was in a cold mountain river, a jungle lagoon, or the open ocean.

Foreword

One of Joe's greatest gifts to fly fishermen is that he opened up the world to all those who followed. Fly fishermen today jump on airplanes to test the waters of the upper Amazon Basin, the trout streams and lakes of New Zealand, and the distant atolls of the South Pacific. But no one dared or thought of this until Joe opened the doors.

Perhaps his greatest accomplishment was helping others. There are hundreds of people still alive who can attest to his generosity. A huge impact on modern fly fishermen was Joe's ability to persuade outdoor writers to expand their horizons and then write about their experiences. For example, he convinced Charley Waterman and Stu Apte to try fishing for trout in the West. Both Florida writers got so hooked that they bought homes in Montana. He was my mentor, and the guiding hand who was most influential in my own career in fly fishing. Few people who met Joe Brooks were not affected by him.

What is so sad is that, though Joe did more than anyone to promote the fishing in the Florida Keys and in Montana, most of the fly fishermen (and those in the business) in these places today don't have any idea what great contributions Joe Brooks made to the fly fishing world. This compendium will help fly fishermen to better understand his many innovations—and if you follow his advice you will catch more fish and enjoy fly rodding even more.

Lefty Kreh
December 2003

Preface

Throughout history, fly fishing has remained the peak of the angler's art. Other weapons of attack on dwellers of lake and stream and ocean may come and go, but when a man has tried every one, if he is a philosopher at all, he will come back to the fly rod. For the light wand offers other inducement than merely winning the physical fight with wily trout or rambunctious bass or some hard-hitting denizen of the seas. The greatest enjoyment derived from the use of the fly rod is not necessarily the fish caught—although it is my contention that, given reasonably good fly fishing conditions, the fly rod will outfish any other rod—the greatest satisfaction lies, rather, in the performance of the cast, the dexterous use of the entire equipment, rod, line, leader, and fly.

No other method of fishing gives the angler the same pleasure from a well-delivered cast, or from watching the leader turn over out there at the end of the forward throw, dropping the fly gently upon the dish-calm surface of a pool. Or the thrill of laying out a long line into a stiff breeze. Or of seeing line and leader follow the direction of the rod and curve around to right or left, as the case may be, the better to light in just the pinpoint spot necessary to get a strike.

There is great challenge to floating a fly over a trout that is rising in a difficult place. To get a hit from such a fish, the fly must go over his position at the right speed, neither faster nor slower than the naturals drifting beside it, nor shifting sideways, but right down the groove, looking smart and unsuspect and very much like some real-life food he might expect to see floating over him. The satisfaction an angler derives from fooling a distrustful trout is one of the things that make fly fishing. As is the lift he gets when a smallmouth black bass whops his popping bug, thoroughly convinced that it is a real, live frog; or just plain mad enough to want to knock that annoying thing for a loop. And the solid thump of a fish hitting a streamer, be it in lake or stream or salt, telling the angler that the lure has gone through the water as he intended, looking just like something that fish wants to eat.

In no other branch of fishing is there this same direct, blow- to-blow contact with the fish, a personal contact that is maintained throughout the fight. For though the long, light rod, dipping and bobbing with every twist and turn of the fish will tire that lunker quicker than either plug rod or spinning rod, nevertheless the fly fisherman makes or breaks his own game by the way he handles the line coming from the reel, and by the amount of pressure he puts on the slender leader tippet, which is, of course, the weakest part of fly-fishing equipment.

Unfortunately there has been a tendency among writers to make fly fishing sound difficult and thus many a would-be fly man has been diverted from this most satisfactory sport. The purpose of this book is to show that with a little practice, fly fishing is, not easy, but quickly learned, and that once learned it pays dividends such as no other type of fishing can offer. If I stray sometimes from the old rule of thumb methods it is because I believe that like everything else, fly fishing changes. The day is past when young ladies learned to walk with a book balanced on their heads and fishermen learned to fly-cast with one tucked under their arm. Today's fly man is free of arm and free of hand. His free-arm casts are efficient and he takes his light fly rod where an old-timer never dared.

Fly fishing was originally limited almost entirely to trout and salmon waters, and most of the lore of fly fishing originates in these two species, but today the lover of the light wand carries it into all types of water. The sunnies and the basses were long since added to the trouts and salmons, and more recently fly rod enthusiasts have moved into the salt. Although to a degree it had been practiced by a few hardy adventurers for a long time, saltwater fly fishing has come into its own only in the past fifteen years. But in that time the tide has risen steadily until now fly fishermen the world over are throwing flies in many oceans and along countless beaches, bays, and lagoons. The saltwater fish definitely have it all over their sweet-water cousins when it comes to putting up a fight, and there are innumerable species on which the angler may test his skill.

We used to consider fish of 100 pounds to be beyond the limits of the fly fisherman's gear, but modern tackle has been adapted to the pursuit of big gamesters, and today the fly man goes after anything he can coax to his fly. With improved tackle, new, stronger knots, new types of flies, and new techniques, the fly rod in the salt has accounted in recent years for tarpon to 151 pounds, striped marlin to 148 pounds, sailfish to 136 pounds. And even as this is being written, some adventurous modern saltwater fly fisherman, somewhere, is out chasing more big game to add to the lists. It takes first-class physical condition to battle such monsters on light gear, and the odds are greater for losing the fish than for landing him, but the battle is worth it—thunderous, tumultuous, and awe-inspiring.

Other chargers of the seven seas have one or another attribute to make the heart jump, either great speed, phenomenal leaping ability, or tremendous power. The bonefish and permit, those flashing streaks of silver, lead the shallow-water speedsters by a city block, while the high-jumping ladyfish and dolphin will be remembered for their contortions for a long time. Found along both the east and west coasts of the United States is another gamefish that might have been especially designed for the fly man's pleasure—the striped bass. A great surface hitter to a popping bug, the big "bull" striper provides thrills no end when he swirls under and finally socks the angler's offering, and the ensuing fight will strain the fly tackle to the utmost.

But saltwater fly fishermen have proven that the fine tackle can take it, and anglers who used to look askance at anything over ten pounds as being too heavy for their way of angling will chase the biggest fish they can coax into a strike. It doesn't mean that they expect to land one of those giants (though secretly they always hope to do so) but it does mean that they want to be in on the soul-shocking hit, see the acrobatic antics of a high-jumping power-house, and watch the line melt from the reel as a silver rocket flashes across a shallow flat, headed pell-mell for the deep.

Throughout this book I have attempted to give the dope on those species of fish most commonly sought by fly fishermen—when, where, and how to fish for them, what to use and how to use it, and to supply any other special knowledge I have picked up during forty years of fly fishing. Most of all, through this book I hope to pass on to the reader some of the thrills and pleasure I have derived from fly fishing and to impart to him some of my own enthusiasm. Where you live, somewhere close to you may be found one or more of the great gamesters of which I write. Have a go at them. Good luck, and tight lines!

Joe Brooks

Introduction

Joe Brooks has been described as "the world's greatest angler" *and* "the world's best fly fisherman." If all this praise had been heaped on someone with a larger ego, he might have been a national franchise by the end of his life. But this was the same man who also passed up a promising career as a professional baseball player and was an impressive athlete in the worlds of football and boxing as well. His entry in the International Game Fishing Association (IGFA) Hall of Fame sums up his life. Brooks is described as "One of American's best all-around anglers and one who did as much to popularize fly fishing during his time as any single person in the United States." The citation also gives a sense of his personal character. "Brooks was known for his wit, his gentlemanly nature, and his devotion to sportsmanship and conservation. But even more, he was known as a master angler."

Joseph W. Brooks Jr. was born in Baltimore in 1901, the year that Theodore Roosevelt came to power and the world declared that this would be "the century of electricity after the century of steam." There was a sense of great expectations, that anything was possible. As a young boy, Brooks seemed to have taken up the challenge by showing that he was a great all-round athlete. In fact, it became evident in his teenage years that he had a chance to be a Major League pitcher. A Maryland native, Brooks had earned himself a spot on the Baltimore Orioles farm team. His decision not to pursue a professional sports career was not for lack of talent. At this time in his life, he seemed compelled to follow a more traditional career in business.

Sports were an avocation rather than a business for Brooks in his early years. But his baseball prowess was still alluded to in his later career as an editor at *Outdoor Life*. As fishing writer Scott Bowen writes in *Outdoor Life* online: "Joe was the magazine's Ted Williams. The guy fished everywhere, caught everything, and he was something of a world-class athlete in his time." He even had a passion for boxing, and could sometimes be found in the gym sparring with the legendary Jack Dempsey. But his real passion was taking a rod and reel and getting on the water.

Brooks talks about his first fishing adventures in his introduction to *Salt Water Fly Fishing*, published in 1950. "I was a dry fly fisherman from way back," he recalls, "brought up on eastern brown trout streams and imbued with all the lore of the purest of the purists." Then, in the late 1920s, he received his introduction to saltwater fly fishing. While working for the family's insurance business, he learned to fly-fish locally in the Susquehanna River below the Conowingo Dam. When the fish were not biting, he would move to other tributaries that flowed into the Chesapeake, such as the Severn, Bush, Gunpowder, and Middle rivers. His mentor was Tom Loving, a sportsman renowned for tying unusual but highly productive saltwater flies. "We used big bucktails for the stripers, smaller ones for the shad, and large streamers and popping bugs for the bass. We had rare sport, and as word got around other anglers began to take a more active interest."

Brooks picks up the story in *Salt Water Game Fishing*. "Tom Loving of Baltimore, Maryland, was the first to tie a fly expressly for a saltwater species. He tied a big bucktail for striped bass and he also tied a two-hooked shad fly, which he used in brackish water for shad.

I was lucky enough to fish with him in the 1920s, and I watched him take many stripers on his fly. We fished the grassy flats of Chesapeake Bay, casting in to banks and islands along sandy bars. We looked for single stripers chasing bait, all the while keeping a sharp eye offshore for school stripers, fingered by gulls. Those were the days: we had the whole place to ourselves, and fish were everywhere." This passion for bass fishing never wavered, and Brooks would later write about his exploits in his first angling book, in 1947, called *Bass Bug Fishing*.

In the late 1930s, Brooks finally had to admit that his real passion in life was fishing and not insurance. He also began to realize that his other passion—writing—could help to support his new vocation. It was a brave choice at the time, according to a later profile in *Collier's* magazine. "When Joe abandoned the insurance business to become a professional angler, skeptics called him foolish to stake his fishing future exclusively on his fly rod. They claimed that only certain kinds of fish would take a fly." Brooks spent the next thirty years of his life proving the skeptics wrong. He landed almost every popular freshwater fish imaginable, and more than seventy species of saltwater fish as well. "Any fish that can be taken on the surface with a hook and line," Brooks would say proudly, "will hit an artificial fly." It did not take long for Brooks to amass the records and the trophies to support his theory.

Brooks was paid modestly for his first writing. Fishing colleagues remember that he used to make $5 a week for his fishing columns in Baltimore newspapers. But as his fame and success were recognized, Brooks's assignments grew in size and scope. His work would soon appear in *Field & Stream*, *The Fisherman*, *True Fishing Annual*, *Fishing Waters of the World*, *Ashaway Sportsman*, and *The Salt Water Sportsman*. Later, he was hired as the outdoor editor for *The Baltimore Sun*. This allowed him to travel and write, and provided a base income for his magazine and book work.

In 1947, Brooks heard about a young river guide on the Potomac who was catching boatfuls of smallmouth bass using bait-casting gear. The guide's name was Lefty Kreh. Brooks booked a fishing trip with Lefty and was soon giving the younger fisherman a lesson in catching smallmouth with a fly rod. Kreh was so impressed that he asked Brooks to help him pick out his first fly-fishing outfit—a South Bend fiberglass rod. Kreh and Brooks became friends and professional colleagues, with Brooks mentoring the young man and helping to shape his career. Brooks and Tom McNally, the *Chicago Tribune's* outdoor editor, soon were encouraging Kreh to pursue a writing career, too. By 1951, he had sold his first column to the *Frederick News Post* and was on his way to becoming a successful fly-fishing writer and author.

Meanwhile, Brooks was using some of the good advice he'd shared in his bass book in 1947. "In September 1948," recalls Brooks, "I landed a striped bass which, as far as is known, is the largest striper ever taken on a fly rod. It came from the waters of Coos Bay, Oregon and weighed 29 pounds, 6 ounces." It took forty minutes to land the fish, which is documented by a photo of a smiling Brooks in the pages of the *Coos Bay Times*. Equally impressive, he caught it using a little shrimp popper that he had developed himself.

By this time, Brooks was becoming nationally renowned. He received invitations to test equipment for tackle manufacturers, and a request to manage the Metropolitan Miami South Florida Fishing Tournament in 1949. He was also traveling to Bermuda, where he continued to dazzle people with his skills as a fly fisherman. Soon he was logging close to 75,000 miles a year fishing. At this time, there were only a dozen writers who were covering outdoor subjects for American newspapers. Brooks and his colleague Kreh were traveling fishermen-writers, pioneers in the field, and becoming much in demand.

By 1953, Brooks was starting to write for *Outdoor Life*, one of the most successful and prestigious sporting journals of the day. His first piece was entitled "The Big Hole," about the Montana trout stream that he called "the best I ever fished." In fact, Brooks even developed a pattern of bucktails that he called his Blond series.

When he was fishing in the rough waters of the western United States, he found that these little gems worked magic on the wild and unpredictable rivers. Brooks maintained a lifelong admiration for the state of Montana and its exquisite fishing. Indeed, he died in 1972 while fishing in Montana and is buried in a cemetery overlooking the Yellowstone River, one of his favorites.

Brooks went where the fishing was good, and these adventures often took him north to Canada. On one of the trips in the 1940s, he met his future wife, Mary, who was also a good fly fisherman and his lifelong companion. Fans of Brooks will find her photo in several of his books, proudly holding up trout and other fish she ably caught on a fly rod. In fact, one of his stories in *Greatest Fishing* is facetiously entitled "Next Time We'll Leave the Ladies Home." On a trip to Cuba, the spouses of the fishermen upstage the "experts" and win their grudging admiration. Brooks dedicated his book *Salt Water Fly Fishing* to Mary, and includes her with admiration and affection in many of his stories.

With the advent of television, the producers were looking for dramatic material to fill air time and hold the attention of male viewers. Outdoor shows proved to be winners, and sporting material was a hit with advertisers, too. ABC's "American Sportsman" and "Wide World of Sports" television series became perfect vehicles for the ruggedly handsome and articulate Joe Brooks. (Some admirers even called him "Hemingway-esque.") They soon hired him as their fishing consultant. "Wide World of Sports" even filmed a classic impromptu fishing contest between two "teams": the famous guide Stu Apte and Joe Brooks, and guide Jimmie Albright (also a friend of Brooks) and A.J. McClane, author of the famous fishing encyclopedia. Apte was the guide for the stars of the day, including the legendary Ted Williams, so the competition made good drama for television.

It certainly did not hurt Brooks's career that he was continuing to set world records for the size and variety of his catches. He posted the IGFA world record for kawakawa in 1958. A year earlier he had landed a 19-pound, 8-ounce permit off Cuba, setting a record for a light tippet in its class. Brooks was fishing in Florida three years later with guide Stu Apte when he set the world record for the largest tarpon ever caught on a fly—148½ pounds. At the time, it was also the largest fish of any type ever caught on a fly rod. Brooks was inducted posthumously in 1998 into the IGFA Hall of Fame Museum, located in Dania Beach, Florida.

Brooks was considered an innovator in all aspects of fly fishing. "In his day," writes Scott Bowen in an online piece in *Outdoor Life*, "Joe Brooks was imaginative and willing to try new things. His championing of the Muddler Minnow, which originated in Montana, was an example." Brooks wrote about this fly in *Outdoor Life* in 1963, and the piece was reprinted in the magazine in May 1999. "When other anglers thought the pattern too plain or dull to catch fish," says Bowen, "Brooks took to the fly and figured out ways to make it work."

Brooks developed other flies when he thought that fish could be enticed by new combinations of feather and fur. Here's the recipe, for example, for an innovative little shrimp pattern that Brooks used for bonefish and tarpon:

> *Thread: Red.*
> *Tail: Two pink saddle tips.*
> *Body: Flat silver tinsel.*
> *Hackle: Pink saddle hackle palmered through body and clipped at top*
> *(hackle extends slightly beyond gap width).*
> *Head: Red.*

The fly was appropriately named the Joe Brooks Shrimp, and it can be found in several of the well-known books on fly tying.

Florida held an intense fascination for Brooks throughout his life. He lived in Islamorada for many years, and he also ran the MET fishing tournament. In 1964 he recruited his friend Lefty Kreh as the manager, which only added to the luster of the event. Much of the popularity and success of such tournaments was also the result of Brooks's now-classic book from 1950, *Salt Water Fly Fishing*. It was reprinted in 2000, with a new foreword by Joe Healy, editor of *Saltwater Fly Fishing* magazine. "This book gave generations of anglers an instruction manual on casting flies in the brine." Healy believed that Brooks had "legitimized the sport of saltwater fly fishing as a discipline," and exposed a mass audience of sportsmen to "an entirely new concept in fishing." Brooks led the charge by landing more than seventy species on flies in saltwater. During the 1960s he also helped to found a new organization, the Salt Water Fly Rodders of America.

Brooks met many influential people in the world of fishing through his adventures in Florida. One of them was Cam Sigler, a fly tackle developer and fellow member of the prestigious Miami Rod and Reel Club. Sigler referred to Brooks as "Gentleman Joe," says Joe Healy. Sigler claims that his entire career was influenced by his hero. "The things he taught were honesty and integrity, in whatever you do." As the sport of saltwater fly fishing gained popularity, the tackle changed and improved, and Sigler was just one of the many beneficiaries of the industry's growth.

When Brooks was not writing or hosting tournaments during the years 1961 to 1966, he was working on three different books, including his mammoth *Complete Guide to Fishing Across North America*. In 600 pages he takes readers on a comprehensive fishing trip of North America, state by state and province by province. In fact, he even includes Mexico, the Bahamas, and Bermuda. Brooks tells his readers where to find the best fishing spots, and what bait, lures, or flies to use in order to catch trophy fish. Although some of the map details and accommodations are now a bit out of date, this guide is still a classic for anyone who travels in search of good fishing.

When the position of fishing editor for *Outdoor Life* came up in 1968, Brooks was ready for the job. He had been contributing regularly since the publication of "The Big Hole" in 1953. By this point in his career he had also published eight books, including *Bass Bug Fishing* (1947), *Salt Water Fly Fishing* (1950), *Bermuda Fishing* (1957), *Greatest Fishing* (1957), *The Complete Book of Fly Fishing*

(1958), *The Complete Illustrated Guide to Casting* (1963), *A World of Fishing* (1964), and *Complete Guide to Fishing Across North America* (1966). He was also finishing his second-last book, *Salt Water Game Fishing* (1968). With all of his writing and television credentials, Brooks was the obvious choice for this quality sporting journal.

In October 1968, *Outdoor Life* published Brooks's first story as their fishing editor. "Heaven Is a Steelhead" is the colorful story of a trip from his home in Richmond, Virginia to the Babine River in British Columbia to fish for monster steelhead with flies. He called them "one of the greatest of all gamefish." Brooks's friend Bill McGuire landed eight in a single day, amidst the "dank smell of the forests" and "the racing rapids." Brooks described the Babine as "stern, remote, and wonderful," with wild fish that showed "a crimson slash along each side from gill cover to tail." This story was later included in *A Treasury of Outdoor Life*, published in 1975, and once again in *The Best of Outdoor Life*, published in 1998.

Brooks held the post of fishing editor for four years, helping to popularize many previously unknown waters, but always returning to some of his favorite haunts and his beloved fly rod. He also took time to give back to the sport that had been so good to him. He served as director of the Outdoor Writers Association of America. He also worked tirelessly to teach young boys how to fly-fish. Back in 1947 he had founded the Brotherhood of the Junglecock with other prominent fishermen in order to conduct three-day fishing workshops. Thousands of young men received their first instruction in fly fishing from Brooks and his colleagues.

In 1972 he attended his last workshop, the 25th anniversary of the organization. Brooks was the last living member of the founding group. Ed Koch, author of *Fishing the Midge*, was president of the Brotherhood that year. "It would be difficult to describe the pleasure he took in watching those youngsters learning fly tying, fly casting, and other angling skills. Joe would go out of his way, any time, any place, to assist a young angler on the path he so dearly loved," wrote Koch.

Brooks also used his platform at *Outdoor Life* to promote the concepts of good sportsmanship and conservation. When Brooks was on a river with friends, he always made sure that they had first crack at the best pools. As Vin Sparano, former editor-in-chief of *Outdoor Life*, once said, Brooks was "a guy without a hint of ego." His tireless efforts to protect important watersheds were honored by Trout Unlimited, and Brooks was cited by the states of Florida and Montana for his outstanding work in conservation.

During his last few years, Brooks worked on the project that many feel is his greatest achievement, *Trout Fishing*, published just before his death in 1972. This book has now achieved the status of a classic among fly fishermen. It was reviewed at the time by Arnold Gingrich, himself a great writer about fishing, who heaped praise on the work: "The master angler puts his reader through the best short course of trout appreciation and understanding that our day affords." Gingrich proclaimed that Brooks's history of trout fishing is "the best job of condensation since H.G. Wells wrote *The Outline of History* in one volume." The chapter entitled "The Trout We Fish For," which is included in this volume, is "so good it makes you almost start feeling for fins." Gingrich concluded that the book was "a worthy monument to a great fisherman." Even Ted Williams, who was notoriously rough on guides and had no shortage of ego, said: "This is a great book—I couldn't put it down." Dan Bailey, a leading authority on trout, said: "The information in this book is the best on the subject. Joe Brooks is not only a fine writer, but is one of the greatest fishermen of all time."

Joe Brooks died on September 20, 1972 in Rochester, Minnesota. Ed Koch, author of *Fishing the Midge*, remembers the day. "I received a phone call informing me that Joe had succumbed to a heart attack." Less than a week before, Brooks had offered praise about Koch's new book. "He thought I'd done a good job and believed that the book filled a need and would be of interest to many anglers. That was the greatest compliment I have received in twenty-five years of tying, teaching, and writing." A funeral service was held on Saturday, September 23 in Livingston, Montana, where Brooks spent his summers fishing. As Koch writes in the acknowledgments to his book, Brooks's rise to fame earned him the title of "the finest all-around fly fisherman in the world. He will live in angling history as one of the great men who have gone before."

But we'll leave the last words to Joe Brooks himself, writing in his foreword to *A World of Fishing:* "In my profession of writing about the outdoors I have been fortunate enough to cast my line in many of the world's great fishing waters. Yet I still find that each trip is better than the last. Each new stream offers fresh enchantment. Each new ocean presents further challenge." Although each of Brooks's pieces is written for those who fish, each one is also written for those who only dream of fishing in these sometimes exotic places. "Through my memories," he reflects, "may you fulfill your dreams."

Editor's Note

Although Joe Brooks wrote ten books during his lifetime, not all of them have been excerpted in this collection. A few are overly technical and do not include the stylish prose or warm anecdotal character of his other books. His Complete Guide to Fishing Across North America, *for example, is almost forty years out of date. Highways have "moved" and rivers have been dammed. Only the section from Brooks's beloved Montana has been included in this anthology, partly as an historical curiosity. Similarly, we have omitted wherever possible the travel instructions from excerpts taken from* A World of Fishing. *Travel by jet airplane and other sophisticated means has made Brooks's "exotic" locales even more accessible than he might have imagined. Finally, there are bound to be a few pieces that are cherished by Brooks fans that did not make it into this collection. It's the editor's hope that readers who are discovering Brooks for the first time will seek out his other books for additional days of pleasurable reading.*

Don Sedgwick

Joe Brooks

On Fishing

Freshwater Fishing

The Trout We Fish For

All the trouts are believed to be of Arctic marine origin, apparently having spread over a wide northern area in prehistoric times as they retreated southward during glacial periods. Authorities believe that the rainbow and cutthroat came south through the Bering Straits to the Pacific coast of the United States, while the brown trout migrated down between Norway and Greenland and spread along the European coast as far south as Spain. The first browns were brought to America in 1885 from Germany and were called German brown or Von Behr trout, after the member of the German Fisheries Society who sent them over. At about the same time browns were stocked in North America from Loch Leven, Scotland.

As the trouts ran before the extreme cold of the glacial era, seeking warmer water, they sometimes moved into rivers and on up to headwater lakes, and in both lakes and rivers they adapted themselves to freshwater living. Many of them stayed permanently in the fresh water but others, perhaps finding a shortage of food or perhaps stirred by some primeval memory of the ocean, traveled back down the rivers and out to sea. Yet when spawning time came, they returned to their river.

BROWN TROUT

The European brown trout that stays at home is still called *Salmo fario* by some ichthyologists, while the migratory or sea-run brown is called *Salmo trutta.* There is some variation in the coloring and markings of the brown trouts that occur in various water locations. In Loch Leven, Scotland, the fish have a somewhat silver coat as compared to the dark hues of the small burn trout found in the runs and becks and lochs of the Scottish Highlands. But if you take such a burn trout and put him in Loch Leven he will soon put on length and girth and blossom out in the same silvery sheen, all no doubt as a result of the increased food supply, plus, perhaps, some difference in mineral content in the water he is living in.

Similarly, in the Rocky Mountain states I have heard anglers insist that there are two definite kinds of brown trout, the German brown and the Loch Leven or lochie. These anglers have pointed out that one is heavier than the other, or darker, or wears different spots. In my own fishing I have not been able to differentiate enough to say whether the brown trout I have caught is a Loch Leven or came from the German stock. I have found much difference in coloration between one river and another and one lake and another. I have taken browns on which the spots were round, while on others they were more like stars. I've seen them with red dots and black ones, and with basic color ranging from light tan to dark brown. I've even fished for browns with apparent physiological differences, but which I believe are nevertheless simply members of the brown trout family. Such is the gillaroo, or "gizzard trout," I encountered while fishing the Drowse River between Lough Melvin and Donegal Bay on Ireland's west coast. While this trout wears the same outward dress as other browns, the gillaroo has a different stomach. Evidently at some time in its history the supply of aquatic insects, freshwater shrimp, and minnows fell off and the trout were forced to feed on the small snails that abound in the river and lough, and on which the trout still feed, in addition to the current standard food. The sharp points of the snails irritated and punctured the lining of the stomach, so nature took over and gradually the gillaroo built its defense. The walls of the stomach hardened so that it has the appearance of the gizzard of a fowl. If you press in on the stomach between the pectorals and the vent you can feel this hard place.

From a strictly scientific point of view I would like to discover if all these markings and other idiosyncrasies of the brown trout are indications of different ancient ancestors or merely mutations due to food and mineral content of the water they live in. But actually, as far as fishing goes, it does not concern the angler because the brownie is the same challenge in whatever guise you find him, spotted or starred, bright or dark.

I long ago lost my heart to the trouts as my favorite species to fish for, and of all the trouts I put the brown at the top of the list. The greatest single mistake made in the stocking of fish in the United States has been the insistence on rainbows over browns. Millions of small rainbows are dumped into streams every year, many of them dead before they even hit the water. So-called anglers follow the trucks and catch their limit fast, because hatchery-reared fish are easy to catch after such a dumping. And these fish reproduce so slightly that the program of stocking must go on year after year, with no possibility of increasing returns, to maintain even a few fish in the river for anglers to fish for. If the same time and effort and money, or even half of it, had gone into stocking brown trout we would have a basis of self-perpetuating fish that could survive even in some of our polluted waters and in waters that have become too warm for the more demanding rainbow.

The brown is the most adaptable of trouts, being able to withstand a wide range of temperatures, more pollution, and able, in general, to take care of itself as far as reproduction is concerned. There was ample proof of that for anyone who was in Montana during the earthquake of August 17, 1959, which dammed the Madison River for a few days and bared wide sections of the river bottom. As the water level lowered the fish were concentrated in pools where they

7

could readily be checked. In this, one of North America's most famous "rainbow streams," which is heavily stocked with rainbows every year, by far the greatest number of trout were browns. Big, fat and healthy. They still are.

But the brown trout is more difficult to raise in captivity, and costs more, so to keep the politicians happy, and let them announce how many millions of tiny fish they have fed into the rivers, we go on dumping rainbows and downgrading the brown as "too expensive to raise," and "cannibalistic." And the final argument is that the brown is too hard to catch.

To demolish each argument in turn: (1) if browns were stocked the cost would diminish in time, as the fish perpetuated themselves, which rainbows cannot do; (2) all fish are cannibalistic, but even so, I have never taken a brown whose stomach held a member of its own family; (3) the difficulty of getting a wily brown trout to take a fly is what keeps fly fishermen going to the river (while the bait and spin fishermen come into their own everywhere they find browns, which hit spinners and spoons with vigor). Every year the biggest trout taken in any given stream or lake will nearly always have fallen to the bait fisherman's worm or minnow.

Another argument I occasionally hear about browns is "they don't jump." Granted that, like the salmon, the rainbow is a fabulous aerial performer; but anyone who has caught browns in clean, fresh water, on flies, knows that they do indeed jump! More browns I have caught have jumped than have not jumped. In fact I could go to the superlative and say that *most* browns I have caught have jumped. A 14½-pounder I hooked in the Chimehuin River in Argentina jumped six times, straight up two feet into the air each time. My biggest, an 18½-pounder from the same river, jumped three times. All over the Rocky Mountains, wherever I have fished, the browns make spectacular jumps. I think that perhaps the mistaken belief about their lack of jumping ability originates with those who fish for the species in warm water or who use big, heavy spoons with weights, to get down deep.

Those big browns of the Chimehuin River in Argentina are an example of the adaptability of the brown trout. The original brown trout stock was sent down there from the United States in 1903. Now spread over twenty-five hundred miles of the Andes, they provide some of the world's greatest fishing for the species.

In 1935 a fine angler named John Lovell, who lived at Estancia Viamonte on Tierra del Fuego, at the southern tip of Argentina, had some trout eggs shipped from England. He planted them in several streams which empty into the south Atlantic. A few years later anglers were taking brown trout in all those rivers; and not much later the special bonus arrived. They began to catch big, fat, silvery brown trout that had obviously been out in the salt, putting on weight in the tremendous larder of the ocean. They were sea-run browns. Apparently that shipment of eggs had contained some of the European sea trout, as well as the river resident breed.

When I first fished the Rio Grande in the early 1950s, one of the streams which had been stocked on Tierra del Fuego, seven of us fishing one day in a big pool on the Estancia Maria Behety took two hundred trout, including both browns and rainbows. All the fish that appeared to be residents of the river were long and slim, and had big heads, the typical conformation of trout that are not getting enough food. Obviously there was not enough food in the river for the numbers of fish. But those that were marked by the salt were plump, silvery, and strong.

We suggested to the owners of the Estancia that they net the pools and remove some of the fish. They did this, and with the addition of increased angling pressure the situation leveled off. The next time I fished there, three years later, every resident fish we took, both brown and rainbow, was fat and fit, and they ranged in weight from four to eight pounds.

Sea-run browns do not stay for a long time in the salt, and they often move in and out of a tidal pool before they make their spawning run up the river. It is believed that after spawning a few stay in the stream over the winter but most seem to drop down that autumn and head out to sea again. In Europe the runs of the sea trout are as popular with anglers as the salmon runs, with which they sometimes coincide. Often the sea trout are harder to catch than the salmon. On the Oykel River in northern Scotland I found that even in mid-August when the salmon were what the gillie termed "dour," unwilling to take a fly, we could catch one or two each day. But not until evening put a pall over things and did away with shadows or any glint of light to betray our presence could we get a sea trout to come to a fly. Most of the British Isles sea trout are taken after dark.

If I ever had any doubts about the extreme awareness of danger that sparks the sea trout, I was put straight one day on the Dovey River in Wales. I had crawled in to the side of the pool, and kneeling there I slowly raised my arm to make a cast. Ten feet out from me a school of about twenty trout flushed like a busted covey of quail and disappeared in a trice, looking like the shadows of a flight of bluewing teal. I managed to get a couple of those Dovey sea trout before the day was out, but only by calling on every trick in the book. I crouched, crept, and crawled, and used a side-arm cast, and a very long, light leader. And even then, many more of them saw me than rose to my fly.

The same situation holds true elsewhere. At the Laerdal River in Norway the sea trout arrive on a split-second timetable, on August 1, each year. Although the anglers know they are there, they never go out in the daytime but wait for dusk, the only "night" at that time of year in the land of the midnight sun. Then, around 7:30 or 8 o'clock, they start to have a chance at presenting a fly in safety to the wily sea-run browns.

All over Europe fishing for sea trout has become so popular that today it is almost as difficult and almost as expensive to get a beat for sea trout as it is for Atlantic salmon. Sea-trout populations, like those of the Atlantic salmon, have declined markedly, making things even more difficult. At some of the more famous lakes in the British Isles, which are frequented by sea trout, as for instance, Loch Maree, it is necessary to book years in advance.

In Scotland I had the pleasure of meeting Charles C. McLaren, former long-distance fly-casting champion of England and Scotland, and a great fisher for sea trout. He had started at it very young. On October 24, 1928, when he was only thirteen years old, he had caught a sea trout in Loch Maree in the Scottish Highlands that weighed twelve and a half pounds and that, by scale count, was nineteen years old, and it is believed to be the oldest sea trout on record. Then on October 12, 1929, McLaren caught another sea trout, this one in the Kinlochewe River at the head of Loch Maree, that weighed fourteen pounds.

It was a good start in a fishing life, and he has never got away from those sea trout. Today he operates an angler's hotel at Altnaharra in northern Scotland, close to Loch Hope and the Naver River, both of which furnish good sea-trout fishing. His book *The Art of Sea Trout Fishing*, published in 1963 by Oliver & Boyd in Edinburgh, is a must for anyone going for these fish in Scotland.

THE SONAGHAN

The European sea trout has his variations, too. In Lough Melvin, in northern Ireland, I encountered the sonaghan, a brown trout that is believed to go to sea only once in his lifetime, then return to his home lake or river. In the lakes they usually go to considerable depth, twenty feet of water, seldom if ever moving into the shallows. Yet they will rise in that twenty feet of water and take a dry. On a visit to Lough Melvin my wife Mary and I caught many of the sonaghan on dries, and were astonished by this lengthy rush for the floating fly, in my experience the longest rise of any fish to a fly. We would cast the fly out and wait patiently, the fly sitting on the surface, and then, splash, he had it, and the fight was on. Those fish averaged about twelve to fourteen inches and each fought very hard for his size, a nice little battler in a family of many mysteries.

Brown trout that make their homes in big, deep, freshwater lakes sometimes take on the same coloring as sea-run trout, probably because of the abundance of food, to better blend into the big, wide spaces, or because of certain minerals in the water. In Lago Huechalaufquen, out of which the Chimehuin River flows, the spawning brownies come out of the lake as bright silver slabs and only after some time in the river do they revert to their true brown trout hues.

RAINBOW TROUT

The natural home of the rainbow trout extends from Alaska southward to the mountains of Mexico. While most rainbows found east of the Rocky Mountain Divide are transplants, there is some possibility that those of the Yellowstone drainage are an exception and that they came to these waters of the eastern slope by ascending Pacific Creek on the west side of the Continental Divide, crossing Two Ocean Plateau above Yellowstone Park, and moving into and running down Atlantic Creek, whose waters eventually reach the Atlantic Ocean.

The first rainbows transported to the more easterly part of the United States were sent from California to Michigan in 1873; and a couple of years later rainbow eggs were also shipped to New York State. Within a few years the Michigan stock was going strong, and later these fish began to show in the Great lakes. In 1898 further fish were stocked in the St. Mary's River between Lake Superior and Lake Huron. The famous Soo Rapids were soon furnishing some of the greatest rainbow fishing in the country.

Like the brown, the rainbow includes many variations, but these are mainly based on scale count or some slight difference in appearance and do not necessarily indicate a different fish. The Kamloops is an example. The Kamloops is so named for a lake in British Columbia where the rainbows were found to be especially robust and fast-growing and which consequently made a very desirable strain for stocking in other waters. Similarly, rainbows found in a few big lakes, which make annual runs into available rivers, are called steelhead in some places. For instance, the fish stocked in the Great Lakes showed a strong migratory urge and roamed far and wide, and were often called steelhead. But I think the name steelhead should be reserved for the true sea-going rainbow, the great sporting fish of the Pacific coast, which runs out to sea to feed and returns to his native river to spawn. Regardless of local names, of course, they are all rainbows, bearing the scientific name *Salmo gairdneri.*

Very little authoritative material has been available on the Kamloops, but in early 1971 a very complete book appeared on the fish, written by Steve Raymond. It does a great deal to clear up the differences between the steelhead and the resident rainbow and the Kamloops. It also gives the best flies for the last.

The rainbows of some of the big western rivers of the United States cross with the native cutthroat, and, while the crossbred fish cannot reproduce, the combination develops a big, healthy, extra-bright-colored and extra-hard-fighting fish. This has been true of nearly every rainbow I have taken that displayed the red slash under each gill plate and the distinctive markings that revealed his hybridization. A large proportion of the rainbows weighing four pounds or better that I have taken in our western rivers have been such hybrids. In my experience the standard rainbow does not grow to such large size in most rivers, with the exception of Alaska.

When the rainbow makes his home in a big lake or goes to sea where he can find extra food, he can grow to sensational size. Wherever you find these big rainbows you find an exceptional food supply. In Lake Pend Oreille, Idaho, which was stocked with fingerlings of the Kamloops trout from British Columbia, this food supply consisted of millions of landlocked kokanee (Pacific sockeye salmon). Those small Kamloops rainbows maintained their normal growth for two years. Then they were big enough to feed on the kokanee, and suddenly in the next two years they practically blew up, sometimes into thirty-pounders.

The rainbow is a fish of the fast waters. He likes plenty of oxygen and is often found up in the heavy water that pours into the top of a pool, reveling in the force of the current. The strength he builds up in this strenuous life gives him the power to make the startling leaps for which he is famous. And when found in his favorite milieu of bright, clear, rushing water he is one of the most beautiful trout on the books, his silvery sides slashed with scarlet and a brilliant greenish cast to the top of his back. Because he is generally a fish of the fast water, the finer points of fishing are not always as critical as with a brown trout, but when you find a rainbow in calmer water, it takes all your skill to get him to hit.

When a rainbow goes to sea, he really builds up size and vigor and the result on the West Coast of North America is the steelhead, probably the strongest fish that swims. Steelhead travel great distances in their oceanic visits, and I have heard of one case where a tagged steelhead was traced on a twenty-five-hundred-mile trip from tidal water of his home river. Even within the river they make prodigious journeys, often following the main stem for many miles, then forking off into a feeder stream, and months later finding their spawning beds and perpetuating their kind.

The steelhead of the Babine River in British Columbia come up the Skeena River waterway to the Babine, and we catch them there two hundred miles from the sea. By this time they have begun to lose the bright silver look of the sea-traveler and are beginning to show their rainbow parentage. There are big buttons of vivid red on the cheeks and the rainbow down each side is aglow. They seem to set the water on fire, and they certainly light the hearts of fishermen.

The time when a steelhead run enters a river differs widely throughout their range. The angler must know the dates of the run into any particular river he plans to fish. Some rivers host a "summer run" in September and October, often called "half-pounders" although this is a misnomer, since the fish range from half a pound to ten or twelve pounds; and a winter run of much bigger fish, in January, February or March—cold fishing indeed. Of late, many northwestern U.S. rivers are experiencing excellent summer runs in June and July.

Strictly speaking, the steelhead we take in the Babine River are a summer-run fish, and they are certainly not half-pounders. While the fish we lose are always bigger than those we land, I am convinced that one steelhead I lost in the Babine in early October of 1970 was an all-time record. I knew from the moment he hit that I would never stop him. But I tried. I followed quite a way downstream but suddenly felt a slack line. I expected to find that he had cut me off on a big rock he went around, but when I reached the spot where the end of the line lay in the water I found that he had merely dropped the fly. That fish had to be at least forty pounds.

The steelhead of the entire Skeena River watershed are a race apart, especially big and strong. The rivers of this drainage, including the renowned Kispiox, produce our biggest steelhead.

Steelheading isn't the contemplative trout fishing of spring creek or limestone stream, or even a big western river. The steelhead follows the Pacific salmon into most of his home rivers, feeding on their spawn. On many of the streams where you fish steelhead you see the salmons—sockeye, humpback, chinook, chum and coho—all bound upstream to perform the last act of their lives, as the Pacific salmons die after spawning. They are covered with whitish blotches of fungus, gaunt and sunken-eyed, many of them already half dead as they dig out spawning beds and deposit the eggs. The sockeyes in particular are brilliant red along the body with contrasting greenish head and tail, the mouths like beaks, studded with sharp teeth, and the males show a decided hump, another manifestation of the spawning phenomenon. Sometimes anglers catch these salmon while steelheading and they give a terrific fight.

The steelhead river is usually running high, sometimes murky, the weather wet and cold. Casts of eighty to a hundred feet are often needed to reach the eddies and broken water on the far side, where the fish often lie. On many of the steelhead rivers such as the Klamath in northern California, the Eel, the Rogue in Oregon, and the Kalama in Washington, you have to throw a fly a long way to consistently take the migrating steelhead.

While the steelhead will take a dry fly when you find him in shallow, clear water, most fishing for the species is done with sinking lines, and the flies are almost universally tied to represent salmon eggs either in color or shape or both. Still, nymph patterns in more somber colors produce their share of fish.

CUTTHROAT TROUT

Another dweller of the west-coast waters of the United States is the cutthroat trout, *Salmo clarki*. This fish, in many species and sub-species, is found all the way along the Rocky Mountain chain from Alaska to California. When you hear a westerner speak of the "native" it is the cutthroat. And while there are many color variations, and they bear local names in various rivers and lakes, they are all readily identifiable by the red slash under each jaw, which slash gives the trout his common name.

Because the cutthroat is a wilderness trout rather than an urban dweller, he is one of the easier members of the family to catch, and his numbers have been decimated by heavy fishing wherever he can be reached. Today the Yellowstone River is probably the only stream outside of primitive areas which supports a good population of cutthroat trout.

As mentioned earlier, the cutthroat crosses readily with the rainbow, producing strong, healthy fish with the good qualities of each. The hybrid is more difficult to fool than the full-blooded cut-throat, bigger in size, usually, and extremely beautiful with the brilliant red throat slashes added to the flashing rainbow on his sides.

In Pacific coastal rivers flowing directly to the sea, the cutthroat acts like the other trouts. He goes to sea, on occasion, and can be caught in coastal water in some places. On this sea voyage they seem to stay closer to the influence of the home river than do the rainbow and brown, moving in and out and hanging around offshore islands. Like the other trouts, the cutthroat that has been to sea is stronger, spunkier, and gives the angler on his beat a great deal of sporty fishing. He is also much harder to catch.

GOLDEN TROUT

The cutthroat has been known to hybridize with another trout, the golden, but because of the limited waters in which the cutthroat occurs, and the rarity of the golden, this is a cross that not many anglers ever see. The golden trout, *Salmo aguabonita*, originated in the headwaters of the Kern River in California, and prefers high altitudes almost exclusively, either high mountain streams or high lakes at the headwaters of mountain streams. From California, goldens have been carried to high lakes in Wyoming, Montana, and Idaho.

The golden has launched more high-country pack trips than any other fish, for anglers seek them for trophies and also for food, as this is one of the finest tasting trout. In most cases the catch will be small in size and limited in numbers, although in some few lakes goldens grow to large size, and a few double-figure fish have been taken.

Perhaps with further stocking the golden will adapt to changing environmental conditions, as other trouts have done on occasion. My wife, Mary, is convinced that a fish she took on a dry fly in the Big Hole River in the summer of 1970 was a golden or a golden hybrid with some other trout. It was neither rainbow, brown or cutthroat, nor Dolly Varden, as she has caught and can identify all those. It had brilliant orange-red sides in a widespread pattern, black-dotted fins, but no white edging that would suggest brook trout or cutthroat, and no throat slashes. She returned the fish to the water quickly, and only after she had done so realized that she could not identify it.

In another instance I know of, an angler brought a golden back alive from the high country and put it in the aquarium at Dan Bailey's Fly Shop in Livingston, Montana, where the altitude is only four thousand feet. The fish survived in fine health for fifteen months. Finally compassionate Dan carried him out to the river in an aerated bucket and released him in one of the sloughs of the Yellowstone.

Brook Trout

The brook trout, *Salvelinus fontinalis*—fish "of the springs"—is well named. He must have clear, fresh, sparkling water. This was the native trout of the eastern part of the United States. Those of us who are old enough to have fished the small streams of the Appalachians and the Adirondacks before dams and pollution destroyed the habitat remember them as the first trout we caught, with a stick, a piece of line, a hook, and a worm. I can still see the first one I took, the trout flying through the air to land on the ground behind me as I heaved back when he hit, my own lightning pounce on him, my awe at the beauty of his red and black dots all circled in halos, and how I carried him home, a six-inch bragging fish, and next morning tasted him, crisp from the pan, the best fish I have ever eaten.

In the eastern states, the brook trout as a native has now been pushed back to smaller streams, upper river reaches, and back-woods ponds, often at high elevations. With the limited food supply the trout often become stunted, 6 or 7 inches being the full adult size in most instances except in beaver ponds and back-country lakes. Nevertheless, they still provide good fly-fishing sport. In shallow water they are alert, knowing themselves susceptible to attack on all sides. But they still can't resist a fly. They zip up from their shelter beside or under a rock, hit, and if you don't hook them, turn and dash back, all in a second, a fleeting flash of wild trout.

That obliging willingness to hit a fly, be it dry, nymph, wet, streamer or bucktail, is a hallmark of the species. Once when Walt Weber, *National Geographic* Wildlife Artist, and his wife, Grace, went to fish the famous Kennebago Pool in Maine, they found that the popular spot was overcrowded that day, all the best places already taken by hard-casting anglers. Walt anchored off to one side, and suggested to Grace that since they were not going to get into the good fishing, this might be the time for her to practice her casting. The big pool lay out in front of them, a ten-foot patch of lily pads behind them. Walt tied on a Royal Coachman dry fly and told Grace to fire away. Out there over the best part of the pool five boatloads of anglers cast, retrieved, picked their flies off the water and cast again, methodically, and with perfect form—and no strikes.

Suddenly the sanctified air was rent by a piercing scream. Walt looked up from tying a tippet on his own leader in time to see a seven-inch trout come hurtling at him from behind.

"I've got one!" screamed Grace.

"On your backcast," said Walt with disgust.

He tossed the trout back.

On her next cast Grace again managed to put her backcast right on top of a hungry seven-incher. He, too, came hurtling through the air towards Walt. Again the screams, and the snort of disgust from Walt. Eleven brook trout from seven to nine inches fell before Grace's accurate backcasting.

It became too much for the stern-visaged purists who were keeping their backcasts well in the air where a properly executed cast should put it. One by one they up-anchored and departed.

Walt pulled anchor, too, and rowed out and settled in the best spot in the pool. On his first cast with a size 10 Brown Hackle dry, a great brook trout rolled up and took. It weighed 2½ pounds.

In the United States the few spots where you can still find good fishing for fair-sized brook trout are those that are difficult to get to. Anglers ambitious enough to walk in three miles to catch them find fourteen-inchers in some of the mountain waters of Virginia, West Virginia, and North Carolina. In Quebec, which has always been one of the great habitats for the species, you can find some really big ones in places which have not been fished too hard. In some of the rivers and lakes of Quebec it is not unusual for fly fishermen to take two- and three-pounders, a few four-pounders, and an occasional one that goes to five pounds. A few fast rivers and fly-in lakes in Maine also produce such fish.

God's River and others that flow to Hudson's Bay in northern Ontario and Manitoba also host big, strong brook trout; and again they are remote, fly-in spots. The more accessible Nipigon Lake and River, in Northwestern Ontario, once produced many big brook trout, and for decades held the world record for the species, with a 14½-pound fish taken in 1916 by Dr. W. J. Cook. These waters still produce some big fish but not the consistent numbers and size of old. Trophy and fly-only regulations continue to preserve Labrador's Minipi river-lake chain as one of the last strongholds of truly large brook trout. Fish in the 6- to 8-pound class can be taken to this day.

Some of the lost eastern brook trout fishing is being restored through a program of stocking, and now, in a few rivers from Georgia up through the Middle Atlantic area, Maine, and the Canadian Maritime Provinces, fair-sized brook trout of this origin can be taken from these stocked streams. They have also been planted in the Rocky Mountain states and have thrived there, especially in lakes. I have taken brook trout up to fourteen inches in the upper waters of the Big Hole River in Montana, in a series of beaver ponds at eleven thousand feet altitude, above Gunnison, Colorado, and in similar high-country lakes in the Big Beartooth Mountains of Montana.

My best fishing for brook trout in either lake or stream has been in Argentina. The brook trout was stocked there from U.S. sources, and in that cold, unpolluted water teeming with food they have grown to the utmost in size for the species. I believe it is only a matter of time until one of these Argentine fish, or one from the Argentine-Chilean border lakes, will take over top billing for the species.

When I fished the Senguerr River and Lago Fontana on the eastern slope of the Andes, far down in Patagonia, in 1957, those brookies came to our dries as if they had been on a hunger strike, and we took a four-pounder on nearly every cast. There were so many fish that probably the food supply has now become somewhat limited and holds them at about this weight, but with more fishing this situation will change and then there will be some really big fish.

The Trout We Fish For

In 1963 I went with an ABC-TV crew to Lago General Paz on the Argentine-Chilean border, to film a fishing contest for the Wide World of Sports program. The Argentine team was composed of Tito Hosman of Buenos Aires and Erik Gornik of Futalaufquen, Patagonia. TV announcer Curt Gowdy and I represented the United States. We won the contest in the last minute of time, but that is not the story. What stood out was the fish we caught. We fished for three days, using both fly and spinning gear. But because of the remote spot where we were camped we had to run two hours down the lake to the best fishing grounds each day, and back again before dark, thus missing the best fishing times, early and late. After dark, travel on that forty-five-mile-long lake was out.

In spite of this loss of the prime times, we landed 54 fish that totaled 256 pounds, an average of 4.47 pounds. The largest, taken on spinning gear, was 8 pounds, the largest on a fly only one pound less. In a few hours on the Corcovado River, which flows out of the lake, a beautiful, clear stream where we could see tiny pebbles on the bottom in twenty feet of water, we took brookies to five pounds on our flies. It was a wonderful place, with high, snow-capped alps at the northern end, the kind of spot where *fontinalis* was meant to live.

In many places the brook trout, just like other trouts, goes to sea; and when he returns he indeed surpasses his inland brothers for size and strength. Newfoundland's resident brook trout of some of the inland lakes is called mud trout and doesn't attract too many anglers. But the brook trout that comes into Newfoundland's rivers as a sea-run fish is something else again. Twenty years ago (1952) when I fished salmon there it was common to see them in droves in the salmon pools, blackening the bottom, so thick they were. The average weight was four to five pounds, and some went as high as ten pounds. And how they would hit a size 12 Royal Wulff fly!

The Labrador coastal rivers also play host to these sea-run brook trout, as do some coastal rivers on Prince Edward Island.

DOLLY VARDEN TROUT

The Dolly Varden, *Salvelinus malma,* named for a reigning English beauty, is a western form of the eastern brook trout. The Dolly takes flies fairly well when found in suitable water, but he really prefers meat and is inclined to lie deep rather than near the surface. Hence the fly fisherman will do better when he goes for this species if he uses a sinking line.

Once on the South Fork of the Flathead River in Montana, I was fishing for the cutthroat trout for which the river is famous. Martin Bovey, angler and photographer, was along and had brought his movie camera.

"I'd like to get some footage of you catching a cutthroat," he said.

I eased into position, and when he had the camera focused on a spot about thirty-five feet upstream from me, I made my cast, dropping the Royal Wulff dry fly out in the current. I saw the cutthroat coming, but instead of taking the fly he continued on into the air. There was a tremendous splash and right behind him out came a Dolly Varden that must have weighed twenty pounds. It missed the cutthroat, but Martin got the pictures and later I saw the film of that hungry Dolly on the trail of a substantial meal.

We did catch a few small Dolly Vardens later on flies, but none on a dry, and none of such size.

GRAYLING

The American grayling, *Thymallus arcticus,* is the only grayling in the Western Hemisphere, though subspecies occur in isolated areas. The only other form is the European grayling, *Thymallus thymallus,* widely distributed from continental Europe to the USSR, but limited to specific clearwater habitat throughout this range. The grayling is found in many of the same waters as the trout and is fished in much the same way. The fish is readily identifiable by the high dorsal, almost sail-like fin, and the small mouth which seems to open into a square O, quite different from the mouth of a trout. The latin name *Thymallus* is derived from the slight odor of thyme which can sometimes be discerned in the fish. Various other tags have been added throughout its range.

The Montana grayling, which is called *Thymallus montanus*, was native only to the Missouri River above Great Falls, but has been stocked in many other rivers and high lakes in Montana, and in Wyoming. The waters chosen for planting are selected with a view to the preference of the species for pure, cold, fresh water. The Montana grayling wear a dull silver coat with faint overwash of purple, and black dots on the shoulders. They do not grow to much size, usually from nine to twelve inches, with an occasional fourteen-incher showing.

The Upper Big Hole River holds more Montana grayling than most rivers of the Rockies. They seem to like the cold water up there in the wild hay country near Wisdom and Jackson in the Valley of 10,000 Stacks. Only the odd one used to come to my flies further down in the Big Hole, but since the dam went out at Divide more and more are showing around Melrose and Glen. The last time I fished this area, in the lower Big Hole, I caught four grayling in one day, my biggest take of them ever.

The Arctic grayling encountered in Alaskan rivers is more brilliant than the Montana grayling and is, indeed, one of the most beautiful of all freshwater fishes. My own first encounter with the grayling, in August 1947, was with the Arctic branch of the family. Frank Dufresne, then Chief of the Alaska Game and Fish Commission, had organized a fishing and hunting trip to Alaska for a group of Outdoor Writers. When we convened at Whitehorse, we were offered a choice.

"Joe, do you want to go to Admiralty Island for giant Alaska brown bear?" Frank asked me. "Or would you like to try the Lewes River for grayling?"

As far as I was concerned, it was no choice. I had never caught an Arctic grayling, and I had been hoping to since reading of its beauty and fly-taking qualities.

"It was grayling that brought me here," I said. "I'll take the Lewes."

Where I hit the Lewes, only five miles out of Whitehorse, the river moves right along, yet the surface was slick and unruffled. All over it I could see the markings of rising fish. I tied on a Black Gnat, size 12, dry, and cast to the nearest feeder. Bang! I had a hit. I struck and missed.

"You gotta be fast," called my fishing companion, Gene Letourneau, of Waterville, Maine, who had waded out into the stream not far from me. "They hit and then they're gone before you know it."

I cast again, and bang again, another fish piled into the Black Gnat so hard I saw his dorsal and knew for sure, then, that these were grayling I was working over. He looped out, waved that angel-wing at me, and slipped back into the water. But I had this one securely hooked and fought him safely through a couple more jumps and finally brought him in.

He must have weighed about two pounds, a fish that was almost cigar-shaped, his back wearing a silver-gray sheen and flaring above it the sail that makes him so sensational, a dorsal fin that stood two and a half inches high and seemed to have been brushed with all the colors of the borealis.

"He should be called the Northern Lights Fish," I said, holding him up for Gene to see.

His mouth opened in an O as I removed the hook, and his pear-shaped eyes opened, too, then seemed to blink in gratitude as I slipped him back into the water.

Arctic grayling of two pounds are fairly common throughout their range, and you can expect an occasional one of three pounds.

These bigger members of the grayling family like the same flies that take the Montana grayling. In the Fond du Lac River and Black Lake, near Stony Rapids in Saskatchewan, we took them on small nymphs and dry flies tied on number 12 and 14 hooks, only slightly larger than those used in small streams.

Many of the lakes and streams in the Northwest Territories produce extra-large grayling. Bud Williams, then owner of Arctic Star Lodge on Great Slave Lake, took one that weighed four pounds, and three pounders are fairly common in this lake. In 1969 one was taken which went a little over five pounds. The world-record grayling came from the Northwest Territories, too, a beautiful five-pound fifteen-ounce fish taken in the Katseyedie River on August 16, 1967, by Jeanne P. Branson. This fish hit a Mepps lure cast with a spinning outfit.

On a recent trip to the Northwest Territories I traced some of the history of the Arctic grayling. It was in 1819 that a young English midshipman named George Bach saw fish rising one summer evening on the glassy surface of Great Slave Lake in what is now Canada's Northwest Territories. Bach had brought a fly rod with him from England—undoubtedly the fourteen-footer typical of English usage of the day—and he wasted no time in putting it together and dropping a fly over those rising fish. One of the risers took and, at least as far as historical records tell, Bach became the first man to catch an Arctic grayling on a fly.

George Bach was a member of Sir John Richardson's staff, on the Franklin expedition to the North Pole, and his catch was made as the party camped at the site of Fort Reliance, on the eastern end of Great Slave Lake. I like to think of Sir John and his young midshipman standing there in the bright Arctic evening admiring this beautiful fish with its flaring dorsal fin that glimmered with rose and gold, hints of yellow, shots of green like an early aspen leaf, and was liberally dotted with purple and blue, some of the dots further enhanced with circles of green and gold and rose.

Both men knew the grayling species in England, but this was a new member of the family to them.

"We'll name it for you," Sir John said. "Bach's grayling." (Sometimes spelled "Back," as is also the river named for him.)

To the scientific generic name of *Thymallus*, which applies to all graylings, Sir John also added *signifer*, meaning standard bearer, both as a comment on the beautiful, extra-large sail flaunted by the fish, and as a compliment to the young seaman's calling.

When early settlers fishing the Ausable River in Michigan came up with a catch they could not identify, they sent a couple of the fish to Washington. There the authorities named it a member of the grayling family, a fish highly regarded in Europe for both sporting and food qualities. When the news of the presence of large numbers of these fish got around, there followed a spree of uninhibited fishing, so widely publicized that the citizens of one of the towns central to the grayling streams changed its name from Crawford to Grayling.

Unfortunately, in that era of belief that nature's bounty knows no limits, the grayling was practically wiped out in Michigan waters within a few years. In an article written by Kendrick Kimball in the *Detroit News* of December 15, 1929, we can read the story of what happened to the Michigan grayling. He quotes Rube Babbit, of Grayling, an old man in 1929:

From 1875 to 1881 my father and I shipped our catches of grayling to a Chicago restaurant, which paid the unheard of price of 25 cents a pound. I'd take fishermen down the Ausable for more than 200 miles in a houseboat. When we reached Lake Huron I'd sell or leave the boat and go back to Grayling and build another one. Those houseboats were equipped with wells, so we could keep our catch alive. Later we built camps on shore, to which we constructed our own roads through the timber. The grayling was the greatest game fish in Michigan and was the only native of the trout family in the waters below the northern tip of the Lower Peninsula. The biggest one I saw weighed around one pound 10 ounces. They averaged a bit smaller.

An Englishman came from his homeland every year to catch grayling. Artists came from the east to paint their beauty. One in particular put up his easel beside the live well in one of my houseboats and took fish after fish from the water, exposing them for a few seconds then throwing them back, so he could catch the exact shades. The log-

gers were responsible for the loss of the grayling. When the pines went, the streams became impure through erosion. Soil was washed into them by the rains, and the grayling could not live in muddy, dirty waters. No longer shaded by trees, the rivers rose in temperature, which also hurt as the grayling needed water almost as cold as ice. When the logs came down the rivers they raked the spawning beds, destroying the eggs or the young fish. In the jams the bark was ground off the Norway pines, filling the water with fine particles that sifted into the grayling gills. I found innumerable dead with festering gills, and in every case the fine particles of bark were the cause. The State has endeavored to plant them below the straits in recent years, but they also died. No, the grayling is gone forever, gone with the pines and the pigeons and the Michigan that used to be.

What happened to the Michigan grayling, then, was well known and should have been a lesson. But all over the country we still allow money-mad people to pour poisons into the rivers. And then we dig into our pockets to pay more taxes to raise fish to plant in the streams those poisons have destroyed, to live for a day, a week, or perhaps a month, in the waters we are still polluting. It's an expensive way to maintain our sport.

In England, particularly in the chalk streams such as the Test and the Itchen, there was a period when grayling were sometimes regarded as pests, competing with the more desirable trout for food. Many a grayling was ignominiously heaved out on the bank to die. But this school of thought rapidly disappeared; the grayling continues to be highly regarded wherever he is found, as a fly-taking, sporting fish, and has earned such fancy terms of admiration as "The Flower of Fishes" and "Queen of the Waters."

The renowned Charles Ritz, Europe's most famous fly fisherman, has stated that he prefers the grayling to the trouts. I cannot go along with him on that, but I do think that the grayling can be very difficult to fool at times, hard to tempt to come to your best-chosen and most discreetly offered fly. One of Ritz's favorite fishing streams for grayling was the Traun River in Austria. Indeed, in this clear, lovely river the grayling is at his best, feeding constantly, and is a particularly challenge to the fly fisherman.

It was while fishing the Traun that I had a good opportunity to study the peculiarity of the grayling's rise as compared to that of a trout. The grayling will often let your fly go by, so you think he is going to ignore it. Then he turns and drifts downstream under it, and corkscrews up to take, a nerve-shattering procedure that always seems to catch you unready and accounts for many missed strikes. So it always pays to let the fly float well through, when you are putting your offering over grayling, and watch it carefully throughout a long float.

I have often heard anglers say that grayling are hard to hook because they have a tender mouth. I believe, however, that we lose a few grayling because the point of the small hooks usually employed either bend or are straightened out under the pressure. Or the hook goes through a bit of flesh over the lip of the fish and pulls out.

The English and the Austrian grayling are a little less brilliant in coloring than their North American counterparts. They are smaller than the Arctic grayling, but average larger than the Montana. And the grayling I found in the beautiful, crystal-clear waters of the Sava and other rivers in Yugoslavia was slightly different again, sometimes almost transparent looking, so you seemed to see through the fish in the water; and was generally a little more brown in overall coloring and the dorsal fin not quite so gay. But, in numbers and response to the fly, they provided some of the best grayling fishing I have found.

Dry Fly Fishing for Trout

THE DRY FLY

The dry fly is designed to match a natural aquatic fly or a terrestrial that has fallen and is floating on the surface of the water. The artificial must look as nearly like the natural as possible, for the trout, and in fact most fish, have eyes that would put the human 20/20 vision to shame. Trout take natural freshwater shrimp, and daphnia, or water fleas, that are not much larger than a pin point, and a size 12 fly probably looks as big as a dinner plate to them, so that a faulty tie is quickly perceived and passed up.

Therefore the dry fly must be fashioned with much thought to size, color, slant of wings, and set of hackle. It should be well balanced so that it will alight and sit perkily on the surface of the water, not being pulled this way or that by the weight of the hook so that it rests unevenly on the water. A good fly does not sit on its tail, nor yet lean on its chin. The nearer the parallel to the water, the better, even though many natural flies come down the current resting on their sides, with only one wing sticking upward.

There are many variations of the dry fly. The most common is the standard upright wing tie patterned after one or another of the common natural flies found on a stream. Many of these same patterns are tied in a "spentwing" variation, with wings outstretched, like a downed natural. It seems to me that spentwing flies would make a better match to the real thing if they were tied to float awash instead of with a full hackle which places the flat wings above the surface. Then there are other dries that are designed to ride the big waters where the current pours in at the head of a pool, large creations that the angler can readily sport in that heavy water, or in white riffles elsewhere on the river. These big-winged ties have been produced by many different people and are called by many different names, but the end result is the same—they are the answer to a great need for a fly that will tempt those lunkers that are up there in the rough water waiting for something substantial to come their way. The Wulff patterns of hairwing flies are proven fish takers in this group, and the Trude pattern, and the sofa pillow, mostly ties with a goodly degree of white to make them easy to see in the fast water. Right up there floating along with them are a couple of big flies that can be fished both above and below the water—the Bailey's bi-fly, the Joe's hopper, and the great muddler minnow which made its reputation as a bucktail fly but is now mopping up on Western streams when used as a dry fly.

Also constructed with an eye to the angler's vision are the bi-visible flies. These are tied in various patterns but always with white hackles at the front so the angler as well as the trout can see the fly. This is a fly that enters almost every trout fisherman's fly box shortly after he reaches forty years of age. Because, size of hatch regardless, it is important in dry fly fishing to see the fly.

To start with, every trouter should stock his fly box with a few basic flies which are consistent fish getters everywhere. One friend once asked me: "If you could have only ten dry flies to fish, country-wide, what would they be?"

This was my choice:

Light Cahill, size 16	*Gray Wulff, size 10*
Gray Midge Hackle Fly, size 20	*Blue Dun, size 16*
Black Flying Ant, size 20	*Adams, size 12*
Red Variant, size 14	*Quill Gordon, size 14*
Black Gnat, size 12	*Jassid, size 20*

This is only the barest necessity, each fly guaranteed to be useful sometime, anywhere. To really meet the vagaries of a trout's appetite, and to give the angler the most from his fishing, a well-equipped fly box also should be stocked with the flies listed below, in many different sizes and patterns.

STANDARD DRY FLIES,
HOOK SIZES 6 TO 20

Adams	*Iron Blue Dun*
Black Flying Ant	*Pale Evening Dun*
Black Gnat	*Light Cahill Quill*
Black Quill	*Mosquito*
Blue Dun	*McGinty*
Blue Quill	*Olive Dun Dark*
Brown Hackle, Peacock	*Pink Lady*
Brown Hackle, Yellow	*Queen of Waters*
Dark Cahill	*Quill Gordon*
Light Cahill	*Red Ant*
Cahill Quill	*Renegade*
Coachman	*Rio Grande King*
Royal Coachman	*Red Fox*
Ginger Quill	*Roberts*
Gray Hackle, Peacock	*Tup's Indispensable*
Gray Hackle, Red	*Willow*
Gray Hackle, Yellow	*White Miller*
Hendrickson	*Whitcomb*
Light Hendrickson	

BIVISIBLES,
HOOK SIZES 6 TO 10

Brown Badger	*Badger*
Gray Ginger	*Ginger*
Grizzly	*Black*

WULFF HAIRWING DRY FLIES,
HOOK SIZES 6 TO 12

Gray Wulff	*White Wulff*
Grizzly Wulff	*Blond Wulff*
Black Wulff	*Royal Wulff*

SPECIAL TIES (DRY OR WET),
HOOK SIZES 6, 8, 10 12, LONG SHANK HOOK

Bailey's Bi-Flies	*Joe's Hopper*[1]
Bi-Fly Yellow	*Goofus Bug*[2]
Bi-Fly Orange	*Dan's Hopper*

FISHING THE DRY FLY

While most anglers class dry fly as the most demanding way of fishing, it is nevertheless the best way for a beginner to start. With a wet fly or a streamer, you are usually fishing the stream by your knowledge of where the fish may lie. But with a dry you are in on all the sights and sounds of the river, going by every signal a fish can flash to you as he eats or swims. The dry fly is also easier to cast than the wet, and the angler can see drag when it occurs and sees the fish strike and is therefore able to set the hook more quickly.

[1] Also called Dan's hopper, Michigan hopper (8 and 10 long shank).
[2] A hairwing fly with divided wing, body, and tail formed by pulling deer hair back over the body and tying it at the bend of the hook. This floats the fly better, and gives it a buggy appearance.

The whole principle upon which dry fly fishing is based is that the fly should come down the stream exactly like a downed natural. Yet there are many anglers who fish for years without discovering that their fly is practically never floating free! It may seem to be moving with the current—but look carefully—is it traveling faster than the bubbles and bits of flotsam on the surface? Is it going more slowly? If either of these things is true, you have drag and the chances of a strike are slim. Is the fly floating downstream opposite you in a straight line or is the fly line bellied out ahead of it, dragging the fly crosswise, even the least bit, across the current toward you, telling the trout that there is something peculiar about that insect? Sometimes the amount of drag can be so small as to fool even a veteran, but never a trout.

Without that natural float, strikes are going to be as few as icebergs in Florida, even when trout are popping so fast in the middle of a hatch that you would think that all you would have to do is throw a fly on the surface and wait for the hit. It seems as if a fly would never run the gauntlet of all those feeding fish. But when a trout comes up and gobbles a natural exactly an inch from your lonely artificial, you begin to get the true story. They are turning up their mandibles at your fly because it isn't a right looking fly. It's either going too fast or too slow or it's going across current. In the meantime, those naturals are coming along as they should and therefore why worry about strange-acting, odd-looking affairs that seem to have a motive power of their own?

True, now and then a maverick trout will rush a fly that is skidding across the surface, and it's true, too, that you can take trout by dabbling, skittering, and various other ways. But these methods are usually productive only under certain specific conditions which will be described later in this chapter. The angler who substitutes such methods for float is betting on chance against skill, and if it's meat he's after, he is going to wind up with plenty of air around the fish in his frying pan.

"What makes drag?" asked my nephew Paul Levering, when I was first teaching him to fly cast.

"Drag is caused when the fly is pulled by the leader and line at a rate slower or faster than the current, or across current," I answered, "instead of riding straight downstream like a natural fly that is at the mercy of the current."

Paul made a cast and dropped his fly on the smooth surface of the pool. It looked good, with wings cocked high, but it wasn't moving. It was resting in still water. Then the current caught the line and bellied it downstream, pulling the leader and fly after it.

"You have drag now," I told Paul.

"But the fly's riding high," he protested. "It looks all right."

"Just because the surface is smooth and the fly sits up doesn't mean you don't have drag," I said. "Look at the naturals beside it."

Paul's fly was moving quite a bit faster and in a different direction. Any trout down there below was going to know there was something different and wrong about that fly. And as if to prove it, even as we watched, a fish came up and took one of those naturals within inches of the strange-acting artificial.

Once more Paul cast and the fly floated through untouched.

"There are at least half a dozen fish rising out there," he said. "You'd think one of them would hit."

"Pick out a single fish," I said "Then figure the water for a good float to him. Forget all the other fish. Concentrate on just that one."

Such a situation is like shooting into a covey of rising quail. If you don't bear down on one, you'll miss them all. Regardless of how hard trout are feeding, if you don't put the fly down the groove to a certain fish, you'll do remarkably little business.

"I'll try that one, then," said Paul, nodding towards a riser about 30 feet out and slightly above us.

"Take a gander at the speed of the current between you and the fish," I said. "It's moving fast, and that's the water that's going to hurt you. It's one of the toughest spots to get a free float—when there's a fast current between you and where you want the fly to float."

"Try the S-cast," I suggested. "This is a perfect place for it."

"What's the S-cast?" asked Paul.

I described it to him.

"It will give you at least a couple of feet of free float, and that should be enough when the fish is hungry."

"Wish me luck," said Paul, getting his line in the air.

He false cast and when he had 35 feet he cast hard and the line shot out, hit the reel as he stopped the rod, and the fly lit as lightly as a bird, 4 feet above the rising fish. It bobbed jauntily along right over him absolutely free of drag. That 14-incher grabbed it without fear and a few minutes later, his face one big grin, Paul was landing his first trout.

Like all rules, the free float edict has exceptions, and one spot where a dry fly does not need to be floating dead center in order to get hits is in the eddy back of a protruding rock. In such an eddy a natural does not float normally, but is pulled and whirled by the varying currents, and for this reason the monster trout that may well lurk there will not be too upset by a fly that isn't floating free. But in such a spot the line is usually grabbed by the current as soon as it lights, whisking the fly out of there before it has time to float at all and before the fish can even see it. In that case, the angler must wade in close and cast a very short line, 12 or 15 or at most 20 feet, then hold the rod as high as possible so that the line is kept clear of the water altogether and only leader and fly are on the surface. That way it is possible to get a foot or two of float, or at least for the fly to whirl lightly around in the eddy, and that is usually sufficient for a strike.

The same technique pays off at the head of a pool. Cast across the fast water and where the current is pouring in hard, hold the arms high, rod in one hand and line in the other. When the current is very heavy you can often obtain a decent float this way even where an S-cast of a mended line would be bellied out of there in a hurry. A line handled this way is free of the water and the dry fly will float naturally down the far side of the current.

A beginner should keep his eyes going the entire time he is on the stream. The quickest way of getting on to trout habits is to watch them feed. In a clear stream you can get a close-up view of how they take a fly. On their feeding stations they generally seem to see the fly as it comes down the current, about 4 feet above them. Then, as it comes nearer they rise a bit higher to meet it, and as it comes over them they drift back right under it and suck it in.

When trout are not on their feeding stations working on a hatch, but are after minnows, they cruise around, usually working the still, shallow water, and they spend a lot of time covering the tails of the pools where the water thins off.

The first time I fished the Big Hole River near Melrose, Montana, I was so anxious to get fishing that I forgot to figure the water. I slipped into the tail of a beautiful-looking pool that was 400 feet long and about 70 feet wide. I waded out to knee depth and after a warm-up cast or two to take the edge off my eagerness, I started to look around. I should have known better. Where I was standing, and as far as I could see, the bottom was smooth and pebbly, with no break anywhere, no grasses, no rocks. This wasn't holding water, this was cruising water, and it wasn't cruising time. That would come later, about dusk. What was I doing here now?

I scrambled out and moved on upstream along the bank and went into the head of the pool about 75 feet from the top. I waded carefully out and at once saw trout rising in the fast current near the head of the pool. From then on I had fun. And just before dark I walked downstream again and in the tail of the pool saw trout cruising, snatching naturals from the surface. This was the time to be in the water. So I went well down below the working fish, waded in and crept up to within casting distance.

Cruising fish call for special treatment. A fly slipping along on the current as usual doesn't always pay off. They will slam it hard if it happens to come across their path, but those fish have left their feeding stations, they are on the make, out looking. You can see the V they cut as they swim just under the surface, and watch the water bulge as they grab a nymph just before it reaches the top. They take an erratic course across the pool, so that you must figure which way your fish is going, then quickly drop the fly about four feet in front of him. Generally he will spot the fly and take it on the go. Sometimes it helps to impart a jiggling motion to the fly with the rod tip, making the fly shiver and shake on the surface, then let it sit quietly, give it another twitch, then bring it slowly along the top to pick it up for the next cast—tease them good! Trout may hit a fly during any of the above maneuvers, and they often hit when you are bringing the fly along the surface because they think it is a freshly hatched fly taxiing across, trying for elevation.

All of these tricks take a little time, a little practice, a great deal of patience. But the amount of work a fisherman puts into them will be more than repaid in the increase in his take. There's nothing quite like the pleasure of looking at a stream at the end of the day and knowing that you've fished it well and taken from it as much as any angler is entitled to take—enough fish for the pan, and a world of enjoyment.

Most trouters fish far too rapidly. A few casts in one pool and then they are off to the next. Small pools, say 50 feet long and 40 feet across, don't take long to cover, but some of the larger ones, 100 to 200 feet long, call for a couple of hours of fishing to work them properly. Many times, especially when fish are rising, I take two hours to fish a pool 200 feet long and 100 feet across. And I have action the whole time.

The approach to a pool is more important than many fishermen think. Before even starting to fish, the dry-fly man should study the pool or run carefully. Trout always lie facing upstream as they feed and therefore the logical approach in order not to be seen, is from the tail of the pool. But somehow the beginner naturally gravitates to the head of the pool. Once there, he either stands on the highest rock, where all the trout in the pool can see him, or he wades noisily out into the center and casts hither and yon as he walks down the middle, flushing trout helter-skelter from their feeding place with every clumsy step.

If you start at the head of the pool, crouch as low as possible and wield the rod horizontally and try to fish from the bank. If there are bushes, stand in front of them so that your movements will not be flashed against a clear sky. Walk softly so that vibrations will not be sent out to be picked up by the fish. It all sounds extremely on the cautious side but if you would take more fish and take them consistently, these things do make the difference.

Even at the bottom of a pool it is always wise to move in with caution. In some pools the water hesitates before dropping over the lip and trout like to lie there, taking their food the easy way, where the water slows and they can rise up to their prey with a minimum of effort. In front of rocks the water also backs up and slows and usually there is a fish there, ready for whatever tidbit the current offers. The fast current on either side of a rock is another natural feeding place for trout, as is the eddy behind a rock. Fishing such an eddy means only a foot or two of float before the fly drags and it is necessary to get close, drop the fly lightly and hold the rod high as you can to prevent the line from catching in the swift current between you and the eddy and thus hastening the drag. But fish hit fast in eddies and usually a float of only a foot will bring a strike from a fish that is there and is hungry.

Fish out the bottom of the pool and work your way slowly up along it, fishing the different currents as you go. Once an angler is in the pool and working quietly along, the fish will usually become accustomed to him and often begin to break all around him, some of them practically leaping into his pockets. It is always startling when a trout rises right up in front of you, and usually it happens just when you are tossing your fly to some spot 60 feet away. It makes you realize—too late—that short, well-placed casts will usually do the trick.

As an example, one day while I was fishing the Taylor River, trout started to rise all around me. I took one fish 10 feet directly upstream from me and after things quieted down and the risers appeared again, I had a hit from a splasher not 15 feet below me. He had made a wave when he broke for a natural and he seemed like a good fish. I sent a downstream cast to him, throwing harder than I needed to for the distance and stopping the rod upright so as to land the line on the surface in serpentine fashion and allow the fly to float naturally over the riser before drag commenced. It didn't go over the riser, however, as he came up to meet it with determination and accuracy. The fight was on and he came out in a sidelong leap that showed me that I had been right about his size. He looked close to 3 pounds—but—another jump and my line flew high in the air as he shook the hook.

Usually at the head of a pool the fast water pours in tumultuously and then a big fly is by far the best. Rainbows are fast-water fish, but you'll find plenty of brownies up there with them, too. In a big, even-flowing pool it usually is best to work the pool from left to right or vice versa, depending on which side the angler is fishing.

I like to cast up and across stream and start with the first cast straight up for about 40 feet, make a couple of casts, then put the next throw 2 feet over to the right, and continue the procedure until I have covered all the water which I can reach comfortably and with accuracy. As the direction of the cast moves across the pool, I shorten the line to avoid drag and wind up that series when the cast is directly across stream from me. Then I move upstream and start the next series of casts at a point just below where the previous series had ended. It's very much like the wet-fly method of "drops" used in Atlantic salmon fishing, only the reverse. That is, the fisherman drops upstream.

There are many small things which, either done or left undone, may mean the difference in a day's take when fly fishing. Most dry-fly men don't get close enough to the fish. They try for long casts and end up with a long line that puts the fly beyond true control. Rather than try for a longer line to reach a fish, the dry-fly man should try for better wading. And though trout are easily frightened, they also forget quickly. Many times when an angler chases a fish off its feeding station, if he will only stand still for a while and wait, the fish will return and start feeding again, and then he will take. Get close to the fish, and keep the cast as short as possible.

When casting to a trout which has been seen in the water or has been spotted rising, it is best to drop the fly several feet in front of him. Give the fish plenty of time to get set to take, allow him to see the fly coming down the current for some distance up the pool. Now and then a trout will take a fly as soon as it lands, but on the whole you do better by letting the feeder see the fly coming from at least 4 feet away.

Try not to make the false casts over the spot where he is lying. Rather, the false casts should be made to the side, and then with a quick change of direction, the fly can be steered to the spot above him where you want it to land. In places where the fish can be seen and the angler is very close to him, a horizontal cast will do the trick, as sometimes in such close quarters the fish may see the rod in the air as it waves back and forth with the vertical cast. Scientists say the trout's area of vision widens like an inverted cone, so it helps fool them when you keep the rod low.

Another error common to many anglers is that they lift the fly too soon after it has gone over a trout that did not take. Ripping the line off the surface right in back of him will fix him for sure, and the angler might as well go on to the next pool and find a new fish to work on. The fly should be allowed to float well below the fish, 6 feet at least, then be retrieved carefully well in toward the fisherman before being lifted for the next cast. Then, with the fly still coming his way, a lift of the arm will pull the line quietly off the surface, and a snap of the wrist will shoot both line and fly and leader noiselessly up into the air.

If the fish has risen to the fly and missed, rather than just not showing interest, then the angler should wait a while before putting the fly back over him again. Give him time to get back on his feeding station and to forget that what he just hit had a most peculiar look. Then the chances are much better for a repeat than they would be if the fly were slammed right back at him.

While fishing the Gunnison River one day I had a most unusual experience. I had made my cast and the fly had scarcely lit when I saw a trout come up for a natural 2 feet behind and directly in line with my fly. The trout missed and the natural fluttered downstream.

He followed and hit at it twice more and missed both times. Then my fly came along and the trout had a go at it. He missed, or perhaps I missed, and then the trout further pursued and finally took the natural. All this fast and exciting action occurred within a 15-foot distance. Completely unnerved, I brought my fly in, hooked it in one of the guides of the rod, got out a cigarette, lighted it, and smoked that entire fag before allowing myself to cast over the spot where that trout had first showed. I thought I saw a flash down below the fly as it went over his former position but nothing happened. I waited at least a minute more before casting again. This time he took hard and my patience was rewarded when I landed a 16-incher.

The dry fly is the ideal way to fish a grassy stream where watercress grows along the banks and matted grass floats in patches on the surface. One day I came upon young Dick DePuy as I was fishing such a spring stream. Three feet out from the far bank a nice trout was rising.

"Take him," I said to Dick.

"I'll catch on the grass," said Dick. "This wet fly sinks fast."

"Try a dry," I suggested.

"How about that grass?"

He pointed to the 3-foot island of it.

"Drop the fly a couple of feet above the fish, let the line fall on the floating grass, and you should get over the fish okay," I said. "Then strike and keep your rod high and you can probably skid him across the surface and in to you."

It worked that way. The 10-inch brownie took on the first float and when Dick struck, the line jumped up from the grass, and holding the rod high, Dick pulled the struggling trout along the top to his net.

"Now you try one," said Dick. "There's another one rising just above where I took this one."

I walked into the water, dropped the dry fly in buoy solution to make it float high and dry. Then I made of couple of false casts and dropped the fly on the surface a couple of times just a few feet away from me and well away from where the fish was rising.

"Why are you doing that?" asked Dick.

"When the fly first hits the water," I explained, "the fly buoy puts a fine film of solution on the surface, and in such clear, still water as this, the fish might notice it and shy off. It's small things like that that may mean the difference in taking or not taking a fish out of a tough spot."

Many anglers fish a difficult stream as if they were afraid of it, stacking the cards against themselves before they even start. They snatch the line and fly out of every danger spot, oblivious to the fact that the biggest trout of them all may well have chosen that very spot as a safety area. For instance, when fishing the water along a log jam, you may think that the fly is about to float down and catch on the logs or brush. But look closer—you will see the water cushioning outwards from the logs and it takes the fly with it, safely along the edge. And it's right along the edge that the lunkers lurk. The angler who fearfully whips the fly out of there misses the chance of a strike from a big one, and probably scares the spots off all the trout around.

It seems as if the dry-fly man's greatest delight is trying to take fish under difficult conditions. He can have a lot of fun thinking and figuring and scheming ways to make them hit. He gets a kick out of taking advantage of the weather, the time of day, the way the light falls.

One day just at dusk Len Kinkie came up to me where I was fishing near Twin Bridges, Montana.

"Can't see a thing any more," he said. "Guess we may as well quit, though I hate to when they're hitting so well."

I looked over my shoulder at the western sky where there was still a faint glow.

"There's still a little light," I insisted.

I dug into my vest for my magnifying glasses, bought at the 5 & 10 cent store for 79 cents. Even with those on, it was hard to tie the fly, but by holding it up against the sky, I made it with a couple of jabs.

"You won't see the fly on the water anyway," said Len.

"Let's cross over the bridge," I said. "To the other side. And then I'll show you. We can get in another half hour yet. We'll be casting against the light then."

We moved into another pool over there, and sure enough, when we cast, our flies showed up plainly, silhouetted against the fading light as long as there was a glow in the western sky. We each took a couple more fish before total darkness dropped the curtain.

When the dry-fly man finds that fish are not rising, he has many a trick to fall back on to tempt the wily, sleepy, or too well-fed trout to hit. He can coax them up by guile, or he can waken them from their sleep, or he can make them mad enough to hit even though they are not hungry.

One time on the Yellow Breeches in Pennsylvania, my dry fly, a size 14 black gnat, came bouncing down a fast glide, 4 inches out from a jumble of logs. The trout that dashed up for it changed his mind at the last second and almost ripped a fin off getting back home again. He was so big he gave me the shakes. Instead of resting him I had to rest myself. But after a few long minutes I managed to put that fly out there again.

My gnat came high-riding down the current as chipper as a birch bark canoe. Four feet down under those logs that wily old buster stuck his beezer out, but he stayed at the foot of the stairs. I kept casting, changing flies a dozen times, but still no soap. Something was haywire.

I got the brain cells working.

The fly was floating entirely free of drag. The leader was long and fine, tapered to a 4X tippet. I was crouched low so that fish couldn't see me. Everything was as right as a teenager. Yet something was keeping him from hitting.

"First of all, there's no hatch on," I mumbled to myself. "So he isn't out in the open on a feeding station."

"That's it!" I almost shouted. "He's deep under cover, hungry to a certain degree, but not enough to come to the table and reach for a knife and fork."

So, I figured, there were a couple of things to do if I wanted to make him hit a dry fly. I could manufacture a hatch by casting time and again to the same spot, floating fly after fly past him, and in that way convince him that soup was on. Or I could put on a size 12 spider, a big powder puff of a fly. Oversize flies will often raise a trout just out of sheer curiosity, and even if he does not then grab the big fly, he is usually aroused enough to take a swipe at a smaller offering that looks bona fide. Similarly, when an angler knows there is a fish, especially a big one, in a heavy current, he can often coax him out by casting a big hairwing fly or a grasshopper type fly to the far edge of the current, then, holding the rod high, skip the fly back across the surface. Many a big buster has come roaring out of the rapids to such an offering, which might very well scare the daylights out of him in calm water but only seems to make him mad, there in the hurly-burly of the current.

Since this particular trout had already showed enough enthusiasm to take a glance at the black gnat, I decided to manufacture a hatch with it. After eleven casts and floats he came out from under the logs. Another eight casts pulled him up within a couple of feet of the surface. He looked ready. He also looked as if he would weigh 4 pounds.

On the next cast he spotted the fly, moved up within an inch of the surface, let go his fin hold in the current, drifted back with it, opened his mouth and inhaled the fly. I raised the rod tip and set the hook, but I couldn't hold him and he slammed back under the logs and broke me off. But what matter? I had fun putting one over on that tough old cannibal. It was the satisfaction of the play, calling the pitch and showing him the right offering in the right way. That's the main course in dry-fly fishing and for dessert there is the moving water, the peaceful meadows, and doing what you like best of all. It's this challenge and satisfaction that make dry-fly men unequivocally name their sport the tops in angling.

Terrestrials

Terrestrials include ants, beetles, daddy long legs, houseflies, inch worms, Japanese beetles, grasshoppers and jassids—and many other insects that are born on the land and become trout food when they blow, fly, fall, crawl or jump into the water. They often come late in the season after the aquatic hatches have had their day, and they come on strong. There is something about a terrestrial that appeals mightily to a trout, be it the juicy crispness of the grasshopper, the tart taste of the ant, or the pepper speck on the tongue, the tiny jassid.

Grasshoppers are perhaps the oldest of the terrestrials used by fly fishermen. In some of our Western states the grasshopper, fished either wet or dry, is liked so much that very little else is used, other than the wooly worm. Even in this day of more sophisticated approaches to trout, and better materials for tying, the old, beat-up 'hopper still takes its deadly toll. There are several different ties of this great fly, the Joe's Hopper, first tied by a Michigan barber, being the most popular.

I have always found grasshoppers particularly good on windy days. I'll never forget one time when I was fishing the Clark Fork of the Columbia River with Bruce Elliott of Rock Creek Lodge, near Clinton, Montana, and Russ Ward, a Missoula tackle dealer. As we walked the grass banks looking for a good spot to cast, the wind began to blow up strong. Its sharp gusts swept a myriad of grasshoppers off the long grasses by the river and blasted them into the stream, where they drifted, struggling on the surface. Within half a minute trout were rising all along the bank, snatching at them. We put on Joe's Hoppers and what a couple of hours we had!

Ants run grasshoppers a close second in the terrestrial line. I have used a size 20 flying black ant, dry, for many years and still call it my favorite on limestone streams, and indeed on almost any type of stream. The smaller ants are used dry, especially those tied on small-sized hooks, such as 18, 20, and 22. The larger ants are generally fished wet, at varying levels beneath the surface. I always like to have in my box the following ants: wet, in hook sizes 8 to 20, black, red, black and red, and white; dry, in hook sizes 18, 20 and 22, black, brown, and cinnamon. The size 12 black ant tied by the Phillips Fly and Tackle Company of Alexandria, Pennsylvania, is one of the best wet flies I have ever used.

Many times when weather, or muddy water, or feeding habits, were keeping fish down, ants have saved the day for me. One such day, Dan Bailey and I hit the Yellowstone when the water was still high and roily after a hard rain.

"It's clearing," said Dan. "But it's not ready for dry flies yet."

He moved on upstream, while I went right in where I was. I soon spotted a few ants drifting by. Some place up above, the flash storm had washed a colony of them into the river. They looked like a choice item for trout and I took the cue. I dug into my fly box and picked out a black ant, size 12. I was busy tying it on the end of a 3X tippet, attached to a 10-foot leader, when Dan called to me.

"Try an ant," he suggested, pointing to the river. He had spotted them, too.

We both got busy. Trout seemed to be everywhere and we caught them consistently. They all acted so hungry that I decided to see what else they would hit. I put on a yellow wooly worm, took one fish on it, and then didn't get another strike for twenty casts. I put on a royal coachman, size 12, wet. I made fifteen casts. No strikes. I tried a leadwing coachman. No soap. Here were three of the best-known wet flies on the Yellowstone River and trout didn't want them. I hastened to tie on the black ant again and in four casts I hung two trout, landed one, lost one. It was ants they wanted.

When fishing an ant, I usually use the same technique as in fishing a wet fly for Atlantic salmon. I start with a cast of about 12 feet, thrown across and slightly upstream, mend the line and as the ant reaches the end of the downstream float, I bring it back across the current in short jerks for about 3 feet, let it swim free for a couple of feet, then repeat the jerks. At the end of the swing through, when the ant is directly below me, I strip it my way for about 3 feet, again with jerks, then pick it up for the next cast. This time I lengthen the throw a foot, repeat the same procedure as before, and continue thus, lengthening each cast till all the near water has been covered. Then I move downstream to about the farthest point where the ant has worked and begin the series of casts all over again.

But if the fish are passing up such a presentation, there are other ways of getting to them. A short cast straight across current, then a retrieve in short jerks just under the surface, will often get a hit. And when fish are rising, sometimes they will not hit a drifting ant, but a cast across and a couple of feet above a riser, brought back in 8- or 9-inch jerks, will get that baby nearly every time.

A few days after I had fished with Dan, I hit the Yellowstone again, this time with Edwin and Allen Nelson. It was clear and fish were rising, taking naturals. We fanned out and started to fish and soon I saw Edwin hook a nice cutthroat on a dry. A pair of rainbows fell in succession to my big number 10 hairwing royal coachman as it danced along the waves of a fast ripple. They looked like brother and sister, both 14-inchers. It was a good start.

Then a fast-moving black cloud dropped its burden, putting the fish down and making us run for the willows. After the rain stopped, the wind came up. It scuffed the surface, making for very poor dry-fly fishing. We only landed one fish in the next hour. Finally we joined forces, compared notes.

"I like a wooly worm," said Allen, showing me the gray one he had just tied on. "They really catch fish."

"You're right," I agreed. "But have you ever tried this?"

I showed him a black ant with a red tail, tied on a number 10 hook.

"There's something that really takes 'em," I said. "It's as hot as a Yellowstone geyser."

"I still like the wooly worm," he said. But he pocketed the ant just the same.

Ed and I went back to dropping our flies on the surface, while Allen moved upstream. Suddenly we heard him yell.

"Yippee!" he shouted. We saw a pound and a half rainbow flash in the air.

"Yippee!" he shouted again, as the crimson-streaked jumping jack reached upwards for a second time.

We watched him land the fish, then turned back to our dry fly fishing again.

"Youie!" we heard him yell, ten minutes later, and we saw another rainbow trying for the moon.

I changed to a big dry fly, then a small one. Edwin was busy tying on different flies, too, but none of them got action. At last we gave in.

"Sure must be pay day for wooly worms," Edwin shouted to me. "I'm going to put one on."

"Me too," I yelled back.

But fifteen minutes later we were still hitless. Then Allen really let out a yell. We jerked our heads around in time to see a huge trout thrashing on top. Allen's rod tip snapped back as we watched and Allen turned and started for shore.

"Where are you going!" shouted Ed.

"I'm getting out of here," said Allen. "They're eating me up. And besides that, that last fish took my fly."

As he splashed up to me, I pointed at the lamb's wool on his vest, where he had an assortment of flies showing.

"You've got another wooly worm there," I told him.

"Wooly worms?" he said. "I've been using that black ant you gave me. How about another?"

Edwin and I got ants on in a hurry. After that we had hits and we caught fish from then on out. The trout menu that day consisted of a single, all-in-one dish—black ants.

Ants are good medicine in high-altitude lakes, too, especially for cutthroat. On a pack trip to Charlie White Lake, near Emigrant Peak, Montana, Eleanore and Arnold Schueren and my wife Mary and I fished from the shore to trout that were swirling within easy casting distance. On dry flies we didn't do much, so I shifted to a black ant and those natives went to town. I had such fast and furious action that pretty soon everyone else wanted in. I dug into my fly box and produced what I had—three black, a couple with red tails, and two white ones. I divied up and we all went back to fishing.

We had decided to eat fish for dinner that night, so we were keeping some for that purpose and when there were enough, the women headed back to camp to start the fire. Arnold and I went on fishing, less carefully now, because we had all the fish we wanted—fishing just for the fun of fishing. We hooked into several pretty good ones that took us under the brush and around fallen logs with which the shoreline was littered. By the time we started for camp, we had lost all the ants.

Suddenly as we neared the tents, we heard yells. We rounded the curve in the path in time to see both women wielding frying pans at a totally unperturbed burro that was busily eating up our dinner fish. He was holding one fish headfirst in his mouth and every time he chewed the tail would flap up in the girl's faces. A couple more whacks with the frying pans finally drove Jack off to finish his dinner with the rest of the pack train, and then a quick count showed us the damage. We were short three fish for dinner.

We had to go back to the lake, and this time, minus ants, it took us almost an hour to get those three fish.

I remember another time, too, when nothing but ants would take fish in one of those high-altitude lakes. We were 9000 feet up, at Lake of the Woods, in Wyoming. Mary and I were in one boat with Pete Redman of Dubois, while his son, Duane, had a couple of fellows from Texas in another boat.

Duane had told us that there were grayling in this lake.

"But sometimes they're awful hard to catch," he said. "Can't figure it out. They'll be rising all around, but they won't take anything."

I dug into my fly box and found five black ants. I gave him two.

"Try these," I said. "Sometimes they're good in these high-altitude lakes."

They were good that day, all right. Mary and I had great fun taking one grayling after the other. We whooped and hollered as we landed them, removed the ants from their mouths, and put the fish back.

Nothing but a great and gloomy silence came from the other boat. We could see the men casting and casting, but with never a strike. They moved closer to us.

"What are they hitting?" asked Duane.

"Ants," I replied. "Haven't you tried the ones I gave you?"

He shook his head.

"I left them in the jeep," he said, "Can you spare a couple more until we go in for lunch?"

"Sure," I said. "Come on over."

I handed him two more. They pushed off and soon their whoops and hollers were blending with ours. They were into fish, but good.

Similarly, although beetles are an occasional rather than a regular food for trout, there are times when almost nothing else will do. During the height of the Japanese beetle migrations, I've opened trout whose belly linings were cut clear through with the bites of these insects before they perished.

A couple of years ago I was fishing the Laramie River in Wyoming, on the Lazy W Cross Ranch, near Glendivy. Strikes were few, and the fish seemed lethargic. Most of those that did show came up slowly and looked the floating fly over carefully, then just nudged it with their noses. I switched to nymphs and if anything, the going was slower. Then I spotted a couple of black beetles floating along. I tied an artificial beetle, black, size 12, on my leader tippet. No hits. Thinking that perhaps those drifting beetles had been dark brown, rather than black, I changed to that color. They scorned the brown beetle, and then a green one. In desperation I put on a size 18, black, and hit the jackpot. For the next half-hour I was busy taking trout. They hit that little beetle like they really wanted it. There wasn't any hesitation, there was no careful scrutiny. They just charged it and took.

Not content with that demonstration, I tied on a size 18 green beetle. They let that color go by. I put on a size 18 brown. They didn't even know it was there. They wanted a size 18 black, and nothing else would do.

Occasionally, when the usual underwater presentations fail to interest trout, I grease all of the leader and the bottom of the beetle with line dressing and let it float on top. At times I bring it back in a smooth even retrieve that makes the beetle look like the real thing skimming across the surface. It works, too. In fact, the angler who isn't afraid to use a little ingenuity can find some mighty odd but successful ways to fish a beetle.

On one occasion when I was fishing a clear spring lake in Montana with Red Monical, we could see the fish cruising so close to the shore that it was like looking at them through a window pane.

We heard a familiar story. "No one can catch these trout," we were told. "The water is so clear that they see you every time, and won't hit."

One look convinced me that regardless of the fly, those fish would not take anything unless it were on the end of a very long fine leader. This place called for a 12-foot leader tapered to at least 4X. Even with that already set up, I added another 16-inch length of 4X tippet, then put on a size 12 black beetle.

Such slick-water beetle fishing also called for the same greased line and leader as nymph fishing, with the last 3 inches of the tippet treated with leader sink. Quietness, a lightly dropped fly and line, patience to wait before imparting even the slightest motion, careful timing of the retrieve, and a sharp lookout for the very slight leader movement that signifies a strike—these are all even more important in still, clear water than in riffles and ripples.

There was a barely perceptible current and I cast the beetle out and let it float there for at least a minute, then moved it my way, very slowly, in 6-inch jerks, for a couple of feet, then let it stay motionless again for another quarter minute. Then I repeated the jerks and picked it up for the next cast.

I worked the black beetle that way for a few minutes, then, when it didn't get a strike, changed to a green, size 14. Immediately I had a fish. After watching me land it, Red went down the shore a way to try his luck. When I next saw him, he had a couple of nice fish taken on the same green beetle.

"I had to do some figuring," he said. "I missed several strikes because I couldn't see the line and leader moving when the trout hit. But I fixed those babies. I put on a number 10 hairwing royal coachman, then tied the beetle on an 18-inch length of 4X tippet as a dropper. The hairwing worked like a bobber, and boy, did it bob when those trout hit. I hooked them good, too."

Even if your fly box doesn't contain a single beetle, and the time comes when you suspect that a beetle is what is needed, there is a way to fake one. Once on a small Eastern stream in Maryland, I was using a size 20 dry fly and couldn't make those bulging trout take it. It was a limestone stream and this was my favorite fly, a black flying ant, and they should have liked it. But those nymph-feeding trout wouldn't take it, nor would they take a nymph when I finally gave in and tried several. They rocked the dries as they bulged right beside them, and they pushed aside the floating nymphs to get at whatever they were eating. But they would have none of what I offered.

I sat down on a log and pulled out all of my fly boxes. I went through them carefully. Down in one corner of a dry-fly-laden section I spotted a small black beetle, size 18. I scattered flies in all directions as I grabbed that beetle and tied it on the 5X tippet.

And I was right! The first float brought a hard strike and I was so keyed up that I laid back on the rod like I was striking a 100-pound tarpon and left that one and only beetle in the trout's mouth.

Disgusted, I staggered back to my log again and fingered through the fly boxes. Not a beetle or a nymph that looked the least bit like a beetle!

Then I saw a black gnat, size 16. I grabbed that baby like it was peaches and cream, cut the wings off, snipped the tail off, and held it up. It looked almost like the beetle that had just brought such a rousing strike. The third time I floated that makeshift thing over a bulging trout, he took. I set the hook lightly, this time, and fought the fish boldly then, because I knew that I had at least half a dozen black gnats in my box that I could metamorphose into beetles. Nature is wonderful, but sometimes man can do a good job, too. To avoid getting caught as I did, you should always carry a few beetles in hook sizes 8 to 14, in black, brown, bronze and green.

Newest in the terrestrial field is the jassid developed on the Letort River in Pennsylvania and described by its innovator, Vince Marinaro, in his fine book, *A Modern Dry Fly Code*. With the help of Charlie Fox, on whose water on the Letort River the investigation and experimentation were done, Vince observed the jassids in the river and came up with matching artificials which were sensational fish takers.

It was in the natural course of events that the discovery of the jassid in particular, and the development of the use of the terrestrial in general, should have taken place in Pennsylvania. For although there are many such waters in Maryland, Virginia, West Virginia, Kentucky, Missouri and Ohio, the Quaker State is the traditional locale of these unique streams. Emerging out of faults in the limestone along the edge of the freestone, these rivers usually run through lush meadows, meandering quietly along with placid pools and long runs that cut channels through the dense stands of underwater weeds and grasses. The streams are seldom over 60 feet across and most of the pools are less than 80 feet long. However, there is usually a good flow of water, and the angler can pick up fish all along the way, from undercut banks, channels in the grasses, smack in the middle or in eddies behind surface-matted grass, or the occasional tree root that extends out into the water. The best way, if the river has a good head of trout, is to loaf your way along, upstream, looking for the rings made by risers. This is the fun way, but if they are not rising, then you simply work the good holding water.

These streams are packed with beds of elodea, a dense weed that is the home of all manner of nymphs, cress bugs, and other types of trout fodder, and there are many other grasses and weeds which harbor food. During the course of their exploratory work, Vince Marinaro and Charlie Fox became aware of a consistent rise of a particular nature. The fish that came up did not seem to break the surface, but appeared to be bulging, humping, and cupping the water, but not breaking it. The rise made a V-shaped form on the surface that slipped down the current and dissolved. At first glance it would appear that they were nymphing, taking the nymphs as they neared the top to ride the surface, break their nymphal shucks and emerge, dry their wings and fly away. But at these times there was no hatch of aquatic flies. The first nymph did not make the surface. Nothing showed. And a steady bombardment of nymphs, cast and fished flawlessly, left those two veterans hitless. Yet the fish went on feeding; on what, the anglers could not see, but always with that characteristic and strange rise form.

The first day that Vince showed me this rise form I noticed that sometimes the V turned into a circle farther downstream.

"That's right," said Vince, when I mentioned this to him, "and if you are not sharp you might miss seeing the V, and cast to the circle, which wouldn't get you a hit because you would be throwing far behind the fish."

How many anglers must have suffered defeat before this same trout behavior on limestone streams, and finally, after throwing the fly box at the rising fish, have gone their way shaking their heads! How many must have searched the water in vain for the fly, or its nymph, on which those trout were feeding! How many have given up, saying "They just won't take anything."

Those rises were really hard to spot. When I was fishing with Vince he had to point them out to me, until I got onto it.

"That's the way it used to be with me," said Vince. "At first I didn't see that rise, or at best, I spotted only the circle drifting down. Then I began to notice the V-shaped rises, always the same, and it seemed to me that there must be something in the water that I couldn't see and that those trout were taking."

"There's one now," Vince said. "Try him."

My leader was 12 feet long and tapered down to a 6X tippet. I tied on a size 22 jassid that Vince handed me. Then I crawled toward the stream bank. Five feet from the water, and from a kneeling position, I made my cast and dropped the fly 5 feet above where the fish had shown. It was hard to follow but I glued my eyes on it, and knowing the line of drift, managed to see the tiny fly, watch it down to where the trout had been working, past that spot, on for 4 more feet. Then I saw movement, a foot below the surface, and suddenly I saw the fish rise right under the fly, and he took. I waited a bit, then raised the rod tip. I was into my first jassid-hooked brown. Working carefully I played him out, and in. Then I gently removed the hook from the corner of his mouth and put him back in the water.

"That's a dividend trout," I said. "There isn't the first show of aquatic insects. No spentwings, nothing that I can see but flat water. Except for those V-shaped rises now and then."

"That's it," said Vince. "Jassids fill the gap."

Early in his investigations, before he knew just what these small insects were, Vince opened trout and found them tightly packed with tiny terrestrials in many different colors. He collected a number and sent them to an entomologist.

"Formerly called jassidae," was the report, "but recently scientists have changed the name to cicadellidae."

Vince chose to use the earlier name, and condensed it to "jassid," and by that title these small insects and their matching flies have gone into angling records. There are myriads of jassids in many colors, so many that there is no need to tie the artificial in any special hue. Almost any color of hackle will do the trick. Personally I like black best.

When Vince first tied flies to match the natural jassid he had poor results. They were realistic flies, but still those choosy trout passed them up. It was not until he conceived the idea that with a fly as small a the jassid, perhaps the form was all-important, plus the way those little naturals floated awash. His next step was to tie the fly without a body. He used a flattened junglecock wing, "junglecock nail" fly tyers term it, which made the wings opaque. Now he had the silhouette only, and by clipping a small V on the underpart of the hackle, he produced a fly which would float in the water, rather than on it, awash like the naturals.

He soon found that this was, indeed, the way the trout wanted those jassids. And from then on, he and Charlie were catching fish from waters that seemed fishless to other anglers. It wasn't long be-fore others in the area learned about the jassid. Soon the fly took its rightful place in American angling lore, and has become known wherever trout fishermen meet as one of the great flies of all time.

The jassid calls for special presentation, not so much a long and fine cast as a short and delicate one. From the first silent, creeping approach to the stream to the especially restrained strike, because of the lightness of the tippet, everything must be keyed to the tiny terrestrial. Only a very light tippet will allow the angler to drop such a fly lightly and loosely, and will allow the tippet to float with a minimum of friction or water disturbance.

For those who aspire to tie the jassid, here is the pattern:

JASSID
Body: Tying silk, any color.
Wings: One medium to small junglecock nail, any color.
Hackle: Two or three, very small, turned as for a ribbing hackle. Any
*   color, as short-fibred as possible.*
Hook: 20 short or 22 regular, model perfect.

The method of tying the jassid is very much the same as that used in tying any of the small beetles, except that the materials used are limited to tying silk, junglecock nail, and hackle, all used sparingly. First tie in the hackle and wind the front, then spiral hackle front, turning the hackles one at a time in open turns, as for a ribbing hackle, and tie off at the neck. Next, clip the hackle, top and bottom, so that the fly has a low-riding appearance, as does the natural. This tie allows maximum support with the fewest possible fibers, 2½ turns being quite sufficient for a jassid to float beautifully.

Another good terrestrial is the daddy long legs. I remember using one of these with great luck in the Omme River in Denmark. When I first looked at that tule-lined, glassy water, I felt convinced that the smallest of flies would be what I needed. I tried them, pattern after pattern, without success. Then Sven Saaby, a well-known Danish artist, came along. He handed me a couple of daddy long legs.

"This is the best fly on the river," he said.

They were large, sparsely tied, on a size 12 hook.

I dropped my first cast into a run along the bank and watched it float serenely along. Then I saw the snout of the trout as he inhaled and I lifted my rod tip. Although I knew he was large when I saw his nose, I could hardly believe it when he came out and really showed me his size. He fought like the 3-pounder he was, but I finally pulled him over the landing net.

Wet Fly and Nymph
Fishing for Trout

FISHING THE WET FLY

The wet fly is at once the hope of the beginner and the veteran. There are many old-timers who will use nothing else, for wet flies have paid off for them over the years with some mighty big fish that seldom rise to dries. And the novice, providing he can wade to within easy reach of a current where fish are likely to lie, and can heave the fly out there to drift in the current, can usually manage to hang a trout, even though his method may involve more dunking than finesse.

Nevertheless, to really fish a wet fly with the greatest success calls for a knowledge of fish lies, their feeding habits, and the ability to cast the fly to the greatest advantage. With the exception of those times when a wet fly is played to imitate a moving bit of food, such as a minnow or shrimp or nymph, it seems to me that the one big thing with wets as with dries, to get consistent hits, is the free float, without any semblance of drag. Therefore, the up-and-across cast pays off best. With that presentation, the fly should float along naturally with the current and the trout will rise to it much as they do to a dry fly, thinking it is what it's meant to be, a downed fly, floating downstream.

On the up-and-across cast I allow the fly to float motionless for almost the complete length of its downward swim, until it begins to swing in below me in the current. Then I often manipulate the rod tip so that it will cause the fly to hop forward in a series of short jumps, a couple of inches at a time, and continue that technique until the fly is directly below me in the water, and then I bring it my way for 10 or 12 feet before lifting it as quietly as possible from the water.

This up-and-across-stream cast permits delivery without letting the fish see the angler. Since fish usually lie facing into the current, the angler is far enough below, or off to the side from them, that they will not so readily spot him. It's true that a good wader can get into the stream and fish a wet fly on down and scarcely disturb the fish except for the ones he drives off their feeding stations as he wades. But the average angler is usually too noisy in his wading, waves his arms too much, and makes no effort to hide, so the fish can hardly avoid seeing him. Sometimes I wonder that many of them catch a fish at all, because they start at the head of the pool, standing on a rock or bank high above the water, in plain view of any trout within 50 feet. And since the trout's eyes are aimed upward anyway, that wet-fly man is at a great disadvantage before he even starts to fish.

But in such a situation a wet fly cast straight upstream, from farther down, would have brought him hits from the very fish that thus spot him. In using the straight upstream cast in fast water, however, a very short line must be thrown in order to be able to retain any control and be ready to strike. A cast of 25 or 30 feet is plenty long enough, and then the line should be stripped at approximately the same speed at which the current is riding the fly down towards the angler—and as he raises the rod, he is then ready for the strike or for the pickup for the next cast.

Sometimes when trout seem to be lazy, they can be stirred into striking by throwing the wet fly across the current and then bringing it back at once in a series of foot-long jerks, much as a streamer fly is fished. This is one of the times when I am convinced the fish hits the fly as a minnow, not a fly.

When using the across-current cast, the line must be mended and the fly led down with the rod tip ahead of the line (*see* Fly Fishing for Atlantic Salmon). With that method the angler has good control of the line, avoiding a belly that would delay his strike to the fish; and the fly is presented broadside so the fish has a better view than if it were hurtling down head or tail first. Then, when the fly starts to swing in below, it can be given motion by imparting short jerks which should attract a trout's attention and cause him to go for it.

Another almost sure-fire method to get a hit on a wet fly is to let it float for several yards, then give it motion for a couple of feet, then stop the strip and let the fly float free in the current again. What the trout think of this one is any man's guess, but it may be that he mistakes the feathery fooler for a fly still struggling, or a wounded minnow, floating, fighting to regain his equilibrium, floating and fighting.

Whichever retrieve seems to be the payoff of the day, that is the one to stick to, as trout appear to follow a pattern. Once I have found out what they want I stay with it till they stop hitting, and then I try something else. And regardless of how the fly is played, it must be played with confidence. With a dry fly, the angler knows what the fly is doing, and if the fish are rising he knows they are there. With a wet fly he must *believe* that the fly is doing what it should be doing, and he must *believe* the fish are there. He must be convinced that they're down there just waiting to knock the hackles off his fly.

Most anglers fish far too fast, passing up chance after chance because they do not figure the water before they start. Every pool and run should be figured out and a pattern set for casting. This not only makes for more pleasant and leisurely fishing, it brings a better harvest from the water.

For instance, sometimes I spend more than an hour fishing a pool 100 feet long. But I cover all the water, starting my first cast up and across current and not too far from me. I fish that cast through the length of the float and then make my next throw a couple of feet farther out. And so on, until I have fanned well out, 60 feet or more, and the fly has gone over practically any lie of a trout within that area. Then I move to a point just below that covered by my first series of floats, and repeat. This is the drop system of fishing a wet fly for Atlantic salmon and it is equally effective for trout. It pays off. It covers all the water and when you are through you are likely to find that you have picked up a couple of fish from spots you might ordinarily have overlooked.

To fish a wet fly properly calls for just as much, or even more, finesse than fishing a dry fly. A dry fly is easier to cast, the angler can see all the action, including the strike. but the wet fly is comparatively heavy and does not have the balance, the padding, so to speak, of the hackles of the dry, to set it down lightly and quietly. The hackles are tied facing backwards and are sparse, and therefore the fly comes down more heavily.

One thing that will help the beginning fly caster is a nicely tapered leader and one that is long enough to take up a lot of the shock of the heavy wet fly, allowing the lighter delivery that is a sure aid to getting strikes. Yet the majority of wet-fly fishermen seem to gravitate to unnecessarily heavy leaders and many a wet-fly addict I meet on the stream is all set up with a short, 6-foot leader running as high as 20-pound test. Even though in some circumstances, such as very heavy water, the fish might not spot this atrocity, the heavy leader hurts the action of the fly. A 9-foot, or preferably a 12-foot, leader would get many more strikes, especially when the water is clear. And for almost any trout, regardless of size, a 6-pound-test tippet should be more than adequate. For average fishing, the tippet can be almost as fine for wet-fly fishing as for dry. And certainly these calibrations are far less noticed by the fish.

Once on Slate Run in Pennsylvania, a good stream for small trout, I ran into a wet-fly fisherman coming down the creek. We stopped and talked awhile, and as we talked, a trout rose across from us.

"Why don't you show him that wet?" I asked.

"Oh, they won't hit a wet when they're rising," he said. "I've tried."

"As far as that goes," I said, "I've fished a dry over risers for many an hour and not caught them. Anyhow, throw it over there and give it a try."

As he got ready to cast I noticed that he was using a leader tippet that must have gone about 20-pound test. He didn't even get a flash in ten casts.

"See?" he said at last.

"Give me that fly," I said. When he took it off and handed it to me, I tied it on the end of my 4X tippet.

"Try this," I said, handing the rod to him.

He hemmed and hawed and said he couldn't cast such a leader as that 12-footer, and the whole thing was too light for him, and so on.

But his first cast went out there perfectly and dropped the size 12 black gnat he had been using just right. The trout took on that first float and came struggling out, a nice 12-incher.

That man looked at me as if he couldn't believe it.

"It's nothing but the leader," I said. "The fish can see the one you've been using."

It isn't often that you have such a chance to show how important the smaller leader can be. Or the trout may be selective and feeding on only one type of fly that happens to be emerging, but they will still take time out to sock a wet if it is presented to them right. Maybe it resembles the nymph of the fly they are taking, or maybe it just looks good, but either way, it's well worth while to cast your wet among the surface feeders.

The exception to the light leader rule comes when the fly is being retrieved in fast, foot-long jerks, in water where a heavy trout might hit in the middle of a strip and break the tippet. But the angler will have so many more strikes on light gear that even in such water it is more fun to keep the wet-fly leader down to a fine terminal point and take the chance of losing a fly or two.

Probably because they are fishing blind, rather than to specific fish, or rising fish, all too many wet-fly anglers fish in a hit or miss fashion. Selection of the wet fly to be used is more a matter of chance than is the case with dry flies, where the angler sees the natural and the fish rising to take it right before his eyes. But many times a careful study of the stream will reveal flies floating down, or bugs or insects which can be matched with a certain wet fly, if not in exact conformation, then at least in color and size. And once a fish has been landed, it is easy to open him up and examine the contents of the stomach and quickly determine what is the main item on the menu that day.

FISHING NYMPHS FOR TROUT

The nymph is the underwater stage of an aquatic fly. Nymphs spend two to three years living under rocks on the bottom of the stream, encased in a sort of shell, then at various times they struggle to the surface, break their cases, and emerge as flies. Nymphs appear in many different forms, some flat-bodied, some round-bodied, and others appear to have built little houses around themselves, or put up nets to catch food.

Nymphs differ in the way they act prior to emerging as flies. Some crawl out on the rocks, while others go up the reeds along-shore and when the fly appears it lays its eggs there. When the eggs hatch, the little creature that is born crawls down the reed again to hide itself in the mud till it is time for the cycle to begin all over again. Still other nymphal forms are often seen floating downstream, riding along the surface as the fly works out of its shell and finally breaks free and flies away—if some hungry trout doesn't get it.

And so it goes, through a vast array of underwater forms of life which for fishing purposes we class together as nymphs. As a result of the great variety, it takes a close study of nymphs to match them with artificials and the tying of good nymphs is one of the most difficult phases of fly tying. Some of the products turned out are also the prettiest things in a fly man's book.

Since the nymph is usually underwater when the fish takes it, or barely to the surface, it should carry a little more weight than dries, and most commercially tied nymphs are weighted. In the case of some of the lighter, unweighted ones, however, anglers frequently pinch on a split shot about a foot above the fly if it becomes necessary to get them down to reach a feeding fish.

While many private tyers turn out nymphs of their own design, commercial tyers in the Eastern part of the country, where nymph fishing has a longer history than in the West, concentrate on the well-known light stone fly, yellow May fly, March brown, Tellico, ginger quill, brown drake, black and yellow, orange and black, black, and the Ed Burke, all tied on sizes from 10 to 14. The smallest nymph I have ever been able to find was tied on a size 16 hook, but certainly there are naturals which would be matched with a size 18 or even 20, if these were available on the market.

On the other end of the line are such really big ones as the Western stone flies, called by various names—salmon, trout, and willow fly—often so large that they are tied on number 6 long-shank hooks. Rocky Mountain tyers have done an imaginative job of imitating natural nymphs. Dan Bailey of Livingston, Montana, turns out a large stone fly nymph on a 2X long, number 8 hook, that is more natural looking than the natural. It is best in the early season while the big hatch is on, but will produce well all year. Some of the best Western nymphs in larger sizes are the Bailey's May fly nymph, caddis fly, the cross guinea, dark olive and cream May fly, all tied on 10 and 12 hooks. Tied on long-shank hooks in sizes 6 to 10, the light mossback with light olive and cream body is a good producer, and the dark mossback with body of dark olive and yellow is one of the best nymphs I've ever fished.

The first dark mossback I ever tried was handed to me by Dan Bailey, who invented this particular tie. He told me he thought it was one of the best early-season nymphs in the West. I started using it and kept taking fish. I tried it in August and September and up to mid-October and throughout all that time I had wonderful luck with it. About that time I went out one day with Dan and we tried the Yellowstone River about 20 miles upstream from Livingston. Dan started about halfway down a 200-yard-long pool and I moseyed on up to the top. I used the dark mossback and was into a good fish at once. I took four in a row and the last one went 3 pounds, a deep-bodied, high-jumping rainbow.

I noticed that Dan wasn't doing much, and then I saw him walking my way, well back from the river. Then he came out in back of me.

"What are they hitting?" he asked.

"The dark mossback," I said. "They've been hitting it all summer and fall, too. In fact, ever since you gave me that one last spring, I've been cleaning up with them."

Dan laughed. "That's typical. I tie the fly but I don't have the first one with me."

I gave him a couple from my box and he went back to his former position and took a fish on his first cast.

Potts of Missoula ties the Sandy Mite, Lady Mite, Mr. Mite, and Buddy Mite, in sizes 6 to 12, to represent nymphs familiar in that area. These are hair hackle ties with either hair or silk bodies with bright colored silk strips laced into the bottom. The hackle hairs are shaped around the hook. And another Western favorite that has proven out elsewhere is the gray nymph in sizes 6 to 12, with a heavy, fuzzy body of muskrat fur, gray hackle, and badger tail.

Nymphs which take fish both in the East and the West and which should always be in the angler's fly box are the caddis, the

Hewitt nymphs, the flat-bodied nymphs in gray and black, and the nymph tied with gray fur body. The little black nymph tied on a number 12 hook is a good one, too. These should be carried in sizes from 8 to 18. And now and then the larger yellow and gray nymphs on size 6 hooks will also take plenty of fish in the bigger rivers.

Nymphs which should appear in the trout fisherman's box are:

NYMPHS
(WEIGHTED AND UNWEIGHTED)
HOOK SIZES 8 TO 16

Alder	*March Brown*
Black and Orange	*Brown Drake*
Black and Yellow	*Ginger Quill*
Caddis	*Tellico*

HOOK SIZES 10, 12, 14, AND 16, 2X LONG-SHANK HOOK

Yellow May	*Olive May*
Tan May	*Brown May*
Black May	*Gray May*

SPECIAL NYMPHS
HOOK SIZES 6 TO 12

Gray Nymph	*Olive Shrimp Nymph*
Fresh Water Shrimp	*Pink Stripe*
Tan Shrimp Nymph	
Pink Stripe	

DAN BAILEY'S NATURE NYMPHS—
HOOK SIZES 4 TO 10, AND 12 LONG-SHANK

Light Mossback	*Light Olive and Cream*
Dark Mossback	*Dark Olive and Yellow*
Black Mossback	*Black and Dark Olive*

NYMPHS
(WEIGHTED)

Large Stone Fly Nymph	*2X Long-shank No. 8*
Large May Fly Nymph	*2X Long-shank No. 10*
Caddis Fly Nymph	*2X Long-shank No. 10*
March Brown Nymph	*2X Long-shank No. 12*
Dark Olive Nymph	*2X Long-shank No. 12*
Cross Guinea Nymph	*2X Long-shank No. 10*
Ed Burke Nymph	*2X Long-shank No. 12*
Montana Nymph	*4 and 6*
Tellico Nymph	*8 and 10*

Whenever anyone says to me, "There are lots of trout in there, but you can't catch them," I reach for my box of nymphs. That's what happened one day a couple of summers ago when I was standing with Randy Skelton looking over the slough back of his grandad's Rock Creek Lodge near Missoula, Montana.

"They're too hard to catch," Randy was explaining to me. "You can always see them feeding, but hardly anyone can catch them."

I soon saw why. It was a lovely stretch of stream with long grasses waving slowly in the quiet motion of the crystal clear water. Gravel beds showed wherever the current moved a little faster. It was the kind of water that calls for 12-foot leaders tapered down to 4X or maybe 5X or 6X. Trout were bulging all over the surface. But obviously this was no dry-fly deal. Those fish were nymphing.

Searching the water near the shore, I found several small gray nymphs. That's what I wanted to discover. Betting that they were the dish right now, I dug out a gray nymph, size 14, that was a good match for the naturals I had spotted. I added another 16-inch 4X tippet to my already 12-foot-long leader. Just before casting I greased the leader down to about 3 inches from the end, then applied leader sink to the last 3 inches. I wanted the entire line and leader to float, except for just enough of the tippet end to allow the nymph to swim an inch or so under the surface.

"Why will they take a nymph when they won't take a dry fly?" Randy wanted to know, as I explained to him what I was doing.

"The same old trout trick," I said. "Selective feeding. They're working on nymphs, taking them right *under* the surface, and they won't look at anything that's riding on top. That's why sometimes you can't catch trout with dry flies even though the air is thick with naturals. They're taking the nymphs before the flies emerge."

"Watch those fish out there," I went on. "Look hard and you'll see that they aren't slapping into flies riding on top, or breaking the surface the way they do when they suck in a fly. The water seems to bulge up, instead."

That meant they were grabbing those nymphs just before they reached the surface, and as they turned their bodies on the take, they put up a swirl that made the water move up, or bulge. Once an angler has seen that and recognized it for what it is, he can nearly always spot the difference between bulging fish and those that are taking surface flies.

Those trout were working about 40 feet out in the current where it ran over gravel smack alongside of a patch of watercress. I dropped the nymph a couple of feet above where I'd seen a rise, stripped in the slack, then held the rod tip slightly ahead of the floating line. With the last 3 inches under water, the line and leader drifted along, acting as a float, a sort of bobber. I knew the nymph was right where I wanted it, 2 inches under water, moving a bit with the eddies, lifelike.

It floated along. No strike. It went on down, reached the end of the float and then swept across the current towards my bank. I raised the rod tip to a 40-degree angle and began to impart short jerks to the line by manipulating the tip. After a foot of that, I let the nymph float free again for a foot, then gave a few more jerks, to imitate the action of a natural nymph struggling to reach the surface, then picked it up and sent it back to the same place it had started from.

This time it didn't go far. I saw the leader jerk forward, raised the rod tip and was into a good fish. He tore downstream, back showing, then busted out in a long, splashy jump. What with his jumping and the hazards of grass beds in that slough, he gave me a rough ten minutes before I finally landed him. He turned out to be a beautiful 2-pound rainbow trout.

Many times when fish are feeding on nymphs, the operation is not quite as obvious as when they are bulging, as they were that day on the slough behind Rock Creek Lodge. Sometimes they are feeding deep, tails up, nosing out nymphs from the gravel, pushing them out from under rocks, then snatching them. If the water is fairly shallow, you can see the whole procedure, but if it is slightly deeper, then all the angler can spot is the flash of their sides as they work.

Trout are just as selective in their choice of nymphs as they are in feeding on dry flies and many times the angler must match the hatch or go hitless. Usually, however, by careful study of the water he can discover what nymph it is that the fish are taking. Or if he has landed a fish he can open it and soon determine what is the main diet of the day. Dump the contents of the stomach into clear water, stir with a knife or a pencil, and the nymphs upon which the fish has been feeding will float free and the angler can then try to match them with something from his fly box.

In one of his great books on fishing, Edward Hewitt said that an expert nymph fisherman could clean out a trout stream. That statement is so true that probably the only saving feature is that there are not many good nymph fishermen. Most of them seem to think that nymphs can be presented to trout without stealth and all that is necessary is to cast them out and let them ride down with the current. It's true that the occasional fish will be taken that way, but to be consistent and make the most of those situations that call for a nymph, the angler must use special tactics.

Sometimes fish will hit only nymphs floating free in the current, and other times they will only take an artificial that matches the struggles of the natural nymph swimming to the top to emerge as a fly. Therefore, sometimes the nymph should be allowed to float as a wet fly, and again it should be moved fast, in jerks, right under the surface. And other times it may be thrown upstream and allowed to float down much as a dry fly, only deeper. At such times strikes are very hard to see, and the angler must almost sense them, or strike every time the line seems to hesitate as if a fish had mouthed the fly. Now and then it will be bottom or gravel, but it pays to strike anyway.

While nymphs are usually fished just under the surface, there are many times when it is necessary to get down into deeper holes, and for this reason, many nymphs are weighted so that they sink slowly. Those who tie their own nymphs can soon discover how much weight to add for best results—usually the amount is very slight and therefore does not interfere with casting.

In deep pools, the nymph should be cast well upstream so it will sink as it comes down with the current. By the time it reaches the angler it will be deep enough to be spotted by the trout. Both leader and nymph always seem to float on top when you want them to go down, and sometimes a good stiff jerk on the line is needed to make the nymph sink, even though there is some danger of disturbing the pool by the commotion. A lot more trouble, but worth the effort, is the application of leader sink to the entire leader. If you are caught on the stream without a commercial leader sink, mud will do the trick, or if you have already landed a fish, then the slime from it will serve even better. And that old saying "Spit on the bait for luck" is no idle talk, either. Spittle on the nymph will also help to put it down.

Lots of times in deep water you never do see the fish working and then all you can do is float the nymph through the pool, deep, watching the line for signs of a strike. If you feel you are not getting down deep enough, a wrap-around lead or a pinch of split shot on the leader will get the nymph down. With that much extra weight, you will think you are getting hit after hit when most of the time it is just the nymph catching on the bottom. But when trout are nosing into the bottom you can really cash in by letting a weighted nymph roll along and bounce off the rocks. You have to strike every time you feel anything on the line and every time the line stops, but if it's a fish instead of a rock, you have him.

Nymph Fishing

To fish a nymph well and successfully is certainly more difficult than to fish a wet fly or a dry, but it generally pays off in bigger trout. And it often produces trout when nothing else will. This was the theory of G.E.M. Skues, the English barrister who pioneered fishing for trout with artificial nymphs. Skues lived and fished and wrote in the same period as Halford, who had so thoroughly touted the art of dry fly fishing as the "only" way to fish for trout in a chalk stream. But Skues was equally vehement in his exposition of the nymph. He spent many years studying the subject, and experimenting. He used to open the stomachs of the fish he caught, place the contents in a shallow white bowl filled with water, gently stir the tightly packed mass until the particles separated and the insects assumed more or less their natural shape. Then he tied artificials to match, fished them, and wrote about how he fished them and how successful they were. He soon had a following as vociferous as Halford's, and became known as the father of nymph fishing.

Many experts have stated that eighty-five percent of the diet of a trout consist of nymphs. It is certainly true that the nymphal forms of the aquatic flies are available to the trout in more phases and for longer periods of time than the other forms. And since there are so many aquatic hatches and each has a larval stage of some kind, the number and variety of nymphs that could be copied by the nymph fisherman could well be described as infinite.

BASIC NYMPHS

Every trouter cannot become an entomologist, and it is not necessary to be one, to fish a nymph. For practical purposes it is possible to fill your nymph fly book with the right patterns for almost any occasion, if you are familiar with certain basic nymphs found commonly in trout waters.

The mayflies, Ephemeridae, are found in most streams that are capable of holding trout and where pollution has not destroyed both the hatches and the fish. The evolution of the mayfly (*see* Dry Fly) is typical of many aquatic hatches, and in spite of its name it occurs throughout most of the warm months of the year. Nearly every trout angler at some time meets a situation that calls for a mayfly nymph.

The stone flies, Plecoptera, are found mostly in fast rivers, where there is plenty of oxygen. In early summer they furnish some fast and furious fishing. They are big insects and bring up big trout. When they are on the water, trout smash into them fearlessly. This is the time when the fly fisherman on the big rivers of the Rocky Mountains can take big fish.

The female of the stone fly drops her eggs into the water individually, not as a cluster, and they then sink to the bottom. After they emerge from the egg, the nymphs stay on the bottom for about a year, during which time they grow legs and wings, in fact everything that will be needed when they enter the world of air rather than water. When they are ready to emerge they crawl out and attach themselves to rocks on shore, and the imago, the perfect insect (stone flies have only two stages, the nymphal and the imago), breaks out of the nymphal case, crawls under a rock or log, and after about two hours its wings are dry. The male finds the female in this situation, they mate, and then the female flies off and drops her eggs on the water, to start the cycle again.

At any time the nymphal form is in the water, Plecoptera is prey to the trout; in fact, an artificial stone fly nymph will take fish at any time of year, not just during a hatch. On a trip to the Williamson River in Oregon, in early July, when no big flies were hatching, the biggest fish I got, a five-pounder, fell to a big nymph tied by Klamath Falls fly tyer Granny Granstrom. Called the Granny's Creeper, it produces at any time of the year.

The caddis flies, Trichoptera, have still a different cycle. The eggs are laid by the female dipping into the surface or dropping them while flying over the water, or by crawling down a reed or a branch of some kind and fastening the eggs to a rock, log, or base of a reed. The small larva comes out of the egg and, in many species, constructs a case around its body for protection, using tiny bits of bark, leaves, small pebbles, sand, and slivers of twigs. It sticks its head and shoulders out of the forward end of the case and crawls along dragging its house behind it.

As it grows it enlarges the case. And then after a year the larva goes into the pupa stage and encases itself in a cocoon of silk and seals it up. Deep in its nest it forms legs and wings, and when it is ready to emerge it bites out the end of the cocoon and goes to the surface and emerges as the imago, the perfect fly, and flies away, to mate. Thus, in this fly, we have the larva and the pupa, or still stage, both nymphal forms that are available at one time or another to a feeding trout, and all suitable to be matched with your artificials.

In my opinion nymphs are usually tied too big, probably because fishermen shy off from the very small sizes, which do indeed sometimes look infinitesimal. It's one thing to fish a small dry fly that is matching something equally small that you see on the surface. It's quite another to be able to picture a correspondingly small nymph drifting along under the surface and to believe that a fish will see it and take it. So we are inclined to go to the larger sizes. But I firmly believe that if more nymphs were used in sizes 16, 18, and 20, more trout would be caught. After all, the small mayflies we match with a size 24 dry fly came out of an equally small nymph—so why back off?

The midge nymph is probably the least used of any of the commercially tied patterns, but this nymph has been taking trout for a long time, tiny flies tied on size 18, 20, 22, and smaller hooks. When you find a swarm of midges, smuts or other small natural flies working above the surface of the water, hovering and falling and rising, you can often use those midge nymphs with telling effect.

One time I was fishing a mountain lake in Wyoming, close to an outlet where a small stream ran out, an ideal place for nymphs to hatch. There were so many midges working about a foot above the surface that it looked like a small black cloud. I had a size 20 Black Hackle dry fly on and I dropped it four times in among those flies, let it sit still on the surface, then gave it short jerks as I retrieved it. Not the first hit. They didn't want a dry. I changed to a size 12 Olive nymph. Still no hits. Then I recalled that in my fly box I had a couple of black midge nymphs. I put one on, a size 20, threw it out there through the ranks of the swarming midges. When it dropped to the surface I let it sink for an inch, then started it back, drawing it slowly along. A fish had it. With that same nymph I took four more trout from beneath those swarming midges. That was a day that was won by having the right nymph with me—a small one.

It is often difficult to find the very small nymphs in tackle stores. You frequently must order them from a commercial tyer, direct, or tie them yourself. On the other hand, there are plenty of large nymphs available, and plenty of these are good fish takers regardless of what is going on in the way of true nymphal activity at the time you are fishing.

One of the great favorites on Rocky Mountain streams is the Gray nymph, weighted. It is made with a heavy, fuzzy muskrat fur body, gray hackle and badger hair tail, in sizes from 6 to 12. Cast and allowed to sink, then retrieved slowly, in pulls and pauses, it produces well in all types of water.

The big stone fly nymphs are great producers in fast water at the head of a pool, and again, they are good regardless of season. I have had great fishing throughout the trout season with various stone fly patterns that Dan Bailey ties, under the name Nature Nymphs.

TIME FOR THE NYMPH

Often you see trout bulging, taking the nymphs just before they reach the surface, and turning their bodies as they do so, thus causing the water to bulge a bit. Novices may mistake this for a rise to a dry fly and wonder why they don't get a hit to a dry that matches the flies coming off the river. But when the trout are working on nymphs they usually ignore the fully hatched fly. So look carefully, and if they are bulging, without breaking the surface, go to a nymph, particularly one tied as an emerger.

When trout are bulging, taking nymphs right at the surface like that, almost at the point of emergence of the dry fly, I like to fish the artificial nymph very much like a dry fly—upstream on a floating line and with a long leader, tapered to a very fine tippet. I like to grease the leader down to within three or four inches of the end of the tippet. The line and leader then float nicely, but that few inches of ungreased leader tippet allows the nymph to sink an inch or two beneath the surface and go over the fish at that depth, right where he has his eyes fixed. The cast should be made well above the bulging fish and the S-cast is the one to deliver it free of drag, just as you like a dry fly to float.

Many times you will be able to spot that telltale bulge as the trout takes your nymph, but as in dry-fly fishing that rise can fool you. The disturbance of the trout bulging will rock the water and fade out well below the spot where he actually took the nymph. Be sure to take time enough to fish that spot of the first bulge of water in your mind, or you may be casting below his station. If you make several casts to the fish and do not get a strike, try extending your throw to drop the nymph from eight to ten feet above where you have been casting.

At all times, keep your eyes on the end of your line as it floats downstream, and when you see that line move forward, or stop, then strike, whether you have seen the fish or not.

Again, as you stand at streamside you may see the flash of a trout's sides, and at such a time you can be sure that the fish is feeding on nymphs that he is digging out of the gravel or snatching as they scurry across it. As the trout noses down and takes, he turns his body and the light glints off his sides, an underwater heliography that gives him away.

When trout are intent on those nymphs down in the gravel, in shallow water, say 2½ to 3 feet deep, you can take them with a floating line. Cast upstream, then pay out plenty of line so the nymph will float deep and into the range of the trout. Or you can increase the chance of getting down there by using a weighted nymph cast upstream and allowed to sink and come bumping across the gravel. Some nymph fishermen pinch a bit of split shot onto the leader about a foot above the fly, and it is effective, as the split shot bounces down the stream bed and the nymph jerks erratically along in back of it with a lifelike action. But if I am going to use weight, I prefer to go to a weighted nymph.

Any time you are fishing a nymph deep in this way, you must watch the line carefully because there is no way to see the trout take your offering. When a trout takes, the line will stop moving or it will jerk forward. Every time you get such a line reaction, that's your cue to strike. Your nymph may only be caught on a rock or bit of grass down there, but on the other hand you may have a fish.

If there is no strike throughout the float, start the fly back in short jerks, keeping this up for several feet, then stop it altogether, then start the short jerks, and so on until the nymph reaches the surface. A trout may hit at any stage of this retrieve.

If I am not getting the hits I think I should to an upstream nymph, I often cast up and across and bring the nymph back immediately, in short uplifts of the rod tip, to make it jerk and dart as I bring it along. It should move not too fast, but briskly, so the trout will have to chase it; and the rod must be kept at a fairly high angle so the bend of the rod can absorb the force of a hit.

On the whole, however, I think that when you make a cross-stream throw, the dead float pays off best; and when you are fishing a nymph in dead water, a fast retrieve is best. In the still water of a slough, for instance, a cruising fish might never even see a nymph that is dropped and allowed to float dead. But pull it across in front of him a foot or so, and he spots that movement, and if it looks right, he comes for it. This is the time, however, when you must use a very long, very light leader because in such still, clear water it is easy to line the fish and spook them.

In general, such shallow-water fishing always calls for a light outfit. I remember once when I fished the Little Pine Lagoon in Tasmania, Australia, with Jim Wilson of Lake St. Clair. We found the trout tailing amid stumps and grasses in water only two feet deep. I got out my 7½-foot rod, matching double-tapered #5 floating line, and used a 14-foot leader tapered down to a 4X tippet. Then I greased the line and the leader down to six inches from the fly, and was ready for business. I dropped a brown and black nymph a foot away and slightly beyond the nearest tailing trout and retrieved it slowly past him, hoping he would think it was a nymph he had scared out of the grasses. It worked, and he chased after it, took with a swirl and a splash, and the fight was on.

For most nymph fishing the leader should be long and light. The trout has a close-up look at a nymph that rides along right in front of him, and he will shy away from a heavy tippet. I like to use a leader not less than ten feet long, to assure that the line will fall far enough away from the fish not to scare him. And for most nymphs I like to go down to a 5X, or at the heaviest, a 4X tippet. The light tippet allows the nymph to swim freely, with a much more lifelike action than if it were riding into the trout's vision on the end of a stiff, straight stick of nylon.

When nymphing fish are lying very deep, on the other hand, and it takes a sinking line to get to them, the leader must be shortened considerably, to six feet only, so the current will not wash the leader high, and drag the nymph up out of the fish's area of interest. The weight of the line should also be adjusted to the river or lake you are fishing, according to depth. The floating/sinking line, of which the first thirty feet sinks while the balance floats, is good for deeper streams and lakes, while the shorter sinking line, of which only ten feet sinks, serves better in shallower water (*see* Lines).

Usually as you walk along the river bank you can find some evidence of a nymph that might have value in that time and place. One day a few years ago I was wandering up the Big Hole River in Montana, having great fishing with a dry fly. Several times during the day I noticed a big, dark nymph floating down the current, and I saw the shucks along the rocks onshore, too. But I was doing so well with a dry fly that I didn't change. Then just before sunset the situation altered. The fish stopped rising to dries. I was at the head of a run where the white water rushed madly into the pool, then subsided gradually and rolled out into a smooth surface further down.

"There must be some trout holding somewhere along this heavy current," I thought.

I opened my nymph book and looked. There were a couple of large nymphs tied by Dave Whitlock: the Whit Bronze nymph and the Whit Black Stone nymph. Dave had told me that the latter was good towards evening and at dark, so I chose that in size 8.

But the current up where I thought the fish would be was very heavy. My floating line was not going to get that nymph down to them. I reached into my vest pocket and pulled out the extra spool I usually carry, loaded with a #6 wet-head sinking line, and complete with the necessary short six-foot leader. I threaded the new line through the guides, tied on Dave's nymph and was ready.

I moved down a bit, to just where the fast incoming water smoothed off. I made my throw upstream for forty-five feet and held the rod high to keep the current from snatching the near line and pulling it in to me, which, of course, would bring the fly nearer to the surface. I stripped off several more feet of line from the reel and wiggled the rod tip from side to side to get it out, then aided it a bit by roll casting to put the line farther out.

Now I knew that the nymph would ride close to the bottom and I turned the rod downstream, following the track of the line. Almost immediately I saw the line shoot forward, and I pulled back with the rod and was tight to a fish. Tight to a rollicking projectile that tore downstream like a bolt from the blue, racing, making the spray leap up from the line as it sizzled through the water. On he went for fifty feet, seventy-five, a hundred, and then he was into my backing. Just about then I saw the line coming up towards the surface and the water flew apart and I saw the deep body of the fish, his long length and sides afire with crimson. That beautiful, wonderful and wild rainbow went two feet into the air and I guessed him at five pounds.

But this was no time for guessing games. I was too busy. He turned the smooth part of the pool into a shambles, in and out, up and down, and I held the rod high and each time he jumped I dropped the rod tip like it was a live coal. That gives slack line, and it is a good move that keeps a wild fish from falling on the leader and breaking it, or from getting a hard, straightaway yank at it, which might snap the flimsy tippet.

I hung on and met all his tactics and gradually he tired and I got him in close. Then he saw me and off he went again, and wound up that flurry with a halfway-out jump. But he was cooling off, and now I slowly pulled back on the rod, and finding him receptive I gave him the butt and pulled him my way along the top, nose out. I unlatched my landing net, held it in the water and pulled that beautifully colored trout into it. He was long and deep, with a small head on his powerfully built body. He was silvery, too, almost like a steelhead fresh from the salt, but liberally sprinkled with black dots, the crimson streak along his side seemed to glow, and the red splash on his gill covers completed a masterpiece that only nature can produce. I gently unhooked him and slid him back into the river where he belonged.

Fishing Streamers and Bucktails for Trout

A streamer is a fly tied with long wings of feathers, and a bucktail is a similar fly tied with hair wings. The original streamers and bucktails were designed to look like minnows going through the water and many were tied to match the long time favorite patterns of wet flies, the Royal Coachman, the Coachman, Black Gnat, Grizzly King, Yellow Sally, and so on down the list of conventional and proven patterns.

Most of the streamers and bucktails are tied on size 8 and 10 long-shank hooks, with sparsely dressed wing or wings. Some have bodies, but others show the bare shank of the hook. One of the most effective bucktails I have ever used was a size 10 white bucktail with only a wrapping of silver tinsel for a body, and a very sparse wing that extended just a bit below the bend of the hook. That fly can be dropped quietly in a very still pool and because of its thinness it doesn't seem to scare the fish.

Besides the wet-fly colors, streamers and bucktails are tied in all white and yellow, and all black—and more and more I, for one, am finding that the all-black streamer or bucktail is a very fine taker of both trout and other varieties of gamefish.

Modern fly tyers have come up with some new and different designed, flies such as the Optic Bucktail, a great steelhead fly with bucktail wing and a built-up head with eyes painted on it; and the Muddler Minnow, a bucktail designed by Don Gapen, the well known tyer. The Muddler Minnow is now widely copied in many materials, but the original was made with a single genuine timber wolf hair wing plus a single feather wing. Although it was tied to imitate the Darter Minnow, when it is in the water the muddler can also look like the buggiest thing you have ever seen. Or it may look like a grasshopper, or another time, like a small mouse. How one bucktail can look like so many different things is a great puzzle, but whatever it happens to look like at the moment, it always seems to look good to the trout. It is as potent a trout fly as anything I have ever used.

That statement covers a lot of territory, especially when you consider marabou streamers. Marabous produce some monster fish. Because of the lightness of the feathers, every fiber seems to move, waving gently, appearing to breathe. When cast across stream and retrieved in jerks 6 inches to a foot in length, the flaunting, tempting liveliness of the tail makes trout hop on it in a hurry.

Marabous are tied in a variety of solid colors and color combinations as shown later on in this chapter, and a number of tyers in various parts of the country have added innovations of their own, for their particular area. An outstanding one is the Silver Garland, tied by Polly Rosborough of Chiloquin, Oregon, for rainbows. This is a weighted marabou with blue and white wings and silver tinsel body, and is a terrific fish getter for almost any species where such a streamer might be feasible at all.

With both Muddler and Marabou being such great flies it was only a matter of time before they were put together in a single tie. Dan Bailey of Livingston, Montana, and his partner, Red Monical, did just that, producing the now renowned Marabou Muddler.

They first tied this fly with the regular muddler dressing, but using a white marabou wing instead of turkey feather wing. Some big fish were taken on it, and then other colors in marabou wings were tried. On one occasion I arrived at the Chimehuin River in Argentina with half a dozen black Marabou Muddlers in my fly book, in hook sizes No. 4, 2, and 1/0. I also had White Marabou Muddlers, Brown Marabou Muddlers and Gray Marabou Muddlers in great numbers. I tried the black one first, and fish piled into it. They tore it apart in a hurry. Charles Radziwill and Bebe Anchorena, who were fishing with me, each borrowed one from me, and the trout took those apart, too. We tried other colors, and took only the occasional fish. Back went the black marabou, and wham, we had hit after hit. Yet another time, when the three of us fished the Rio Grande on Tierra del Fuego, it was the Gray Marabou Muddler that got the hits from the big, silver-bright sea-run brown trout that were in the river.

The Gray Marabou also proved itself on the Missouri River in Montana, when Gene Anderegg of Ridgewood, New Jersey, used a 1/0 to land a walloping 10-pound brown.

So all the marabou muddlers pay off; and size does not seem to make too much difference. I've caught some very large fish on a No. 4, and others on a 1/0.

Another marrying of successful patterns produced the spuddler. Dan Bailey and Red Monical had both used the spruce-fly streamer to take many large trout. They had both noticed that it did more damage when fished on a sinking line. On the other hand, the muddler seemed best when fished on a floating line. They decided to combine the dressing of both flies, with the accent on copying the Sculpin Minnow which the muddler basically represents—a minnow that lives under the rocks in rivers and lakes. The spuddler has the flattened bucktail head of the muddler, and the bucktail hackle. The wing is the same barred wing used in the spruce fly, and the tail is black bucktail. The body is light tan wool. Like the Marabou Muddlers, the spuddler proved itself immediately, and has been one of the great producers of recent years.

Bucktails are usually made of deerhair which is hollow, and therefore they float very well even when tied on large hooks. In fact sometimes it is necessary to give the rod tip a hard jerk to pull the bucktail under the surface.

Of all the hairs used for bucktails the deerhair seems to have the most sparkle, looks better in the water, and deerhair wings do not seem to wrap around the hook as easily as do some of the other hairs used in tying bucktail flies. In this regard, both streamer flies and bucktails should be examined frequently during casting, to be sure that the wings have not wrapped around the bend of the hook, as this destroys both appearance and action, and a fly so entangled will seldom draw a strike. When wings hang up in this manner, I pull the hair or feather upwards from the hook where they are tied to it. This helps for a while at least, to make the wings ride high and wide, free of the bend of the hook.

Many flies designed for fresh water have proven equally efficient in the salt, and conversely a number of streamers and bucktails designed for fishing the ocean flats have turned out to be highly effective in fresh water, especially for big trout and salm-on. One big white bucktail, the Platinum Blonde, and an equally big fly made of yellow bucktail, called the Honey Blonde, have proven just about the best flies I have ever used for really big trout.

They were originally tied for striped bass and in an effort to make the fly large and extra long-winged, one piece of bucktail was tied on top of the 1/0 hook and immediately behind the eye, and another length of bucktail was tied just in front of the bend of the hook. Over a long number of years it has continued to be a terrific number for stripers and has also proven a great fly for big trout. In the Chimehuin River in Argentina I have taken many brown trout from 10 to 18 pounds on a 1/0 Platinum Blonde; and my friend Bebe Anchorena used a Honey Blond to land a 24-pound brown there.

The blondes are also great for sea trout. Everywhere they are fished they produce bigger than usual fish.

Similarly, big multiwing streamers with three and four feathers on each side of the 1/0 hook are sure attractions for big boys. These streamers work in the water, closing in on the hook when the angler strips line, spreading out again as he stops the retrieve, so that they appear to breathe. They are used in salt water with telling effect and while many a freshwater angler will look at them askance, they surely do have the power to bring hits from big trout, too.

The first time I produced those big flies at the Chimehuin River in Argentina, I brought down the house.

"What's that, your shaving brush?" howled my fried Jorge Donovan.

"Funny, eh?" I said. "Just wait!"

"We use small flies," said Jorge. "A big bundle like that will scare them out of the river. They'll run up into Lake Huechulaufquen and hide on the bottom."

"Wait a while," I said again.

I was using a 9-foot rod, a WF-8F line and a 14-foot leader, starting with a 30-pound butt section and tapered down to a 4-pound-test tippet. I threw that big bucktail across the current at the head of the pool and started it back. I had only taken three 2-foot-long strips of line when something hit that fly so hard that it almost knocked the rod out of my hand. It was something big.

That baby turned it on for a downstream dash that made the water fly from the speeding line. Then he showed himself, a beautiful brown trout that jumped 2 feet in the air and seemed to hang there as if pinned up. And that's what I thought. "What a pin-up, and I'll take it!"

After fifteen minutes I got him in, took the hook from the corner of his mouth and gently put him back again.

"What are you doing?" asked Jorge.

"I'm releasing him," I said. "He was a great fighter."

"Releasing a 10-pound fish," said Bebe Anchorena. "That's good."

"But what am I doing, just standing here?" he said suddenly. "How many of those flies do you have?"

"Cut me in, too," grinned Jorge.

We used those big flies down there in Argentina for a month of fishing. We took big brown trout and rainbows and landlocked salmon with them, and in the Rio Grande River on Tierra del Fuego we caught sea-run brown trout that hit them like a trip-hammer every time one of those big streamers was pulled across their noses.

While big streamers and bucktails are the answer in big water for larger than average fish, the smaller, more sparsely tied ones will pay off best in clear and shallow water. There, the lightest presentation possible with a small fly will get results when a big fly might chase the fish out in a hurry. Nevertheless, some of these streamers manage to have a bulky enough look to tempt good-sized fish. Some of the long-winged flies used in Maine are tied on tandem hooks and are designed to look like the smelt upon which the landlocks feed. They have been proven flies for this game fish for a long time, and practically all the blue-winged ties in this group are good, with the supervisor probably being the best known, and the Wilson Special, while not so well known, being equally as good for getting hits.

In either bucktail or streamer the Mickey Finn is a good early-season fly, and is also good in discolored water, as indeed are almost all the yellow or black flies.

A well-stocked streamer and bucktail book will include most of the following:

STREAMERS,
HOOK SIZES 6 TO 12, LONG SHANK

Black Ghost	*Wilson's Special*
Gray Ghost	*Mickey Finn*
York's Kennebago	*Red and Yellow*
Lady Ghost	*Red and White*

Black Nosed Dace

Colonel Fuller

Supervisor

Red and Barred Yellow
 Wings

Yellow and White

Black and White

MULTIWING STREAMERS,
HOOK SIZES 1 AND 1/0

Red and White
Red and Yellow
Yellow and Barred
Yellow Wings

Black and White
Black Hackle Barred
 Orange Wing

MARABOU STREAMERS,
HOOK SIZES 6 TO 12, LONG SHANK

Black
Red
Yellow

White
Black and Yellow
Red and Yellow

BUCKTAILS,
HOOK SIZES 6 TO 12, LONG SHANK

Black Prince
Prince Charlie
Brown and Yellow
Brown and White

Black and White
Red and White
Red and Yellow
Mickey Finn

BLONDE BUCKTAILS,
HOOK SIZE 1/0

Platinum Blonde
Honey Blonde
Black Blonde

Strawberry Blonde
Argentine Blonde

MUDDLER MINNOW,
HOOK SIZES 1/0, 2, 4, 6, 8, 10

Brown Muddler   *White Muddler*
Yellow Muddler   *(Missoulian Spook)*

MARABOU MUDDLERS,
HOOK SIZES 1/0, 2, 4, 6

White   *Gray*
Brown   *Black*

If you want to catch lunker trout, use big streamer flies. When a trout reaches 2½ to 3 pounds, he has done with midges, freshwater shrimp, and other small fry. He wants to gulp down something big enough to make his stomach sac press against his sides. Occasionally a 4-pounder will take a size 10 hairwing and once in a while he might even go for a size 18 or 20. But generally speaking, trout that big don't play for peanuts. They want the works.

Streamers bring out the yen for meat in these big boys and with the right presentation and retrieve an angler can get strikes from hook-jawed old busters that weigh in up in the heavyweight division. They are so hungry for substantial food that even if their stomachs are stuffed tighter than a Pennsylvania food locker the day after deer season, they still will grab another minnow that they can't even swallow and will swim around with the tail sticking out of their mouths, waiting for the swallowed part to dissolve so they can handle the rest. And believe it or not, those big-eyed aquatic so-and-sos, with that remnant of a partly digested meal still protruding from their throats, will hit a streamer. When I opened up one 4½-pound lunker last year, what did I find? Two field mice each about 5 inches long, two minnows each about 4 inches long, and one 5-inch minnow with its tail just showing in the trout's throat. Here was this jasper making like the filling of a knockwurst and he wants a bucktail, yet!

In streamer fishing the handling of the retrieve means defeat or success. You must make the lure imitate the actions of the natural food upon which the trout feed, so that they go for it totally unsuspecting. Streamer fishing calls for rod tip work and line manipulation that will make the fly out there act like a minnow. It should be retrieved in short jerks to make it look like a minnow darting erratically around the pool, or in longer strips to ape a more leisurely swim. A lure that is allowed to sink and is then played very slowly can be made to look like a minnow nosing the bottom for food, and an extra-fast top-water retrieve makes the artificial dash across the surface, faking a natural minnow that is rushing along the top, trying to escape some great, toothy-mawed 5-pounder.

The angler should try all types of bringbacks until he discovers just which one will do the best job that day. I usually start with the cast across the current, mend the line, then let the fly float downstream broadside and without any motion. When it reaches the end of the float and starts to swim my way, I impart 6-inch jerks to it, then when it has finally swung in directly below me, I bring it back my way slowly and evenly for about 3 feet, then pick it up for the next cast. You can expect a thudding hit at any stage of that play.

Another effective cast and retrieve is upstream and across, bringing the fly back in 2-foot-long jerks, fast, right to the rod tip. Often a fish will follow such a retrieve and hit it just as the angler is about to pick it up for the next cast. And sometimes in a low clear stream it is a good move to cast directly upstream. This cast requires the same care and stealth in approach as does dry fly fishing, but often such a throw and a slowly retrieved, sparsely tied bucktail will take trout when all other methods fail.

One of the fish-teasin'est ways of all is to figure where a fish should be lying in the current, cast the fly to that spot and instead of bringing it back all the way, just retrieve it a foot or two, then let it float downstream again, retrieve it a foot or so again, and repeat the whole procedure. It takes patience, but it's usually worth the effort in bringing hits that won't seem to come by other methods just then.

That retrieve paid heavy dividends one day when I fished the East Branch of the Antietam River with Bob Wishard of Waynesboro, Pennsylvania. The stream meandered through lush meadows, and at the bends the current had cut under the banks, making deep holes and swell hiding places for trout. At such a bend a brush pile provided shelter for fish. I watched Bob work a yellow and brown streamer in and out of one of those spooky-looking spots, giving it action that made it perform for all the world like a small minnow lying there just above the log jam and darting upstream, then dropping back, waiting for food to come to it in the current. Bob teased a trout so much with that retrieve that at last it zoomed up from out of the black hole and hit the fly so hard he was carried into the air by the force of his rush. As soon as he fell in again, he jumped and landed on top of the brush, snapped the leader and lay there on a big log, flapping, and finally slipped back into the water.

Bob's face was white.

"With all that water around, he has to jump on that bunch of logs!" he grumbled. "That trout weighed 3 pounds at least."

Later we both took a couple of good fish in the same way, by assuming that there was a lunker under every log pile, and teasing them out with a streamer.

During the spring when the streams are high and roily, and after rains during the summer, streamers are fairly commonly used by Eastern anglers, but few of them are used at any other time. Yet even when the water has dropped and is clear and a hundred anglers are walking along the banks of a 30-foot-wide Eastern river, a wide-awake trouter can get hits with a streamer. In clear water, a sparsely tied bucktail on a number 10 or even a 12 hook is very effective when used with a leader tapered down to a 5X tippet. These thinly clad numbers tied with wings of black and white, brown and white, blue and white, and brown and yellow, will do a swell job of making lazy trout hit.

In discolored water, on the other hand, all yellow, all brown or all black seem to show up best. Once on Beaver Creek in Maryland, the water turned so brown following a heavy downpour that we were ready to quit fishing.

"Sometimes I've caught trout in very muddy water with this fly," said Bill Snyder, holding up a brown hackle.

"Not in water this muddy," I said.

Bill tossed his fly midway out in the pool. A fish shot up through that muddy mess and took the fly like he had seen it through gin-clear water. Bill was so surprised he struck too hard and left the fly in the trout's mouth. But he had proved his point. I grubbed into my streamer box and brought out an all-yellow number, tied it on and was in business at the first hole upstream. A 14-incher roared up and knocked that Yellow Sally silly. In the next hour we landed nine fish.

After that I took three dark colors and held them in the water, then took a couple of other flies with neutral colors and held them beside the dark ones. The yellow, brown, and black showed up five times more plainly.

To fish streamers the angler needs a bigger rod than is used for dry fly fishing but it is not necessary to go into the heavy equipment that some fishermen seem to think. Using a small streamer in a low, clear stream, an 8-foot rod weighing 4 ounces, with a DT-5-F line and a 10-foot leader tapered down to as low as 4X will do a workmanlike job. The tippet may be upped to 3X or 2X depending on the size of fish you are getting hits from. Sometimes when the line is being stripped, a big trout will sock the streamer, and the combined pressure of the pull and the hit will break the leader. So with a light leader you stand the chance of losing a few fish, but you will get more strikes, too.

The larger streamers are difficult to cast on a small rod and with a long, fine leader, and in order to throw them effectively, an 8½-foot rod weighing as much as 4¾ ounces is needed, and should be fitted with a WF-7-F line. The 10-foot leader should start off with a heavy butt section and then fade down to a 4X tippet (*see* Tackle). Just before and right at dark, an even heavier leader is all right as in the evening light the trout don't seem to be scared by the larger tippet diameter.

Hook sizes in streamers should range from 12 all the way down to 1/0. Many times it is the size of the fly rather than the color that seems to make the difference between hits and no hits, so the streamer fisherman should carry a large assortment of both colors and sizes. Some day it will pay off heavily.

Out West, trout fishermen have always favored big wet flies and wooly worms, and with these they catch plenty of big trout. Yet if these same fellows would use streamers, I believe they would find the size of their fish increasing.

I well remember the day I introduced a Montana fishing pal to streamers. Len Kinkie had fished dries, and wets and nymphs, but the big Black Ghost I presented to him scared him.

"What is it?" he said. "Trimming for a gal's hat?"

"Trimming for a trout," I assured him.

It was just before dark. Len went up to the fast water at the top of the 300-foot pool while I worked down toward the tail. I was busily casting when I heard a shout. My head snapped around in time to see Len walking towards the shore, rod held high. Out in the current a great trout jumped clear and threw the hook.

"That was the biggest trout I've ever hooked," Len told me later. "He was 10 pounds. I know now what you mean about streamers."

Speaking of big streamers and big fish always makes me think of a certain pool on the Yellowstone River. If I'm within a couple of hundred miles of it, regardless of time or inconvenience, I'll head for it pronto. From that pool I've taken enough big trout—and put most of them back—that if they were laid end to end they would reach from Denver to the Rio Grande.

The last time I waded out into that pool was 4:00 p.m. on October 19, my last day of fishing before heading east. As always, I was expecting to sink my barbs into a 16- or 17-pounder.

Since I was sure there would be some big fish working there just before dark, I tied on a 2X tippet. I started at the head of the pool, dropping a size 1/0 White Marabou 20 feet out in the fast water and let it float a bit before bringing it back in fast, foot-long jerks. I lengthened the second throw 2 feet. And the next one another 2 feet. When I had 50 feet of line out, I floated it through and waded down to about where it had swung across on that last cast. Then I started the series of casts again. That way I was covering all of the holding water.

The first cast on the next series brought a strike when the marabou was only 20 feet away. That rany hit almost on top and threw water 3 feet high when he took. Then he hung there for a second, heavy, and then my rod tip snapped back and the flyless leader shot high in the air. He had broken me off on the hit.

I tested the leader and put on another marabou. I started the series of casts from where I was. This time it took three casts and then again I almost jumped out of my waders when a hook-beaked beezer poked his nose out and clapped his mandibles at me. He missed the fly but he didn't miss giving me the cold chills. He looked bigger than the other.

I rested him for three or four minutes only, and then sent the fly over the spot where he had been and once again a fish had it, and once again the tip bowed down and stayed there a minute and then flaunted another flyless leader in my face.

I burned then! I was sure that every one of those fish went over 5 pounds. I put on a 1X tippet, cast again and once more got the same treatment. And that one took my last marabou.

I cut off the 1X, leaving just the heavier part of the tapered leader, and tied on a yellow and brown streamer. On the first cast a big baby out there took, rolled on the leader, and once again I was fit to be tied. The sun was away down, peeping over the top of the Gallatins, shadows already across the river, and back of me I heard a deer bleat.

This time I cut that 12-foot leader in half. I must have been up to at least 8-pound test after all that clipping.

While I was tying on a muddler, a fish rose 30 feet in front of me. I cast and he was waiting there with his mouth wide open. I didn't have time to strike because he started off so fast. He slashed across the fast water, then ran down with it for 30 feet and came out in a going-away jump. All I could see was a dark blob down there and as

I dropped the rod tip he fell back in and went away again, fast.

He did everything a trout should do to get off. But somehow I gradually started to gain on him. He came upstream and I reeled fast to keep him coming, to get fly line back on the reel. When I got him close, he jumped right in front of me and threw water in my face and then went off again in a slashing drive across current, and then swirled on top and started to shake his head back and forth.

At that nasty maneuver I gave line in a hurry. Then he hung there in the current and I couldn't make him bat an eye. It was a draw for a couple of minutes and then I fooled him. I suddenly gave him slack and he slipped down with the current, and while he was wondering what happened, I tightened up and pulled him off balance and got him coming my way. He tried to get his head again but I held him and skidded him sideways now, in close, and up on top and into the net. He weighed 3¼ pounds, a nice fish to end the season.

As I waded ashore with him, I heard the sound of a rise out there in the current back of me. It made a noise like the thud of a rock falling on frozen ground. I wanted to go back but it was too dark.

"I'll get you next year," I said aloud. "I'll start fishing right here and I'll use a size 1/0 muddler, or maybe a White Marabou."

Because I know it's big flies those big lunkers want.

A recent streamer-type fly that has had great success is the Big Hole demon, first tied in 1964 by rancher Nick Naranchi, of Twin Bridges, Montana. This fine fly looks something like a low-water Wooly Worm, and it brings lots of hits from big trout. It is fished across current and allowed to drift free for several feet, then a slow jerk is given to make it look alive and make it swim across the current in an enticing manner. However, most strikes come when the demon is floating still.

Dan Bailey ties two versions of the pattern, one with black and badger body, one with black and furnace body. Both are good. I use them on hook sizes 2, 4, 6, and down to number 10. Like all good patterns, this one was soon carried far and wide, to scenes far from the Big Hole River, for which the fly was named. Bebe Anchorena fished

Montana the summer of 1965, and he took a couple of dozen Big Hole demons back to Argentina with him, and there he and Charles Radziwill cashed in with them, landing sea trout to 10 pounds.

There are many long-known streamers and bucktails that are temporarily forgotten because of the success of some new fly. Last year I broke out one such, the Bailey bi-fly, and fished it with such success that I won't forget it again. It can be used either wet or dry, but I have the best luck when I fish it as a streamer.

In general, trout fishing must be done with great quiet, and therefore the popping bug is seldom considered a good trout fly. Yet even big brown trout, smartest and scariest of them all, like a big popper, properly administered in the right place.

Two winters ago, while fishing the Chimenuin River in Argentina, I was taking a string of 6-, 8-, and 10-pound fish on large streamers, enjoying the best trout fishing I've ever had in my life. But I knew there were bigger ones there. Bebe Anchorena and Jorge Donovan of Buenos Aires, who were fishing with me, had told me about the heft of some of those trout.

"Every year," said Jorge, "someone catches brown trout up to 25 pounds here in this river."

"Last year a friend of mine caught a 26-pounder," said Bebe. "He was plug casting with a spoon."

Suddenly I thought of popping bugs. I wondered. And I tried. I got out a big popper, one with a total length of 5 inches, from eye of the hook to end of tail.

It was a windy day. The water on the lake above was white-capped and dark clouds blotted out the mountains and raced over the low hills. It was a rough day to tie into a rough fish, and that was what I wanted to do. Here in the river the water was bouncing with 6-inch waves, and I thought how perfect a spot this was to use a big bug, because it had the bulk a big brownie would like and the waves would not allow too loud a pop, to maybe scare off a suspicious fish.

I cast that big popping bug across current 70 feet, bringing the rod tip almost down to the water so the wind wouldn't blow the bug off course. I let it drift for maybe 10 feet, then retrieved it slowly, in foot-long pulls, trying to make the bug skip softly along. Suddenly I saw a big brown shape out there standing on its head. The rod tip went down violently and the reel began to sing and I was into a big trout. He went 8½ pounds.

I didn't see the next one because he hit in the middle of an incoming wave that still wore a frothy top. But I felt the strike more than the other one. It was a sort of double hit, as if he turned and missed and then took a second try. Or maybe he was hooked the first time, then turned fast and yanked his head around as he did. Anyway, I had all I could handle for the next ten minutes weathering his first frantic fight. Then it turned into a slug fest and it was fifteen minutes before I slipped him ashore, a good quarter of a mile downstream. He was a 10-pounder.

"Give me one of those poppers," said Jorge, who had been going right along with me.

"Me, too," said Bebe.

I handed a popper to each of them, and they left on the run for the next pool.

I had only brought three poppers with me, not expecting to use poppers on trout, so that left me with only the one I had been using. I decided to save it for some special occasion when I thought there might be an extra-big fish around. That occasion came only a couple of days later. I had fished down river for a good half mile without a hit. Then I came to a pool that was so fishy looking that there just had to be a big trout in there.

Out came that big popper. On the third cast I saw a great fish in back of the bug, his cavernous mouth open. I saw him bring his upper mandible down. I struck. Three quarters of an hour later I landed that baby, an 18½-pound brown trout that was 35 inches long and had a girth of 22 inches. A few days later I took a 15-pounder on the same bug.

Those were the two biggest fish of the trip. Popping bugs? You bet!

Landing Bass on the Fly

Whether lake or river dwellers, both smallmouth and largemouth black bass are great fly-rod fish, mostly because they feed on so many different forms of life that can readily be matched with artificials. And they have such tremendous appetites that while they may sometimes get selective and go for one dish only, they can still be had by matching the hatch, whatever it is.

They like frogs, the different types of minnows such as shiners, darters, chubs, and small catfish. They eat leeches, nymphs, small eels, natural flies, and all kinds of things that fall into the water, such as ants, worms, bugs, even mice, and small snakes. And one of their favorite snacks is old pinchnose the hellgramite. The largemouth is such a stuffer that when hunger pangs assail him he's sudden death to almost any living thing that comes near him. He'll eat his nearest and dearest relatives, and has even been known to snatch a squirrel running along a log in the water, and to take birds of assorted sizes.

With such a wide variety of items to match or imitate, the bass fisherman should have a well-stocked fly box and when he's so armed, he's certain at some time or other to have fine sport. There will be days, of course, as with any kind of fishing, when hits are few and far between, and a fellow should have gone to the movies, or "stood in bed"; but in general, with the right equipment plus a little thought and the right technique, he can have a banner day with bass.

And because one or the other of the basses is found reasonably close to almost any spot you can name in the United States and Canada, the bass fills a mighty void for the thousands of avid fly-rodders. The largemouth does more than his share to provide sport by moving into brackish water in sounds, bays, and river mouths; and there, with that touch of salt to spark his fight, he seems greater than ever.

If I were to choose a single fly-rod artificial for both smallmouth and largemouth black bass, it would be a popping bug. A popper does something special to a bass as it makes a popping sound, caused by water action against the collar.

Probably the best-working model is the bug made of balsa wood. This has lightness for casting and for effective lure play, even in large sizes. It can be popped or slid or skidded across the surface, or pulled under, according to the way it is constructed, and generally can be played with real zip and pep so as to appear to be something very much alive. Other materials may be more durable, but none performs with the same lifelike actions as does the balsa wood popper.

The new plastic popping bugs, however, while a little heavier per size, also do a workmanlike job and are more durable and retain their finish better. And in Southern canals, tiny poppers made of either balsa, plastic or cork, all with rubber legs, get a great play from fishermen out for bream but taking bass on the side.

Because bass are found around weed beds so often, there are now quite a number of weedless poppers on the market, and they are good because they give the angler the confidence to cast into grass patches and among lily pads, knowing he will not hang up and will be able to play the popper properly. It will "walk" across the grass and lily pads, and that's where some mighty nice bass are often lying.

Popping bugs vary greatly in size, from the little bream getters just mentioned, which are sometimes only the size of a thumbnail, to whopping big foolers that are primarily designed for the big maws of the largemouth but are frequently just as effective for smallmouths.

The action is built into a popper by the tyer, according to the way he wants it to work. Some are designed to be played with loud pops, while others are planned to make little noise—hence are often called "sliders"—and are meant to be just pulled across the surface, rather than popped.

One of the best bugs for largemouth, and smallmouth, too, is the skipping bug, first tied of cork by the writer back in the late '30s for striped bass. I soon found that it was ideal for freshwater bass. Its long, round body lies flat on the water when not being popped, the weight of the hook held up by the deerhair tail so the bug floats level on the surface. When you give it a twitch it looks like a wounded minnow trying to swim away. I now have it made of balsa wood in three sizes, 3/0 for big largemouth bass, 1/0 for both large-mouth and smallmouth, and on a #1 long-shank hook for smaller smallmouth. The best colors are red head with the balance of the body yellow, and a yellow tail; red head with white body and tail; all white; and all yellow.

When the skipping bug hits the surface, it's best to let it sit for a few minutes, then give it a slight pop, then let it stay still there maybe twenty seconds, then another pop, and then bring it back in a series of pops until it is close enough to pick up for the next cast. A bass will hit at any point in this retrieve, either when the bug is moving or when it is lying motionless on the surface.

With this, as with any popper, it's important to tune in on the bass' wave length. Don't pop the bug so hard that it will scare him. When a bug hits the water a bass usually swims away for several feet, then turns and gives it the eye. Then a slight pop interests him and he moves in. Another pop and he's ready. Sometimes a doubtful bass will wait until your series of pops has convinced him that thing is getting away and then he'll charge and take. You can't taunt him too much. Even when he's half asleep you can make him mad enough to come out, if you keep popping the bug lightly, time and again, over his hole in the grass, his cave under a tree, his lair under an old dock. When you tease him like that it is not long before he gets his dorsal fin up and charges, so hard and fervently that sometimes he'll knock the bug a couple of feet into the air, open his wide mouth and make a fair catch of that high-kicked, buggy punt.

Another bug I first tied back in the early '40s, this one aimed at smallmouth, is the spouter. You seldom find this one on the market, but many bass-bug fishermen have tried it and found it so good that they make their own. It is a great bug for river fishing, its face shaped to cut into the current like the bow of a boat, and with slanting shoulders, so that when you give it a pop, jets of water shoot up. It picks up easily and casts well, having a minimum of wind resistance. The spouter is made on a No. 1 3X long hook with cork body ⅝ inch in diameter by 1 inch long, in each case with a feathery tail. I like it in robin's egg blue for smallmouth, and all yellow for largemouth, but all brown, brown with yellow tail, and all yellow are also good.

Yellow seems to be one of the best colors to use for bass, but robin's egg blue is also good, especially for smallmouth. And black is greatly overlooked. Black has always brought me plenty of strikes, and yet there are probably fewer professionally made poppers in black than in any other color. Combination colors that pay off are the bugs with head of red on a yellow body, red on white, and blue on white. These bugs have the face and maybe a quarter-inch of color painted all around the head part of the bug, then the rest of the body and usually the tail of deer hair are in the other shade.

An excellent strike getter is the all-black popper with yellow dots all over it, and another one is all white with black dots on sides and back. There is considerable doubt in my mind that the bass ever see those fancy designs on the sides and backs of bugs, but the fishermen like them, both the tyer and the buyer, and they do catch fish.

The fisherman who goes for bass with streamers and bucktails should stock his fly book with a wide assortment as to both color and size. Bass are sometimes quite selective, and the angler should be equipped with several of each of certain basic patterns, so that if he loses a couple he will still have more of what those fish are looking for.

Larger editions of the trout flies, usually tied on No. 2 hooks, are excellent bass streamers. I believe the essential difference is that, in general, the more sparsely dressed fly is better for bass. Many bucktails are tied with so much hair that the wing looks dead, and acts that way, too. Even with good rod and line manipulation it still doesn't have the dash to get hits. But a sparsely dressed bucktail, with hair tapered to a point at the end of the wings to give it a minnow-like appearance, results in some slamming strikes. Bucktails seem to expand somewhat in the water and these lightly dressed flies then take on added stature. Some of the best luck I have ever had with bass came to an ordinary white bucktail, sparsely tied on a No. 2 hook.

Similarly, too many feathers in the wings of streamers make the fly ap-pear too bulky in most smallmouth water and scare the fish off rather than enticing them into striking. However, even though the dressing may be skimpy, considerable length is good in these bass flies.

The standard all-time successful colors are the winners in bass streamers and bucktails. One of the best of all is a blue and white bucktail, the top half blue and the lower half white. The all white, the all yellow, the brown and white, and the black and white are all good producers. The yellow is especially good in discolored or roily water, as are the black and the brown. Black is a universally good color for both smallmouth and largemouth bass, and in waters where black leeches occur as a natural food, then the black marabou will produce plenty of action.

The muddler minnow, designed for trout, has turned out to be a great fly for bass. Smallmouth black bass must see it as a grasshopper, or a stone cat that lives under the rocks in the river, or a river runner, darter, or the sculpin for which the imitation was first tied. The muddler can look like any of these. It may also look like a very small mouse. No wonder those smallmouth go for it in a big way.

In a river the muddler is fished in the same way for smallmouth as it would be for trout. Throw an S-cast across current, let the fly sink a bit, an inch or two beneath the surface, then start it back straight across current in short, fast jerks, and keep it coming until it is close enough to pick up for your next cast. If that doesn't bring hits, try dropping it out there across the current and letting it float along without motion, then as it starts to swing across the current, make slow pulls of a couple of feet, which speeds the fly. Then for the last part of the retrieve, give foot-long jerks until the fly swings below you, then bring it upstream in those same jerks until you wish to pick it up for the next cast. Nothing gets you action better than trying different types of retrieves, faster or slower, dead floats, fast jerks, slow jerks. A well-mixed bag of tricks gets you the bunting.

While dry flies are not widely used for bass, there are certain situations when smallmouths will knock the feathers off them, and occasionally the largemouths, too, will go for a big dry. When you're after smallmouths in rivers, a size 6 dry fished as it would be handled for trout, with accent on the perfect float, will often produce wonderful results. Many smallmouths are found in little meadow runs that hardly seem big enough to hold fish, yet from such places I have taken smallmouths up to 3 pounds, and it is fun with a light outfit and small flies.

As in trout fishing, this kind of water calls for a quiet approach and careful delivery, and to fish these small waterways I use an 8-foot rod, a DT-5-F line and a leader tapered to a 3-pound-test point, or roughly a 4X tippet. Dry flies that work well are the standard patterns of Royal Coachman, Black Gnat, Light Cahill, Ginger Quill, and the hairwing dries, all on size 6, 8, 10, and 12 hooks.

As is the case with dry flies, only a handful of anglers ever use nymphs for bass, but when the occasion calls for them, and when properly played, nymphs are good items for smallmouth. Only a few patterns will be needed in the bass fisherman's book, however, because if the bass are hitting nymphs it will usually be either the large gray nymph, or a large black one tied on a No. 4 hook. This particular one matches the hellgramite on which bass feed so avidly and brings thudding strikes. And nymphs tied to represent the large salmon flies, trout flies, and willow flies of the West are also good with smallmouth.

When bass go deep during the heat of a summer day, or when the opposite is true—the air is chilled and the water cold in spring or fall—a sinking line will help to get the fly down where the fish lie. Even a chilly smallmouth hates to see a good-looking fly go past without telling it just who is boss. In the shallower parts of the rivers, in water from 4 to 10 foot depth, the Scientific Anglers Wet Head sinking/floating line (*see* Fly Lines) will get the fly down and the floating section will enable you to mend the line and to pick up the sinking head that much more easily. The same applies in lake fishing.

When bass are hitting on top, I'd rather use a popping bug, and if they're just below the surface, then my choice is a streamer. But there are plenty of times when the fish are lying deep and seem to need something to stir them up, and at such times there is nothing quite like the fly and spinner combination to produce results. This tandem pair is designed to look like a minnow, with the flashy spoon to catch a dormant bass' attention and get him moving.

It takes a good stout rod to throw such a fly because nothing but a strong tip would stand the constant strain of lifting the heavy lure from the water and casting it repeatedly. Perhaps this is one reason that this oldtime favorite of bass fishermen is so seldom used today. In many places it is next to impossible to buy ready-made flies of this kind. Yet I remember one day last summer on a northern Ontario lake when I tried everything in the book without any luck, and then dug that old spinner rigged with a Colonel Fuller wet fly out of my box. It had been lying there for a couple of years, unused. But that day it brought the previously lazy smallmouth roaring up for it, to give me one of my best days of the season.

Even when it is not possible to find the ready-made flies, it is easy enough to purchase small spinners of the type used in both trout and bass fishing and to attach a favorite fly to them. The spinners should be in size No. 2 for clear water, or No. 3 for roily or muddy water. Bronze, silver or gold color is a matter of seeming indifference. It is the flash that counts. Sometimes, especially when the water is very heavy or discolored, a tandem spinner will attract notice and bring strikes.

Flies to be used with these spinners should be tied on hooks with a straight eye, as a turned-down eye will not allow the fly to ride freely, but instead forces it to one side, thus preventing good action.

Some of the most successful flies to combine with spinners are listed below. All are wet flies, tied on 1/0 hooks; 2/0 hooks are satisfactory in many cases, but the extra size is not necessary and extra size means extra weight, making the fly just that much heavier to throw.

PATTERNS FOR FLY AND SPINNER COMBINATIONS
HOOK SIZES 8, 10, 12

Colonel Fuller	*Royal Coachman*
Lord Baltimore	*Coachman*
Brown Hackle	*Black Gnat*
Gray Hackle	*Red and White Streamer*
Yellow Sally	*Brown and White Streamer*
Professor	*Colonel Bates*

With all the spinner combinations, the retrieve should be slow and steady, so that the fly swims, drops, swims, drops, while the spinner gives out the glint to draw the eye of the fish to the wounded minnow which I suspect this combination represents.

106

Sometimes if this fails to catch their eye, a smooth, slow retrieve will stir them. The important thing is that the spinner blade be moving from the time it enters the water until it is lifted from it.

FISHING FOR SMALLMOUTH BLACK BASS

Two of the best smallmouths I've ever caught came to big poppers. One was taken from an Ontario lake only a few acres in size, one evening when I dropped a yellow popping bug on the mirrored surface and popped it only once. While the tiny waves were just starting to roll out from it, I had a strike that tossed water all around and out came a big-headed, pot-bellied smallmouth that was ready for just about anything. It took me a long time to get him in. He weighted 5¼ pounds, one of the biggest smallmouth black bass I've ever seen. When we got in to the dock, I looked down his throat. A broad tail was sticking out.

"Look," I said to Frank Bentz who was fishing with me. "Full to overflowing, and he still socks a bug."

I took a pair of pliers and clamped down on that protruding tail and carefully pulled out the half-decomposed carcass. It was 7 inches long, what was left of a bullhead.

"They sure like big things to eat," I said. "And this shows that you can make them mad by working a big popper, too."

"That fish had to be mad, all right," Frank agreed. "The way he was packed he couldn't have swallowed a no-see-um."

A year later I was fishing with Frank again, with the same model bug, and for the same species, smallmouth black bass. We were with Fred Narvel at Port Deposit, Maryland, and we were fishing the Susquehanna River below the Conowingo Dam. We had been working the shoreline with poppers and getting enough fair-sized fish to get a big bang out of it.

Then I put on an extra-big popper and the minute it dropped, in close to the shore, it looked as if a landmine had exploded. Then, as my nerves jolted back into their grooves and my eyes stopped spinning, I saw the shape of a great, bronze-backed fish emerging above the splashes of water, a long, wide, ferocious smallmouth, the biggest of all.

That was a fight, too, because he was as powerful as he looked, with the spunk of a great fighting species to back him up. But I finally brought him to net. He weighed 6½ pounds, the largest smallmouth I've ever taken.

The greatest charm of fishing with poppers is that they bring the bass within sight of the angler as it hits. The popping bug lets him in on the whole works. He has the fun of manipulating the bug to coax the fish to it, then he gets a bang out of the strike, right there in plain view, and then the excitement of fighting the fish near the surface.

But the bug must be worked right to produce results. A popping bug, especially a big one, without proper play, is as impotent as a sea cucumber. Most novices at the popper game just throw the bug out and bring it back at once in a series of pops, maybe for 5 or 6 feet, and then pick it up and cast again. And usually they rip the line off the water so hard that they scare the scales off any nearby fish. Bringing it back so fast doesn't give the fish time to get to it and the undue surface commotion discourages him from even trying. Most fish, on seeing a bug drop to the surface, swim away and then turn to see what's happening. If they see the bug resting quietly there, or making only a slight dent in the surface, they'll usually swim back to see what's cooking, and that's when the angler has his chance. And unfortunately, that's the time the novice chooses to rip the line off the water, and then the fish is suspicious for sure. In fact, he's convinced that all is not as it should be.

But an angler who knows how to put a popping bug through its paces can make it talk the right language to make that bass come up and sock it, make him so mad he wants to grab it and smash it flat. So the popper should be rested quietly a moment, then popped gently, then brought back in a slow retrieve of interspersed pops and rests. If that doesn't work, then try a faster retrieve. Make the bug act like a minnow skipping across the surface. Use small pops across the top.

Use a big, hard pop now and then, one that really kicks up a commotion and makes a big fish think that there's something he wants.

But always remember that there is plenty of attraction for bass, both big and small, in a still lure. Especially in hot weather, the slower the play the better. The bug should be stopped dead and allowed to lie on the surface for as long as half a minute. Sixty per cent of all strikes come when the bug is not moving, but resting quietly on the surface.

While it is hard to choose between the two, I believe that it requires just a shade more finesse to fish for smallmouth than it does for largemouth. It's true that as summer wanes and fall moves in, the smallmouth bass really go on a feeding binge and during this splurge they wage the best fight of their careers. So that at such a time their behavior is a little more erratic than that of the largemouth. I remember one day in particular when I drove in on the Virginia side of the Potomac River, about twenty miles from Washington, parked the car and began to wade upstream. The water was seldom more than waist deep over the whole river and only occasionally was it necessary to wade around a deep hole. I loafed along, using a popping bug, casting only to risers. With arm-length strips of the line I brought the bug back across the surface as fast as I could, barely popping it, imparting more of a skid than a real pop, keeping the bug moving without a real pause at all.

The first smallmouth that hit fell on that fast-moving bug so hard he almost knocked the rod from my hands. And in the next two hours about fifteen more bass did the same thing. Then they slacked off and passed up not only that retrieve but every other kind of retrieve I tried.

Then I noticed that there had been a change in the way the fish were rising. Earlier, they had been dimpling the surface, but now they were leaping all the way out of the water. I soon saw why. Snake doctors were flying about, hovering a few inches above the surface. Those bass were jumping for them. So I put on a 2X tippet and tied on a spentwing Adams dry, size 6.

That turned the tables. They hit it hard and often and for the next hour I had the time of my life floating that big dry over them. But at last that ceased to be the medicine, too. The fish went down, and even though I moved upstream to show my flies to new and less wary bass, I couldn't connect. Yet I knew they were around.

Then I thought of an old-time trick that often sets reluctant trout on fire. I tied on a big spider fly and tossed that small powderpuff out about 50 feet. I imparted quick jerks to it as I brought it back, made it jump across the current for 2 or 3 feet at a time, then let it sit still for a few seconds, then gave it the business again. Soon I had a 3-pounder chasing that fly, all but turning himself inside out in his efforts to get it. So I stopped the fly altogether and wham! he had it. He smothered the fly with spray and when the hook went home he came out, red eyed as a mad bull, and once again I was in business. For half an hour, from then until dark, I had the time of my life fishing spiders.

Time and again when for one reason or another the bass have been down, I've taken them by using that varied, jerky retrieve with spiders, variants, and big hairwing flies, not only on rivers but on lakes and ponds as well. A fly played in that manner seems to bring out a playful spirit in bass. They like to chase a windblown natural across the surface, like a puppy after a ball, or a cat playing with a string. Sometimes I've found them with five or six naturals in their mouths, not swallowed, just sticking there. So apparently it's not the food but just the game's the thing, with smallmouths.

Hair frogs are great top-water lures for smallmouth black bass. Although it is little used these days, I think that Joe Messenger's famous Hair Frog, tied many, many years ago, has probably caught more smallmouth bass than any other single lure. Fished fast across the surface, it looks like a swimming frog. Smallmouth tear into it with wild abandon. Very similar to it is another great hair bug called the Weberfoot, after its designer, my friend Walt Weber, wildlife artist for the *National Geographic Magazine*. This bug is also fished in fast, foot-long jerks across the surface, with many changes of speed to interest fish that are not coming good. The body is shaped like a frog, the legs slanting backwards from the body and bound with thread and lacquered about half an inch from the end, so they look like feet. When you strip the bug the legs pump back and forth, giving a very lifelike action. Eyes are painted on the bug and the whole result is a very juicy-looking morsel. I like the No. 2 and No. 1 hook size for smallmouth, and the 1/0 regular shank for largemouth.

When fishing a Hair Frog, or any other hair bug, the angler should always have a good supply on hand, as they soon become wet and then they are hard to cast and lose their buoyant action, start dragging their feet, so they lack the fire to make a smallmouth forget his cunning and go for them hard.

Many anglers grease the underside of the Hair Frog before starting to fish, and this keeps the frog from becoming soggy for quite a while. If you do only have one and it becomes wet, you can often squeeze most of the water out and return it to some of its original life.

As I mentioned earlier, when I find that the bass are not coming to a popper, I usually turn to streamers. I recall one such day on the Susquehanna below the Conowingo Dam when we had used poppers for some time and although we had taken the odd bass, we were surely not setting the world on fire. Then we turned to streamers. I tied on a fly with a 3-inch-long yellow wing and a brown body, on a No. 1 hook.

I started casting it in among the rocks, dropping it less than a foot from shore and bringing it back straight across current, fast, in foot-long jumps. The long feathers really had action, flipping back and forth in the current. I cast for five minutes without a strike, then the whole tribe of Susquehanna smallmouths seemed to be located along about a hundred yards of shoreline and each one of them made at my fly. They just about tore the feathers off the hook. My partner was having the same experience. We never were sure just what those smallmouths figured the streamers to be—maybe they thought they were small walleyes, or catfish or sauger, or even chub, or some of the saltwater minnows that strayed four miles from tidewater. Or maybe just those flaunting feathers brought them roaring up.

And certainly the way the streamer is played makes the difference, as I remember another day on the same river, when every strike came when the fly was played in the exact opposite to the method just described. Frank Bentz and I had fished all morning without taking anything more than a couple of 10-inchers. But fish were moving because as we waded and cast to the shoreline, we would now and then see the wave put up by a good sized fish as he got out of there.

We had tried almost everything in the box, and finally Frank was starting all over again, with a white bucktail on a size 4 hook. He made a cast, let the fly drift free in the current, and turned to say something to me. Bang! A 2-pound smallmouth latched onto that drifting streamer and busted for the ceiling. Frank landed that one. We kept on fishing. No more action.

Then Frank turned to me.

"Maybe they want it just fished like a wet fly, without any action," he said.

"Give it a try," I agreed. "After all, that other one hit while the fly was floating with the current."

And it turned out that was what they wanted that day. They wanted their streamers without any action. We both fished that way and both got some nice bass. So there's nothing that beats trying new ways as well as new flies, to get to bass that are not cooperating.

Even when an angler thinks he knows just what the fish are going to hit, it always pays to watch just what's going on in the water. Once while fishing near Point of Rocks, on the Potomac, Walt Weber and I were using our favorite popping bugs, but with little success. It was a still, hot day. The glides, slides, and runs looked dead calm, only the bounce of the riffles giving any life to the surface of the river. There wasn't a sign of fish life.

Yet when we waded in the shallower water we could see the waves that several bass made as they went out ahead of us.

"They're here," said Walt. "They just aren't hitting."

At that moment we both saw a couple of swirls along the shoreline, close by. Those fish didn't break through the surface, they just pushed it up.

"They're bulging," I said. "Just like trout."

"Nymphing!" said Walt, and we both dove for our tackle boxes.

We added an extra 2 feet of 2X tippet to the end of our leaders and then greased the leaders down to within 4 inches of the end. Then we put on gray nymphs tied on No. 8 hooks.

Walt made the first cast, to one of those fish we had spotted. He dropped the nymph 3 feet above the bulge and let it float free with the current. Down it came. Our eyes were glued on the end of the floating leader and just under it we could picture the nymph, 2 or 3 inches below the surface, jiggling around a little in the current, lifelike. Then the forward motion of the leader stopped and it seemed as if a giant hand had grabbed it and pulled it forward.

"He's there! He's on!" yelled Walt, striking.

A 2-pound tiger-striped smallmouth came out and walked across the surface on his tail. He splashed back in and dashed away for 20 feet, then came out in an end-over-end leap. He tore down the shoreline, then cut out below us, headed for deeper water. When he hit the fast current, he jumped again. Then he hung there in the current, resting.

Walt kept the pressure on and finally pulled his head our way and got him moving. That stubborn fish dashed for shore and jumped again in water so shallow that he must have bumped his belly on the bottom. But at last Walt got him in. He was only the first of a nice string we took on those gray nymphs.

Since smallmouths live mostly in clear-water lakes and rivers, and have eyes like a hawk, they present a special problem during the bright part of the day. In the shallows, particularly, they can spot motion in a hurry, and fishing for them there calls for just as careful an approach as fishing for trout. The angler who wants to connect in such water must work cautiously, avoid noise or excessive commotion in the boat or in wading.

The value of being quiet when fly-rodding for bass was convincingly demonstrated to me one summer when half a dozen of us who lived in Baltimore used to go to the Upper Potomac near Shepherdstown, West Virginia, for weekends of smallmouth fishing. Usually we would line up in the river and start down, six abreast, flinging flies in all directions. We caught plenty of fish because there were plenty of them in there—and solely for that reason, I believe. Because six men fishing together in a stream make a lot of commotion. But the fish we caught were mostly 8 and 9 inches long, with a few up to 15 inches.

It was fun, for there is nothing dull about the fight of even that size of smallmouth. But we wished we would catch some larger ones occasionally.

"There are no big ones in here," said one of the boys.

"Want to bet on that?" asked Walt Weber. "I'll bet we could come out here on a week day, just a couple of us, when the river is quiet, and take some good fish."

Bets were laid, and later that week Walt and I slipped out there. We eased into the river quietly, waded carefully, avoiding excessive grinding of gravel under our boots, and made no false motions for wary big boys to spot. There was no one on the river but ourselves.

We took several smallmouths apiece in the 2-, 3-, and 4-pound class. And in almost any water where the small ones are found, you can count on some hard-hitting bigger ones, too, if you get there at the right time and fish the right way.

In large rivers such as the Potomac, the Shenandoah in Virginia, and the Great Cacapon in West Virginia, the shorelines are frequently big producing areas. To avoid spooking the fish that are lying or feeding alongshore, the angler should stay well out from the shore, at least 50 feet, and work slowly downstream, casting directly across current in to the shore. The fly will go downstream in the current, then swing in below with plenty of real-looking action. A fly cast directly downstream, as would be the case if the angler were wading inshore and casting to fish just below him, would look lifeless. The fly should be retrieved in slow, even strips, and brought well in before being picked up for the next cast.

When smallmouths are feeding in the shallows along the shore of a lake, as they often do on summer mornings or evenings, then a quiet, stealthy approach is doubly important. Always when a fish is in shallow water he is warier than at other times. He knows he is open to attack from many angles, so he swims and feeds with both eyes cocked, ready to shoot off to safety. At such times a fairly long cast is advisable, both to reach the spot where you know there is a fish, and to avoid frightening any that might happen to be between you and the known smallmouth.

"What do you call a long cast?" one angler asked me.

"Anywhere from 65 to 70 feet," I said.

"How about these 100-foot casts you hear people talking about?" he wanted to know.

"There's such a thing as casting too far," I told him. "For efficient fly or bug play and for a quick strike, and for line work in general, I'd say that 55 to 70 feet would be the best distance to cast. Over 80 feet the strike impulse takes too long to get to the fish and he may spit out the fly before he's hooked. And the greater the distance away, the harder it is to see the flash of a fish as he goes for the lure, and so you may strike too late."

In other words, the shorter the cast, the more control the angler has over line and fly, and the easier it is for him to hook his fish. So he has to judge the conditions and cast accordingly, remembering always that the shorter cast is surer and easier to handle.

Often on rivers I creep up close enough to get off casts of only 40 feet. And if I were to choose one over-all perfect casting distance, I would take 50 feet. At that distance you have control; it's hard for the fish to see you but fairly easy for you to see him.

Another important thing to remember in clear-water fishing for smallmouths is that the terminal tackle should be light. Going light on fly leaders for bass means tapering down to 3X, which works very well with dry flies and nymphs on rivers. Generally it is better to go a bit heavier when using streamers or bucktails on big water. A hard strike from a smallmouth while the lure is being retrieved quickly across current will snap the leader where it is tied to the fly, if the tippet is too light.

On such big water there are usually swirls and runs, broken surfaces and bubbles which tend to prevent the bass from seeing the leader too readily anyway. Then a slightly heavier tippet is called for—say 4-pound test. But there is seldom, if ever, any need to put on a heavier leader than that. A 4-pound-test tippet will hold almost any smallmouth in existence, and the finer the calibration of the last section of the leader, the better action can be given to the fly. A stiff, heavy leader end makes the streamer appear dead and will certainly be spotted in a hurry by a suspicious bass. And the bass leader should be tapered just as carefully as the trout leader; in fact, a properly tapered leader is all the more important in casting the big flies and poppers used for bass.

While the smallmouth is undoubtedly one of the readiest hitters, there are times when they cross you up, and for no apparent reason refuse to hit. Don Gapen and I ran into such a situation in a little lake on an island in Lake Superior, near Nipigon, Ontario. This was not smallmouth country, but Don knew where there were some bass in a lake and he frequently took guests from his nearby resort to this lake for a change from trout and northern pike fishing. But that day we cast poppers for an hour without a hit. We tried bucktails, streamers, nymphs, dry flies. Don put on a spinner and fly combination and tried that. Nothing happened. We tried fast retrieves, slow retrieves, with equal lack of success. We went back to popping bugs again, hoping to stir up those lethargic bass.

"It's been pretty hot," said Don. "But still, we should get a hit or two, at least."

We were both sitting there feeling pretty disconsolate, and as we sat, Don had left his popper lying on the surface of the water about 50 feet out from the boat. It must have lain there a full minute, and then he started to retrieve it.

"Bam!"

A two-pound smallmouth came roaring out, clamped down on the popper and the fight was on. After he had landed that one, Don threw the popper out again and I did the same with mine, and then we just sat there and grinned. Don pointed to his watch.

"We'll give them a full minute," he said. "That's what they need. Time. We haven't been waiting long enough."

If you've ever sat and waited for a bass to hit, while you watched the second hand of a wristwatch make a full circuit of 60 seconds, you know that a minute can seem like an hour. But that's what we did. And it paid off. And has paid off many more times, with lazy bass.

"They must have been down there looking at the bugs all the time," said Don. "But they're lazy with the heat and it takes quite a while for them to make up their minds to hit."

"Well, we can wait," I said. "It's never too long to wait for small-mouth."

Later in the day, when air and water had cooled a little, those bass returned to their normal willing form and knocked the spots off our poppers, and for the last half-hour before dark we were mixed up with a bunch of wild-eyed bass that didn't care what kind of temptation we offered. They took everything, to remind us once again that in spite of their peculiar behavior earlier, they were the same old rambunctious, hard-hitting, high-jumping smallmouths that make anglers all over the United States and Canada just as wild-eyed as they are.

FISHING FOR LARGEMOUTH BLACK BASS

Probably more words have been written about the largemouth black bass than about any other fish, except perhaps the trout. It's not because they are harder to make hit, or that they wage a tougher fight, or that they jump higher, or bore deeper, or shake their heads more than others. It's because of two things—wherever an angler lives in the U.S.A., he can find them nearby; and wherever he finds them they are ready takers of lures. They are the fish kids cut their teeth on. They are the fish, even more than sunnies, that most anglers catch first.

While the largemouth goes by many different names, there's never really any question as to who he is. He's the same forthright guy everywhere, a buster with a great hunger, with eyes larger than his very big stomach. He has an appetite that will make him try to swallow anything from a mouse to a manatee. The hungrier he gets, the madder he gets, and when he's mad he looks mad all over. His scales stick out, his fins beat violently, his lower jaw juts out more than usual, and his eyes get as red as a mad bull's. He bristles. He is full of a hot-headed desire to knock the heck out of anything that goes by. So, when your popping bug or other feathery fooler is near, boy, oh boy, does he sock it!

The farther south the largemouth is found, the bigger he gets. Wherever he isn't ice-bound, he feeds most of the year round, and down in lower Georgia and Florida he is sitting at the dinner table all the time. They grow big in Texas, too, and that state rightly boasts of the outsize hunks of bassy fish-flesh that swim its water. This was brought home to me once when I fished with Andy Anderson of the Houston *Press*. That day Andy and I were casting away, talking up a storm and in general having a good old get-together.

"Gosh!" cried Andy, suddenly. "Did you see that?"

I looked in time to see him with one foot on the gunwale, one arm on a tree branch, like he was going to climb up to get away from something.

"What?" I stammered, thinking of snakes and sea serpents.

Andy pointed. I looked, and where he was pointing I could still see the receding waves that could only have been pushed up by a monster bass.

"Come down out of that tree," I said, "and cast back there."

It was a tough place to put a bug but Andy did it. In fact he did it eleven times, and then, deep down, something moved. Two small whirlpools showed on the surface, about 2 feet apart.

"He'll hit soon," I said. "Throw on back. He just swirled down deep."

"Probably just a little one," said Andy.

"Little?" I shouted. "Did you see how far apart those little whirlpools were? Only a big bass makes swirls like that."

My excitement was beginning to get to Andy. His next cast was a bit off line but he brought it carefully back, tried again and made a bullseye. The bug had hardly lit before the water flew apart as that big bass rammed his wide open mug through the surface, inhaled the bug, turned and tore across the top, headed for the sanctuary of a maze of criss-crossed tree branches just under the surface. Andy put the heat on, leaned back on his rod, and held. The tip bounced down to the surface, hung there, then as the bass slowed, the pressure brought him to the surface and Andy got him coming our way. He looked like 20 pounds to me.

Even when I put the net under him and lifted him into the boat, he still looked that big.

"A fair fish," said Andy. "Let's put him back."

"I don't mind putting him back," I replied. "But what size do you call a big fish, in Texas?"

"Wal," said Andy. "We call anything over 15 pounds a big fish. This one's only about 9."

I kept mum because I didn't want Andy to know that any largemouth over 5 pounds seemed very big to me. But this was Texas.

When he does get over 10 pounds, the largemouth seems to be all mouth and gut. His maw looks as big as the entrance to the Luray Caverns. And when he's big like that he gets a bit lazy, often basking like a walrus, or lying around moping in the shade of a log or a lily pad. On hot days when the sun moves around, he changes his position just enough to keep up with his shade patch, making even that small move under protest and you imagine you can see him grumpily wipe the sweat from his brow with a limp fin.

In order to make such a lazy bass hit, a lure must be played very slowly—in the case of a popping bug, with long pauses between pops, and many changes of pace to arouse his interest or anger; and in the case of a streamer, with a tempting, flirting action.

But when he is hungry, you just can't take the fly away from him. And if he's a brackish-water largemouth, as well as being hungry, he's twice as rambunctious as usual. There's no more evil-tempered fish than the bigmouth in brackish water. The sea seems to add a little salt to his disposition, and when an angler disturbs his slumbers or merely interrupts his train of thought as he lies among the weeds, he may expect that fish to come up with wide-open mouth to fix that pesky noise maker. He'll even come back a second time if he's mad enough. And it isn't hard to make him mad enough.

Many times I have fished Currituck Sound out of Poplar Branch, North Carolina, working the island and little lakes among the marshes. The fish in there always seem ready, to the point that they'll almost climb a bush to get at a lure. On one trip there, I saw the swirl of a big fish right against a bank.

"He's grabbed a soft crab," I thought.

My guide eased me into casting distance. My cast started off all right, but it went too far and hung on the reeds that grew up from the water, directly above where the fish had struck. I pulled back with the rod, the bug came loose and jumped a foot onto a single reed, then slipped 3 or 4 inches down it. I pulled back again, and up the reed went the bug, like it had hands. That bass came out then for that bug and I fancied I could hear his jaws bang together as he tried and missed. When my nerves stopped jumping I pulled some more and that bug started swinging, monkey like, from reed to reed. And below it, sticking his ugly old head out and following it, was that bass. He kept after it for 6 feet, and then it fell to the water. He busted it quick and as I set the hook he jumped, fell over a bunch of floating grass and pulled free.

I sat down till my heart began to give an all quiet signal again. Then I cast back there, just to see if perhaps that 12-pounder was still anxious for that bug. He was. He took it on the first cast, as soon as it hit the water, and I landed him that time. He weighed 7 pounds 5 ounces, a far cry from the 12 pounds my bulging eyes had imagined him to be. But he was still a good, walloping big largemouth.

Largemouth are easy to finger. No use to waste time working stretches of flat beach, unbroken sandy places, muddy flats devoid of vegetation or cover. Old bigmouth is out with the things he likes to eat. He's hanging around under or alongside moored boats, docks, logs, fallen trees, channel markers, rafts, pilings, drop-offs, grass beds, both secure and floating along banks and under rocks. Once in Shirley Mill Pond in Virginia, Moses Nunnally showed me just how accurately the largemouth can be spotted. Moses took me out on the pond and pointed out what he called "hurdles."

"We put a pile of cedar bushes down there, held by four poles to keep them from floating away," he explained. "Looks something like an underwater race track hurdle, and it provides just the sort of spot where bass like to hang out. Cast 4 feet beyond that stake to the left, and exactly 2 feet out from it. That's where he'll be."

My cast wasn't quite exact, but it was close. I didn't even have time to pop the bug. There was a swirl and I struck. A big, wide mouth showed for a minute, then the big bug flew back at me. I had only nicked him.

"Too bad," said Moses. "A 6-pounder." He started the motor. "But there's another one right over here."

We moved farther down the shore.

"See that lap?" said Moses.

"What's a lap?" I wanted to know.

"It's the top half of a tree," he explained. "Cut off so it falls in the water. Makes a swell place for fish to hide."

"That one?" I asked, pointing to a freshly downed tree lying against the shore.

"No," said Moses. "The one beyond that. That's a new one that you are looking at. Next year it will be just right. There are about 200 of them in the pond right now, a few that fell naturally, but most of them we chopped."

"Put the bug right in beside it," he went on. "Bob lives there."

Seeing the look I gave him, Moses laughed. "Bob's a 7-pound bass," he explained. "I know him so well I have a name for him. Of course there's just a chance he won't hit, but he's there."

Bob was there. And Bob hit. He was a well-stacked 7-pounds, a top-conditioned largemouth.

We had drifted a considerable distance from the lap when I put him back but Moses told me that he'd go right back there, and be there the next time we came by.

"Suppose we had put him back farther away," I said. "How far would he travel to get back to where he lives?'

"I know two bass named Peggy and Jock," he said. "They used to live on a point down the lake. Each time I caught them there I'd carry them to the other end of the pond in the live well, and then release them. But the next time I came past their home point, there they would be.

"I caught them so often," he added, "that I guess they began to wonder where their home really was. They moved down the lake where I was always putting them back, and now I catch them there and bring them back to the point, and they swim right back down the lake again."

"Just a couple of mixed up kids!" I laughed.

But there was nothing mixed up about the way Moses could spot those fish, and that's the way largemouth are—if you know where they like to live, and if there are fish in there at all, they'll be where you expect them to be.

Largemouth go for a big lure. Especially the weighty old-timers can't be bothered with small stuff. They only stir their stumpy fins for an article of food big enough to bulge their bellies. They like the large popping bugs and streamers and bucktails, and they like streamer-spinner and bucktail-spinner combinations. But while these big lures bring lots of hits, the angler must use caution in presenting and playing them. When the fly hits the surface, the nearby bass will start swimming away, but invariably he will turn back after a bit and look to see what has fallen there. If the lure is quiet, like a bug that has dropped and is resting, he will come back and generally grab it. Sometimes if he is a little suspicious, a slight quiver of the bug will chase his fears away. But always, after making the cast, be sure to rest it awhile before beginning to play it—whether using streamer or popping bug.

In my book the all-time greatest bass bug, the one I think is a mile ahead of any other for largemouth, is the Gerbubble Bug, invented in the late 1920s by Tom Loving of Baltimore, Maryland. Because it is difficult to make, and because the pattern has seldom appeared in print, this wonderful bug is little used. It's one I think every bass fisherman should try. The Gerbubble Bug picks up lightly, pops well, sits low in the water, and the fringe-like hackles on the sides and the flirting tail make it a potent bit of medicine for bass. Loving tied it on a No. 2/0 hook with cork body 9/16 inches high, 11/16 inches wide and 7/8 inches long. It has hackle fringes projecting from the sides, and a feathery hackled tail. He painted his bugs an overall brown with red, white or yellow tiny circles or dots here and there; or all white, or all yellow, with the same added small eyes and circles, and matching feathers. This makes the bug look more natural than some of the bright colors painted on many bugs, and which I think are designed to dazzle the angler rather than the bass.

Another bug that can look like many different kinds of food to a bass is "The Thing." This is a bug that features five moosemane legs, each 3 inches long, on the top side of the cork body. When you throw it out and it lights on the surface, the legs are all straight up. As you watch, they fall on the surface, slowly, on either side of the cork body. It looks for all the world like a bird landing on the water and folding its wings. Sometimes I think the small fish flee before it, believing it to be a fish hawk. But it's something else again when you show it to a lunker. He'll sink his fangs into it. Some of the biggest bass ever landed in Virginia and Maryland waters have hit The Thing.

A number of commercially tied popping bugs feature a fine wire weedless attachment, looking like two delicate legs extending back under the body from just below the face. When these wires hit the reeds or heavy grass they ride the bug up so the hook doesn't catch on these obstacles. But you can maneuver any of the good poppers in such weedy spots if you handle them carefully. When you cast a popper in to a stand of upthrust reeds, play it very slowly as it nears each single reed. This brings the head of the bug up against the reed, and as you pull gently the hook will move out and the whole bug will get safely by.

With the bug, a good half-minute rest before giving it the first pop pays off, especially during the warm months. The majority of strikes come when the bug is not moving, but resting quietly on the surface. Sometimes a bass will see a lure coming through the air, move under it and grab it as soon as it hits, but usually they want to look it over carefully before picking up their knives and forks. Glutton-like, they want to bolt it down in a hurry, but gourmand-like, they want to savor it a bit, and they want to be sure it's not tainted meat.

A streamer should be allowed to sink almost to the bottom in shallow water, or a good long time if it's deeper, before it is started back. And even if the first cast doesn't produce, a second, or a third, back to the same spot will bring a hit. The largemouth is not the hardest fish to make hit a fly but he can go down, like any other fish, and being the stubborn creature he is, when a bigmouth is down, he's really down.

Even a veteran angler fishes far too fast. One quick cast, a fast retrieve, and away he goes to the next likely spot, never realizing that the fast retrieve gets the lure out of there too soon, maybe when the fish is getting interested. A bass wants to think things over a bit, he wants his suspicions lulled, he wants to be convinced that the fly is really something good to eat. During the hot months the lure can hardly be played slowly enough. I've waited a full minute, and never less than half a minute, before giving a popping bug action. It seems an hour, when you want hits, but it's that way or else.

School bass behave quite differently from the singles. At Welaka on the St. John's River in Florida, schools of largemouth cut the surface up as they feed on shad minnows, and along with the bass, sticking their long, slender snouts out and feeding at the same trough are beaucoup needlefish. They like shad minnows, too.

"A.P." Oliver knows the first name of every bass in that area. Besides being a fine angler, an excellent guide, and a student of fish behavior, A.P. is fun to fish with. Not much misses his keen eye and usually when the other fishermen are drawing blanks, A.P. is boating fish. When I fished with A.P. we were ninety miles from the river mouth, yet there was still tidal action. We cut the motor and soon saw fish working a short way off.

"Do they always school here?" I asked.

"Generally from October to April," A.P. said. "But in 1952 they were thick around here all year."

We were close to the breaking school now. I cast a popping bug to a spot where I had seen a rise. By the time the bug hit the surface, I saw top-water disturbance only 10 feet away.

"They move fast," said A.P. "You gotta get to them in a hurry."

But before I could even pop that bug, a 2-pounder hit and came on out, shaking his head so hard that he threw the insecurely hooked tenite bug a foot into the air. When it hit the water again, another bass was waiting and gobbled it fast, jumped and also threw the bug. I looked at the hook, but the fault wasn't there. It was my fault.

I cast and had another hit, and this time I pulled in a 3-pound fish. As I took the hook out, an inch-long shad minnow pulled out of his mouth, then another, and another, all fresh.

"Can you beat that!" I said. "Here's a guy stuffed to the hilt, so full that he's making like a machine grinding hamburgers, and he still wants his plate refilled!"

I threw him back into the water and when he hit he disgorged at least half a dozen more shad minnows. These last were a bit more of the chum variety—a bit used, so to speak.

Another school showed suddenly, thrashing the top 20 feet away. They sounded, and I cast uptide from where they had showed.

"That's the wrong place," A.P. advised. "Cast downtide from the fish. They follow the shad minnows that swim with the tide, and hit them from behind."

Sure enough, they showed again 10 feet farther downtide, going away from us. A.P. started the motor. My nerves jumped.

"Hey!" I shouted. "Hadn't we better row after them? The motor will put them down."

"Not these school bass," said A.P. "It doesn't work that way here. The motor doesn't scare them, but if I were to cut it and start rowing, then they would go down."

It was hard to believe but that's the way it is.

"Look," I said. "It's raining over there."

A white line showed on the surface a hundred yards away where raindrops were slapping hard into the water.

"That's bass," A.P. said. "Look at them feed."

The disturbance was in a straight line for a hundred feet and altogether there must have been two acres of water jumping up. As we came nearer we saw that the water was being splashed a couple of inches high as the bass, completely berserk, rammed open-mouthed into a tightly packed, frenzied schools of shad minnows. We could hear the sizzling sound when A.P. cut the motor, and now and then we saw a minnow knocked high in the air. It was vicious. These might be school fish, but they were the same old extra-hungry, extra-big eaters, the same old largemouth black bass. Then everything went down and here and there patches of foam were left, so it looked like the circus grounds after the tents are down and gone, the scattered pieces of paper, the bits of cardboard cups.

We left the school fish then and worked the shoreline for big stuff under stumps and floating vegetation. And while the school fish were mostly small, there are some bass in that river that will pry your eyelids wide open. You never know what will happen, or when. It's bass fishing that keeps you guessing, and it certainly keeps you casting because if you want action, the school fish will furnish that, and if you want size, the huge hunks along the shoreline will provide that, too.

Bass school all over the South, in the TVA lakes, in big rivers in Texas, and in the bigger lakes and rivers of Florida. On Lake Okeechobee they are continually moving into the bays and along the shoreline to spawn. For nine months of the year they keep moving in, furnish good fishing, spawn, and then go back to the big part of the lake where it is hard to find them, hard to get a hit.

On one trip to Lake Okeechobee with Captain Bill Johnson of Clewiston, we took his charter boat, the Seven Seas, towed a couple of skiffs, and ran down to Moonshine Bay. The water was from 2 to 5 feet deep and reeds stuck up everywhere and pepper grass lay on the surface in great patches. This type of fishing called for a weedless attachment so I tied on a popping bug that was already rigged that way. It had rubber legs, a yellow tenite body, white bucktail tail. I cast it out, and started it walking across the surface. It looked alive and it didn't walk very far before a mite of a bass flew up and hit it. That bigmouthed youngster wasn't 8 inches long.

We worked all the open spaces in the reeds, all the little pockets that looked bassy enough to hold 10-pounders. We fished for fifteen minutes without a strike aside from that junior edition. Then I dropped the bug on the pepper grass and a five-pounder tore up and engulfed it and dove for the bottom.

After that almost every time we dropped a lure on that pepper grass we had a hit. The bass would come up, grab the bug, jump once, then dive and tangle in the grass. We would have to row over, catch hold of the leader and pull gently, bringing up a huge wad of grass with each fish. Half the time the bass would be entirely covered with grass and weeds and wouldn't even kick as we took the hook out and dropped them back in. With their heads buried in all that greenery they must have thought they were hidden from us.

The next day Bill took us to Fisheating Creek, also near Clewiston. It was a bassy looking place, pretty enough to make us want to take pictures of it, with or without fish. There were great live oaks with wide limbs dripping with Spanish moss. Rimming the creek were huge cypress trees, thin trunked at the top, fringed with leaves, and tapering outward fast at the butt. On the ground, all around, were cypress knees. The early sun slanted through the trees, sifting through the hanging tendrils of moss and cutting through the leaves in shafts. The morning mist rose from the water like incense, giving the whole thing a cathedral atmosphere.

But we shook our heads briskly and soon shapes of huge bass covered the picture, shattered the calm. We were bass hungry. We dashed for the water. Bill and Hoit Agey took the boat and Dave Roberts and I slipped upstream along the shore. Dave eased into the first nice looking bit of water and I went on until I came to a round pool rimmed with water hyacinths. It looked like what I wanted.

On my first cast, the big yellow popper had hardly hit the water before the surface was smashed into a thousand particles. A bigmouth jumped, shaking his head, gill covers flaring outward, red gills showing, the big yellow bug showing, too, in the corner of his mouth. He was a 5-pounder and fought like double that. I took three others from that pool before moving upstream.

Fisheating Creek lazed through bottom land in a million twists and turns. I had to wade the creek a dozen times and still wasn't very far from where we had parked. The fishing was terrific.

I stayed at it till dark and had to use my flashlight to get back to the car. As we put our rods away, we talked over the day.

"Best bass fishing I've had in a long, long time," I said. "I even had to kick them aside as I waded."

"Yah!" said Hoite. "I can see you kicking bass out of the way."

"No fooling," I said. "Once I felt one bump into my leg and I kicked him."

Hoite laughed. "The next time you feel something bump into you in those hyacinths," he said, "brush it aside with a 15-foot pole. That was a cottonmouth you kicked, for sure."

In the autumn, in the colder parts of the country, largemouth seem to go on orgies of eating everything within reach, everything they can stuff down their wide throats, as if to store up fat to tide them over the winter months. For a while, then, they seem to hit harder and fight harder, and for the angler it is one of the best times of year to be out. The bass lose a lot of their summer sluggishness then, and are ready and willing to chase after a fly. They hit so hard and so often that the lucky fisherman who is in on those days comes to believe that he has discovered the all-time secret of catching bass. And then the next day they are down, and he begins to understand. This was their last mighty binge, just before curtains, and as the cold continues to work on them, only a deep, slow-moving streamer or bucktail will get any response at all.

BRACKISH WATER LARGEMOUTH

Where largemouth black bass go into brackish water they provide anglers with some extra-special sport. I remember one day not long ago when I fished for largemouth at Currituck Sound, out of Bertha, North Carolina. Met Lupton, who was guiding me, jockeyed the skiff broadside to a small island fringed with reeds and grasses.

"This bank is loaded with bass," he said.

I made a false cast, then shot the line out. The leader went over a clump of reeds that rose from the shallow water close to shore, and the gerbubble bug landed with a splat on the surface back of them. I lifted the rod tip. The leader pulled across the reeds and the popper rose from the surface, climbing one of the stalks like something alive. There was a swirl under it and I almost struck. I pulled again, gently, hoping the bug would fall on the water. Instead it swung out into the air as the leader slid across yet another reed. I could see water movement as the bass followed. Then the bug dropped to the surface. Water flew. I struck and missed.

I cast right back and again the bug went over the reeds. As I started the retrieve it swung from reed to reed as if it were a monkey traveling the jungle lanes. I gave an extra-hard jerk and the bug landed on the surface 2 feet from the reeds. There was a walloping hit. I lifted the rod and felt him.

He busted out in the air, a bulldog of a bass close to 6 pounds. He fell back in and swept along the bank as if looking for something sharp on which to cut the leader. He jumped again, and when he fell back in I pulled back with the rod and turned him. He came our way slowly, doggedly, then made another lunge and came halfway out of the water. He was tiring and I used the butt of the rod to keep him coming. Met grabbed him by the lower lip and lifted him up to remove the hook. We let him go.

The brackish-water largemouth is widespread throughout the country in a thin band wherever salt and fresh water meet a great gamefish overlooked by many anglers. They are in tidewater and below, wherever a river floods down lots of fresh water into the salt, or in sounds where winds move salt water into a freshwater area. The upper part of the Chesapeake Bay is a good place for them because the mighty Susquehanna pours in there. Nearby, the Elk and Northeast rivers are veritable pipelines of fresh water pushing well out into the bay, and all this sweet water spreads out and mingles with the salt over the famed Susquehanna flats. Another good spot is where the tidewater pushing in through Oregon Inlet is moved by winds up into Currituck, Albemarle, and Pamlico sounds in North Carolina, and as far as Back Bay, Virginia. Still further south the brackish-water largemouth finds suitable habitat in the mysterious mangrove-studded bays of the Florida coast where the freshwater streams of the Everglades pour into the gulf of Mexico. Where you find this mixture of salt water and fresh in comparative shallows, within the range of the largemouth, there you find him adapting himself to the brackish water. The salt brings him an extra supply of minnows, baitfish, shrimps, crabs, and small eels.

Too much fresh water moves the brackish bass a bit farther toward the salt, but too much salt can do them real harm. In 1935 a hurricane brought the sea rolling over the Outer Banks of North Carolina into Currituck Sound. The brine killed off a lot of bass. But within a few years, as the salinity of the water returned to normal (about 4½ percent), there he was again, that hard-hitting, bug-eyed, devil-may-care, ever-hungry slammer.

In sounds and marshes and along the mainland and island, these brackish-water bass run 1½ to 2½ pounds, with a sprinkling of 4- and 5-pounders, and a few weighing 7 and 8. Ten-pounders are taken occasionally but they are few and far between. Regardless of size, their strike, especially to a surface lure, is a rocker. A touch of salt gives the largemouth extra ginger, makes him more of a gamefish.

Practically everywhere within their habitat, 25, 50, 75, and even 100 fish may be caught in a day. Fishing alone in Currituck Sound, I once took 32 bass without moving the skiff. I just worked the water 5 feet deep between two islands. Another time when I was at Currituck with Walt Weber, *National Geographic* wildlife artist, we took turns fishing and landed 75 bass in one day on one single Gerbubble Bug. One two different occasions we each took 100 bass. All, of course, were returned to the water.

Good brackish-water bass fishing begins in mid-April in most places and continues until the first part of October. If it stays warm in the northern part of their range, the fish will continue to hit, but when colder weather chills the water they go deep and become sluggish. May is perhaps the best month in their northern range, and that's a good time to be out in the marshes. As you cast you see the long-billed marsh wren, a tiny wooer, rise straight up 10 feet in the air on fast-beating wings, singing his mating song; then, overcome by it all, sink back down to his perch on a reed.

You hear the chattering cry of the clapper rail, the raspy wail of a galinule. Add all that to the swirls you see as bass break and feed.

Since brackish-water bass usually inhabit the shallows, you often have a problem with dingy water. Strong winds roll up waves that sweep the bottom and stir the mud. But there's a way to overcome this. Search out heavier growths of weeds that reach right to the surface. Dotted here and there within these patches of weeds and you'll often find spots that are bare of vegetation. Within these protected circles the water will be clear.

While they will hit many kinds of lures, top-water and sub-surface, the nature of the bass's home grounds makes the fly-rod popper the most effective lure of all. You can work a fly-rod popper in around reeds, close along the bank, around mounds of mud and grass, and back into little bays and coves amid the irregular growth of swamp sedge. It goes in there easily, floats on the water, responds lightly to rod and line play, and is easy to get out again without hanging up, because of the wide gape of the hook.

In spite of the fact that these bass have plenty of water to move about in, they run true to form by taking up residence in certain spots, migrating only with the rise and fall of wind-controlled tides. You'll find them off points, which they seem to use as feeding stations, and around duck blinds, where they are often just resting in the shade. They move to cooler spots when the sun goes around, half asleep, but not so sleepy that they'll miss a well-placed bug offered with a minimum of commotion. They lie along the edges of weed beds, under rocks, and all manner of floating live boxes, logs or downed trees. You find them almost anywhere they can locate something to lean against or on which to scratch their backs.

There is little use in fishing long, flat stretches where the bottom is smooth and without the cover that bass like. Unless you see fish working, it's usually unproductive to fish a fly in water 6 feet or more deep. The exceptions are the guts that run like a network of veins through the marshes. In them the water may be 6 or 7 feet deep, but you'll find largemouth lurking close along the upslope of the banks.

In many places you can put on hip boots and walk the banks of the guts, streams, and man-made canals, watching for risers and casting ahead to good-looking spots. Such places often hold large bass.

One of the most effective ways of bringing hits is to drop a bug as close as possible to tuckahoes and lily pads. It's fun to drop your offering smack on top of a lily pad, let it sit a moment, then yank it off. Suddenly, before it has gone a foot, there's often a resounding strike. Bass seem to think that anything sitting on a lily pad is something good to eat.

During the hot months poppers should be played very slowly. Bass evidently feel the heat, and, like people, don't want to move around too much or too fast. In the summer the best fishing is from daybreak on for a couple of hours, and again a couple of hours before dark. Things are cooler then, the bass more active. In the cooler weather of early spring and autumn, a faster retrieve often does better. In the fall the fish are on the prod, feeding heavily to store up energy for the cold days ahead. Cast in to a dock, boat or bank, let the bug sit still when it hits, then give it a single pop, then start it back in a series of pops, fast all the way until you pick it up for the next cast. One pay-off retrieve is to cast 50 feet or less, raise the rod tip as high as you can and make short strips of the line. The bug comes part way out of the water, sways from side to side, tail swishing. It's a beautiful and tantalizing-looking bug just then, and no wonder it makes bass tingle all over and rush up and strike.

Regardless of the speed of your retrieve always remember to let the bug sit that first few seconds after it hits the water. I've watched bass from a dock when other anglers were casting to them. When the bug lands, the bass will slowly swim 4 or 5 feet away, then stop, turn, and eye the resting bug. The angler gives it a slight pop. The bass beats his fins a bit more rapidly. He's casing that thing up there. He wants to be sure it's what he thinks it is. Another slight pop eases his doubts and he rushes for it.

When bass go down and spurn the best surface offerings, you can sometimes save the day by tying on a bucktail or streamer in red and white, red and yellow, blue and white, all brown, all yellow, or all white. I like them on hooks that range from 1/0 through No. 1 and No. 2. Cast these to the same places you would drop a bug, keep the rod tip high on the retrieve in shallow water, and bring the fly back in slow, foot-long jerks. This seems to be the best all-round retrieve for streamers and bucktails, but if it brings no strikes, then experiment a little. Try a fast, even retrieve, make the fly dart forward in erratic jerks, start it back slowly, then speed it up. Mix up your offerings until you find the retrieve they will hit. The strip method of retrieve is best for this because it enables you to bring the fly back at any speed—slow, fast, extra fast. You have control of the line at all times and you are always ready for the strike or the pickup for the next cast.

Boca Fever

In a few hours I caught the two biggest trout of my career. Yet the Argentine fishermen hardly rated them as keepers!

We came over the hilltop and there was the lake, and the river pouring out of it.

"The boca!" shouted Jorge Donovan.

"The boca! The boca!" yelled Bebe Anchorena and Andrew Gordon.

All three were Argentines who knew their country's rivers well. If they could become so excited about their first trip of the season in the foothills of the Andes Mountains, then what they'd been telling me must be true. This was the place where the spotted monsters lived.

Unlike many South American fishing waters, the rivers in the Junin area lie at a comfortable 2,500-foot altitude. They're the world's greatest trout steams, most of them seldom fished. In a month I saw fewer than a dozen anglers. I'd drive fifty miles along great, trouty rivers and not meet one.

These rivers flow out of vast lakes containing enormous trout. Thirty- and 35-pound fish are taken by the few trollers who venture out on these lakes, but boats are few and the water usually too rough for comfort. But the rivers—the Chimehuin, the Alumine, the Collon Cura, the Quilquihue, the Quillen, and the Malleo—are jam-packed with 4-, 5-, and 6-pound browns and rainbows. These aren't considered keepers, and a 9-pounder is just part of the day's catch. A competent angler can be sure of a 10-pounder and, now and again, a 12-, 15- or maybe 20-pounder. Tiring of that, you can drive, in three hours, to the Traful and the Limay, two of the greatest land-locked salmon rivers in the world.

The choicest spot on a river is the boca, the first pool just below the lake from which the river runs. "Boca" means mouth, and in the Argentine foothills the place where the water pours out of a lake to form a river is called a boca—Boca Lolog, Boca Chimehuin, and so on. Big fish? The word "lunker" must have been coined by a fellow fresh from a boca.

"This is the Boca Lolog," said Jorge that first day. "The water is so clear that you'll be glad the wind is putting a riffle on it."

Riffle? Three-foot-high waves were rolling in and the wind was blowing the tops off them!

"There are some fish in the bocas all summer—that is, in January, February, and March," Jorge continued. "But I'll take March as the best month for the biggest fish. That's when they're getting ready to drop downstream to spawn."

That sounded strange. I'm accustomed to fish that run upstream to spawn. But there are few large feeder streams above Argentine lakes into which a trout can run, so they go down into the broader rivers. Still it seemed strange that they should reverse the usual direction of run, since these trout are descendents of fish brought from other parts of the world and planted in Neuquen Territory lakes in 1903. Lake trout and whitefish were also planted, but have disappeared. The landlocked salmon, browns, and rainbows thrived.

When the browns and rainbows first leave the lakes for the bocas, they are a bright silver, like fresh-run Atlantic salmon. They are firm and sleek and pack the wallop of a Firpo. That's because they dine well on two-inch-wide greenish crabs that look like heavy, clawed editions of our crawfish. The lakes and rivers are loaded with them. The fish also take natural flies, nymphs, and minnows about 1½ inches long, called puyen.

"Let's go," said Bebe. "You start right here, Joe."

I stepped into the water. It was cold. I moved out, and a big wave slopped water all over my right side. I eased my way to within casting range of the channel, got a good firm grip on the gravel bottom with my felt-soled waders and looked the situation over. This could be the home of big trout all right. Water was sliding out of Lake Lolog through a 250-foot-wide exit to form the Quilquihui River.

I got line out and shot the big 4-inch red-and-yellow streamer fly out for sixty-five feet. I started it back in foot-long jerks—just two of them. There was a terrific swirl under the streamer. Startled, I struck prematurely. The high-riding fly left the water and shot my way. I stripped in line and waited, giving that trout time to get back to his feeding station. When I cast again, he let the fly come halfway back, then hit it so hard that he almost jerked the 9-foot fly rod from my hand. He headed downriver for four hundred feet, then came out in a startling end-over-end jump. He was pure silver, a big rainbow.

He jumped again, as high as a kite, swapped ends, sizzled off on another 150-foot run, greyhounded, came back my way, changed his mind, went downstream, came out in a straight-up try for the sky and threw the hook.

I'd never before been tied to a rainbow that big. He must have been nine pounds. I was numb all over, and it took me a long time to reel in the line.

Ten minutes later I saw another fish slashing at my fly. I kept up the slow, steady retrieve. He socked it and ran up past me, headed for the lake. Then he jumped clear, and as certainly as the other had been the biggest rainbow I'd ever had on, this was the biggest brownie. He looked to be ten pounds.

He lit and kept on for the lake, but after a hundred feet I turned him. This time he ran downstream, and kept going until he was a couple of hundred feet below. Then he came halfway out, sank back in and kept boring off, taking line slowly from the reel.

I couldn't hold him, so I started walking after him, keeping the line tight but not able to gain any back. I eased into the shallower water, reeling fast, ran down his way for a hundred feet, stopped and reeled some more. Then I lay back on the rod. He was a hard-mouthed, big-jawed bull of a brownie, but I finally turned him and headed him my way. At least I saw the leader come out. I kept skidding him shoreward until he was out of the water and lay still. Reaching down, I put a handful of fingers into his gills, carried him ashore and weighed him. He went 9¼ pounds.

As is usual when fishing is good in the Andes foothills, clouds were low. A misty rain had started driving at my back; my right side, where the water had splashed me, was like ice. I tightened up my collar and turned back to the business at hand. A few casts later I saw a big brown shape in back of my fly. He hit like a triphammer, stuck his snout out and began shaking it until I thought the rod would come apart. But I dropped the tip fast and he drifted downstream, then got a finhold and tore off as though someone were jabbing him with a pitchfork.

He ran for 130 feet, stopped and shook his massive head again. I went after him. He ran some more. So did I. He gained on me, and I got stuck. There was a deep hole in front of me, and I had to walk fifty feet toward shore to get around it. Luckily he'd found another hole further down and was resting in it. I went on down, reeling fast, and got opposite him. I got him moving again, going downstream slowly; so I knew he was tired. I tightened the drag. He was too big to play with, too big for gentle handling. You can't baby a bosco like that one. You have to play him boldly, or he'll get off. I put a bend in the rod, and the pressure finally got him. When I skidded him up on the gravel beach, I wished I hadn't kept that little 9¼-pounder. This one weighed 10¼.

I sat down and mopped my feverish brow. In a distance of little more than a hundred feet and in less than an hour and a half, I had landed the two best trout I'd ever caught. No one back home was going to believe me. And in the next half hour I took two more nice rainbows, a 5-pounder and a 7½-pounder.

You only have to see a few fish like that and hear about a few more to get boca fever forever. Last year a spoon fisherman on the Chimehuin Boca came up with a 21-pound brown. In the Boca Lolog another spoon angler took a hook-jawed brownie that weighed 26½ pounds. A couple of years ago, still another spoon fancier, on one day, took a 20-pound brown trout, two of 15½ pounds, two rainbows and two browns of 13 pounds, three rainbows and two browns each running 11 pounds, and one 6½-pound rainbow. Fishing like that doesn't happen every day, or even every year! But those big ones are there, and this fact makes any angler's temperature jump.

It's said that the Limay Boca, head of the great Limay River, has the biggest rainbows in all Argentina. Thirty- and 35-pound rainbows have been caught by trollers in Lago Nahuel Huapi, the lake that feeds the Limay, and those big fish sometimes move into the boca. This is one of the few bocas where skiffs are used, and from them you can see the fish through the crystal-clear water, great hulks that every now and then rise up and shine as they bust for the heavens.

In all the Argentine bocas I fished, big flies proved much better than smaller ones. The big fish scorned small stuff. After the first day on Boca Lolog we seldom used anything smaller than a 4-inch-long fly tied on at least a number 2 hook. We even used larger streamers, some with wings five inches long and tied on a 1/0 hook. The bigger the fly, the bigger the fish seemed to be. They wanted bulk. And while occasionally a big fish is taken on a small fly, browns and rainbows of 9 pounds and up seldom hit a fly smaller than four inches. Best colors are red-and-yellow, blue-and-white, brown-and-white, red-and-white, all yellow and all white.

The next day, on the Boca Chimehuin, Bebe took a 10-pound rainbow; Jorge, an 8½-pound brown and a 7-pound rainbow. Andrew took a 6-pounder of each. I landed a 7-pound brown and a pair of beautiful rainbows that went 7 and 8½ pounds.

In the gin-clear water of Andean streams, fish do not hit during the bright part of the day, from one until six o'clock; so most anglers fish in the morning, come in for dinner in the middle of the day, have a siesta, rise at four for tea (another full-fledged meal), then wend their way streamward for the evening fishing. Anglers often stay out until eleven; so the evening meal may be served at midnight.

The Boca Lolog was wonderful, but the Chimehuin became my favorite. This pool was eighty feet across and two hundred feet long. Waves bounced into it from the lake, but on the five-foot-deep channel there was only a riffle. The wind that roars into that boca, like a blast from the polar regions, all but blows you over.

"When it's from the north," Jorge told me, "it's wrong. Then it's blowing up river and into the lake. You never catch fish on that wind."

"But we only get north winds about three or four times a season," said Andrew. "Most of the time it's a west wind, and that's the best wind for the bocas. It's west today."

It was west, right enough, and cold, pushing up three-foot waves that doused us. Over the lake, huge billowing black clouds reached up high. Below them other clouds blotted out the mountains. We could see water pouring out of them.

"We're going to get it good," I remarked.

"Not necessarily," said Andrew. "Those storms seem to hang over the lake. Most of the time they never reach the river."

He was right. We felt the dampness of the storm, but it stayed up on the lake. Where I was fishing, the wind was coming at an angle, and I really had to put the rod to it to make any kind of throw. But with the 9-foot glass rod and GAF line I managed to put the streamer out about 50 feet, to a spot where the water poured past a rock. As I started it coming, a wave hit me and almost knocked me flat. I kept the fly coming, picked it up and cast again. For twenty minutes I fished without moving from that spot, and I didn't have a hit or a follow that I could see. Yet I had a hunch there was a big fish near that rock. I showed it everything I had. No luck. Then I looked deep in my tackle bag and came up with a 5-inch fly-rod popper, a devil to throw in the wind, but just the right medicine for a big trout. I tied it on, wound up and put it out there. I started it back slowly and then saw a great shape in back of it, a long brown form that appeared from nowhere and put its nose on that moving bug and followed after it. I stripped again, slowly, so as not to make it pop and maybe scare that thing away. I stripped again—the shadow followed.

Sweat burst out on my brow and suddenly I was cold all over. Should I stop stripping, increase the speed or pop the bug? I decided to stick to the retrieve that had got him interested. I kept stripping and hoping. Then that fish came down on the popper with a thump that jolted me so hard that my feet slipped from under me and I fell sideways into the fast current. I was loaded with clothing; if I ever got caught in there, I'd never get out again. So I made an all-out effort and scrambled back to my feet.

Then I became conscious of a singing reel and realized that I was sill clutching the rod in my right hand. The fly line was all gone and the backing was leaping from the whirling reel. Below me the bottom shelved up; so I scrambled down, got into ankle-deep water, and chased that fish. He went out of the tail of the pool into water that dropped off to 15-foot depth, and kept right on. Traveling like a bat riding a gale, he went through the second pool for 150 feet, then came into the air. Even at that distance, he looked like a horse!

He kept boring away, taking line again. I had to go down the shoreline after him. But I kept reeling and put the pressure on. It took twenty minutes more to get him in close, and then he half-rolled in the shallows and I thought I'd lose him after all. But I held the line tight and somehow managed to keep the leader clear of sharp rocks. I skidded him into inch-deep water, reached down and grabbed him through the gills.

Until then I hadn't known there was anyone else around. But a crowd had gathered. Jorge, Bebe, and Andrew were there, and Don Jose Julian, proprietor of the hosteria, came hurrying up with scales.

"Fifteen pounds," he announced.

I was shaking so hard that my teeth were rattling.

"What's the matter?" asked Jorge. "Are you cold?"

"Boca fever," Bebe laughed. "He's got boca fever."

I knew it was true and that I'd never again be really content until I got back to fish these fabulous bocas again.

But the time had come to go, and after dinner that night I went to pay my tab. I found Don Jose apologetic.

"There has been a slight rise in price," he said. "When you first arrived the charge was $1.40 a day for everything. But then it went up to $1.50. However," he added, "after the rise in price, all wine was free."

It happens that I do not drink wine. But I still contend that ten cents a day was a small premium to pay for Utopia.

Argentina

Big trout are the dream of every angler, and big trout where anglers can get to them are like gold in the national vault. That's the way I see the trout of Argentina. I believe that within a few years that country is going to discover that an investment made about 60 years ago in some brood fish from the United States is going to pay good solid dividends. From a standing start, in rivers which were the natural habitat of only one species, a rather negligible perch-type fish (the brood stock imported from the U.S.A.) have reproduced and flourished to the point that today Argentina can claim to have more big fish of the species salmo and char than any comparable area in the world. In Argentina there are thousands of miles of rivers and hundreds of lakes crowded with tremendous brown trout, huge rainbows, great leaping landlocked salmon and strong, brilliantly colored eastern brook trout. In the course of a single day on many of the big rivers the angler may expect a dozen 3 pounders, two or three 7 to 9 pounders, maybe a 12 pounder and maybe one that goes 20 pounds. When he hits the brook trout waters he can be sure of plenty of 2 to 8 pound fish, and weights as high as 14 pounds have been reported.

Where is all this fishing? Throw a noose around the eastern slope of the Andes, in a long, narrow loop down through Patagonia in southern Argentina, and to the Argentina side of the island of Tierra del Fuego, and you have it. That makes thousands of miles of hard-to-believe fishing in hundreds of lakes and rivers.

Granted it's 5000 miles from the United States, which is obviously the market for this kind of fishing. But what is 5000 miles in the day of the jet? The distance from the United States to these lakes and streams may be long, but once there, you find these Argentine waters are at a comfortable altitude of only 2500 to 3500 feet. Practically all of them are adjacent to good roads, are easy to wade and at worst can readily be fished from the banks because there is so little underbrush. Even the lakes, which are the source waters of the rivers, seldom lie at more than 4000 feet and these, too, can usually be fished from the shore.

Many years ago Prince Charles Radziwill, formerly of Poland, took his wife and several friends for a picnic on the shores of Lake Huechulaufquen. While the ladies in the party were busy brewing a pot of "mate," the national drink comparable to coffee in the United States, Charles made a few casts with his spinning rod. Standing in one spot, in less than half an hour, he landed an 11 pound and a 12 pound brown trout.

In that same lake 35 pounders have been taken by trollers from the boats available along its 27 mile length. And further evidence of the spotted monsters that dwell therein are the fish which move down into the "Boca," as Argentines call the first pool below the lake, each season from December to April. As if to add to angling convenience, these fish have reversed the direction of their spawning migration—this is one of the few places in the world where the trout move downstream to spawn.

At this time fly rodders take many fish from 15 to 24 pounds, and spinners have come up with browns as heavy as 26 pounds. One of the outstanding catches in a river "boca" was a series of fish taken in a day and a half by Willie Best, a rancher from Bolivar, Argentina. On that phenomenal visit to the Chimehuin Boca he took a 22 pound brown, two 15 pounders, four 12 pounders, four 10 pounders and one 6 pounder.

These were not just lucky windfalls. In 1955 I used a fly to take an 18½ pounder, a 15½ pounder, a 15 pounder and a dozen fish between 10 and 12 pounds. In 1956 the fish were smaller. My best was 14½ pounds, followed by a 14 pounder and a dozen between 10 and 12 pounds. Bebe Anchorena took a 13½ pounder, a 13 pounder and many in the 8 to 10 pound bracket. All around us, fishing the same rivers and lakes, other fishermen were bringing in big beauties. Hardly a day passed without a trout of better than 12 pounds being brought in to the Hosteria. Four and 5 pound fish were throw-backs.

Even the kids were getting in on such fishing. One evening at the Boca, just at dark, I heard a cry for help from the Corner Pool. I rushed over and there stood Carolina Anchorena, Bebe's 13-year-old daughter, right at the edge of the stream, her casting rod bent double.

"I have one on," she said. "But I can't land him. The bank is too steep."

"Pull him in close," I said. "I'll get him for you."

I scrambled down over the bank to the water while Carolina pulled the fish in. I almost fainted when I saw its size. I had been expecting a 2 or 3 pounder. This fish gave a mighty swipe of his tail and threw water all over me. But Carolina hung on, yanked back and pulled him in so that his head rested on the rocks. I hastily shoved my fingers into his gills, got a good grip and lifted him up. I thought his whole length would never leave the water.

I struggled up the bank with him.

"Good one, eh?" said Carolina.

"Good is right!" said her father five minutes later as he hefted that fish on the scale. It was 13 pounds even.

Bebe himself has caught a lot of tremendous trout at the boca, big browns in the hallowed 15 to 20 pound class. In February of 1962 he topped his list with a beauty that will take a lot of beating. One evening he was fishing downstream, fishing seriously, concentrating on putting his fly in the right spots. At the pool below the bridge he shot one out almost to the other side, a very long line. He started the fly back. Something came up, slowly, like a whale, and took on top. Bebe struck. The fish sank down as slowly as it had risen on the take. It sulked.

Bebe put harder pressure on and that started him. He came to the top, tried to jump, but instead thrashed on top, throwing so much water that Bebe couldn't see him.

"He was big," Bebe told me. "Really big. I thought he would go 14 or 15 pounds."

The fish went rushing downstream, turned and gave a gigantic lunge forward, went down again and didn't move. But Bebe was in trouble. That lunge had made the reel overspin and the line was tangled badly. He started walking downstream, untangling the line as he went, too busy to watch where he was going. He fell to his knees once, got up and kept going, still untangling line. At last he got it all free, reeled it onto the spool and pulled it tight to the fish.

It was like pulling on a dead weight. Nothing moved.

"I thought I had lost him or that he had the line around a stone," Bebe told me. "My stomach hurt and so did my knees where I had fallen down. I went down the bank below and tried to pull him backwards. Nothing moved. I tried pulling back on the line and then giving slack. I worked on him for 10 minutes. At last I was sure he was off and was about ready to really pull, to get the line back. Then he moved . . . just a short spurt and then stopped again."

But it was the beginning. Bebe started to pump him and he came, little by little. When he got near the surface he shot downstream on another long run and stopped near some tree stumps.

"My ears were buzzing by then," said Bebe. "And it was getting darker and darker. But I kept on working at him."

By the time Bebe had the fish coming the moon was up, giving him better light. The fish rolled on top and he saw its white belly.

"I knew I had a chance then," he said. "I eased him closer and closer, and there he was. I gaffed him."

As he lifted the gaff that monster fish gave a flap, jumped off the gaff, pulling Bebe forward and almost into the river.

But the fish was all in. It just lay there and Bebe gaffed it again.

Bebe's two daughters, who had been watching from the other side of the river, shouted to him, asking how big the trout was.

"Fifteen pounds," he answered. Then, taking a better look. "He's bigger than that. Maybe 20 pounds."

The girls laughed. They didn't believe him.

Bebe took out his spring scales which will weigh up to 20 pounds. He put the fish on them. The scale went down, bang, and hit the bottom.

"He's over 20," Bebe shouted to the girls.

That fish went 24 pounds even, the largest brown trout known to have been taken on a fly anywhere in the world.

Not all Argentine streams produce such heavyweights. In the Collon Cura, a great, long and wide river, the fish are small as Argentine standards go, probably because there are too many fish for the food supply in the river. But what trout fisherman will complain when he takes a 3 pound rainbow on every fourth cast? There are so many rainbows in that river that it is easy to take a hundred a day on flies.

The Quilquehue, near Junin de los Andes, is a small stream, again as Argentine standards go, and it's as clear as crystal. It's a dry fly man's dream, running through country that is very beautiful, similar in many ways to parts of Montana and Wyoming, and it holds some wonderful rainbows and browns. In the Boca of the Quilquehue, called the Boca Lolog after the lake out of which the river flows, I had just about the best and fastest "big fish fishing" I have ever found.

That time we hit the Boca Lolog on a windy, rainy, and very dark day. I started at the head of the Boca pool, wading out into the lake almost to the top of my waders. I began casting a big streamer across current where the lake water poured out and formed the river.

I had a hit before I had made two strips of the retrieve. A 10 pound rainbow jumped out and then dashed off downstream a mile a minute, then cleared the water again and threw the hook. I reeled in, too stunned to think. Automatically I started casting again and immediately had another hit. It was a heavy fish that made a couple of lunges with his long body and pulled my big 9 foot rod this way and that until I thought the tip section would come off. Then the fish got his bearings and ran up into the lake for 100 feet, reversed and ran down past me for another 100 feet. He was on his way and I didn't think he was going to stop, but the line came up, and out through the surface roared the biggest brownie I had ever seen until that time. Then he went on downstream some more, moving slowly, but still going. I followed after him. He jumped again. I fought back. I was now 200 feet below where I had hooked him. After a half hour fight I finally beached that beautiful brownie. He weighed 10¼ pounds.

In quick succession, then, I caught a 5 pound rainbow, a 7 pound rainbow, a 12 pound brown, a 10½ pound brown, and a 9 pound brown. And all these fish were hooked in a 200-foot stretch of pool. It was hard to believe.

Of course, even in such rivers there are off times, and the bright of the day is the off time at the Boca Lolog. I went back there daily for the next three days and didn't raise a fish. Then on the fourth day the weather blacked over again and once more those big fish were on the rampage and it was like Old Home Week. The biggest that day was 13 pounds.

The reason for this wonderful "bad weather, good fishing" is obvious to any trout or salmon fisherman as soon as he sees a couple of these Andean rivers. The water is so clear that every pebble stands out on the bottom like a boulder. What smart trout is going to hit in such water during the bright of the day, when the sun shines smack on the pools? He can see up just as well as the angler can see down and nothing will fool him then. Those trout can be taken in the morning and up to about 1 o'clock, but then the fisherman must bide his time until about five before he will get any further action, and the best fishing is from six o'clock on. However, the angler need not grieve for a few lost hours at mid-day because during the Argentine summer months of January, February, and March it doesn't get dark until 10:30, so that between the long hours of daylight and a few stormy days thrown in, at which time the fish will hit regardless of it being mid-day, he will get all the fishing he can stand.

While most of the fishing is in rivers which are below the lakes, there are some, like the Paimun, which run out of the hills above and feed the lakes. The Paimun River empties into Paimun Lake, which is a sort of arm of vast Lake Huechulaufquen. It comes rolicking down through a stand of beautiful beech trees, a particularly lovely stream. The pools peter out rapidly up river so that there are only about four good ones for fishermen to work. Above that the stream becomes narrow and winds its way through boulders and among dense clumps of bushes. My friend Bebe Anchorena says that an Indian told him that "Paimun" means "Here they come," and when they named that river I'm sure the Indians meant "Here come the rainbows."

On my trip to the Paimun I started to fish at the first pool above the lake. I dropped a size 8 gray Wulff in the white water where it rolled into the pool, and watched the fly come buoyantly back, riding the waves, then settle into a slow float, wings cocked, saying "Come on!" in Spanish to the trout.

Immediately I saw a fish rise. He sucked the fly in and I struck. He bounced right out, fell back in, then came out again. He was big!

And he was just about the jumpin'est rainbow I'll ever tangle with and he could fight close in, too. But first he wanted to see what the lake looked like. He ran down through the pool and jumped just offshore, immediately in front of Lou Klewer, Outdoor Editor of the *Toledo Blade*, who made the trip to Argentina with me.

Lou had just stepped out upon the bank and what he thought when he saw that silver slab with the red streak down its side, I never did find out because he disappeared into the underbrush as if scared by some prehistoric monster.

That fish kept me busy for a long time, but at last I skidded him up on a sandy spit and weighed him: 12 pounds 5 ounces. A nice rainbow on a dry fly. And I took two more from that pool, both around 10 pounds.

When I moved up to the next pool I found out what had happened to Lou. He was sitting on a rock, camera poised.

"Take one there," he said, pointing to a spot in the current out in front of him. "I have my movie camera focused on that spot."

"You're not asking for much, are you?" I said.

"There are a dozen big rainbows in there," he said. "I can see them."

I cast my fly where he had pointed. When it floated over those fish one of them took it and the fireworks were on. They were of short duration because this was another 10 pounder and on his first jump he threw the hook. But Lou was satisfied. He got the jump.

We were probably the only party to make the trek in there to fish that year because to reach the Paimun it was necessary to take a boat and go up Lake Huechulaufquen, and since there was no place to stay overnight the trip had to be completed in a single day. Even so it's not nearly as tough a trip as many an angler makes in North America to catch trout a fifth the size.

Just because the fish are so numerous doesn't necessarily mean that the fishing is always easy. There is usually a pretty fair wind blowing and tackle must be suited to the wind as well as to the size of the fish. While an 8½ foot rod is right for some of the smaller streams, something larger is necessary on the larger waters. Most fly fishermen use a 9 foot rod weighing 6 ounces, a GAF (WF9F) line, a reel capable of holding 200 yards of 18 pound test backing as well as the fly line, and a tapered nylon leader. For better casting in the wind the butt section of the leader should be heavy, the leader tapering from a 30 pound test butt section, through 25, 20, 15, 12, 10 and 8 to a 6 pound test tippet. Butt and tippet sections should be longer than the others, the tippet especially, in order to provide better fly action as well as for invisibility.

All kinds of flies are used. Many of the Argentinians use Atlantic salmon flies and do very well with them. And almost any of the standard wet flies produce well. Hook sizes range from number 6 to number 14, seldom smaller. But it is the big streamers and bucktails, with 5-inch-long wings and tied on a 1/0 hook that get the big fish, bearing out the theory long propounded by experienced trout fishermen that big trout, and especially big browns, like a big mouthful and that it takes a big fly to interest them.

The multiwing streamers are terrific, streamers tied with red hackle and white wings and white chenille body, or red hackle, yellow wings and body, and also the yellow barred rock winged multiwing streamer. These flies have four feathers tied on either side of the hook so that when the fly is pulled forward they fold in on the shank of the hook, and when it is stopped they flare outwards thus giving a lifelike action to the fly, a real come-on for big trout.

Another successful fly is the Platinum Blonde. This one has a silver tinsel body and sports two 4-inch-long white bucktail wings, one tied immediately in back of the eye of the hook and the other tied just before the bend of the hook. That tie gives both length and fullness to the fly and when it is stripped in with foot-long pulls, the wings work with an up-and-down motion. The Honey Blonde, equally as good as the platinum, is tied the same way but with the wings of yellow bucktail. Both of these flies took some of our biggest fish.

Dry flies that bring plenty of action in Argentine waters are the Royal, Black and Gray Wulff, Brown Bivisible, Black Bivisible, Gray Hackle with yellow body, Black Gnat, Light Cahill and Red Variant, all tied on hook sizes from 6 to 14.

Spinners use medium spinning rods and spin reels large enough to carry 200 yards of 6 pound test monofilament. While some plugs are used, the majority of spinners cast big spoons, preferably with copper or gold finish. Some of these spoons are 6 inches long and with those big, flashy lures anglers have taken 20, 21, 25, and 26 pounders each year.

Most spinners use 6 pound test monofilament line, although more cautious anglers do go a bit heavier, to the 8 pound test, feeling that they are a lot safer when they tie into one of those big lunkers.

Even though spin lures work deeper in the water than do flies, nevertheless it still holds true that the late afternoon and evening fishing is away ahead of the bright of the day for this method as well as fly fishing.

As if such wonderful brown and rainbow trout fishing were not enough, another import from North America, the landlocked salmon, stocked in 1903 from Lake Sebago in Maine, has run wild in a number of Argentine waters. Today this species, one of the rarest and most ardently sought by anglers, is a sure-fire hitter in half a dozen Andean streams, notably those in the great Lanin and Nahuel Huapi and Futalaufquen Parks.

The Limay, which flows out of Lake Nahuel Huapi, is a big river and holds correspondingly large salmon. The Traful, flowing into the Limay at Confluencia, is probably the best all-around land-locked salmon river in the world. Catches of 10 or 12 fish a day, weighing from 6 to 12 pounds, are not unusual.

Clinging to the tastes of their ancestors, these landlocks go for the Atlantic salmon flies. The Honey, the Jock Scott, Blue Charm, Silver Tip, Thunder and Lightning, Black Doctor, Silver Doctor, Silver Gray and Mar Lodge are all good producers. Some of the more unorthodox flies take them too—one day I saw Bebe drive the fish wild with a big platinum blonde, a white bucktail. He took half a dozen fish on it that day, topping them with a 12½ pounder.

In the Traful I found that the average weight of the fish taken was close to 6 pounds. I heard of four fish, each weighing better than 23 pounds, which had been landed during the previous eight years. Any one of them would have broken the world record for landlocked salmon if they had been submitted for recognition.

In March, 1963, I made a return journey to the Traful. We fished on the Estancia La Primavera. Our host, Felipe Lariviere, was not too optimistic when he welcomed us.

"You have come at a bad time," he said. "The waters are very low and hardly a salmon is in the river."

Just the same, Bebe and I threw on our fishing clothes, snatched our gear and rushed to the river. I took the Leonoro Pool, Bebe the Pool of Plenty, just below.

I tied on a skating spider, a two-inch-long Adams hackled dry fly, and chucked it across current. I watched it light on the still surface, then stuck my rod tip high up and with short jerks of the tip made that fly get up on its tiptoes and shake and quiver and skate in foot-long glides along the top. It looked like a thing alive, a sure bet to make any nearby fish drool.

Three casts later a landlocked salmon did spot it, rushed, and came halfway out as he took. I was into him and he busted right on out, a long, silvery fish that had taken a finishing course in advanced acrobatics. He was in and out of the water. He turned his body this way and that, and upside down. He stood on his nose, then on his tail, did half-gainers, and wound up with some fancy body flipping that threatened to pop his scales. Then he went under, zipped down the pool, sulked; then flashed back upstream, twisting his body as he went, like a trout nymphing. He began to tire. At last I got him in and tailed him. He was 8 pounds, a nice weight for my first landlocked salmon on a skater fly.

The wind came up then, so I changed to the honey, an Atlantic salmon fly first tied by the late George Phillips, which had proven very good on our first trip to the Traful. It was no different now. They greeted it like a long lost friend. All the time, in his pool Bebe was having the same wonderful fishing, and he proved again the fatal powers of the Platinum Blonde when he took a fine 10 pound fish on it.

We had three days of that kind of fishing, taking about 10 fish a day each, with an average weight of 7½ pounds, and the top fish 12 pounds.

The eastern brook trout has done equally as well as the other imports to Argentina, and can be found in many lakes and rivers. The average is a good 3 pounds, and 8 and 9 pounders are not unusual, while in a few lakes in Patagonia they run as high as 14 pounds, and perhaps better—for many of these lakes have scarcely ever been fished.

Patagonia is that part of Argentina extending from Neuquen Territory south to the Magellan Straits, and lying between the Atlantic Ocean and the slopes of the Andes. It takes its name from the original inhabitants of the area, the Patagona, reputed to be the largest people the world has ever known, and according to stories, reaching 9 feet in height.

Here, where the continent narrows down, there are many great lakes in the Andes, pouring their waters to the Atlantic through mighty rivers. Towns are few and far between and those which do exist are tiny native villages with few conveniences. The main exceptions are the fair-sized town of Esquel in the north of Patagonia, and Rio Gallegos, in the south. In both these towns there are hotels and supplies are available, and there are good guides to be found at Esquel. The usual jumping off place for a trip in Patagonia is San Carlos de Bariloche. This is a popular resort town and has plentiful hotels of all kinds, stores, lake fishing in Lago Nahuel Huapi on which the town is located, and is on the railway line from Buenos Aires.

On my first trip to Patagonia, in 1957, we were able to obtain a car and driver at Bariloche for $12.00 per day. It was a 1947 English Ford, a bit on the rattley side. However, since that time the situation has improved with the manufacture in Argentina of Kaiser jeeps and station wagons, which are ideal for fishermen, and which can be arranged through guides at Bariloche.

The initial part of our drive when we left Bariloche on that first trip was through mountainous country, often on very narrow, steep, and winding roads. We were glad of the small size of the car, which even so sometimes seemed to overhang the cliffs along which we skirted some of the lakes. Eventually we came down out of the mountains and steamed onto the Pampas, a great, level plain with many cacti and clumps of sage-like brush. We left behind us a small hamlet at the foot of the mountains and were off onto the Pampas, the wilds of Patagonia, with nothing to be seen for miles in any direction. We had gone about 35 miles when suddenly the car plunged off the road into the gravelly pampas and jolted to a stop.

"The steering gear has broken," said Hugo, the driver.

While thanking our good luck that this had not happened on one of the mountain passes, we still realized the difficulties of the situation. The nearest town was 35 miles behind us and, as Jorge Donovan and Charles Radziwill, our travelling companions, pointed out, this was a road where there might not be another car for days. Nevertheless, there was nothing to do but wait. We had a little food in the car, and some water. We had just settled down in gloom when far away to the south we saw a long line of dust.

"A car!" yelled Jorge. "A car!"

In a few minutes a truck drew up beside us, one man driving, another standing in the back, rifle in hand.

"We are hunting puma," the rifleman explained to Jorge. "Sometimes you see them from the road."

Jorge broke into a torrent of Spanish, the men nodded and pointed back the way we had come. Suddenly Charles, who is an engineer, and Hugo, scrambled under our car. In short order they had the steering gear apart, and carrying the broken rod they climbed into the truck and away they went, headed for the town we had passed 35 miles back.

Within four hours they returned.

"Would you believe our luck?" said Charles. "There was an electric welder in that town! He repaired the rod in no time."

He and Hugo installed the rod and after only a six hour delay we were on our way again. We stayed that night at the town of Esquel, and next day made it about 200 miles farther south to Senguerr, where we planned to fish the Senguerr River and Lago Fontana, out of which the river flows.

We started our fishing right where the river poured out of the lake. It was about 100 feet across, with rock formations running crosswise and forming deep pools. Jorge was the first to cast and the first to hang a fish, a spunky fighter that made his rod bounce. When he landed it we figured it for a good 4 pounds, a brilliantly colored, fat, and healthy looking eastern brook trout that thrived in these waters so far from his natural home.

Meantime, Charles had walked downstream 100 yards and suddenly he shouted. We looked down to see him fighting a fish, a heavy one from the look of it. By the time I got down there he had it ashore, another beautiful brookie, a pound better than George's catch. And that's the way it went all day, brookies one after the other, from 2 to 5 pounds, almost as fast as we could land them and get the fly in the water again.

The drop-off from the shore in the lake was about 30 feet out and it was here that the fish would hit. Apparently they were patrolling the line of the drop-off. If we put a fly to them there, they would take. In the clear water we could often see the fish swimming and once I saw a whole school go by, as thick as minnows. I cast. I saw a fish go for it—and struck too soon. The fly jumped back my way a good 8 feet. Another fish zipped out of that school and grabbed it and I was in another fight.

"Up at the other end of the lake they come bigger," Jorge told us as we ate our dinner round a campfire that night.

But we didn't have time to go and prove or disprove his words. That's one thing about fishing—there's always an excuse to go back another time.

On my next visit to Patagonia, however, I didn't even get to Lago Fontana. It was in March, 1963, and I fished Lago General Paz, which lies on the Argentina-Chile border, 150 miles farther north. The lake is reputed to hold tremendous eastern brook trout, and a fishing team, composed of Curt Gowdy, TV and radio sportscaster, and I, made the trip down there to fish against an Argentine team for the cameras of Wide World of Sports. The Argentine team was made up of a well known guide and landscape artist, Erick Gornik of Futalaufquen, and fine angler Tito Hosman of Buenos Aires. They had fished down there before and had taken such good fish that they were hopeful that during the contest we could break the 14½ pound world record for brook trout, established by Dr. W.A. Cook, in the Nipigon River, in Ontario, Canada.

We were quite a crew, riding down through Patagonia in two jeeps and two trucks, loaded with fishing tackle and camera equipment. There were Mort Neff, the producer, cameraman Bob Wood, sound man Lenny Lencina, and Roone Arledge, Executive Producer of Wide World of Sports, all for ABC. Erick Gornik served as guide and his wife did the cooking. His young son Raul and an agricultural student on vacation named Helmut were on hand to keep the boats and motors in order. And Panagra Pilot Captain Don MacArthur, who had made a lot of the transportation arrangements, came along to see that everything went smoothly. We stayed at Esquel the first night out of Bariloche, and reached the eastern end of Lago General Paz in time to make camp there the second night.

The rules of our fishing contest were set up so that each angler received a point for each pound of fish taken. A bonus of five points was given each day to the team which came up with the heaviest single trout. Those fish which we released were estimated as to weight by the two anglers competing together. On the first day everyone would use spinning tackle; the second day we would all use fly, and the third day was up to the angler. He could use either or both, one for a while, then the other. At the end of the first day Argentina led, 54 points to 44. The second day they were again on top, 50 to 41. This put them 18 points ahead at the start of the final day. Then things turned. The Argentines couldn't get going, and Curt and I crept slowly up. With seven minutes to go, the contest was tied. And right then I lucked into a 6½ pounder and by the time I landed him there was just one minute left. So after three days of angling, the U.S. team won by six points: the final score was U.S.—136 points, Argentina—130 points.

In all, during those three days we took 54 fish to a total of 256 pounds, making an average weight of 4.47 pounds. Each team took 27 fish. The heaviest was an 8 pounder which I took on spinning gear. The heaviest on fly weighed 7 pounds and was taken by Curt Gowdy. To show how even the fishing was—the individual totals on our fish were: Brooks—76 pounds, 16 fish; Gornik—72 pounds, 15 fish; Hosman—58 pounds, 12 fish; Gowdy—50 pounds, 11 fish.

The fish were deep in the water and we used sinking fly lines throughout the tournament. Because we had to travel a couple of miles each day by outboard to get to the best fishing, we had to leave the fishing grounds each day just when the trout were beginning to rise. Therefore our fly fishing was not as exciting as it might have been if we had been able to be on the spot at the right moment. But the lake was dangerous at night, with many protruding rocks. A storm might blow up, and even though we all wore life preservers, if we were thrown into the lake the chances were that we would never come out, it was that cold. So caution prevailed, as it should with outdoorsmen, and we played it that way.

On our way out, we fished the Corcovado River briefly, a beautiful stream that empties out of Lago General Paz. It was crystal clear, so you could see the pebbles on the bottom in 15 feet of water. There Roone Arledge took several very nice fish on dry flies, his biggest going 4 pounds; and again, as at the lake, we felt that had we been able to fish it longer and at the right time, we could have come up with much better fish.

So we didn't come close to the world record, but we saw enough to suspect that there's a new top weight brook trout swimming around there just waiting for the man who comes at the right time, with the right offering.

During our first trip to Patagonia, we had time for a very short visit to the famous Futalaufquen Park, often called the Alps of America. We rode in a big, modern steamer up the rivers and across beautiful Lake Futalaufquen to the town of the same name and stayed there in a modern resort hotel. Then, through arrangements with the National Parks Director, we headed to some of the less known waters of the area, in search of landlocked salmon that we had heard might be found in some of the lakes of the interior.

With a Parks Commission Warden guiding us we travelled up the lake in a big skiff powered by a 1920 vintage motor, and from the lake went up a stream we knew only as "Number 1 River." With our big skiff and small motor and five people in the boat we could barely make it against the hard push of the current. Looking over the edge of the skiff I could see that the water was about waist deep, but getting shallower every moment. I kept my shoulders hunched, expecting to hear the propellor hit a boulder at any moment.

Then Williams, the guide, headed the skiff for shore. Suddenly a slight movement in the bushes showed us why. In there, a tall, handsome man sat astride a big, black horse. This was Jim Austin. Like Williams, he was a descendant of an early migration of Welsh people to Patagonia, and he was here with his horse to tow the boat up through the rapids, while we would wade behind, as the brush onshore made it impossible to walk there.

The hike through the water lasted for about half a mile, then Austin unhooked the boat from the great chain attached to his saddle and signalled us on. We piled into the skiff, Williams cranked up the little motor, and away we went again. Twice more we came to rapids where we had to bail out and push the boat, and once we went up what was virtually a waterfall. Then we were in smooth water and not far ahead we could see the opening into a lake.

Up there, Jorge, who had gone ahead on foot as we worked the boat over the last rapids, was signalling madly. Then suddenly our motor caught and started and we saw him drop his arms and stand there disconsolately.

"There were a dozen huge landlocked salmon lying here at the mouth of the river when I came up," he said. "I kept very quiet, then I realized that the sound of the motor would spook them and I tried to stop you. But I was too late. They've gone out into the lake."

We fished blind in the lake for a couple of hours, hoping to locate those salmon, but never did, and had to leave in order to get down river again before dark. That's just another place on my list of fishing I want to go back to.

Still farther south in Argentina, in the Rios Gallegos, on the tip of the continent, just north of the Straits of Magellan, there is some wonderful sea-run brown trout fishing. We stayed at the Grand Hotel, also called the Hotel Rossi after Juan Rossi, its proprietor, in the town of Gallegos, but it is also possible to stay at a farmhouse or ranch and hire a car and driver to go to the river each day. As everywhere in Argentina, when you take into consideration the rate of exchange, these services are extremely cheap.

There is a hundred miles of good fishing from the town upstream. From mid-January through March the sea-run brown trout run into the river from the South Atlantic. There are many smaller ones, but there are even more that are great hulks of fish weighing from 8 to 20 pounds. Juan Rossi, who is an ardent trout angler, rates his top catch at 18 pounds. No wonder he chooses to live in Gallegos, no matter how lonely it may be for the rest of the year. During the summer he can get to this kind of fishing in 10 minutes. Or he can drive 60 miles upstream to try new pools that hardly anyone ever fishes.

Jorge Donovan, Lou Klewer of the *Toledo Blade*, Bebe Anchorena, and I fished the Gallegos with Percy James of the Bella Vista Estancia and we had a field day for four days in a row. The top sea run was a plump 14 pounder, and to round out the excitement we caught rainbows to 8 pounds and resident browns to 10!

So much of the world has been opened up to fishermen by the airplane that we are inclined to think there are no longer any outposts to discover. But in the eastern half of remote Tierra del Fuego, lying just across the Magellan Straits from Rio Gallegos, there is outpost fishing for many generations to come. There, in the part of Tierra del Fuego that belongs to Argentina, in the Rio Grande River, seven of us took 200 trout in two hours, from one 800-foot long pool.

We stayed at the Estancia Maria Behety, owned by Carlos Menendez Behety. The 250,000 acre ranch had 150,000 sheep, and its shearing shed, the largest in the world, held 7000 animals at one time. The winters are so cold that there is a winter-kill of 15,000 sheep annually. The ranch employed 250 men, mostly from the Chilean island of Chiloe, and their living quarters were a town in themselves, with a bakery, machine shop, movie theatre, quarters for married folk and others for bachelors.

The Rio Grande, which runs for 20 miles through the Estancia, holds more trout than any river I've ever fished. There are so many they are underfed. The river needs heavy fishing to remove some of the fish so the average weight may rise, for some of the resident fish are long and thin. This river also boasts a tremendous run of sea run brown trout, big, silvery bruisers, that the Argentines call "una plateada," the silver one. They come in fresh from the sea, packing a terrific wallop, ready for anything. Why the stay-at-homes don't take the hint and run with their brothers to the sea is an unknown question; but a majority of the browns do stay in the river and fight for food and survival.

Even though they also have the opportunity to go to sea, the rainbows in the Rio Grande are stay-at-homes, too. But it doesn't hurt their fight. They turn on the works, and the works from a 10 pound rainbow is something to see.

As is the case on the mainland, trout were not native to Fuegian waters. They were planted there in 1935, 1936, and 1937 by the late John Goodall, an Englishman who had settled at Viamonte. This was the home of the Bridges family, descendants of Lucas Bridges, the first missionary to and settler of Tierra del Fuego, and the author of the historic book *Uttermost Part of the Earth*.

Goodall planted rainbows, landlocked salmon, and brown trout in many lakes and rivers, notably the Rio Grande, the Ewan, the Menendez, the Rio de Fuego, and the great Lago Fagnano. Today there are probably more trout per hundred feet of stream or lake, here in Tierra del Fuego, than any place in the world. These rivers are badly in need of fishing, to improve the size and quality of the fish.

It's a long trip to Tierra del Fuego—6451 miles from Miami—and the weather is rough and cold most of the time. But to the outdoorsman as well as the fisherman, it is an unforgettable experience to visit this strange land that is only 700 miles from the Antarctic. Here the storms blow in bitterly from the south and the sheep is the only domestic animal which can endure the climate with any equanimity. Yet wild life is everywhere in an amazing variety of forms. Geese and ducks fly in and out, or alight and feed, by the tens of thousands. Birds of many and strange species are as thick as mice in a granary. This is the home of the black throated swan and the 20 pound steamer duck which is so heavy it is flightless. Even such tropical birds as the flamingo are to be seen in flocks of more than a hundred, calmly feeding in ponds here and there.

Adding a final touch of wilderness to this bleak but beautiful countryside is the guanaco, cousin to the llama, the fleetest and most graceful of animals, that runs like the wind on feet that never seem to touch the ground.

Perhaps one reason for the continuance of all this wild life is the fact that there is almost no resident population beyond the few ranchers on the immense, almost boundless sheep ranches. At Viamonte, the Bridges family residence, there are still a few Ona Indians, the last of the original inhabits of the area, a tribe whose members were probably the greatest trackers the world has ever known. These and a handful of Yahgans, the southernmost Indians in the world, are all that remain of the two groups of peoples who originally inhabited Tierra del Fuego in the days when the only fish in the streams was the Argentine perch—and the brown trout, the rainbow, and the landlocked salmon were unknown.

New Zealand

The Maoris call New Zealand "Aotora," the Land of the Long White Cloud, because at landfall their first pioneering canoes sighted a long white cloud over the island. Trout fishermen today are inclined to call it the land of the long trout; since trout were first planted there in the early 1900's it has developed a reputation as one of the world's top trout countries.

"There's one spot that should certainly be fished by anyone who visits New Zealand," Bill Bramley of Aukland told me when I arrived there. "That's Dan's Creek at Turangi.

"It starts to get good in February and is at its best in March when the big browns move in. You have to go at night for those big fellows. You should hear them—it sounds like a dog falling in!"

That was a fine way to talk to a fellow who had three days in New Zealand, in January.

"You should fish Lake Taupo, too," he said. "The season is open now though the fishing's best in May and June. The fish are all of good size—at least they're good enough that our minimum size limit is 18 inches."

I didn't say a word, thinking how big an 18 incher would look in a lot of rivers I've fished, and here they were barely keepers.

Then Bill went on to tell me about the time his young son came home from his school in England for a holiday, and went out to Lake Taupo to try his hand. He chose the spot where the Tongariro River flows into the lake.

"He was casting left handed because he had sprained his right wrist, so you know his technique wasn't very good," said Bill.

"Well, he cast out there and right off he hooked a big fish. He was standing in the middle of a long line of anglers and the fish really tied their lines in knots. I bet there were a lot of angry fishermen there but he was just a boy and no one said a word. Besides, they could tell he had a big one."

Eventually everyone got their lines untangled, the schoolboy still had his fish, and he managed to land it. It was a brownie, 9 pounds, 12 ounces.

"Wouldn't that rock you?" said the lad. "That's my first fish."

A lot of disgruntled experts went back to their fishing. Meantime, the boy moved over to the mouth of a small run where the water was only about two feet deep and started casting there, figuring he had done enough damage where the experts were. Within an hour he had his limit of 10 fish, the smallest 2 pounds and the largest the 9 pound 12 ouncer. As he picked up this impressive load and started back for the lodge, he happened to look over his shoulder.

None of those fisherman had noticed him at the mouth of the little stream, as they cast into the bigger water at the mouth of the Tongariro. Then one of them spotted him with that string, homeward bound, and called to the others. There they stood, mouths open, watching that rank amateur head home with his limit, topped by that whopping big close-to-ten-pounder.

My own fishing in New Zealand wasn't in a class with that but I did get into some rainbow fishing that would keep most of us happy for a long time.

I stayed at the Bridge Lodge, at Turangi, a short distance above the spot where the Tongariro River pours into lake Taupo. Of some 40 streams that feed Lake Taupo, the Tongariro is by far the largest. It is, in fact, one of the most renowned fishing streams in the world. In the 16 miles from the lake up, there are 50 well-known pools. These pools or "reaches" as they are called locally, are easy to approach, either by road or trail, the roads and angling sign-posts and such facilities being maintained by the New Zealand Anglers Association and the Internal Affairs Department. Only fly fishing is permitted in the river.

That first night at the lodge I met Charles Harding-Tilley of London, England, who told me that he had been fishing in this neighbourhood for the past nine years.

"You can't beat it," he said. "I'd like to show you some of the fishing tomorrow."

After breakfast next morning we put our waders on, our rods up and walked slowly along the banks of the river, heading for the best fishing water farther downstream. At a bend in the river I saw a nice looking gravel bar and thought I'd step out onto it and make a cast. I started forward and had one foot raised to step down off the bank when Charles yelled at me.

"Stop!" he shouted. "Stop!"

My foot froze in mid-air. I thought of snakes but my searching eyes could see nothing.

"Don't step down there," Charles said. "That looks like a gravel bar but it's really a raft of floating pumice. The water is deep underneath it. You'd sink out of sight."

New Zealand is a land of volcanoes. When they explode, as Rauephu did in 1945, the violence of the explosion blows the guts out of the rocks down in that inferno, turning them into pumice, light-as-wood remains of the molten rock, and showers them over the countryside. Now, knocked loose by some heavy rainstorm upstream, this pumice had come floating down the river and piled up here, looking for all the world like a gravel bar.

165

The volcanoes send out great showers of volcanic dust, too, and sometimes after a heavy rainstorm, if you look down as you wade, you can see this dust moving along the bottom like a cloud, pushed up by the current. You'd think that eventually this condition might affect the food supply in the river, yet all the fish I caught were sleek and in fine condition.

"Start here," said Charles, finally, as we approached a good-looking pool. "I'll go back upstream a way and fish there."

I tied on a Phillips red and white multiwing streamer and shot the fly out some 65 feet. I started it back in slow, foot-long jerks, knowing the feather wings were working, breathing, closing in on the hook shank as I stripped, flaring outward as I stopped the strip.

I saw a swirl right in back of the fly, kept it coming, and then felt a hard, thudding strike. I struck back and felt a good big fish. He showed me he was big, all right, when he came out in a high up leap, his side one flash of crimson. When he fell back in he headed downstream fast, riding the current, going like the wind. He jumped again, 100 feet out, slashed across the current, jumped once more, then held, broadside. I put the rod to him, started him coming back. It took five more minutes to land him, a husky 5 pounder. I slipped him back into the water.

Then I stepped out about knee depth in the water to make my next cast. As I did so, I saw a motion out of the corner of my eye, and looked up—and jumped hastily back. A big rock was bearing down on me! Then I realized what it was, stepped forward, and when that spongy bit of pumice bumped my knee I just pushed it aside, grinning to myself at the scare it had given me. Floating rocks are a hazard a fisherman "down under" has to get used to.

After 10 minutes of casting with no results, I switched to a number 2 muddler minnow fly, had a strike and fought it out with a nice, golden 3 pound brownie. A half hour later I had a rainbow that went 4 pounds. Then, as my fly floated just under the surface I saw a big shape under it, and suddenly there was a tremendous splash. I didn't feel the fish and kept the fly coming. I was shaking good and hard. That had been a really big fish. But though I got the fly out there again, covered the place he had hit, and all the neighboring water, both upstream and down, I couldn't raise him again.

Charles came down then and we fished some 150 feet apart, working the current where the river came into the lake. Charles took two rainbows in the 3 to 5 pound class. I took another 3 pound rainbow. Then things slowed and we headed back to the lodge.

"We'll have an early lunch," said Charles. "This afternoon I want to take you to a fine little dry fly river which holds some 5, 6 and 7 pound rainbows."

"Let's not wait for lunch!" I said.

"We'd better have them put up some sandwiches for us, too," Charles said. "We may stay there late tonight."

The Tokaanu River flows through land belonging to a Maori farmer, who had given us permission to fish. It's a slow moving, crystal clear meadow stream, lined with bushes, but with open spaces here and there where you could make a cast from the bank. At least that was what I thought as we meandered along its crooked course.

"You start here," said Charles. "Work on upstream and keep going till I come for you. I'll go down a good three-quarters of a mile before I start. That way we'll both have untouched water to fish."

I walked quietly in to the bank of the river. Fish were rising, making large concentric circles that raised goose bumps along my spine. Carefully I got ready and carefully made a backcast. Three great boils burst, out there. The three fish that made them rushed up the pool pushing a wave in front of them. It told me the story. Those fish had eyes like a kiwi. There would be no casting from the bank on this stream!

I walked back from the pool and staying well back, went on up to the tail of the next pool. There I eased into the stream and edged my way into casting position, to work the tail of the pool first. It was thin water and spooky fishing. Line slap would put down those scary New Zealand rainbows.

I was using an 8 foot fly rod, an HDH floating line, and a 15 foot long leader tapered to 4X tippet. A size 14 Blue Dun looked good to me and I hoped these trout would feel the same way. I made a cast.

It dropped about 10 feet up in the pool, with nice S curves to insure a good float. The fly was sitting up prettily but it floated on through without a strike.

Then I saw a fish rise about 20 feet off to the right of where I had dropped that fly, and so close to the bank that he moved the overhanging grasses as he came up and took a natural. I cast to him, landing the fly quietly about 4 feet above him, close in to the bank. Once it hung up for a second on a bit of grass and I quietly pulled back on the rod tip, freed it, and watched it slip along, still free of drag, nudging the bank, hesitating, then going on. It went over that trout and he came up and took. When I tightened, out he came, a fine rainbow, at least 9 pounds. He fell back in with a splash, rushed upstream and around the slight bend into the pool, forcing me to go after him. I managed to hold on and keep a tight line and when he jumped again I dropped the rod tip fast. He lit running this time and dashed down and out of the pool, tossing water all over the place as he skidded through the shallows on the way down. He stopped at the head of the next pool and I went his way, walking fast, reeling fast, anxious to get below him. I made it, pulled back and turned him, and now his sprints were not so fast and so far.

I finally got him coming and pulled him over the maw of the landing net. I thought of keeping this one, he was such a beautiful fish, but he was better off swimming in this great river so I carefully took the fly out of his mouth and released him. I still think he was 9 pounds, maybe 10.

From then until Charles came to get me, I took fish in each pool where I could approach quietly and get off a decent cast. It was the kind of fishing I'd dreamed about having in New Zealand, only I hadn't really imagined it would be with dry fly.

Charles, too, had sensational fishing.

"One of my best days," he said. "This is what brings me back, year after year."

I could well believe him because I was already figuring how I could come back the next year.

The following day we fished with Dufft Patean, one of the best known of the Maori guides on Lake Taupo. Before we started to fish, Dufft made a few casts. One of them, made from a sitting position, covered a good 100 feet. That's throwing a fly a mile in any man's language!

"All the Maori guides like to fly cast," Dufft said. "We would rather fish than eat."

He told us that where the river came into the lake he and his father used to spear rainbows up to 25 and 30 pounds in weight. Spearing was legal in those days, of course. Now Dufft is an ardent conservationist.

Casting a big Phillips red and yellow streamer across the current at the mouth of the river, that morning, we took a series of fat and fighty rainbows to a top weight of 6 pounds. In the afternoon, Dufft paddled us slowly alongshore so we could cast to risers he thought we would find in the shallows.

Right away we saw the telltale swirls and in short order Charles had a nice 5 pound rainbow. We were using a streamer fly that New Zealanders call the Mrs. Simpson (because it's so deadly), dropping the fly within a foot of shore and bringing it back in short jerks. Within a couple of hours we landed 20 rainbows between us, ranging from 2 to 7 pounds.

Lake Taupo has had a spotty career for several reasons. There's a great natural supply of food in the form of many hatches as well as crustaceans, and a small gudgeon minnow called the bully. When Taupo was first stocked with trout about 50 years ago, they developed so fast and grew so big that the food supply began to suffer and consequently the trout began to deteriorate. Authorities then netted the lake, removing many tons of fish, and since then smelt have been introduced to provide additional food. With this and the increasing numbers of anglers taking a considerable quantity of fish from the lake, a reasonable balance is being maintained.

There is no doubt, however, that the natural aquatic fly supply was somewhat damaged by the effect of the downpouring of pumice and volcanic ash after the explosion of the volcano Rotorua. The fly hatches have varied greatly since then.

The flies most recommended locally are the Sedge size 10, Claret Spinner size 12, Red Tipped Governor size 12, Cocky Bondu size 12, Greenwell's Glory size 12, and the Red Spinner size 12. The Mrs. Simpson, the Hairy Dog, the Partridge and Claret are all regarded as especially good when the smelt run is on.

The season opens at Taupo on October 1st and runs through to the end of June. May and June are the peak months, though March and April can show a good run of fish going upstream to spawn. In September and October they come down again as kelts, fish that have spawned. There is a limit of eight fish per day, and a minimum size limit of 18 inches.

I didn't have time to cover any more of those famous New Zealand trout waters, but when I do I've promised myself a few days on the Ngongotaha.

The Ngongotaha—pronounced Non-go-taha—River, which flows into Lake Rotorua, rates as one of the best fishing steams in New Zealand. This small stream is only 25 to 45 feet wide, slipping through 15 miles of breathtakingly beautiful meadowland. Every bend is marked by a deep pool in which lurk brown and rainbow trout that if they came up and clapped their mandibles at you would cause you to run for shelter. My good friend Max Stevenson of Pittsburgh had some fabulous fishing on the Ngongotaha the season after I was in New Zealand; and one evening he really hit the jackpot on the Governor Pool.

"Wish you had been there," Max told me later. "I had a field day.

"On my third cast with a size 8 Goofus Bug a fish took, jumped and almost made me run for the bank, he looked so big. I wondered if my 3X tippet would handle this brownie. He was a jumper, too. He fought all the way, came out of the water five times, rushed from one side of the pool to the other. After about 15 minutes, when he began to tire, I thought of my landing net—good for 15 inches but not for fish like this. There was a patch of watercress at the side of the pool, over shallow water, and I led the tiring fish in to that, but he took one look and headed for the middle. I got him back twice more and he went out again, before he at last turned on his side and let me skid him onto the cress and then pick him up and walk up the bank with him. He was a beauty, my biggest trout, a wonderful fat and fit brownie that weighed 8 pounds 2 ounces.

"I rushed back into the river and started fishing again. For 10 minutes nothing happened. It was getting dark and time was running out."

Max changed flies then, tried a Joe's Hopper. No hits. He switched to a size 4 Muddler and worked down the fast water at the head of the pool as his last try of the evening. On his third cast he had a slugging hit. A brilliantly colored rainbow arched for the sky, and he had two hands full of acrobatic fury.

Max weathered runs, jumps, broaches and tailwalking. At last the fish tired and Max took him down to the same patch of watercress and skidded him up.

"This one weighed 6 pounds 12 ounces," said Max. "A big brown and a big rainbow, all in about an hour and a half of fishing. That was a day!"

Max also reported very good fishing in the lakes in the Rotorua area, particularly at the mouths of the Ratotiti, Okataina and Tarawera Rivers.

In fact there's so much good fishing in New Zealand that unless you have quite a long time to spend, you almost have to choose one small area and limit yourself to the waters there. Two of the spots especially recommended to me by New Zealanders were the Matarua River, near the town of Gore, and the several rivers emptying into the Pacific south of Christchurch. In the Matarua they claim there are more trout than in any other river in the country. The fish are not exceptionally large, but can be taken literally by the dozen in weights from 2 to 5 pounds.

The rivers south of Christchurch offer some fine salmon fishing, particularly the Waitaki, which is at its best in February.

Scotland

The first place to which the British Travel and Holidays Association had routed us in Scotland was Loch Leven, the home of the brown trout and the lake from which came most of the seed for the brown trout planted in the United States, and, indeed, in most waters of the world where this species was not native. As is the case nearly everywhere in Europe, we rented a "beat" meaning a certain area to fish on the lake.

On Loch Leven there were 44 boats, headquartered at the town of Kinross, where we stayed at a pleasant inn called the Green Hotel. The boats cost approximately $20.00 from 8 a.m. till 11 p.m., and since this is one lake where fishing is usually good all day long, you could hardly fail to get your money's worth. In two days, with all 44 boats on the water, 2380 fish were taken, all over 12 inches long. The best day for a single boat was 80 fish.

"We fish two anglers to a boat," said Gillie Frank Ford (no relation to Henry, he hastened to assure us). "And it takes two gillies. The boats are heavy, 20 feet long, and use 15-foot sweeps, one man to each oar."

He introduced the other gillie, 16-year-old Don Storro.

"Don is just starting to guide," he said. "I've been on the lake 25 years. My old partner retired, so Don came with me. We'll probably be together now for the rest of my working days."

They packed our gear into the big boat and rowed us upwind for about a mile, then turned the boat broadside to the wind and leaned on the oars. We started to drift across the lake.

"There are many drifts across Loch Leven," said Don, "but this is my favorite."

He pointed to a small island downwind of out boat, where we could see the tumbling ruins of a castle.

"That's where Mary Queen of Scots was imprisoned for so long," he said. "In those days the water level was much higher, so the lake came right up to the walls. The castle stood in the midst of the water, no land around it at all."

On the near shore he indicated a very old cemetery.

"That watchtower was built in the days when grave-robbing was quite a profession. Medical students from Edinburgh would raid the cemetery for newly buried bodies, for research. Even with a guard in the watchtower, those students would sometimes snatch a body.

"And that hill on the far shore is Witches' Hill," he said. "They used to hang witches from those trees."

The older gillie laughed.

"Those aren't the reasons it's his favorite drift," he said. "Those are his landmarks. He likes the drift because it's the best for fishing. See that slick where the wind has knocked the waves down?"

We saw the place he meant. The wind had piled flecks of foam into a long white line at the edge of the slick.

"Drop your flies into those suds," said Frank. "The fish often strike into the flies that gather there. Use a short line. Twenty-five or 30 feet is all the distance you need. Keep your retrieve even, so the bobber fly dances on the water and the other two ride just under the surface.

"You'll no do well on this lake with a single fly," he said, when he saw me tying a grey Wulff to my leader tippet. "You'll want one of our special casts with four flies."

He produced a couple of casts, as a leader is called in Europe. These were equipped with four flies, all very small and tied on size 16 double hooks.

"They're the favorite fly patterns here," said Frank.

He named them from the bobber down.

"The Grouse and Claret, the Butcher, the Woodcock Mixed, and the tail fly is the Greenwell's Glory. We use small flies in the daytime, then go to size 12 at night."

In our fishing on Irish loughs a few weeks earlier we had become familiar with this multiple fly set-up, although in Ireland only three flies were used. I will always be a single fly man at heart, but our experience in Ireland had shown us that under mid-summer fishing conditions, at least, the multiple flies did seem to get more action. And the same thing eventually proved true on Loch Leven. I tried a few casts with single flies and raised an occasional trout, but not with the same consistency as we did with four flies. So I stuck with Frank's suggestion.

Between 2.30 when we left the dock and time to quit that evening, we had caught 20 trout between us, the largest 2½ pounds. While Loch Leven holds tremendous numbers of trout, they do not run to great weights, the largest ever taken weighing 11 pounds 12 ounces. Five to 7 pounders are caught occasionally but are exceptional enough to cause something of a sensation. But you can be sure of lots of 2½ to 3½ pounders, which is good fishing in any man's language.

It's hard to believe that a lake only 4 miles long by 3 miles wide can continue to produce so many fish, day after day, year after year. The explanation probably lies in a combination of circumstances—no predators and plenty of food. Eels, which used to work their way into the lake from the sea and feed on the small trout, no longer can do so because of pollution far down the Leven River below the lake. And pike, which also used to feed on the trout, have been netted out. So the trout have it all to themselves, a plentiful supply of food ranging from crustaceans to minnows, plus any number of aquatic flies and nymphs.

"In June and July we have a hatch of white moths that is so thick it looks like smoke above the trees," said Frank. "We call that hatch 'the fisherman's curse' because while it is on the trout will take only the natural moths and so far no really good imitation has been found."

Once we left Loch Leven and headed north, we soon reached the Highlands. Here the roads switch back and forth up long grades through the famous Scottish glens, winding for miles along the ocean inlets that bisect Scotland so that in many places they seem to run clear across the island. It is these many inlets that provide the river access for the salmon for which we had come to northern Scotland.

The scenery was wild and lonely, with mists hanging over the mountains and the purple bloom of heather along the roadside. Always, peeping through the heather you see the woolly faces of Highland sheep and occasionally come upon a herd of the now rapidly disappearing Highland cattle, beautiful beasts with long, shaggy locks hanging over their eyes, looking like taffy-colored musk-ox.

Every few miles we would see the telephone kiosks of the Automobile Association, where you can call for help if you have car trouble. We had been driving several days before we realized that the friendly salute which the AA motorcycle patrol men gave us as we passed meant that we were members, through the courtesy of the company from which we had rented our car, and that our membership was indicated by a small badge beside the license plate. As we headed deeper into the Highlands we were glad of the security of this knowledge, for towns were few and only occasionally would we see a tiny white farmhouse as we drove.

In spite of the increasing loneliness of the countryside, the roads were good, though so narrow that even the small British cars could not pass. However, frequent pull-outs had been constructed, each one marked with a white flag visible from well ahead, and when two cars meet the nearest one to the flag pulls in and lets the other go through, a sort of leapfrog game with rules that everyone, without exception, respected.

We had decided to start our salmon fishing in Scotland at Lochinver, on the extreme northwest coast, and work our way back, ending at Prestwick where our Pan American plane departed for the U.S.A. We had reservations at the Hotel Culag, a big, substantial brownstone establishment sitting right on the water's edge, at the mouth of the Inver River. The hotel controls fishing rights in both the Inver and the Kirkaig Rivers. When we arrived we found that the Inver was completely booked, but we had a beat on the Kirkaig.

"You have the middle beat this afternoon," the manager told us. "Tomorrow you will have the top beat, and the following day the lower beat. That way, when you are finished you will have fished the whole river."

The Kirkaig is short and fast, plunging down from a misty falls far back in the hills, a falls so precipitous that the salmon cannot get up it. From the Falls Pool the river pours through a narrow, steep-sided glen until it finally flattens out just before reaching the sea. The first day, our beat started at the Heather Pool, a favorite resting place for salmon. A fine head of water came in at the top, moving rapidly along the far bank, a good 60 feet away, then widening, so that it called for a 70 foot cast to drop the fly where it would do the most good.

I started at the top and worked down 20 feet without a hit. Then there was a streak of silver at the fly, so sudden that I almost struck. And that's not the thing to do with a salmon or you'll pull the hook right out of its mouth. I stopped in time and held the rod still while the fish took and moved upstream, and then the belly of the line in the water pulled the hook home in the corner of his mouth. I felt him, and he must have felt the hook because he got out of there in a hurry. He jumped in a flurry of water so I didn't get a good look at him, but in a second he jumped again, only 40 feet out, and this time I saw he was a nice 10 pounder. It was 15 minutes before I had him on the grass. There I gently removed the hook and put that salmon back in the water.

In Europe hardly anyone ever releases a fish. The salmon are treated as a crop and those who control the rivers take care to see that they are not overfished either by nets or sportsmen. Salmon, especially, are nearly always kept, either for the angler's own use, or to be sold. But brought up in the tradition that a fish released adds to the future of sport fishing and that a sportsman never sells a fish, I frequently found myself putting them back in the water.

Later that day Mary took an 8 pounder and I landed another that looked about 7, a pretty good take for a mid-summer's day. As we passed the Island Pool on our way back to the hotel, we saw Allen McKay, a 17-year-old boy who was also staying at the Culag.

I braked to a stop.

"What luck?" I called.

He reached down in the grass and picked up a nice salmon, about 8 pounds.

"My first salmon," he said, his face splitting in a wide grin. "This is only the second time I've fished for them.

"You know," he said, with a suddenly serious expression, "I don't know if it was second sight, or what. But I had been casting all afternoon and suddenly I said to myself, 'In five minutes I'm going to catch a salmon.' Then a bit later I said: 'On the next cast I'm going to catch a salmon.' And I did!"

We wished him luck and drove on, chuckling. That boy was a real angler in the making, sure that he was going to catch one on the next cast. I didn't tell him that every time I threw the fly in the pool I had the same feeling, and that each time I cast I also sent out a prayer for a hit, out there with the fly.

When we arrived back at the hotel we found another happy angler, M.A.G. Morkil of London, who had been fishing Loch Culag. He had used a fly to take one of the prettiest sea trout I have ever seen. It went 7 pounds 8 ounces. It was deep and thick through the shoulders, and though its color was fading to the characteristic brown trout hues, there was still enough of the silver sheen to show that he had been to sea.

From the Kirkaig we went to Altnaharra on the far north coast of Scotland, and stayed with Charles C. McLaren at his Altnaharra Hotel. McLaren is an authority on sea trout, having caught thousands of them, including the oldest sea trout on record, a 12½ pound fish that was proven by scale count to be 19 years old and to have spawned 11 times. Charles McLaren took this great fish at Loch Maree when he was only 13 years old. At that time his father owned a fine fishing hotel on the loch. Charles had his own hotel at Altnaharra, with wonderful sea trout fishing in Loch Hope, and salmon fishing in the Mallart River. We were too early for the sea trout season in Loch Hope, but got several nice salmon from the river.

These two fish can be very confusing to anglers who have not caught trout fresh in from the sea. At this time they resemble the salmon so closely that it almost takes an expert to tell them apart.

"But you can always tell the difference, one way or another," Charles told us. "If you want to take the time you can count the scales on an oblique line from the rear end of the adipose fin down to the lateral line. Salmon generally have from 10 to 13 scales, sea trout have from 13 to 16. Another way is to look at the maxillary, that bit of hard gristle that extends along the top of the mouth. If it extends back beyond the eye it is a sea trout. If it stops at the eye, it is a salmon. The sea trout has a small head but a bigger mouth than a salmon. Also, generally the tail of the sea trout is straight or only slightly convex, while that of the grilse or small salmon to about 8 pounds is forked. As it grows bigger the salmon tail becomes almost straight—but by the time a salmon is that big you're not in any doubt as to what you've got."

In Scotland, the sea trout fishing is generally good from June throughout the summer till the end of September, while salmon rivers vary, usually having their best runs in February and through the first two weeks of May. But there are plenty of rivers such as the Inver and the Kirkaig and the Mallart which fish well all summer, especially if there is enough rain to keep the river level up. There are also many rivers which are called "spate rivers," too low most of the time to hold salmon, but which rise with a rush when there is a heavy run-off of rain, and the fish take advantage of this rise to come roaring up the river.

For our last week in Scotland we had reservations to fish the Oykel River on the Balnagown Estate in Sutherlandshire, not far from Altnaharra, but flowing to the east coast of Scotland. Balnagown is what is known in Scotland as a "sporting estate," catering to both salmon fishermen and grouse shooters. The upper half of the river is fished from a lodge called Benmore, and guests there also fish Loch Ailsh, out of which the river flows. We fished the lower half, staying at Balnagown Lodge, a small but extremely comfortable inn at Oykel Bridge. As we had found throughout the trip, the meals were universally good and very inexpensive. At Balnagown all meals were served buffet style and after one glance at the buffet, loaded with everything from oatmeal porridge to shiny golden Scotch-kippered herring for breakfast, and great roasts of beef, pork, and lamb at night, we were glad of the parade back and forth to pick up our courses.

In Scotland we also had salmon cooked in every way possible, our favorite being an hors d'oeuvre of smoked salmon sliced paper thin and served with equally thinly sliced well-buttered oatmeal bread. I ate it at every opportunity and only laid off when Mary caught me trying to jump the falls of the Oykel.

The lower part of the river, which we fished, covers 20 miles of water. There were six beats, some with as many as 7 good fishing pools within their limits. Mary and I would have adjoining beats each day and by switching at noon we could cover a great deal of water. At the end of six days it was as if we had fished 12 beats.

The head gillie, George Ross, was the son of a gillie and in turn his own son was now putting in his first season at the trade.

"August is the poorest fishing month here," George told us frankly. "There are fish in the river but they are very dour at this time."

We assured him that we understood this but had to take our chances as it was summer fishing we were interested in.

"I assign one gillie to each beat for the whole season," he said. "In that way the gillie learns the lies of the salmon thoroughly and can be of more help to the angler so he doesn't waste time casting to dead water."

That first morning I fished the Junction Pool with David Whyte as my gillie and once more I had it brought home to me that no matter how much you fish there's always something new to be learned. I had gone through the pool without a strike and reached the tail where the water deepened and slowed so that there was hardly enough current to put the fly over a fish in a seductive way. I was about to go ashore and start over again, but David stopped me.

"Sometimes they lie in there," he said. "But it's hard to get a good float. Try backing up the pool.

"Where the current is so slow that you want to give the fly some motion, we back up the pool," he explained. "If you stripped line to get action, the fly would not cover the water properly. But if you cast across current and let the fly float down, then, holding the rod still and keeping it pointed out, start to move sideways up the pool—move one foot about 2½ feet, bring the other up to it; then another step, and so on—that's backing up the pool. The fly comes through faster, but smoothly, and will cover any salmon in there."

It seemed a very small point and I didn't get any fish in that pool, but subsequently I found that it was surprising how often I raised a salmon I hadn't even known was there by "backing up the pool."

As George Ross had told us, this was the poorest time of the year for salmon. We had to work for every fish. In the slicker pools we could cast for hours and be happy to come up with one salmon and a couple of sea trout. But things changed at dusk and fortunately we were far enough north that dusk ran on till nearly midnight, and in the long twilight hours we had plenty of action.

One of the most exciting parts of the evening fishing was that at this time you never could be sure whether it would be a salmon or a sea trout that would hit your fly. In the daytime sea trout are every bit as wary as their fresh water brown brothers and it takes some fine tackle and exacting angling to get them to hit. But when dusk drops over the moors, then the sea trout get a gleam in their eyes, though even then these eyes are as sharp as an owl's and you almost have to go down to a maximum of a 3X tippet.

Then there's the problem of whether to strike or not to strike. With a salmon you don't strike or you'll pull the fly out of the fish's mouth. With a sea trout you must strike quickly or the fish will spit the fly out and be gone before you know you have him.

On our last day at Balnagown we were lucky enough to have the top beat, which includes three pools, the Junction, the George, and the Falls pools, three of the best.

In the Junction that morning I had a small salmon and a sea trout and Mary had two sea trout. In the George, where we fished through the bright of the day, we rated zero. But all day we saw salmon moving up and we could hardly wait to get to the Falls Pool after dinner.

The Falls Pool is named for the falls where the Oykel salmon break their journey on the upstream spawning run. Every time I looked into that pool it was full of fish. They would come leaping over the rapids at the tail of the pool, moving up from the George. We could see them broaching, slashing, and splashing towards the falls. There they would throw themselves at the torrent of water that dropped over the cliff and try desperately to scale it. When they found it impossible they would move back and forth along the bottom of the falls looking for a spot where the climbing was easier. Time and again they would throw themselves into the face of the white water, only to be dashed back. Often their leaps took them clear out on the rocks at the side of the falls and there they would flap and struggle till finally they made it back into the water. And every once in a while we would see one that had found the right tail-hold go soaring up, right in the face of the torrent. He had made it and was on his way to the spawning bed above.

When we reached the Falls Pool that last night, although the sun still shone on the hills above, it was already dark down in the gorge. And there were midges by the millions.

"When the midges bite, so do the salmon," said Gillie Donald Morrison, wiping from his brow the handful of the little insects that had suddenly covered him like a shadow.

"Same everywhere," I said and spat out a mouthful.

After that we were silent because we had already had dinner and didn't care for the taste of midges anyway.

I made my first cast and let the fly start its float. A salmon hit it at exactly the same moment that 10,000 midges bit me on the ear at once. I slapped the midges and jerked the fly out of the salmon's mouth.

"Ye pulled his nose," said Donald accusingly.

Then he slapped his own ear so hard he nearly knocked himself over.

"Don't blame ye," he muttered.

Just then I was into another salmon. The midges were forgotten. That fish tore line off in bunches as he rushed up the pool, took a look at the falls and decided he couldn't make it, then shot back past us like a bullet. He was headed for the rapids below. I held on and gave him all the pressure I dared, and when he stopped short of the drop-off, I reeled quickly and got tight to him. Back to the falls he went, then back to the rapids again, while Donald and I clambered across the rocks like billy goats. For fifteen minutes that salmon kept us jumping.

But one last hard try at the falls seemed to completely wind him and he came down the pool that time on a tight line. I eased him shoreward, Donald scuttled down the bank, and as I brought the fish in he put home the gaff and lifted. It was a nice 10 pounder.

That was the first of three good salmon and four hefty sea trout we took that night in spite of the midges, or perhaps because of the midges. We were only bothered with those pesky creatures on two days while we were at Balnagown and both those days were red letter ones for fishing. Like all fishermen, it's the fish I'll remember, and not the midges.

Iceland

"It is best to use a small fly in this river," said Einar Farestveit. "My favorites are the Black Doctor and Blue Charm, size 10."

The river, the Ellida-A, was only 5 miles from downtown Reykjavik, but it was reported to be loaded with salmon up to 12 pounds and is one of the most sought after rivers in Iceland.

My wife and I had found ourselves with three days to spare on the end of a European trip and when our plane dropped in to Iceland to refuel we decided on the spur of the moment to take that time to see what Iceland had to offer in the way of fishing. It is usually very difficult to obtain a beat on any salmon river without considerable advance notice, especially in June, when we were there. But through the good offices of Einar, who was the agent for Pan American World Airways at Reykjavik, we were lucky enough to get a half day "beat"—that is, permission to fish a certain stretch of water for a certain period of time.

The Ellida-A is only 70 feet across at its widest so we had put up 8½ foot fly rods with GBF (WF8F) lines and 14 foot leaders tapered down to 5 pound test tippets. Now we took Einar's advice and tied on size 10 Black Doctors.

During the walk upstream to the point where our beat started it was hard to keep back from the river bank. The Elida, which from the road had appeared to be a mere trickle, had plenty of water in it. It was slick and slow running, with here and there big turns, producing wide, deep pools, and there were occasional riffles with nice pools below. Our first pool, however, was very flat and the water was so dark because of the heavy cloud overcast that I couldn't see the bottom. I'd have to guess from the swirls in the water where the pool proper was and where the salmon should lie.

On my first cast I dropped the fly about 15 feet out and let it drift downstream. The water had a good flow, after all, taking the fly along fairly fast, just under the surface. This was better than I had thought.

I lengthened my next cast by 2 feet and again the fly swam through without bringing a hit. The third cast was halfway down the pool when the salmon looped up, showing the top of his head as he took. I let the line belly down in the current between rod tip and fish. Then I felt him and out he came, ran up the pool, jumped again, turned and sliced off to the left as he went on a sizzling run down that pool and into the one below. I was already reeling as fast as I could and running after him. He jumped again, and again I dropped the rod tip so he wouldn't fall on a tight leader and break it.

Now I was just across the pool from him and had only 50 feet of line out. That was the way I wanted it because in this narrow, winding stream he could break me off if he went around a bend or if the line caught on a tuft of grass or around a jutting rock. Luck had been with me, but now when he felt me pulling back on the rod he took off upstream and back into the pool he had just quitted. Up I went, as he dogged it there, reeling, trying to keep clear of all those dangers. When I was 20 feet in back of him and out in the open, I laid back on the rod and pulled him my way. He made one hard lunge across to the other side, then sashayed my way. He was tired and I kept him coming, held the rod back and pulled him in to my feet. I reached down and tailed him, picked him from the water, a fine looking 8 pounder, my first salmon in Iceland.

At the end of the 4 hours we were permitted to fish the river, we had taken a dozen salmon up to 12 pounds, wonderful fishing any way you look at it!

Iceland has more fish per foot of river than any place I've ever fished. And since there's scarcely a tree in the whole country, it's a fly fisherman's paradise. You can let your backcast roll out as far as you want, and as long as you keep it from hitting the ground you're safe. Because the rivers are small, long casts are not necessary; so again the fly fisherman gets a break. His only problem is the wind and that is easily enough circumvented in the flat terrain where it is easy to move around and take advantage of the wind rather than fighting it.

While all Icelandic rivers do not hold salmon, most of them do. The size of the fish is not outstanding, though a 37 pounder has been taken on rod and reel, and there is a record of a 48 pound fish being caught in nets. But in these narrow, apparently shallow, but often deceptively deep rivers, a 10 pound Atlantic salmon can keep you mighty busy.

In addition to the salmon there are sea trout, or sea-run brown trout, and sea-run char. The trout go from 3 to 15 pounds, the largest on record being a 28 pounder. Charr vary from 2 to 8 pounds. Besides these river fish, the many lakes and the inland rivers between lakes hold native brown trout and charr averaging 2 to 4 pounds, with some of both species running as high as 10 pounds, and an occasional trout reaching even 15 pounds in such lakes as Myvatn, regarded as the best in Iceland.

The season for salmon is from June 1st to September 15th; for brown trout, May 1st to September 1st; and for both sea trout and charr, fishing is open from April 1st to September 15th. There is no fishing license required, you simply pay the terms of your beat. Once in a while you can find a farmer who will let you fish his share of the river for a morning or afternoon.

Iceland, which lies just short of the Arctic Circle, belies its name in many ways. Because of the nearness of the Gulf Stream there's so little snow in winter that skiers only get out a few times in a season to enjoy their sport. Yet there are three major icecaps on the island, which never melt. Square in the middle of one of those icecaps is a big hot spring, in fact geysers all over the world take their names from Iceland's Great Geysir. As if nature wanted to compensate for the constant coolness of the climate, these geysers, pour out steam here and there all over the island. The old part of the city of Reykjavik is heated by steam from the geysers and in the small inland town of Hveragerdi we saw banks of steam-heated greenhouses where fruits and vegetables as exotic as the banana are raised.

There are 170,000 inhabitants of Iceland and before I'd been in Reykjavik a day I was convinced that they all fish. Not too many years ago the rivers were practically all leased to visiting anglers. Icelanders were too busy with commercial fishing. Then suddenly they started to go in for sport fishing, and today almost every salmon river in the country that is at all accessible has its fishing club, the members banding together to buy the fishing rights of a stream from landowners. One club in Reykjavik has 700 members, so many that they have to plan their fishing months ahead, drawing lots in midwinter for their days astream. The number of rods is limited each day and on each beat, so that in a club such as the one at Reykjavik, members get only three days fishing a season and these days are divided into six half days instead of three full ones.

When one member of that club was kind enough to give us his turn on the Ellida-A, I soon saw the reason for the Icelanders' enthusiasm. That morning was one I'll long remember.

When we got back to Reykjavik that afternoon we found a note from Albert Erlingsson who has a tackle store on the main street. Albert has fished practically everywhere in Iceland and has a wide acquaintance with farmers and land owners who will lease their waters. He had good news for us.

"My friend Helgi Juliesson has got you a beat on the Laxa in Leirasveit," he said. "One of the best rivers in this area. Helgi speaks little English but I'm sure you'll get along fine just the same."

Iceland

Iceland is one country where, even though many people speak a certain amount of English, language is still something of a problem. Even if one spoke Norwegian, which is fairly closely allied, Icelandic has many peculiarities seldom encountered in other languages. As one Icelander said to me, you have to know everyone in Iceland by his or her first name before you can make a phone call. I soon found out what he meant. It isn't too involved if you understand the system—this being that John Smith's son Bill will not be named Bill Smith, but Bill Johnsson; while the same John Smith's daughter Katherine will not be Katherine Smithsdaughter nor Katherine Johnsdaughter but the daughter of his wife, and since his wife's name is Mary, then John Smith's daughter and Bill Johnsson's sister will be named Katherine Marysdaughter. All of which can be mighty confusing to plain Joe Brooks or any visiting angler.

In addition, an Icelander's conversation is liberally sprinkled with an "ow!" sound as if, just as he finished his sentence, he had a sharp pain. "A" in Icelandic is pronounced "ow" and means river, and the "a" is attached to the name of the river. When your fisherman friend says he'll meet you at the Laxa (locks-ow) he means the Lax (salmon) River. Since every second river in Iceland is named for the salmon, each one has to have an added description taken from the territory in which it is found. After getting all this through my head it was easy enough to take a map and discover that the Laxa in Leirasveit lay across the bay from Reykjavik in the District of Leirasveit.

"You take the ferry to Akranes," Albert told us. "Helgi will meet you there. There's a nice hotel where you can stay the night so you'll be ready to fish early in the morning. Helgi has two beats for you, one for the morning and another for the afternoon."

When our ferry docked at Akranes, Helgi had no trouble recognizing us. We were the only passengers loaded with 8 fly rods, 3 cameras, two big packsacks and a tackle bag. He stepped right up, hand outstretched in welcome. We packed ourselves and luggage into his car and headed for the town. The hotel was clean and modern and a double room cost less than we had been paying in Reykjavik.

Dinner was excellent, including the invariably delicious smoked salmon. It was served by two good looking Icelandic girls who somehow managed to understand our sign language between giggles.

"I'll pick you up at seven in the morning," said Helgi. "If that is not too early."

Mary and I were standing outside with our gear piled against the side of the hotel when he arrived. It took about three-quarters of an hour by car to reach the river. On this side of the bay the land was not quite as flat as around Reykjavik and the river was bigger than the Ellida-A and came tumbling down from distant hills to the green fields below. When we reached our beat we walked out on a high cliff and looked down at a falls. As we watched, a salmon came out and jumped into the face of the white water.

"That's where your beat begins," said Helgi. "You may fish from that falls downstream for two miles."

I was using the 5 ounce, 8½ foot fly rod again, and the water looked so clear that I tapered the tippet down to 4 pound test. Then I waded out at the head of the pool right under the falls and starting casting.

Halfway down the pool a fish came up, refused, and made a big swirl as he turned and went back to his lie. I rested him for a couple of minutes, then changed to a Silver Gray, size 6. Then I started the series of casts about 5 feet above where he had showed, just in case he had moved upstream a little. I worked down, put the fly over his former position, but no go. He passed it up. Or maybe he had dropped back. So I put the fly down another 10 feet. He wasn't there or he didn't like what he saw.

"I'll show him a little twinkler," I decided.

I dug into my fly book and came up with a number 12 Silver Doctor with a jungle cock feather tied into its shoulder. It seemed to send off sparks as it went merrily down the current, alive and beckoning.

The salmon must have liked the way it looked. This time there was no mistake, he wanted that fly and he took it hard, dashed down the pool and went down and sulked. He wouldn't move and I couldn't budge him.

When I finally walked along the shore till I was 15 feet below him and laid back on the rod to pull him out of his sulk, he came alive again and made a series of jumps, as beautiful a display of aerobatics as I've seen in a long time. He finally splashed in at the face of the falls, bored off to the left, then came back to the right, jumped again and came dashing my way. He looked about 10 pounds and acted about 20.

Finally he tired and I skidded him up on the gravel, took the hook out and put him back. About five pools farther down the river Mary and Helgi waved congratulations. Three hours and 11 salmon later I reached them. It had been wonderful. Mary had also taken her share, 6 salmon, the largest 12 pounds.

"It is one o'clock," said Helgi. "Your time on this beat is ended. But this afternoon we go to another where you have the hours from 4 until 10 tonight. Up here so near the Arctic it stays light all night at this time of year."

The afternoon's fishing was even better than it had been in the morning. We both got into and landed some nice fish, and the last pool of our beat brought me a slashing hit from the best salmon so far. He hit, jumped once to show me his size, and then went down through five pools and over a falls with me running behind him. I was almost out of backing by the time he stopped, and then he was on the far side of the river below a falls, with so many rocks between us that I couldn't play him from where I stood.

I went in and started across but halfway had to turn back because the water dropped off over my head. Finally I found a place higher in the pool where I could make it across and at last climbed down the bank on the side of the falls where the fish lay, resting his nose in back of a rock. I got below him and, with only 25 feet of line out, put on the pressure. He shot out of there like a rocket, got in the fast water in the middle of the stream and rolled in the leader. I gave line and he floated down, unwinding as he went. But once free of that nylon girdle he really came to life. He raced to the other side, dodged an up-jutting rock, leaped clear over another, did an oblique to the left and almost beached himself in front of me.

He corrected that in a hurry, got up on his tail and danced across the surface, throwing water in all directions. A salmon like that in a small pool is something to see! By the time I got him in it was 10 o'clock, but with that 20 pounder under my belt I didn't mind too much.

We made it back to the ferry, ate our way across the bay in the lunchroom aboard, and were asleep at the City Hotel in Reykjavik by 2 a.m., still the shank of the evening, Iceland style.

The next day we went for sea trout.

"Salmon rivers are in such demand that you must book them months ahead," John Sigurdson told us at the Pan American Airways desk at the airport. "But you can nearly always get on a river where there are sea trout. We'll ask Gunnar Kristjansson to drive us to the Olfusa. It's a glacial river, quite milky, but you catch lots of trout there and occasionally a salmon, too."

The first spot we fished was very murky, except for a band of comparatively clear water along the shore.

"When the sea trout are in they swim up that clear water," said Jon. "Cast there and if they are in you'll catch some."

A number of other fishermen were there ahead of us. Some of them had their rods set in holders which they had designed themselves, long metal spikes with the top ending in a curl into which a conventional spinning reel would fit securely. They baited their hooks with worms, cast the bait out, set the reels in these holders and went back to the bank to smoke and eat and exchange fishing talk. When one of the set-lines had a hit, everyone piled into the river again, ready for action.

The best time for sea trout in this river is from the first of April to the middle of May. Then the fishing usually falls off until the end of June, when it improves again and remains good until the end of September. Since we were there in July we couldn't blame the season for the fact that we caught no fish. It was just one of those days. We cast and cast without a strike. At last Gunnar suggested that we go down closer to the mouth of the river.

"I know the farmer," he said. "It will cost you perhaps a dollar each, but it is a very nice beach and usually good fishing."

We drove over rolling hill country, rough and bleak looking, yet beautiful in its own way, then slipped over the brink of the hill country and looked out on the vast grassland of the coastal plain, green and lush, with the river winding through it and in the distance the lagoons that marked the sea. Halfway down we passed the farmhouse. Gunnar went in and paid three dollars for the three of us who would be fishing. Then we drove on down the winding road till at last the grass gave way to dunes and finally the road led out onto a wide expanse of beach.

"I'll drive you across the sand now because it's low tide," said Gunnar. "Then I'll leave and come back for you later. If I stay here through high tide the car will get stuck."

We went on up the beach till we saw two flags about 200 yards apart, sticking up in the water. Near one of them a commercial fisherman was just beaching his skiff.

"We stopped at the farmhouse," John told him. "They said to check with you because you might be netting. But if it's all right, we'll fish."

"I'm netting between those two flags," he said. "You can fish anywhere else you like."

We went down the beach a hundred feet from his flags and started casting. Because of the 15 mile wind blowing right in our faces we had to put up 9½ foot rods with matching GAF (WF9F) lines and had our leaders cut down to 9 feet, but maintained a 6 pound test tippet. Both of us tied on red and yellow multiwing streamers on 1/0 hooks. John was using a spinning outfit and a large gold spoon. He started casting, connected at once and before long he had a 3 pound sea trout flapping on the beach.

"Three pounds of good eating," he said.

The bay was wide here, the mouth of the river being a good two miles across; but as we cast out we soon saw that the current of the Olfusa hugged the shore so that, although it seemed like casting out in the ocean, our lines were carried along very rapidly. The current was cloudy with glacial water so we could not see the flies but we just kept slowly moving along, casting, retrieving, slowly and carefully.

After about 10 minutes something hit my fly so hard he rocked the rod in my hands. I struck and felt a heavy fish. He ran towards shore and almost beached himself before he swapped ends and went the other way. Then he came out in a beautiful jump and seemed to like it up there because he came out again and again. It took me 10 minutes to beach that fish, a good 5 pound sea trout, as pretty as I've ever seen.

I worked on down the beach and soon was into another, a 4 pounder, while a couple of hundred feet away Mary was landing a 3 pounder and another that went 5. After an hour or so of this activity we saw the commercial fisherman, Asgrimur Agnarsson by name, coming down the beach, while far across the flat Gunnar approached, plodding through the ankle deep tide. The commercial man was bringing us a little refreshment, a slab of some kind of dried fish whose name we couldn't understand and whose nature we could only guess at from the toad-like skin on the outside of it. Gunnar had come to tell us that it was time to leave, as we still had a long drive back to Reykjavik.

"Agnarsson says he's sorry you must leave," he interpreted for us. "He wants you to come back soon. He says if you look in his skiff you will see something that will bring you back soon.

Agnarsson was right. As we walked back up the beach towards the distant car I went over and peered into the skiff which he had been beaching just as we arrived. In it lay a beautiful 25 pound Atlantic salmon.

"He caught it in his nets just before we arrived," said Gunnar. "He says he often gets them like this."

I gabbed my rod and started back down the beach but Gunnar stopped me.

"Too late," he said. "Too late. We must go now. There will be another time."

You can bet on that!

Tumble Rocks!

Adventure with a mighty salmon at the foot of the famous falls of the Humber River, Newfoundland.

On the Gander River in Newfoundland, I saw a run of fresh salmon come into the Joe Beggs Pool. I noticed their splashing down in the rapids below, then saw them come greyhounding toward me. A couple of them jumped high, as if in joy at striking the quiet water. Near the middle of the pool one came out clear on a 40 degree slant, then bellywhopped in again. In back of him, another sloshed along the top for two lengths.

The salmon I had been working on must have heard them coming. He jumped out, too, a long, deep fish with a caudal as broad as an axe blade. Then the main body of those fish hit him and he busted out on a bee line for the rapids above. The speeding pack chased after him.

I knew that if I could have caught one, the tiny sea lice that only live 24 hours in fresh water would still be on him. And maybe his sides would show net marks, or there would be scars to show where he had leaped into the face of a falls and banged hard into the rocks, or he might have a gash from a marauding seal. This was their first wild, thrilling run from the sea. They were strong and bright from the salt and they wouldn't stop until they reached some special pool, perhaps miles above, where they would settle down for a week, or a month, or two months, until some insistent, internal clamoring drove them on again, up and up, to shallower water, to gravel beds to spawn.

I was almost sure there wasn't a salmon left in the pool after that wild parade, but just to be certain I made a cast. There was a swirl and I struck and yanked a five-inch salmon parr right out of the water. I wet my hand, took the parr off the hook and placed it gently back in the river. It would be three or four years at least before that "peel" of the salmon would be charging upstream like the wild ones that had just rolled through. Meantime, he would live in the river, feeding on flies, growing stronger for two or three years until he was ready to go to sea. And some day, out there, maybe in three yeas, maybe in five—no one knows for sure—he would feel the pull of home, and then, from out there in the salt, it would be his time to return to the stream where he was bred.

Some anglers think that it is the memory of his parr days that makes an adult salmon hit a fly; for even though they take artificials, and poachers are known to have caught them on worms, their stomachs are empty whenever they are taken in fresh water and it is commonly believed that they do not eat after they leave the salt.

Whatever the reason, the Atlantic salmon hits a fly with such abandon, mixed with such discretion, that he is regarded by many as the top game fish. To take salmon consistently, and, in fact, any way but accidentally, you must know the country and the river and the pool you are fishing.

Newfoundland is a small fly country, and flies tied on anything larger than a number 4 hook are seldom needed. The bigger flies are used during the run-off of snow water in the spring, but in Newfoundland the rivers are usually low and clear by July 1st, and they keep dropping until only the low water flies on small hooks, or even small trout flies, will take fish.

To take a really large salmon on one of these small flies is the thrill of a lifetime. One of Newfoundland's oldest guides, Micmac Indian Jim Johns, tells of fishing a 75-year-old doctor who took a 44-pound salmon from the Gander—the largest ever taken on that river—on a size 12 Cowdung, a trout fly. The doctor fought that fish from 6 p.m. until midnight, and they followed it upstream for 2½ miles. They landed and Jim built a fire while the doctor worked the fish in. At last it was ready for the net. Jim reached—and there was a hole in the net and the big salmon went on through. Finally the doctor brought the fish in again, and this time Jim jumped on it, drove his hunting knife into it, and carried it ashore.

Some of the best wet flies to use in Newfoundland waters are the Silver Doctor, Silver Grey, Mar Lodge, Blue Charm, Logie, Black Dose, Black Doctor, Jock Scott, Dusty Miller, Cosseboom, and the March Brown. The moosehair flies, tied locally, have paid off recently in Newfoundland. The wing is made of moosehair but otherwise they follow the body pattern of the regularly tied salmon flies. Some use jungle cock but there seems to be a movement to defrock that feather, and Newfoundlanders claim they catch just as many salmon without it. The moosehair flies are certainly cheaper and as they are equally effective, it looks as if they will take over the Newfoundland market.

There are three flies that make salmon mad, or so it seems from the way they charge them: the Thunder and Lightning, the Green Highlander and the Durham Ranger. On my first trip to Newfoundland, I fished Petrie's Rock Pool on the Gander with Roy Petrie of Grand Falls, after whose father the pool is named. Roy handed me a Durham Ranger.

"This one makes them see red," he said.

And it did. On my first cast for Atlantic salmon, a fish shot up, mouth open like he was going to take me instead of the fly. I was too frozen to strike, which was probably just as well, because I would have pulled his head off. Anyway, he had it and was down through the pool and into the next one before I could speak.

But there was nothing wrong with Roy's voice, and to the tune of "Keep the tip up, drop the tip, let him go, watch out!" I fought that fish in and finally landed a five-pound grilse. I sat and looked at him for along time—a thoroughbred of the river, spawned from a long line of silvery thunderbolts, a steeplechaser with countless water barriers behind him.

"A grilse," explained Roy, indicating the forked tail. "When he's a salmon, his tail will be square. In Newfoundland, we class six pounds and under as grilse."

In Newfoundland waters, the sizes most needed in wet flies are 8 and 10. Some anglers still use the double-hooked wet flies but, like the big, heavy, two-handed rods, that type of hook is on the way out. The single hook drops lightly, holds better, and swims better than the larger, heavier ones.

When the water warms and drops, the dry fly comes into its own. The best patterns are the Grey Wulff, the Brown Wulff and the Royal Wulff, with the White Wulff occasionally getting results. The big hair flies float well and show up well, in sizes 6 to 12; and other good dries are the Grey Hackle, the Grey Hackle with red body, the Brown Hackle, the Brown and also the Black Bivisibles. The hair-bodied flies in grizzly, grey and ginger are good. There are dozens of dry flies that will bring hits from salmon, but with dries, it's the shape of the fly, and the way it rides down the current that count, and therefore a large selection is not necessary.

All the salmon flies in the world will not help you if your trip doesn't coincide with the run of fish in the river. Usually the date of the run varies only a day or two from year to year, but occasionally natural conditions will hold the fish back, as in 1954 when an unusually large number of icebergs in White Bay and elsewhere along the Newfoundland coast delayed them as much as ten days. It also pays to know the place where the fish stop on their first drive upstream.

For instance, salmon enter the Humber River about June 20th and don't stop, or come within the angler's reach until they come to the Big Falls Pool, 20 miles above the town of Deer Lake. Once they reach there, the fishing is fabulous. In late July they begin to stop in all the pools and the Lower Humber holds some monster fish, mostly above 20 pounds.

Salmon come into the Serpentine on the west coast of New-foundland also about June 20th and run up to the first falls before stopping. On the Gander they make the run about the end of June and don't stop until they hit the pools immediately below the town of Glenwood. On South Brook the first salmon is usually caught about June 27th, and the same date goes for nearby West Brook and the Indian River, both of which empty into Hall's Bay.

A bright day is bad news for the salmon angler. From 1 p.m. until 6 p.m., particularly, when the sun is on the pools, the salmon will lie in plain sight, their snouts in back of a rock. Then it seems as if nothing will make them rise. Once at Grant's Pool on the Ser-pentine, when I was alone, I decided to try a "kill or cure" medi-cine. I went ashore, picked up a couple of rocks about the size of tennis balls, and threw them into the tail of the pool. Then I walked up and tossed two more rocks into the fast water at the top.

I waited a couple of minutes up there and then started a series of casts. On the third float, a salmon took, careened up, shattered the surface into a thousand jigsaw pieces, and threw the hook. Then at the tail, at the drop off, I saw another one rise.

I hitched on a size 10, low-water Silver Doctor and skidded it across his snout. He grabbed it the first time and hopped out, and I dropped the rod tip as that acrobatic broadjumper covered eight feet in a going-away leap. He hit and bounced right away, and once again I dropped the tip. I didn't want him to fall on my three-pound-test tippet and break it; nor did I want him to get a straight-away pull, because then a sudden charge or jump would snap the leader. If he was well hooked, the slack I was giving him didn't mat-ter; and if he wasn't well hooked, it wouldn't matter anyway. But he didn't get off, and at last I got him into dead water and skidded him up on shore. He was a sleek fourteen-pounder, a bright fish that woke up hungry when he was rocked.

During the first few days on the stream, almost every novice salmon fisherman, and many an expert, loses more fish on the strike, than he hooks. Salmon don't always take with a rush. They ease up on the fly and suck it in, or they take it so quietly that you think a parr is there instead of an older member of the family. If you delay the strike, they will hook themselves. And with either wet or dry flies, it pays to wait until you feel the fish before striking. But it's tough to wait and it's easy to get excited, strike too fast, and lip the fish.

Once, on South Brook, I saw a couple of salmon rising in the tail of a pool I was just starting to fish. I went below, tied on a size 8 Grey Wulff and started casting. On my first float, the fly had a bit of drag and I saw three salmon, one after the other, come up for the fly, refuse, and sink down. My fingers started to do a tap dance on the rod grip and when the first salmon busted out at the fly on my next cast, I struck so fast he couldn't even get to it.

I was shaking up a fit now, so I made myself walk away to rest the pool and try to get a grip on my jumpy nerves. Three minutes later I went back and struck too fast again. But I felt the fish this time. I was doing a bit better.

I figured there was still that third salmon that I hadn't scared, so I pulled two extra feet of line off the reel and made the cast. I didn't touch that extra line as I guided the fly over the fish with my right hand holding the rod, my left hand well away from the line. When the fish took, I couldn't snatch the fly away, for there was that two feet of slack. And when it came tight, the hook went home and I had a seven-pound salmon.

In small streams, like South Brook, you must go fine in tackle and fish the pools quietly. A fifteen-foot leader tapered to a 4-foot section of 4-pound test nylon will fall lightly and not scare the fish. For, contrary to what many fishermen believe, salmon do scare, and though they may stay right in plain sight, once you've scared them they're as down as a broken elevator and you can't raise them with a drag line, much less a fly line.

More and more 8½-foot rods with HCH line to match, and with long, light leaders are showing up on salmon streams in place of the old, two-handed, heavy outfits. It makes for more strikes, more fun, and a fairer break for the salmon, though I sometimes wonder if they need a break, any break at all. They can do things to you that no other fish can do. Like the one I hooked more recently.

We were fishing the Big Falls Pool on the Humber, classed since time unremembered as one of the greatest salmon pools in the world. The first three days were too bright for good fishing. Each day we took a few grilse in the morning, and again at dark. But it was dull going.

Then on the third night the wind changed and started blowing from the east. It howled and wailed through the pines and you could feel the chill in it. We shivered and dug deeper into our sleeping bags. In the morning it grew still colder and mist flew off the falls in clouds.

"We'll do better now," said my guide, Edgar Eastman.

That morning we took a couple of 8-punders, a 9-pounder, and five grilse from 2 to 4 pounds. We went in at mid-afternoon for dinner so we could be out for the evening fishing.

It was getting colder by the minute. The mist swirled low over the pool and blew heavy from the falls. Before we went out we put on extra woolen shirts and our heaviest coats. It was almost cold enough to see your breath.

As we pulled up towards the falls, I wiggled into my bow seat and pulled my coat tighter about me.

"It's blowing off the ice," said Edgar.

He meant the ice in Greenland, and the bergs in White Bay, only 25 miles away. I shook a little harder while he poled the canoe up into the pool. He dropped the rock, let the line out, and then, sure of his position, made the line fast. We were anchored now about 50 feet above the drop off in probably the best spot in the pool. Anything could happen here.

I turned and looked at the 12-foot wall of water above us, stretching from one side of the river to the other. As I looked, a couple of grilse leaped into the face of it, four-foot tries, and then a bigger fish shot up, a 15-pounder, quivering all over. He almost made it. He fell short of the top by two feet.

It was a thrilling sight, the salmon busting up into the face of that tremendous fall of water, through it, head on, and into the rocks beyond, falling back, bruised and banged, and going up for another try. This was it, the greatest salmon pool in the world, and the salmon was the greatest fish. I squared away to cast.

Then Edgar almost scared me out of my wits.

"Can you hear them?" he whispered right in my ear, as he crouched in mid-canoe.

"Hear what?" I asked.

"Shh!" he said. "The rocks! They're tumbling! Hear them!"

I listened, and sure enough, faintly, I could hear a rumbling, like rocks rolling against one another, down there, deep.

"When the rocks tumble," said Edgar, "That's when the salmon hit. The big ones."

"Look out," I said. "I'm casting."

I dropped a size 8, low-water Green Highlander 15 feet out to the right. A six-pound grilse met it before it had floated a foot. I landed him. Ten minutes later I took a four-pounder. Then I had a terrific fight with a ten-pound fish that jumped and threw the hook.

Suddenly, "Look!" said Edgar.

I had seen it, too. In a slick spot between two rocks, right where the water poured over the tail of the pool, a great salmon came up in a head and tail rise. He looked as long as a canoe paddle. This was the one the tumbling rocks had promised.

I dropped the fly six feet above where he had showed, just in case he had moved upstream when he rose. Then I lengthened each successive cast a foot. Wherever he was, I wanted that fly to cover him, and in the right way. I mended the line, let the fly down with the tip of the rod guiding the floating line. I was using the greased line method of salmon fishing, the way of showing the fly broadside to the salmon, so he'd take on the first rise. I kept a slack line so I wouldn't get excited and strike too soon. I knew that if he took and I gave slack, the current would belly the line downstream and pull the fly into the corner of his mouth.

Then I made the cast that would go over the spot where he had showed. I held my breath. He took, and I was into him. From a standing start, that fish went to 40 miles per hour. He ran 20 feet and then I saw the line coming up and I got ready for the jump. He broke through in a terrific leap, five feet up, four feet forward. He looked like the butt end of a 20-year-old birch tree.

"Forty pounds!" I yelled.

"He's a dreadful fish!" said Edgar. "Play him easy."

I was too busy to answer. That fish rushed past us, headed for the falls. I turned with him and the blast of the east wind blowing off those icebergs slammed into my face, but I was too excited to feel the cold.

The salmon rushed on, reel click going in high.

"He's going to jump the falls!" shouted Edgar. "Watch him!"

I was watching him, all right, but I could no more have stopped that run than held back a steamroller with a willow twig.

He came out, straight up into the face of the falls for nine feet, hung there for a second, then fell back into the water. Seconds later he was jumping ten feet below us. I reeled fast, trying for a tight line, but he was on his way back to the falls again.

Once more the blast of cold air hit my face, and then he came out for five feet this time, as if just taking a look-see, and then veered off to the right.

"He's making for the fish ladder," said Edgar.

That salmon was heading for the right side of the falls, where steps had been blasted out a couple of years before. He made a jump up into it, then we saw his back as he hopped over the second step.

"Look at him!" I yelled. "Look at him! He's going home!"

"Home is right," said Edgar, seconds later, as the fly shot back in our faces.

I reeled in the vacant line and leader, wiped the spray from my face, and a few tears, and tested the 6-pound test tippet for fraying. It was in bad shape, so I tied on another and put on a size 8, low-water Green Highlander.

I cast it out.

A grilse hit it hard, bounced out and threw the fly a mile. It was 9:45 and almost dark. I reeled in.

"Let's go, Edgar." I said. "Let's go in and boil up."

Because, right then, no other salmon would do.

Twenty years from now, I thought, as we ran the rapids home-ward, I'll be sitting by a campfire and saying: "That time on the Humber was terrific. The wind was blowing from the east, off the icebergs. And a mammoth salmon hit my Green Highlander and ran the Great Falls."

"It was a shame to lose him," said Edgar as we toiled up the hill to camp.

That night I dreamed about a big, husky salmon that swam up to me, touched me on the shoulder with a fin, and said, "Thanks for letting me go."

"Letting you go!" I said back to the 40-pounder. "You had me groggy from the start. All I did was hang on."

"Well, anyway," said the salmon, "I've thanked you."

And the last I saw of him was his great, silvery body, like the butt end of a thirty-year-old birch tree, jumping over the falls with yards to spare.

Add a Little Salt

When a brook trout goes to sea, he returns to his native waters fat and sassy and full of fight. The scene is laid in Newfoundland.

My guide, Edgar Eastman, and I walked down to the sea. We passed several of the best salmon pools on the Serpentine River without stopping. We'd heard that the sea-run brook trout were bunched at the mouth of the river waiting for high water to start their upstream run. And I wanted to catch one of those brookies in the salt.

We reached the tidewater pool and went on down to where the river emptied into the ocean through high-piled gravel bars, a narrow outlet that a good broad-jumper could cover in one hop. The sea was calm, and evidently the tide was making in because where the river flowed out, foot-high waves piled up as the two currents bucked each other. If there were any hungry brookies around, that was where they would be.

I tied a red and white bucktail to my 4-pound test tippet, a good-sized fly dressed on a No. 4 hook, and I edged in to about 40 feet from the moving water and made my first cast into the sea for a brook trout. It dropped two feet the other side of the current and

I brought it back in slow, foot-long jerks, working the rod tip to give the fly action.

Then there was a swirl at the fly, and as I tensed I saw a flash of silver. I felt a thudding shock that numbed my fingers on the rod grip; my left hand, stripping line, was yanked forward. Then the rod dipped down almost to the water and the reel started clicking, slowly, then faster, then a steady stream.

"I've got him!" I yelled.

"You bet," said Edgar.

That fish ran 60 feet in six seconds, a dizzy dash down the river current toward the open sea. Then he veered to the left, across current, and over there he got broadside to me and sat back and pulled. I pulled too, but I couldn't budge him. He began to shake his head so hard that I had to give him slack by dropping the rod tip. Then I raised it again, gingerly, and he was still there. He was moving up-current now, toward the river mouth, slowly, so that I could reel line in and still have it tight. But he didn't like fighting that current, so he turned and waltzed down the shoreline.

"How big do you think he is?" I asked Edgar.

"Maybe four pounds," he said. "A nice sea trout."

"It can't be a brookie," I said. "They don't fight as hard as this fish. Whatever he is, he's seven or eight pounds."

I got him turned at last and kept him coming. But he still had other tricks. He started rolling in the leader, and that was tough to handle, but eventually it was that very trick that did him in because he got the leader twisted around his gills so that he couldn't fight.

He was a beautiful fish, a brookie for sure, and about four pounds, just as Edgar had said. But in this sea-going version, the characteristic bright reds and oranges of the brookie were overlaid with a skim of silver so that the markings hardly showed.

"A lot more silver than I expected," I said.

"It takes about a month in the fresh water, and then you can't tell whether or not he's ever been to sea," said Edgar. "By that time, he's as bright as a maple leaf."

These sea-run fish are the eastern brook trout, *Salvelinus fonti-nalis,* the native of the east, the same fish that is called speckled trout, squaretail, and brook trout on the mainland. The mud trout of New-foundland is the same fish, too, deriving its uncomplimentary name from its habit of lying over mud in ponds and backwaters of rivers.

Their original habitat was the eastern seaboard of the United States from Georgia through Canada, and as far west as Manitoba and Michigan, but free-handed stocking has taken them to many parts of the world. In 1947, while fishing the tidewater pool of an unnamed river along the Inland Passage of Alaska, I hooked into one of these transposed easterners far from his home grounds, but as fat and saucy as they come. Here, too, as in coastal steams from New England to Newfoundland, some of the brook trout leave the rivers and go to sea, and whenever they do so, they give an account of themselves on their return that is considerably better than the fight made by those of the species that stay in their native fresh water.

The first brook trout to stick his nose into the sea must have been a venturesome fish. Probably pickings were lean that year and he was hungry. The river was almost devoid of all the things he had formerly lived and grown fat upon. The nymphs he used to dig out of the pebbles and stones on the bottom, and the naturals he took from the surface, and the minnows he used to chase and catch in the shallows—all were few and far between. So he had worked his way down to the tidewater pool, and found better for-age. But he didn't like the feel of the salt on his gill rakers, so he quickly beat it back to the pure water of the pool above. But hunger got the better of him and he returned to the tidewater pool again, and for a week he kept nosing into the salt, getting used to it, finding more food than he had ever seen.

Several times he retreated to the pool above, to taste again the sweet water there. But each time that hunger drove him down he became more accustomed to the sea water and began to swim fur-ther out in the bay. And one day, he moved along with the outgoing tide and slipped down the shore until he was ten miles away from the river mouth, a full-fledged sailor, quite at home in the salty seas, feeding on smelt and capelin, growing fat and strong.

It was hunger that took him down to the sea in the first place, but an even more compelling urge eventually brought him back. A month and a half after he first went into the ocean, something stirred in him, insistently, the urge to spawn. And he started back to the river where he was born.

Again he tarried at the tidewater pool, going in and out of the tide, this time getting used to the fresh water. Then, with a goodly high tide he made the bore into the river and headed up. He was "fontinalis," a fish of the springs, and that was what he was looking for, springs or seepage that would maintain a constant temperature as protection for the eggs that would be deposited on the gravel beds away up in the smaller parts of the river.

And the continuance of his species attended to, he would winter over, and with the spring, with the breakup of the ice, he would head down again and out to sea in quest of the great abundance of food there.

In the old days, Newfoundlanders used to take trout by the barrel during the winter season, and one old timer told me that the fish were so hungry during this period that they would take any bait from a piece of red flannel on up.

"But rabbit's tongue was best," he stated. "It was red and tough and we could catch half a dozen on one tongue."

To protect the fish during their winter stay in the ponds, lakes, and rivers, and during their run to the sea in the early spring, it is now legal to take sea run trout from May 24th to September 15th only. The daily limit is 24 fish, except in the Serpentine, Fox Island, Castors, and Western Brook, where due to the enormous size of the fish, the legal creel limit is 8 sea-run brookies per day.

The runs that really provide the fishing come into the rivers in late July and early August, and the fish come in successive waves, usually in schools of about the same weight, ranging from little fellows five and six inches long, to giants of the species, some of them reaching twelve pounds. Fish eight and nine inches long carry roe or milt and are capable of reproducing their kind.

Once at South Brook, with Fisheries Warden Art Butts, I watched six-inch brookies leap up the face of a two-foot high falls.

"They're full of spawn, too," said Art. "Even those tiny fish. They're on the way up just like the big fellows."

I cast and caught one of them, just to look at him. A sheen of silver overlay the brookie markings, proof that he had been to sea. He was firm and fat and strong, as befitted a little fish that was performing an amazing journey, ten miles or more upstream through rapids and over falls. I put him back, knowing that with good luck, one day this little beauty might give someone a sporting battle, when he was three or four pounds, or more.

While the west coast rivers of Newfoundland have the reputation of holding the largest sea-run brook trout, at South Brook and around Gambo anglers bring in an occasional big one as well as the two pounders which are general there. Rocky Schulstad of Grand Falls took a 5¼-pounder at South Brook last summer, and several of that size were brought in at Gambo, as well as one 11-pound fish.

Rocky ties a number of flies especially for sea-runs, and one in particular is worth describing. I call it the "Traverse Brook Sea Trout Fly" because that's where I first saw Rocky using it. The dressing is as follows:

Tail—yellow, golden pheasant
Tag—silver oval tinsel
Hackle—red, palmered along length of body
Body—claret floss
Wing—caribou hair (light)
Head—black

Generally speaking, in the early season the red-bodied flies or streamers, dressed on large hooks, sizes 4, 6, and 8, pay off. Then in the late summer small flies dressed on size 10 and 12 hooks are in order and even as small a fly as a size 16 will do business. Practically any of the trout patterns used in United States and Canadian waters will take sea run brookies. The Silver Doctor, Parmachene Belle, Cow Dung, Black Zulu, Terra Nova (silver body), Jenny Lind, Dark Montreal, Bumble Bee, Marlodge, Royal Coachman, Gray Hackle, Brown Hackle, Professor and Quill Gordon, in sizes 10, 12 and 14, all produce, as do the various streamers and bucktails that are in common usage for the stay-put members of the brookie family.

The red and white, black and white, all black and all white bucktails are sure fire, and the muddler is away up in front as a strike bringer. The black, white, and yellow marabous are excellent flies, and the Grey Ghost and Royal Coachman streamers all produce plenty of strikes.

The best dry flies for Newfoundland sea runs are the Royal, the Brown, the Gray and the Grizzly Wulff patterns, and the hard-to-beat old reliables, the Gray Hackle and the Brown Hackle. The bivisibles do well, with the Black and the Brown taking top billing, as also do the hair-bodied dry flies in grey, grizzly, and black. Dry flies should be dressed on size 12 to 8 hooks.

The ideal fly rod for sea-run brookies in rivers is an 8-footer, weighing 4 to 4½ ounces, and fitted with an HDH nylon fly line and a 14-foot leader tapered down from a 25-pound test top section to a 3-pound test tippet. Such tapering makes the leader easier to cast and prevents the line from slapping down near the fish. In this sea run fishing, as in all trout fishing, a finer leader and lighter presentation will bring more strikes.

The reel should be large enough to hold 100 yards of 10- or 12-pound test nylon squidding line for backing, as well as the fly line. You never know when you might tie into a big one and have to follow him downstream; or, fishing for brookies where you do, you might hang a salmon at any time.

For bigger water, and for the salt, and along the beaches, an 8½-foot fly rod, weighing 4½ to 5 ounces, with a matching HCH fly line is needed. The same backing mentioned above will serve on this outfit, but in the heavier water it is advisable to end the leader with a 4-pound test tippet.

The last time I was in Newfoundland, as I was sitting at the lunch counter in the airlines terminal, a tall young fellow in Pan American World Airways uniform came up and introduced himself.

"I'm Cal Osmond," he said. "What are you here for? Atlantic salmon, I suppose."

"Partly," I said. "But also sea-run brookies. Ever fish for them?"

"Do I! I was brought up on them."

Cal remembers catching them when he was a kid, at Bluff Head near Gambo, about five miles from Traverse Brook. And he and a lot of fellow members of the Gander Rod and Gun Club know the answers still, on the salt water brookies.

"This summer I went back there, and it was just like old days," he said. They still hit best on high tide and at dusk. I caught them from half a pound up to 3½ pounds."

At Bulley's Cove, about eight miles from Point Leamington River, near Botwood, he found sea trout that walloped his streamers and fought like they had been training for just that occasion. Those two-pounders didn't know when to quit. And at Campbelltown Estuary, Cal discovered the top spot in a summer of good fishing. There, he waded out into the salt and tied on a Norsklure, a famous Norwegian salmon fly that he had found to be sure death to Newfoundland brookies—a fine representation of the capelin, a six-inch-long, smelt-like bait fish found in the shallows around the island. It has tandem hooks, the front a number 2 and the one at the rear a number 10, and it is dressed with olive green wings and a silver body. In the water it looks alive.

That was a dish-calm day and Cal could see fish working, see the waves they made as they swam slowly along just under the surface. He dropped his first cast three feet in front of a "wave" and started a series of foot-long strips. The wave speeded up and hit the fly with a thump.

That trout knew all the tricks and tried them all, but Cal beat him down and brought him in, a fine three-pounder. That afternoon he landed nine that went from 2½ to 3½ pounds, all on that Norsklure that looked so much like a capelin. The two fish he kept to eat each had a single capelin in the stomach.

Undoubtedly the capelin is the mainstay of both the sea-run trout and the salmon in these waters, and "Capelin For Sale" signs that appear in front of every Newfoundland grocery store are as good a forecast as any that the sea runs are in the bays. At Hall's Bay I saw the surface riffled by thousands of capelin coming to the shallows to spawn. They swam in circles, working, spawning and dying. We could see the dead ones lying belly up on the bottom while countless others swam over them to deposit their milt and roe and so join the silent ones in the bottom. Local people were dipping them up in buckets, to be fried and eaten like smelts.

But while it's top fun to catch brookies in the bays and estuaries, and at the mouths of the rivers, there's something about moving water and the woods around that belongs to brook trout. And when you find them there, in the river where they belong, but strong and hale and just returned from a trip to the sea, that's an extra dividend.

The year after I had fished the mouth of the Serpentine with Edgar Eastman, I went back there again with Jim Young of Flat Bay doing the guiding. This is one of the rivers where the runs come in wave after wave, 2-, 3-, and 4-pounders, and some that go 5 and 6—not many, but enough to provide great angling—and in back of all these assorted sizes come the chiefs of the clan, great 10- and 12-pounders, huge slabs of fish-flesh, almost impossible to believe.

When we reached the Dump Pool on the first morning, I had hardly gotten my rod rigged up before I heard a shout from Jim.

"Quick!" he shouted. "Look at this."

He pointed to a great dark spot showing on the bottom. It extended half way across the pool and well down towards the tail.

"Those are big sea trout," he said. "Thousands of them."

I took off the low-water Jock Scott I had just tied on my leader and got out a size 10 Royal Wulff.

"I'm going below them," I said, "and show them this dry. If they are going to hit at all, they should hit this."

We walked well back from the pool, and eased in below. I dropped the fly on the outer edge of the dark spot and a fish rocketed up and took just like that.

He flipped over and dove right into the middle of those closely-packed sea run brook trout and a great hole appeared for a moment, then closed in again. My fish was already across the pool, taking line. Then he did a complete circle of the pool as if it was a race-track, a sea-strong trout with the bit in his teeth. Then, well below me, he surfaced and began shaking his head. I gave him slack and ran down his way because I knew the three pound test tippet couldn't take too much of that in such fast water. At last I got a tight line on him again and then when I put the pressure on, he began to tire. When we finally netted him, he was a nice three pounds.

We went back to the pool and on my third cast another trout roared up and grabbed the fly; and he, too, dashed into that bunch on the bottom. They scattered, and this time stayed scattered. They didn't like being the target for those dive bombers.

When I landed that one, it was a 3-pounder, too. "Probably a school of 3-pound fish," I said.

"There could be some bigger ones there, too," Jim told me.

A little later as I was about to pick up the fly, a big, wide mouth clamped down on it. I didn't have time to set the hook—he took so fast—and before I knew it he was half-way up the pool and flying.

"That one's seven pounds!" shouted Jim.

"The big one you said could be there," I grinned.

Then that racing trout turned on a dime and came back our way. And somewhere along the line the hook dropped out of his mouth. He didn't even show to wave goodbye.

For consolation, I took five more from that pool, all three pounds, and one that hit three and a half. That kind of fishing makes you forget losing a seven pounder—almost.

Northern Lights Fish

Seeking the grayling, the fish with an angel's wing for a dorsal, from the Yukon to the mountain lakes and streams of Montana.

"I wonder how they got such a beautiful dorsal?" said my friend Gene Letourneau. He was holding up an Arctic grayling that he had just pulled from the Yukon River.

"That's easy," I answered. "Thousands of years ago the first gray-ling was swimming in primeval darkness. Suddenly a great light shone in the skies, blazed and then faded, then burst out again in many colors. The grayling rose to the surface for a better look, and his dorsal fin stuck out. The northern lights looked down at that drab bit of fish flesh. A pity, they said. Such a dull-looking fish. Let's light him up. And like a flash they swept down and painted that grayish-hued fish with their own colors."

"And the grayling thanked the northern lights," grinned Gene, "and swam away to take a dry fly."

The grayling is the fly-takingest fish of them all. He goes for flies as a Scandinavian goes for coffee. All you need to do to catch one is put a fly on the end of your leader tippet and cast thirty feet

215

out into any of the waters in which he lives. Maybe it's the short feeding season in the cold northern water which is his natural habitat. Perhaps it's because the limited amount of food other than flies and nymphs in this water has conditioned him to flies. Or maybe he just prefers flies over other catchable items, the way a kid prefers candy. Whatever it is that gives him his ravenous appetite, a grayling is always ready. He greets a fly like a long-lost relative.

My first encounter with the Arctic grayling took place within the city limits of Whitehorse in the Yukon Territory. Bill Ackerman, Jack Mahony and I, all from Miami, drove shiveringly out to the Lewes River, a branch of the Yukon, and stopped to fish in sight of the famous gold-rush town.

"What are grayling like?" we asked Sam McBride, local outdoor scribe, who was showing us around. "How do they act?"

"Like houseflies to flypaper," he grinned. "They hit often and get stuck."

"How big do they go?" asked Jack.

"Seldom over two pounds," Sam replied. "But in some spots here and in Alaska, too, they run as high as six pounds. The average right here will be about fourteen inches."

The river was a hundred feet across, and the pool that Sam had chosen for us was a good three hundred yards long, clear and slick as a mirror. Fish were dimpling all over it, sending out concentric circles. It seemed as if a gentle rain were falling, so numerous were those rises. I gave myself a shake. This was it—the dream of a lifetime, coming true.

On the advice of Sam, we had all tied on size 12 Black Gnat dry flies. Before I even got mine in the air I heard simultaneous shouts from my two fishing pals. They were both into fish. In the quick glance I shot their way I saw water splashing and the flash of Jack's fish as it jumped clear. Then I jerked my head back and started casting.

When my Black Gnat dropped, it didn't even have time to shake the water off its hackles before a grayling had it. I struck and was busy with a good fish. It darted around, jumped into the air, thrashed on top, ran my way, and finally slowed down enough to let me skid him into my landing net. He was *Thymallus signifer*, the Arctic grayling, largest and most colorful of the whole family. He was 16 or 17 inches long and his big dorsal stood up like a sail, three inches long and almost as high.

I marveled at the color. It was purple-tinged, with a jagged line of rose along the top edge, and overall were numerous dark-blue dots, all circled in pink rings. Beneath that, his body was cigar shaped, whitish, with black dots on either side along the shoulders, and the whole thing just faintly tinged with brown. He had unusually large eyes for his size and a small mouth that opened in a square O as I took out the hook. I held him up to my nose for a brief sniff of the thyme odor that gives them their scientific name, then popped him back into the water. We wanted grayling to eat that night, but this was my first and too pretty to kill. He gave a grateful flip of his tail and swam away.

My next cast got an immediate strike, and I missed. The force of the strike jerked the fly my way a couple of feet, and when it stopped another grayling was there to nab it. I missed again and then started to strip the line back for the next cast. As I raised the rod tip, still another fish socked that fly just as it was leaving the water, and I pulled that one clear out. But it fell back in again, free, and then, as I started to recover line again, I had still another hit, and this time fought it out with what proved to be a fine, fat, and able 14-incher.

After ten minutes of that kind of fishing, I took a quick look around to see that no one was watching to question my sanity. Then I took off the Black Gnat and tied on a Dark Montreal, wet, on a No.12 hook. I was trying to find a fly they wouldn't hit so hard!

But that one didn't do any better. It had hardly touched the water when one of those hungry grayling with the neon dorsals climbed aboard. They tore it into shreds. And no matter what I offered them, it was the same. Once in a while I would stop for a breather and look around. It was cold and still. I remembered some Robert W. Service: "And the icy mountains hemmed you in with a silence you most could hear."

It was like that now, still and quiet, with only the liquid voice of the water running over pebbles along the shore behind me. Although it was early September, the thermometer already read 19 above. Across the river I could see snow on the peaks above timberline. The water was icy and I was chilled to the bone. Only the gold and yellow and brown of the changing aspens, vivid splotches against the somber pines, fed some warmth to my eyes. The cottonwoods along the river were colored up, too, and between them the river ran deep, cold blue, shot with purple, and here and there the reflected gold of the aspens and cottonwoods. No wonder grayling liked to live here.

Then I heard voices and Jack and Bill were in back of me, waving and telling me to come ashore. Time to get back to the Whitehorse Inn, and that grayling dinner. It was tough to wade out and leave a pool full of rising fish, but my tingling legs and deadened toes told me I was ready to look up a roaring furnace. There would be more fishing tomorrow. Meanwhile we got warm enough to do a job on three plump grayling apiece and found they were just about what many people claim—easily one of the best eating of all the freshwater fish.

During that brief Alaska-Yukon trip, anglers in our party caught plenty of grayling almost everywhere they fished. In those northern waters they cover a wide range, occurring in every major drainage system north of the Gulf of Alaska. They are found in British Columbia, the Yukon Territory, are common in most of the Alaska Peninsula and in the Bristol Bay and the Kuskokim watersheds. They are in all the freshwater clear streams along the Arctic Coast from the mouth of the Yukon to Demarcation Point. They thrive in the tributaries of the Yukon and cause angler traffic jams in the big river itself. They do well in the Tanana, Koyukuk, and the Kantishna. Wherever they are found, they seek the crystal-clear streams and shun those that run milky with glacial silt.

In those cold northern waters they are in a semi-dormant condition for a period of at least five months, while snow and ice close them in, not eating, just putting in time till the spring breakup. When ice-out occurs, they go on a feeding spree which makes you wonder where they pack it all, and which, in short order turns them into a little fish with a big paunch.

During the same trip, Gene Letourneau and I had a field day with better than average grayling at Otter River Falls. Those we had caught in the Yukon and its tributaries had averaged about 14 inches, but up here, 125 miles north of Whitehorse and ten miles off to the east from the Alcan Highway, they went several inches better, although our biggest grayling from each river measured the same, 18 inches.

Viv Gray of Cleveland, and Ham Brown of Baltimore were fishing with us, too, and having plenty of sport, and that day Ham landed what proved to be the prize rainbow of the trip. But we were so busy with grayling that we could hardly take time out to watch the fight, even though that rainbow did tricks that made his scales fly through the air. We had no time for anything but those hard-hitting fish with the angel's wing for a dorsal. This was the first time we had been able to get into them, and it might be the last.

But that shows how wrong you can be. It was only a year later that I waded out into a Montana stream in search of *Thymallus signifer tricolor,* the Montana grayling. Originally grayling were found in both Michigan and Montana as well as the Yukon and Alaska areas. Because of their willingness to swat a fly, plus fishing pressure and the gradual overall warming of the rivers there, the Michigan grayling is now extinct. The Montana species was native only in the Missouri River above Great Falls, but now has been transplanted to many other localities in the state, notably in some Yellowstone Park waters, the Big Hole River in southwestern Montana, and the Belly River in Glacier Park. They are numerous in high mountain lakes and in other streams, too, where cold water prevails year found, yet where, for the two-week season required for the eggs to hatch, the water temperature goes above 50 degrees. Planted in such places by the Montana Department of Fish and Game, they are spawning naturally and doing well. But if left alone, unaided by creel limits and seasons, and where fishermen in numbers could get to them, they would be caught out in a hurry.

The same thing holds true in other states, such as Wyoming, to which Montana grayling have been introduced. Because of their willingness to take a fly, only three things can assure their continuance in goodly numbers: rigid supervision by the state fish and game departments, the shortness of the season during which anglers can fish for them, and the remoteness of the waters in which they thrive.

The newcomer to grayling waters will have no trouble in identifying his catch. The Montana grayling, while not as vividly colored as the Arctic member of the family, has the same bluish head with a bronze tint over it, and his back is purple and blue blending into silvery sides, with black-dotted shoulders. So far he might possibly be confused with the Rocky Mountain whitefish that occurs in many of the same streams, but when you reach the dorsal fin, all confusion ends. The grayling fin stands up purple and green, edged with that eighth of an inch of jagged rose, and is lined with purple and blue dots, some showing faint circles of green and yellow. They do not grow as large as the more northern grayling, ranging mostly around eight and nine inches, with an occasional one that reaches fourteen inches.

The upper waters of the Big Hole River, between Wisdom and Jackson, are literally teeming with these little fish with the big fin. On my first trip there John Krause of Jackson, who knows the surrounding meadows like his own back yard, directed us across fields and around irrigation ditches till we were completely lost. But John, with an uncanny eye for landmarks, knew where we were.

"You want grayling," he said. "Well, I'll take you where I know you'll get grayling. Plenty of them."

The Big Hole ran for miles through those great meadows, meandering along with riffles and four-or-five-foot-deep pools, slipping past banks where over-hanging bushes provided ideal cover for fish. It wasn't more than fifty feet across anywhere, a far different river than down lower where I had fished it for brownies and rainbows.

The first pool we chose was slick and clear, and fish were rising all over it. Here and there we saw a snout stick up as a fish took a natural. Bill Browning, who was with me, wanted pictures for a movie he was working on, and if ever there was a natural spot where you could be sure of photogenic, real-acting fish, this was it. While Bill set up his camera I edged in at the bottom of the 100-foot pool. I made a false cast and dropped the fly about four feet above where I had seen a rise. The float had hardly started when the water opened up and two six-inch fish jumped out, one on either side of the fly, collided in mid-air and fell back in.

"Shucks!" said Bill from the bank. "I wasn't quite ready."

"Well, I can't promise you that again," I said. "Even with grayling."

I turned back to my fishing just in time to see a fish take my still-floating fly, a size 16 Black Gnat. I set the hook and the rod tip stayed down. This was no 6-incher. This was a heavy fish with lots of gumption. He slashed away to the right and then came out in an end-over-end jump. It was a grayling about 14 inches long, and his sail was flapping in the breeze. He went away so fast and strong that I had to give him line. Again he jumped, and then went deep and lay there in the current, trying to rest up a bit. But I hauled back on the rod and pulled him off his couch, and after a couple more half-hearted tries at jumping, he gave in. I skidded him into the landing net, took the hook out and held him up for the camera, then put him back.

"I think I got him on the jump, with that fin up," said Bill. "That sure is a beautiful fin. I wonder what its purpose is."

"Probably uses it to swim with," I suggested. "But more likely, from its coloration I'd be inclined to think it might be a nuptial thing—an attraction for the other sex. It probably becomes brighter just before and during the spring spawning season."

"They sure fade fast when the fish dies," Bill observed. "But I've noticed something I've never known to be true of any other fish. Even when a grayling is dead and has faded, if you put him back in the water for a minute or two, all that vivid color flares up again."

Fish were so thick in that pool that in a short time Bill had all the pictures he needed. "Now I'll fish," he said, stowing the camera.

"Let's fish together," I suggested. "Two strikes and out."

"Good enough," he agreed.

We worked slowly upstream, fishing the same pools, taking turns. Bill started and caught four fish before he missed two strikes in a row. It was my turn. I missed two strikes in a hurry and dropped back to make way for the other team. Bill took three fish this time, then missed a couple of fish.

I held up a size 18 Light Cahill I had just tied on. "I won't miss so many strikes now. That size 12 hook I was using is a bit too big for these small fish. This fly should hook them better," I added as I shot it out over the pool.

It worked, too, I caught three fish, then missed two strikes. Bill caught five more. I caught four in a row.

"This is fun," I finally declared. "But I'm going to put on a size 10 fly and try for a big fish."

"Me too," said Bill. "We'll change the rules. We'll take turns until we catch a good fish, and then it's the other fellow's pool."

I made several casts, and each time small swirls bubbled under the big fly. One larger fish knocked it an inch into the air. I threw the next cast in where the water ran deep-looking against the far bank and watched it ride the current, just a couple of inches out. I had a hit and knew it was the big one I was looking for. I struck hard, set the hook and yanked a 5-inch grayling out of the water. He literally flew our way, missed Bill by an inch and fell in the pool in back of us.

"You should be ashamed," said Bill. "Manhandling a little fish like that."

"I thought it was at least a five-pounder when it hit," I grumbled.

Once more the fly started on its journey and once more a fish came up and swallowed it. I struck with a gentle, uplifting motion of the rod this time and was into another nice fish. He was a grayling, and he bounced out obligingly and gave me a look at the whole fourteen inches of him, then headed for a hole under the bank. But I held on, and the rod tip absorbed his rush, pulled him back. I played him for another four or five minutes before I brought him to net.

This was certainly a great spot for grayling. Farther down the Big Hole the previous year I had run into a few of them scattered among the big browns and rainbows, but this was their home ground. Every cast brought a strike. Occasionally it would be an eastern brook, up to a pound, and now and again a rainbow, but basically this was grayling water. They were five to one over other fish in that part of the stream.

That seems to be the way in most waters where they do thrive. At the famous fishing town of Dubois, Wyoming, I asked Duane Redman if there were any grayling within reach.

"Lake of the Woods is full of them," he said. "It's a long, tough trip, so be ready early."

The lake was high up in the mountains, so high that it was tough going even for a jeep. We went up and up, over precipitous slopes that would daunt a chimney sweep, over rivulets and rivers and snow banks and mountain divides. Duane took that mountain-goat-on-wheels through some places that would have scared the pants off a space cadet. But although we couldn't walk for a few minutes after dismounting, we finally did make it, pumped up the rubber boat we had brought, and shoved out into the lake.

The surface was dimpled with rising fish, and those grayling acted just like grayling should. They climbed aboard the familiar Black Gnats as fast as we could drop them on the water. We caught fish steadily for an hour, nice fat grayling running between nine and fourteen inches. They were full of pep and as willing as anyone could wish. Then around the middle of the morning they suddenly laid off. We went ashore, ate and rested up before starting out again to see if we could waken those drowsy fish. For half an hour we had poor luck. But suddenly, as if someone had rung a bell, the surface broke into a thousand dimples. The fish were up. A grayling just can't stay down for long. We took them on Light Cahills, size 16. We took them on an Adams, size 14, and even caught some on a Gray Hackle, size 20. We tried nymphs and they worked, too. We used ants and they were good. Those wild-eyed bozos hit everything we showed them.

While grayling, both the Arctic and the Montana varieties, will take almost anything you show them, when they go down during the midday heat, or when the barometer is off, or when fishing pressure has scared them from the surface, it takes a bit of figuring to decide what type of fly to use. Then there are certain flies that pay off in the long run. Over the years, the black flies have proved best, including the Black Gnat, the Black Flying Ant, the Black Hackle, and even a Black Bivisible have been high up on the list of strike bringers. They seem to prefer dark colored nymphs, too, although the Gray Nymph is always good, and the yellow one frequently. Beetles in black and brown finishes do well. When those lusty grayling are in the mood for blondes, the Light Cahill and the Brown Hackle and Royal Coachman will do the job.

All the flies should be tied on hook sizes 18 to 12 because, despite the avidness of its strike, the grayling has a small mouth and is difficult to hook. With the small flies, I like a light outfit, a 7½-foot rod that weighs 3 to 3½ ounces or an 8-foot rod weighing up to four ounces. The line should match the rod—an HEH for the smaller one, and an HDH for the 8-footer. Leaders should be nine feet long and tapered to a 4X terminal point.

This past summer I fished the grayling waters near Jackson again, with Howard Cox of Cincinnati.

"I've never seen a grayling," Howard told me as we put our rods together. "Do you think I'll get one?"

"Well," I said, "You know how fish are. Sometimes they just won't hit." "But," I hastened to add, "if you don't catch one here, and right away, I won't wet a line all day."

We walked to the first pool.

"I'll stay with you till you catch your first one," I said. "Then I'm going fishing too."

The surface was covered with dimples, and Howard took a ten-inch grayling on his first cast. I departed on the run for the next pool.

Later in the day we met up again. I stood and watched Howard. He was laying out a beautiful line, dropping the fly on a dime, having strike after strike. Yet, as I watched, seven fish struck, made fights of varying lengths, threw the hook, and got off. He wasn't performing the way he had when I left him.

"What's the trouble?" I asked, wading out beside him. "How come so many get away?"

Howard turned a big wide grin on me and held up his fly. "I cut the barb off," he said. "I'm catching so many and I'm afraid of hurting them."

"Me, too," I said, holding up mine.

We kept just enough for dinner, took them to the Diamond Bar Inn and had the cook fry them for us. After we had laid down our knives and forks, we leaned back, as relaxed and happy as it's possible for a fisherman to be when not in a trout stream.

"Where else ——" began Howard.

I was ready for him.

"There's a land where the mountains are nameless and the rivers all run God knows where ——"

"The Yukon, eh?" mused Howard. "You've been there?"

"Yep," I said. "And do you remember? 'And I want to go back and I will.'"

Montana

Montana rates as one of the top fishing states of this western area. The standard fish taken in Montana waters are brown, rainbow and cutthroat trout, and Rocky Mountain whitefish. In some of the higher lakes golden trout have been stocked and in certain lakes and rivers you may also find eastern brook trout and grayling. In a few of the lakes silver salmon have been introduced, while in the warmer waters of the more shallow lakes found in the northern part of the state, and above some of the man-made dams, besides the trouts there are walleyes, northern pike, largemouth black bass, sauger, and, on occasion, crappie.

Through the mountains, foothills, and valleys of middle and western Montana run many of the greatest fishing rivers of our country: The Yellowstone, Big Blackfoot, Bitterroot, Big Hole, Gallatin, Jefferson and Madison, the last three joining at Trident to form the mighty Missouri. In many of these steams the average trout will run more than a pound and in some as high as 2 pounds; 4-, 5-, and 6-pounders are taken each week from the Yellowstone and Madison Rivers and these, along with others in the state, produce an annual high quota of 10-, 12- and even 15-pound fish.

Montana is also loaded with smaller rivers and so great is their fishing potential that even these streams will yield a more than occasional 4-pounder.

Augmenting the fishing possibilities of the rivers are countless lakes. Such large bodies of water as Flathead Lake, Georgetown Lake, and Duck Lake turn up some tremendous fish, as well as producing in quantity. There are also innumerable smaller lakes, some mere mountain potholes, all of which produce trout of one kind or another, and some of which add bass, pike, walleyes, perch, and kokanee salmon.

With few exceptions the bigger and better waters in Montana are easy to reach. Good roads parallel the Yellowstone on either side of the river from Big Timber all the way down to Gardiner, which is the northern entrance to Yellowstone Park and Wyoming. You can drive for miles along the banks of the Madison. Main roads skirt the Missouri, the Gallatin and the Jefferson, around Three Forks. In the Missoula area, fine roads approach close to the Big Blackfoot, the Bitterroot, Clark Fork of the Columbia, Rock Creek and others. Good main highways and secondary routes traverse the state north and south, east and west, reaching into even remote areas. In many cases it is possible to fish right where you park your car alongside the river, while in others a short walk will put you in a good pool. In places where it is necessary to leave the main roads and walk or drive on private property, the angler should treat that property with the same care he would give his own, taking care not to damage fences or frighten cattle. He should close each gate behind him—or if he finds the gate open, leave it open. Most ranchers are willing to allow fishermen on their property when asked, and the exceptions are usually those who in the past have suffered damage at the hands of thoughtless visitors.

The more remote spots on the larger rivers can be reached by boat trip. Most float fishermen use big rubber life rafts, although oc-casionally skiffs are also used. The anglers cast as they float

downstream, working the shorelines, one man at the oars to control the boat, the others doing the casting. When a good pool is
reached, they beach the boat at the head of the pool, get out and
fish it thoroughly at their leisure, then get back into the boat and
go on downstream to new water. This is an effective way of fishing and enables the angler to reach water that is seldom fished,
but a float trip should not be attempted without a guide unless
you know the river thoroughly. Float guides are available at
almost any town near good floatable water throughout the state.
As the number of guides is limited, the angler who plans to be on
the river at the height of the season should make his reservation
early. Names of guides, outfitters and people able to advise on
floating in the various rivers will be listed with the detailed
descriptions of those rivers.

Montana is famous for the many pack trips available to high
mountain and wilderness areas, most of which offer exceptional
fishing. In some of the rivers and lakes far back in the high country you can take 1½- to 2-pound cutthroat on nearly every cast. In
others you'll find Dolly Vardens running from 5 to 15 pounds.
Again you may choose a lake where the dazzling-hued golden
trout has been stocked, or where your offerings bring up brilliant-
colored eastern brook trout. Back in this high country you will lis-
ten to a serenade at night as cautious coyotes, a half-mile from
your campfire, bark and yodel, hitting a note higher than high C,
telling in their own inimitable way how wonderful is nature among
the peaks.

The Western Montana Outfitters and Guides Association pub-
lishes a folder which lists the areas where such trips are available and
supplies the names of those outfitters who serve each area. The price
of such a back-country trip may run high, but it is well spent with
these men who have been packing into the hinterlands for many
years, are equipped with good horses, tents, bedding, and cooking
utensils, and who know the trails and the fishing thoroughly. They

are alert, competent men who see to the comfort, safety, and enjoyment of those they guide.

Because of the altitude, even summer nights will be chilly and the camper needs warm clothing. In really high areas the pack-trip season is also limited by snow to July, August, and early September.

Throughout Montana, summer temperatures rise into the 80's and very occasionally into the 90's, but late afternoons, early mornings, and evenings are cool and fishing clothes should be chosen accordingly. Blue jeans are a more or less standard uniform, with a cotton shirt for midsummer, wool for spring and fall, and a windbreaker or sweater for warmth when needed. For comfortable fishing, hip boots are necessary on the smaller streams and for lake-shore angling, while to fish the larger rivers effectively, chest-high waders are essential. In all cases felt soles or hobnails will provide added safety on slippery rocks.

Montana is basically a fly fisherman's country, but spinners and bait fishermen take their full share of fish. The 8½-foot rod is ideal for fly casting on Montana lakes and rivers when the angler expects to be throwing the larger, wind-resistant dry flies or streamers and bucktails. A GBF line matches this rod and the leader should be soft nylon, tapered down from a 30-pound-test to the smaller X classifications. The heavy butt section allows for better casting, acting like a continuation of the fly line, while the lighter tippet provides better fly placement and less visibility to the fish, an important consideration in most of Montana's crystal-clear mountain waters. A 9-foot rod, matched with a GAF line, is also used on the bigger waters; for the small rivers, and when using small flies, an 8-foot rod with HDH line will prove efficient.

While there are always special flies which have proven themselves on the individual streams or lakes, there are also certain basic patterns the angler can stock in his fly box and be prepared for almost any eventuality. A generous assortment for Montana fishing should include the following:

Dry flies
HOOK SIZES 8 TO 20—

Adams	*Black Gnat*
Light Cahill	*Royal Coachman*
Gray Hackle	*Yellow Body*
Light Hendrickson	*Hendrickson*
Iron Blue Dun	*Ginger Quill*
Mosquito	*Tup's Indispensable*
Gray Wulff	*Grizzly Wulff*
Sure Strike Special	*Red Trude*
Donnelly's Light Variant	*Red Variant*
Multi-Colored Varient	*Black Spider*
Ginger Spider	*Blue Dun spentwing*
Adams spentwin	*Light Cahill spentwing*

HOOK SIZES 18 AND 20—

Black Jassid	*Black Flying Ant*
Gray Midge hackle fly	*Blue Dun Spentwing*
Humpy	*Sofa Pillow*

Wet flies
HOOK SIZES 8 TO 16—

Gray Hackle	*Yellow Body*
Brown Hackle	*Coachman*
Royal Coachman	*Black Gnat*
Western Bee	*Cowdung*
Blue Dun	*Leadwing Coachman*
March Brown	*Professor*
Mosquito	*Ginger Quill*
Black Woolly Worm	*True Woolly Bear*
Black and Orange	

NYMPHS
SIZES 10, 12, 14, 16—

Gray Nymph	*Ed Burke*
Caddis Fly	*March Brown*
Phillips Black and Yellow	*Phillips Black and Orange*
Large Stone-Fly Nymph	*Ginger-Quill Nymph*
Yellow May	*Brown May*
Black May	*Cream Mayfly nymph*

ANTS
HOOK SIZES 8 TO 16—

Black	*Red*
White	

BEETLES
HOOK SIZES 10 TO 14—

Black	*Brown*
Bronze	*Green*

STREAMERS AND BUCKTAILS
HOOK SIZES 6 TO 12, LONG SHANK—

Black Ghost	*Gray Ghost*
Black-Nosed Dace	*Red and Yellow*
Red and White	*Black and White*
Muddler	*Mickey Finn*

BIG BUCKTAILS
HOOK SIZES 1 AND 1/0—

Platinum Blonde	*Honey Blonde*
Red and White	*Red and Yellow*
Muddler	

MARABOU

HOOK SIZES 6 TO 12—

Black	*Yellow*
Black and Yellow	*White*

Montana spin casters usually find that a 6½- or 7-foot rod and a good reel, either open or closed face, equipped with 200 yards of 4- or 6-pound-test monofilament line will see them through all their lake and stream fishing. The choice lure of the moment in any given location can readily be ascertained at the local tackle shop, and besides these the spinner should have a basic assortment of ⅛-, ¼-, and ½-ounce spoons and spinner-type lures such as the Mepps, size 0 through 4, with the 2's and 3's proving most popular; Thomas Cyclone; Goldfish in small sizes and also in the ½-ounce, which has proven very good for big trout; Flatfish; and Daredevil. The smaller lures are used in small rivers, the larger ones in the bigger rivers and in the lakes. Many anglers never think of using a ½-ounce lure for trout, considering them too large. But big trout like a mouthful, and many a lunker is brought up from the deeper pools on a ½-ounce lure.

Baits which are fine producers all over Montana are grasshoppers, dead or alive, the live being best; live sculpin minnows; red worms; shiner minnows; hellgrammites; stone-fly nymphs; and maggots. Eggs are illegal, as are live sucker minnows, though suckers with the heads cut off may be used. Bait fishermen should check the Montana Fish laws carefully, as minnows are not allowed in many waters and it is the angler's responsibility to know the law on the water he is fishing. Annual changes should be checked with the Montana Fish and Game Department, Helena, Montana.

Fishing is good in Montana throughout the open seasons listed by the Fish and Game Department. However, the bigger rivers are subject to a runoff of snow water from the mountains and this comes later than the easterner usually expects. For instance, the water in these rivers will be low in May before the snow has really started to melt in the high country, and there will be good fishing then. But when the snow begins to melt on the higher slopes the runoff swells the rivers and gives the water a dingy color. When the runoff really gets going there is often so much force to the current that it is almost impossible to fish. The smaller streams run off quickly, so there is usually good early-summer angling in these, but some of the larger rivers stay high until mid or late August.

For all Montana rivers, then, the best fishing period is from July 15th to October 15th. Throughout this period the weather is usually fine, and especially after August 15th, when the big rivers become low and clear, you can get in some fantastic fishing. Boiling it down still further, the most productive thirty days for big fish would be from September 20th to October 20th. As mentioned previously, fishing in the high mountain lakes is at its best earlier, as September and October will be on the cold side in the high altitudes.

Montana is big-game country and the angler may expect to see antelope in the drier sections, deer almost anywhere in ranch country and in the willows along the rivers. Bear and moose are common in many sections, particularly those adjacent to national forests and parks, and both animals should be treated with respect. The fisherman need have little fear, however, as long as he minds his own business, quietly goes his way and allows the animal to do the same. In a few wilderness areas there are grizzly bears, which are always potentially dangerous. The angler who is going into such areas must exercise extreme caution. Elk may also be encountered in the high country. They are very shy of human beings and rarely present any problem.

The Rocky Mountain rattlesnake, which is the least venomous of the rattlers and rarely causes death, is common in parts of Montana and anglers should always be on the alert, even though these snakes tend to keep to the high, dry land and only occasionally are seen along a river. In fifteen years of Montana fishing the writer has seen only four rattlers and these were all on dry, rocky terrain. Nevertheless, in any area where snakes may occur the outdoorsman should always watch where he steps.

LAKE FISHING IN MONTANA

There are a number of large lakes in Montana which have earned special attention from anglers. In recent years Duck Lake, just a few miles south of the Canadian border, near Glacier National Park, has blossomed forth as one of the really great rainbow lakes.

Fly fishermen, spinners and bait fishermen all have good luck at Duck Lake. Rainbows up to 12½ pounds have been taken by the casting methods, the spinners using large spoons, and the fly men leaning heavily to the tan Woolly Worm and the Duck Lake Special. Anglers fishing with bait favor nightcrawlers, barnyard worms, and maggots, often fastening the latter on the hook of a Woolly Worm fly and trolling it behind the boat. Spring is the best time at Duck Lake, March in particular producing many monsters in the 15-pound class.

Another large Montana lake which has a history of producing big fish is Georgetown Lake, near Anaconda. The majority of fish taken at Georgetown now will be cutthroats averaging about 1½ pounds, augmented by some eastern brook trout, Montana grayling, and silver salmon which have been stocked. But there are also some enormous rainbows that reach 14 and 15 pounds.

Georgetown produces well all summer, on standard flies, nymphs and spinning lures, as well as bait, but the peak of the fishing for the big rainbows is in late September and through October. One angler took a string of big rainbows there on spin tackle on November 11th—eight fish that weighed from 8½ to 14 pounds. For this late-season, big-lake angling, spin fishermen use fairly large spoons, while fly fishermen use big streamer flies on 2 or 1/0 hooks, and, when weather conditions warrant, big dry flies.

It should be remembered that this lake is at an altitude of 7,000 feet, and it can be very cold, so the angler should come prepared with plenty of warm clothing. Sometimes in the fall, when snow flurries blow across the lake, you will find the fishermen wearing gloves.

Flathead Lake, in the northern part of the state, is an immense body of water. Some years ago a "sea monster" was reported to have been seen there. The consensus of opinion is that the monster was a giant sturgeon, but who knows? Perhaps some lucky angler will discover what it was one of these days, but in the meantime the lake provides plenty of good sport with cutthroat, lake trout, and Dolly Varden trout and kokanee. This being one of the most scenic areas of the state, there are numerous motels along the way as well as the towns of Ronan, Polson, and a little further north at Kalispell.

In the drier parts of Montana, where the state slopes off eastward into wheatlands and dry grazing country, there are a number of dams for power and irrigation, which have created lakes. These are mostly on the Missouri River. Canyon Ferry Reservoir, near Helena, has good trout and bass fishing, and Fort Peck Reservoir, also an impoundment of the Missouri, has all types of fish, from trout to bass, walleyes, pike and sauger. There are some paddlefish there, too, but these are not classed as game fish and are taken mostly by snagging.

Smaller impounded lakes occur here and there throughout the state, ranging from the Tiber, Fresno, and Nelson. Reservoirs in the north, which offer such warm-water fish as bass, walleyes and sauger, include the Ruby Reservoir, Hebgen Lake, and Ennis or Meadow Lake. These last three, in the heart of the trout country, give up good-sized rainbow and brown trout. Most lake fishing is done from boats, but in places it is possible to work these waters from the shore, or even wade, with reasonable success.

There are innumerable mountain lakes in Montana, most of which offer good fishing. Dailey's Lake, thirty-five miles south of Livingston, turns out some good rainbows, although heavy fishing has reduced their numbers somewhat, as this lake can be reached by car. To reach most of the high mountain lakes, however, it is necessary either to make a major hike or use a jeep or pack horse and carry a rubber life raft in order to fish the lakes adequately. This kind of fishing is best arranged through a guide service; then you can take your pick of lakes with rainbows, cutthroat, eastern brook trout or goldens. Some of the favorite areas into which anglers like to make these pack trips are the Hell Roaring Country accessible from Livingston or Gardiner; the Red Lodge area, accessible from Silver Gate, Red Lodge, and Cooke City; the Ruby Mountains, accessible from Laurin, Alder, Sheridan, Twin Bridges or Virginia City; the Gallatins, which can be reached from Bozeman; the Madison Range, reached from Ennis or West Yellowstone; and the Glacier Park area, which will be covered separately in this chapter. Several lakes in which golden trout have been stocked can be reached by pack trip south of Bozeman.

The standard Montana spoons and baits are successful in these high lakes. Best-producing flies are the Phillips Black Ant, Black and Red Ant, both on #12 hooks; the big dry flies such as the Royal or Gray Wulff; Red Variant; a big Spider skipped across the surface; and the black and yellow, the brown, and the gray nymphs.

RIVER FISHING IN MONTANA

The Yellowstone River is the best known of all Montana Rivers. It runs from headwaters in Yellowstone Lake within Yellowstone National Park, "down north" for fifty-five miles to Livingston, where it makes a big bend westward and traverses the entire state to join the Missouri on the Montana-North Dakota border. The best fishing is in the first hundred miles outside the Park, where the river runs through rocky gorges and Yankee Jim Canyon, then through the luscious ranch country of Paradise Valley. The fishing extends for about fifty-five miles below Livingston, to Reed Point, where the water has warmed sufficiently that trout fade out and trash fish take over.

The Yellowstone has always been one of the great trout rivers of America. Indians once gathered along its banks to catch fish. Early mountain men, roaming its reaches, saw cutthroat as long as their legs. Pioneer settlers took them by the hundreds. Today's fish population is slightly different. The cutthroat is still common in the higher reaches, especially within the boundaries of Yellowstone Park, but the rainbow and the brown are the most common catches now in the balance of the river. Brown trout were first introduced in 1906 by the state authorities, and so well has the brown fared in the Yellowstone that in spite of the fact that there has been no further stocking of browns, this fish is today the most plentiful one in the river.

Shortly after the browns were first planted, the state began to stock fingerling rainbows and they still annually plant 500,000 of the species. They do reasonably well for a year and provide a lot of good sport. Some few survivors grow to bumper size, so that during the course of a season rainbows in the 4-, 5-, and 6-pound class are taken from the Yellowstone, with an occasional one even larger.

An interesting development resulting from the stocking of rainbows has been the appearance of the hybrid rainbow-cut-throat. Of course this fish cannot reproduce, but the hybrids grow to big weights and combine the best qualities of both ancestors. They fight harder than the cutthroat or the rainbow, jump more than the cutthroat, and seem to survive better than the rainbow. They have added immensely to the angling scene in the Yellow-stone river.

Because of a sudden descent of muddler or sculpin minnows into the Yellowstone from feeder streams, the size of the brown trout in the Yellowstone jumped. Almost every brown trout you open will have at least one of these minnows in it. As a result of this great natural potential, plus these developments, the Yellowstone offers probably the best trout fishing in America today.

Add to the trouts the Rocky Mountain whitefish and you have the fish population of the Yellowstone. The whitefish, which reaches top weights of about 4 pounds, is regarded as a nuisance by some anglers, but it is a great taker of flies, spinning lures, and bait and puts up a fair fight. It provides good sport on a dry fly as this fish has a very small mouth and is hard to hook. For this reason the whitefish is a good "practice fish" for the fly man. They taste excellent in the cold season, or when taken from really cold water, and are regarded as the finest fish for smoking.

The best fishing period on the Yellowstone is from April until the runoff of snow matter from the mountains discolors the water, usually in June; and again from late July until the weather becomes too cold for comfortable fishing or for the fish to feed well. The top period is usually from September 20th to October 20th.

In the fishable stretch there are many pools, rapids and flat runs, offering a great variety of fishing. Wading is good throughout and in some parts of the river float trips are feasible. Two major towns, Gardiner, the northern entrance to Yellowstone Park, and Livingston, fifty-five miles downstream, offer motels, laundries, restaurants, churches, grocery stores, garages and service stations. There are also a few dude ranches within reasonable access of the river.

Of the numerous tributaries of the Yellowstone, the Boulder is the best known. This river enters the Yellowstone on the east bank near Big Timber. The Boulder is formed by the confluence of the East and West Boulder, the latter a good fishing stream in itself. The Main Boulder has cutthroat, brown, and rainbow trout plus the ever prevalent Rocky Mountain whitefish. The average catch will be from 1 to 2 pounds but browns up to 7 pounds are taken annually. The West Boulder is a smaller stream but offers excellent angling for cutthroat, rainbows and an increasing number of browns. Both these rivers are at their best in the fall, during late September and October when the big browns move in to spawn. These fish are hungry and hit hard and fight like fiends.

The Shields River enters the Yellowstone about five miles downstream from Livingston and can be reached via U.S. 89 to Wilsall. The river holds some good brownies and also gives up the odd rainbow.

A number of other fishable streams are tributaries of the Yellowstone. Big Creek flows in on the west side a couple of miles south of Emigrant, upstream from Livingston. This is a fine mountain stream and holds cutthroat, rainbows, and some browns in the lower reaches. Eight Mile Creek, across the river from Emigrant, offers some good cutthroat fishing and, though it is a small stream, occasionally 2 pounders are taken. Well downstream, entering the Yellowstone near Columbus, the Stillwater River provides occasional good fishing for moderate-sized browns.

Along the Yellowstone and its tributaries, the stand-out fly patterns are: dry flies—Black, Gray and Grizzly Wulff in size 12; Light Cahill, size 14; dry Grasshopper, size 12. Wet flies—all black or orange and black Woolly Worm, size 12. Nymphs—gray, black-and-yellow, all brown, sizes 12 and 16; and the bigger Mossbacks, sizes 8 and 10. The best all-round fly is the Muddler fished an inch below the surface, although on the Yellowstone some anglers use a sinking line and reap a rich harvest along the bottom with both this and other flies. Aside from the Muddler, the Edson Tiger, Black Prince, Brown and Yellow Bucktail and Multiwing Streamers on 1/0 hooks are good for big trout, and in the fall the Platinum and Honey Blondes on 1/0 hooks should not be overlooked.

The Big Hole River rises in the Bitterroot Mountains and runs through the great "Valley of 10,000 Stacks" in western Montana, one of the greatest hay areas of the West. Early settlers referred to such wide valleys as "holes," hence the name Big Hole. Up in this meadow country in the top reaches of the river there are rainbows, some eastern brook trout, and a great many grayling. The stream is small, winding, and easily fished with hip boots. Since it travels mostly through ranch land, permission to fish should be requested from the ranchers, both out of respect for their privacy rights and because of the fact that when irrigation is in progress, your car may well get bogged down if water has been let in across the path on which you entered. In the lower part of this Upper Big Hole, the river parallels Highway 278 and there is good angling beside the road.

At Divide the Big Hole enters a canyon and from here down it is a much bigger river. The best fishing is from Divide all along the way for seventy miles to where the Big Hole joins the Jefferson River just below Twin Bridges. There are miles of wonderful pools, making this a particularly attractive river for fly fishermen, especially in the late summer.

Below Divide there are many brown trout, some few 5-pounders being taken, and lots in the 3- and 4-pound class. The largest brown ever to come from this river went 17 pounds. Rainbows are also stocked and provide good dry-fly fishing. The largest on record to date was a 7-pounder.

Whitefish are plentiful in the larger pools and some grayling have worked down from the Upper Big Hole, especially into the canyon, so the angler may expect to augment his catch with an occasional fish of this species.

Fly men fishing the Big Hole use all the standard Montana flies, but the Red Variant has proven particularly good as have large Spiders skipped across the surface. In the late fall, some tremendous fish are taken on big streamer flies, particularly the Muddler.

Spinners find smaller spin lures more successful in the low, crystal-clear water than larger spoons, which take fish in a murky stream. Best baits are grasshoppers, minnows, night crawlers, and smaller worms.

Anglers fishing the Big Hole can get up-to-the minute information about what's going on in other streams such as the Beaverhead, Ruby and various small creeks in the area, such as the Alder, which runs from Virginia City down into the Ruby.

The Jefferson River is formed about three miles below Twin Bridges by the confluence of the Big Hole and the Beaverhead Rivers, with the added waters of the Ruby, which enters the Beaverhead only a short distance higher. The Jefferson is a fairly large, shallow, and slow-moving river. It flows through the hay meadows and pastures past Whitehall to Cardwell and Jefferson Island, and on to LaHood, paralleling U.S. Highway 10 to Three Forks, and on to Trident where, along with the Madison and Gallatin, it pushes its waters into the Missouri.

There are few rainbows in the river and it holds multitudes of Rocky Mountain whitefish and even some trash fish such as carp, but the brown-trout fishing is better than average and at times the pools are alive with rising fish. When the Jefferson is low and clear, it is one of the best rivers for brown trout in Montana. The average catch will go a pound and a half, with 3- and 4-pounders taken every day. Some 5-pounders are caught annually, and the biggest known to come from the Jefferson weighed in at 12 pounds.

Many of the pools are long and flat, furnishing great evening angling for cruising trout. There is a good fly hatch throughout the summer, and when the water is low and clear it is a good fly-fishing river. The low and clear state can be expected in late August and throughout September, though even then it can be affected by storms in the Ruby Mountains, which cause mud to pour into the Ruby and then down into the Jefferson. This condition usually clears up a few days after the storm. All in all, the best fishing period on the river is from July 15 through October.

Jefferson browns will hit all the popular Montana dry flies, streamers and bucktails, the standard spoons, and bait of all kinds. The river may be fished from Twin Bridges, already described under the material on the Big Hole River; or the angler may stay at Whitehall, Three Forks, or at LaHood.

The Ruby River rises in southwestern Montana in the mountains of the same name, flows down into the Ruby Reservoir, then continues below the lake to run down through the meadows in back of Alder, Laurin, and Sheridan. A few miles north of Sheridan it joins the Beaverhead. This is a very good river, easily reached from Highway 287 between Ennis and Twin Bridges, and carries a good head of trout. There is good fishing in the river above the reservoir for brown and some rainbows, with fish from 14 to 16 inches being not unusual. This is high-meadow fishing with plenty of space for the angler, but the trout are easily frightened and even heavy footsteps along the bank will send them scurrying. The careful, quiet angler is the one who will come in with the true picture of what the Ruby has to offer.

There is some fishing from the lake shore and, below the reservoir, all the way along to the Beaverhead there is good fishing in the Ruby. In some of the hard-to-reach stretches you are apt to have a rise from a crooked-jawed old brownie that will scare you. Nine- and 10-pound browns have been taken from the Ruby.

The Beaverhead River is another meadow stream which holds some good fish, and stretches of this river are seldom fished. The Beaverhead is a continuation of the Red Rock Creek, which flows down from the Lima Reservoir in the extreme southwestern part of the state. Red Rock itself is a narrow, winding stream and holds plenty of brown trout in the 1- to 2-pound class. It traverses ranch land for almost its entire length and permission to fish must always be obtained. Near Dell it joins Sheep Creek and together with waters from several other small creeks forms the Beaverhead. The best stretch of the Beaverhead is from this juncture down to a short distance above Dillon, and there are many places from which you can reach the river along Highway 41 out of Dillon. Pound fish are the average and 4- and 5-pounders are taken each year. This river is often murky in color and is therefore regarded more as a bait-fishing stream. However, fly and spin casters take their full share of fish; in fact, in the late season flies produce extremely well.

The Madison River has long been recognized as one of the great trout streams of America. It rises in the Yellowstone National Park, entering Montana at the extreme southwest corner and flowing due north to Trident, where it joins the Gallatin and Jefferson to form the Missouri. Several dams on the Madison have changed its character somewhat so it does not have the crystal clarity of its original state, and the raising and lowering of the water level in these dams causes fluctuations in the fishing, but it is still one of the top rivers, turning up many huge rainbows and browns each season. Contrary to prognostications at the time, the earthquake of 1959, which caused part of the river bed to be dry for several weeks, did not harm the fishing.

The fish life of the Madison is composed of browns and rainbows. Although the river was originally renowned for its rainbow fishing, it is the brown you will now take most often. There are also a few grayling.

The best fishing is during early July when there is a phenomenal hatch of stone flies on the Madison. The big-eyed browns go wild for these tasty morsels and fish of 4, 5, and 6 pounds are caught on artificials which match the hatch. Then good fishing continues throughout the summer, except when too much water is let out of the dams and the water level rises. This situation may last for a few days or a week, at which time it is well for the fly angler, at least, to spend his time on neighboring streams or visit some of the high mountain lakes.

Large flies are usually the most successful on the Madison, the most popular being the Sofa Pillow, size 10 Gray Wulff, and the Trude, in dries; and the #4 and #2 Muddler in wets. Spinners lean to spoons with telling effect. Minnows, grasshoppers and nightcrawlers are all popular with bait fishermen, and there is a great natural supply of crawfish in the river.

The Madison River can be fished from headquarters at West Yellowstone or Ennis, much of the river running close to Highway 287. In West Yellowstone you can arrange float trips on certain sections of the river (part of it is closed to floating), and local tackle shops have all the information as to the best flies and lures of the moment.

One tributary of the Madison which is particularly worthy of note is Odell Creek. Odell holds some substantial trout, 2-pounders being taken with great regularity. Permission to fish Odell, except in the immediate vicinity of the highway, must be obtained from the ranchers. Once close to the stream, the angler must work very circumspectly because this is a small and narrow river and the fish hear the slightest noise.

The Missouri River, carrying all the waters of the Gallatin, Jefferson, and Madison, is a big river, necessitating chest-high waders in most places. Parts of the river offer good fishing, notably the twenty miles from Toston Dam to Townsend. From Hauser Dam to the Gates of the Mountains is probably the best stretch for fly fishing. Between Canyon Ferry and the Hauser Dam there is good trolling or casting from boats. Boats may also be used below Canyon

Ferry, but there are none below Hauser until Beaver Creek because of rocks and shallows. From there to the Gates of the Mountains it is again possible to use a boat.

Brown trout and rainbows comprise the fish in the Missouri, with the addition of some bass below the bridge at Townsend and in some of the reservoirs. From Wolf Creek all the way to Ulm there is excellent trout fishing, and from Ulm to Great Falls it continues fair.

Highway 287 and Interstate 15 parallel much of the river, but in some sections to reach the river it is necessary to drive about five miles off the hardtop on dirt roads. There is also entry via a secondary road which runs from U.S. 90 near Three Forks, up through Clarkson, Lombard, and Toston.

Like so many rivers which have been dammed, the Missouri is not as clear as most of Montana's trout streams and this determines the choice of flies and lures. Big spinning lures and the larger flies, streamers, and bucktails pay off. Again the Muddler comes through as a mighty good fly on the Big Mo. Best baits are night crawlers and minnows, while grasshoppers do well in the late summer.

Like the Yellowstone, the Missouri is open to fishing year-round. Late July and August are regarded as the slowest fishing months of the year; the best fishing is in September and October, and from April into July.

The Gallatin River is formed by many small rivulets in Yellowstone Park, and continues to be swelled by numerous small tributaries until it reaches a good size by the time it approaches U.S. Highway 191 between West Yellowstone and Bozeman. It flows north as far as Gallatin Gateway, then turns westward to flow past Manhattan. Just below Logan, at Trident, it joins the Madison and the Jefferson to form the Missouri.

The top part, along Highway 191, holds rainbows and cutthroats. As the river comes out of the canyon at the foot of the mountains and hits the valley floor, brown trout appear and some good ones are caught there every year. The average size of the rainbows is about ¾ of a pound; the browns go 1¼ pounds. However, rainbows up to

3 pounds and browns of 4 and even 5 are caught occasionally. The largest rainbow known to have come from the Gallatin weighed 4½ pounds; the largest brown 9½ pounds.

Small dry flies are good on this river, both the upper and lower stretches. Back of Belgrade the Gallatin winds slowly through hay meadows, fed here and there by a smaller, incoming stream, usually a spring creek, and the rainbows through here have a decided liking for size 16 and 18 dry flies. The best patterns are the Blue Dun, the Iron Blue, and the Light Cahill. The browns in this lower section go for bigger dries, the Royal Wulff, Grizzly Wulff, the Pink Lady, and the Grasshopper fished dry. The Muddler does yeoman duty, too, especially in the lower reaches.

Spin fishermen on the Gallatin River generally use small spoons and some use a bubble with a fly. Both presentations take fish. Bait fishermen use the same steady producers commonly popular through Montana—night crawlers, minnows, and grasshoppers.

Rock Creek starts high up in the mountains of Deer Lodge National Forest and comes tumbling down through Lolo National forest till it debouches into the Clark Fork of the Columbia at Clinton, on U.S. Highway 10, about twenty-two miles east of Missoula. In all, this beautiful mountain stream provides sixty-five miles of wilderness fishing for rainbows. They average under a pound but it is not unusual to take them to 3 and 4 pounds, and the largest on record went a hefty 6 pounds. In the lower reaches brown trout have moved up from the Clark Fork to spawn, and while they are not taken in great numbers, they come big, averaging a good 4 pounds, and a 10½-pounder has been recorded. There are also Rocky Mountain whitefish. The stream is crystal clear with well-defined pools, calling for careful fishing. This is an area where the angler may expect to see moose and bear, and caution should be taken accordingly.

All the standard flies listed for Montana in general are good, with emphasis on the Blue Dun and Red Variant, in sizes 12, 14, and 16. The best fly for the big brownies in the lower reaches is the Muddler, size 4. Spinners use small spoons for the rainbows but go to half-ounce lures for the browns in the lower stretches. Grasshoppers and worms are used by bait fishermen and these account for some big fish. Rock Creek is at its best from July 1st through October 31st.

The Clark Fork of the Columbia may be fished from the same headquarters. This stream rises in the hills near Anaconda and flows westward along Highway 10. However, due to irresponsible dumping of waste, both vegetation and fish have been destroyed along a great deal of its length. A clean-up program, instituted by the mines at the instigation of sportsmen and the state authorities, has resulted in considerable improvement. Now some good browns are being taken from the Clark Fork just west of Missoula and twenty-two miles east of Clinton, where Rock Creek adds its pure waters to the Clark Fork. The average brown in the Clark Fork will weigh 2 pounds and the largest known to have been taken weighed a hefty 10 pounds.

The best time to fish this river is from August 1st to October 31st, and while many flies will produce, the #4, #2, and 1/0 Muddler are outstanding. Spinners use all the large spoons, and bait fishermen are successful with all the conventional baits.

The Big Blackfoot River is formed by the joining of many small streams which flow down from the mountains of Lewis and Clark Country in west-central Montana. The Blackfoot joins the Clark Fork of the Columbia at Missoula and can be reached by U.S. 20 east from Missoula towards Ovando.

The Blackfoot is one of the most beautiful rivers in Montana, its crystal-clear water pouring over many wide gravel beds and through rolling hills and pleasant pasture lands. The angler who works back from the road will see mule deer and an occasional black bear. It is also a big river, and chest-high waders are necessary in order to reach the best positions for fishing many of the pools.

Rainbows in the Blackfoot average a pound, with an occasional 2- to 2½-pounder and the odd one up to 5 pounds. There are also a few browns in the lower Blackfoot, near Missoula.

The river is fishable all along the line. The best time is from August 1st through October. Dry flies, small bucktails and nymphs do well, and the smaller spinning spoons are effective rather than the big half-ounce spoons used for browns. Rainbows like their flies and lures served up in smaller doses. Bait fishermen take their limit with nightcrawlers and grasshoppers.

The Bitterroot River parallels U.S. 93 from the Idaho border to Missoula. The main part of the stream is formed at Connor where the east and west branches join and from there, till it joins the Clark Fork of the Columbia at Missoula. It continues for sixty-five miles, gathering water from the myriad feeder streams which pour down out of the Bitterroots, the mountain range which forms this part of the border between Montana and Idaho.

In the upper part of the Bitterroot River there is good fishing for eastern brook trout as well as rainbows, and as you work further down the browns put in their appearance. The brook trout average ¾ of a pound, with 1- and 2-pounders taken now and again and the biggest going 4 pounds. The average rainbow will go 1 pound, while 2- and 3-pounders turn up occasionally. The biggest on record weighed 6 pounds. The browns grow big in the Bitterroot, with a fine average of 2 pounds, 3- and 4-pounders taken frequently, and the largest known a hulking 10-pounder.

All the standard Montana flies are successful, with emphasis on the Royal Coachman and Red Variant dries, and the small bucktails and streamers in the brook-trout area. When they reach brown trout waters, anglers go to slightly larger flies such as the Muddler and Spruce Fly. Spinners vary their offerings in the same way, the small spoons for the upper stretches, the larger ones when they may expect to find the big browns. Bait fishermen take their fish on nightcrawlers and minnows, and grasshoppers are particularly good in the late summer.

Big Spring Creek, near Lewistown, lies considerably to the east of the major river-fishing area of Montana yet it is one of the really great trout streams of the state. This gigantic spring rises from the ground some ten miles southeast of Lewistown and flows northwest to join the Judith River, which in turn runs northward to the Missouri. In the ten miles above the town there is terrific fishing in crystal-clear water. Fish are rising most of the time, both rainbows and browns, ranging from ¾ pound to 2 pounds, and this part of the river yielded the largest fish ever taken in Spring Creek, a gigantic 18-pound brown. While this fish was taken on a worm, the upper part of Spring Creek is a dry-fly man's ideal stream. Because of the clarity of the water it pays to go down to a 4X or 5X tippet when dry-fly fishing. The most common hatch can be matched with a size 16 or 18 Blue Dun and the same fly with a spent wing does well. However, sometimes a size 16 Light Cahill or a Red Variant is the fly that will do the trick.

Below the town, Spring Creek also offers fine rainbow and brown trout fishing though the water is not so clear here. But the fish on the whole average a pound bigger, rainbows going 1½ to 2 pounds and browns a bit heavier. Three- and 4-pound fish will often be taken in the same day from the same pool. Down here the best flies for browns are the large streamers and bucktails and the Muddler, but they will also take the standard dry flies, the Gray Wulff and Royal Wulff being perhaps the best. The rainbows prefer the smaller flies, particularly the Red Variant and size 12 Blue Dun, and occasionally a size 16 Blue Dun or Light Cahill.

The ranchers along Spring Creek at Lewistown have gone all out in co-operating with anglers, providing parking places and putting stiles over the fences to make access to the river easy. Visiting anglers should be careful to use these stiles and not damage fences, and to observe the signs which indicate that certain fields should not be entered. The co-operation of the ranchers in this area is an outstanding example of landowner-sportsman relations, and the fisherman should do his full share to preserve such a situation.

The Mussellshell River also lies in the drier eastern slopes of the foothills. It can be reached via U.S. Highway 12 from White Sulphur Springs to Harlowton and the good fishing does not extend much below this point. However, in the higher waters brown trout of 2 and 3 pounds are caught regularly. A great deal of the area is posted, and permission to fish must be obtained from the ranchers.

The Smith River, lying a little further west and fed by streams from the Jefferson National Forest on one side and the Helena National Forest on the other, has a reputation for some exceptional fishing. It can be reached from White Sulphur Springs on the south or from Ulm on the north where the Smith joins the Missouri. However, as with the Mussellshell, a great deal of land along the Smith is posted and access is difficult. Some few anglers float the river while others obtain permission to fish from some of the ranchers. Two- and 3-pound browns and rainbows make the fishing exciting and it is not too exceptional to come up with a 5-pounder.

The North Fork of the Sun River, lying just northwest of Helena, in the Lewis and Clark National Forest, provides some very fine rainbow trout fishing. The fish average about 1 pound, with a goodly dividend of 2- and 3-pounders. The fishing is best suited to the fly and very little spinning or bait fishing is done. Best flies are the Red Variant, Blue Dun, Light Cahill, Ginger Quill, and the Iron Blue Dun, in sizes 14 and 16. A size 12 dry of any of the standard Montana flies will also take its share of fish. The best part of the river lies north of the Gibson Dam and is accessible by jeep or pack trip.

Lower down the Sun, in the Gibson Dam and in the big water below, there are some rainbows, but the water is often muddy and what fish are taken are usually caught on bait or big spoons.

The Flathead River, in the northwestern corner of Montana, near the Canadian border, is made up of three branches, the Middle Fork, the South Fork, and the North Fork. The Middle Fork lies north and east of Flathead Lake, forming the southern border of Glacier National Park, while the South Fork is to the south and east of Flathead Lake and pours into the reservoir formed by Hungry Horse Dam. This reservoir, in turn, spills its waters into the North Fork of the Flathead, which is then further swelled by its conjunction with the Middle Fork about twenty miles above Hungry Horse. This North Branch then parallels the western boundary of Glacier National Park right to the Canadian line. The waters of the Flathead are chiefly famous for the fine cutthroat fishing they provide, but Dolly Vardens are also taken. Where the river runs within the boundaries of Glacier National Park, special fishing regulations apply.

The Middle Fork is readily reached from U.S. Highway 2, between West Glacier and East Glacier, but access to the South Fork is usually by pack horse and consequently provides some wonderful wilderness fishing, with cutthroat to 2 pounds rising to almost every cast. Like most of the Flathead waters, it offers ideal dry-fly fishing. When you are trying especially for Dolly Vardens, deep-swimming flies or spoons are more successful. The South Fork lies within grizzly country and anglers should go in only with competent outfitters.

The Swan River parallels the course of the South Fork of the Flathead, just to the west, lying between it and Flathead Lake. The Swan has long been recognized as a fine rainbow and cutthroat river and is particularly noted for a run of brilliant, crimson-sided cutthroats in the fall. The average fish will run 1 pound, the largest 4, and the rainbows are about the same weight.

This is a fairly narrow river with much brush and crystal-clear, sparking cold water, and requires careful fishing. Flies of the standard Montana patterns are more successful than spinning lures or bait, except in some of the deeper pools. Access is by U.S. 326, which runs north from U.S. Highway 20, about forty miles east of Missoula. Several smaller streams in the area also furnish some fishing and Swan Lake, into which the Swan River empties, holds both rainbow and cutthroat trout.

The Kootenai River makes a big loop through the extreme northwest corner of Montana. It is paralleled by U.S. 37 throughout most of its length, providing easy access for fishermen. This river offers good fishing for rainbows and cutthroats which run up to 2 pounds. It is particularly good fly water, with all the standard dries paying off, but spinners take their share with small spoons, and bait fishermen are most successful with grasshoppers.

The Thompson River, just south of the Kootenai, is accessible via secondary road from Thompson Falls, or via pack or foot trail in its northern limits, from U.S. Highway 2 about fifty miles west of Kalispell. The Thompson holds the same fish as the Kootenai.

Saltwater Fishing

Inshore Saltwater Fly Fishing

Light tackle fishing in the salt is still new enough that the fisherman who goes after ocean swimmers with a fly rod attracts plenty of attention. Yet the true story of saltwater fly fishing goes back a long way. A book entitled *Fly Fishing in Salt and Fresh Water*, published in 1851 in England, mentioned the taking of whiting, pollock, mackerel, bass, and gray mullet on flies. To merit such mention, fly fishing the salt must have been conducted well in advance of the publication date of this book. And why not? The art of fly fishing got its start in the freshwaters of England, and had been practiced there for centuries. It makes sense that some adventurous angler would take his salmon outfit to the salty bays, lagoons, and inlets and shallows to see what was there that might hit his flies. Who actually hooked and landed the first salty fish on a fly will probably never be known.

On the American scene, *Salt Water Sportsman Magazine* reports that Genio Scott, author of *Fishing in American Waters*, wrote of fly fishing for stripers in 1875. Only a few years later, according to Tarleton H. Bean, who wrote the chapters on marine basses for the book *The Basses, Fresh Water and Marine* (edited by Louis Rhead and published in 1905), members of the famous striped bass clubs of the New England coast now and then used flies, sometimes trolling them, and other times casting them into a strong current, "using a considerable length of line and manipulating it on the surface of the water." They used gaudy flies and black-bass tackle.

At an equally early date, around 1875, at least one fly fisherman was taking shad on trout flies below tidewater on the Susquehanna River, as was reported in Baltimore newspapers.

In his book *Camping and Cruising in Florida*, published in 1884, Dr. James A. Henshall says that in 1878 he fished the vicinity of Fort Capron, Florida, and took "crevalle of 5 pounds, sea trout of 10 pounds, redfish of 5 pounds, bluefish of 4 pounds, snooks or sergentfish of 6 pounds, ladyfish of 2 pounds, and tarpon of 10 pounds" all on flies. This comes close to giving him the honor of landing the first saltwater fish on a fly in U.S. Continental waters.

Not long afterwards, Frank S. Pinckney wrote a book on tarpon called *Silver King*, published in 1888, in which he says that Dr. George Trowbridge of New York had caught a baby tarpon weighing 1 pound 3 ounces on a fly. That puts Trowbridge right up there on the heels of Dr. Henshall.

Around 1900 the Dimocks, A.W. and Julian, father and son, caught tarpon regularly on flies, and Julian took some of the greatest pictures ever made of leaping tarpon, pictures that are phenomenal when you consider the equipment available in those days. The Dimocks' fine *Book of the Tarpon* is a delight to read.

To my personal knowledge, Tom Loving of Baltimore began to consistently take shad on flies in the 1920s, and by 1922 was tying flies especially for shad, striped bass, and brackish-water largemouth black bass.

Another fly-rod pioneer, Colonel L.S. Thompson of Red Bank, New Jersey, fished at Long Key in 1926, with Captain J.T. Harrod, one of Florida's greatest guides. The colonel caught plenty of tarpon to 20 pounds, using Royal Coachman flies, and he also latched onto a couple of bonefish, although, as J.T. says: "We thought it was an accident, so we didn't try for bonefish but instead concentrated on the tarpon."

By the time the now renowned Rod & Reel Club of Miami Beach, Florida, was started in 1928, some of its members had already taken tarpon on a fly, and snook in the shallow waters of Florida Bay and the canals around Miami. Two of the earlier fly fishermen who did a valuable job in bringing the shallow saltwater fishing possibilities to the attention of fly-rodders were Red Greb and Homer Rhode, of Miami. And far out on the West Coast, pioneer Oregon fly-rod men were working out ties for the imported stripers and shad, as well as the resident silver and king salmon.

But these were lone riders, and it was not until 1947 that the main body of fly fishermen came awake to the knowledge that in the salt was a whole new world for them to explore, and that, as a result of that upsurge in fly fishing the salt, commercially tied saltwater flies began to appear. Since then a standard set of flies has evolved, all of which do a good job in the ocean shallows, and in some cases over the ocean deeps as well.

Saltwater fish seldom, if ever, feed on real flies which have fallen to the surface of the ocean, and there is no aquatic hatch similar to that of a freshwater stream or lake, and therefore there are no dry flies tied for salt water. Rather, flies for the briny have been designed to imitate such common forms of ocean-going fish food as minnows, crabs, shrimp, small worms of the ocean, sand fleas, and so on, and saltwater fly fishing is therefore almost entirely confined to streamers, bucktails, and popping bugs.

Most saltwater streamers are tied with three or four saddle hackle feathers on each side of the hook so that as the streamer is retrieved in foot-long jerks, the feathers will work, closing each time a strip is made, and flaring outwards again when the pull is stopped. These flies, known as "breathers," are often as much as 5 inches in overall length, tied on 3/0 hooks.

The breathers are good numbers for tarpon, striped bass, channel bass, snook, jack crevalle, big snappers, ladyfish, and many other less commonly sought game fish of the seas. Smaller editions of the same breather flies, tied on a 1/0 hook, are also used for bonefish when the fish are in fairly deep water, this hook having sufficient weight to get down to them. But when bonefish are in very shallow water, a bucktail tied on a No. 1 hook or even a No. 2 hook will float better, and not catch on the bottom so readily. And when the fish are feeding on extremely low tide, then even lighter hooks, as small as No. 4, are used.

In the Bahamas the flats are extremely shallow at low tide. When bonefish come up on them to feed there is often so little water that their backs are sticking out. A fly tied on a heavy hook would sink too rapidly and catch on the bottom, so the No. 2 or No. 4 hooks are in order. In some cases, anglers even use Palmer-tied flies there, so that the hackle makes a shield sufficient to prevent the point of the hook from hanging up on weeds or coral.

Another tie which solves some of the problems of fishing the very shallow flats is a Pink Shrimp. These little numbers, on a No. 4 hook, are tied with the hair wrapped around the body of the hook and enough of it protruding underneath to make it almost weedless. It floats high in the water, and is perfect for shallow flats.

Like the bonefish, other saltwater species require different flies according to the water in which the angler is fishing for them. Snook in deep water take the bigger bucktails and streamers, but in canals, when they are feeding on schools of small minnows, herding them into the bank and then striking into them open-mouthed— then a small, inch-long bucktail on a No. 1 hook most nearly matches the minnows. Some enormous snook have been taken on such small bucktails. And in like manner, the flies designed for tarpon vary considerably in size. Fishing for baby tarpon, from 2 to 20 pounds, calls for a 1/0 hook, while for their bigger brothers, the 3/0 is better and if you are going to tangle with 100-pound or better tarpon, you should go to the 4/0 or 5/0 hook.

Poppers are potent lures for almost every saltwater species, in one circumstance or another, and because of the thrill the angler gets when he sees some big, hard-hitting ocean fish sock a surface lure, they are widely used. Some poppers are built so they will skip across the water making plenty of commotion, looking like a small fish jumping and tailwalking in an effort to escape some predatory monster that is on his trail. Others have cork bodies and bullet noses and are called sliders because they go along the top without noise. These are good in canals and in tight spots such as openings in the mangroves where a hard-popped bug might scare the fish.

One of the best producers for snook is the 3/0 skipping bug. There is something about the action, the noise of the pops, the look of the wounded minnow, of this bug, that gets a quick response from big snook. They fly out from under overhanging mangrove limbs, or from under a log, and take this surface fooler with a lunge and a clank of formidable jaws.

In addition to these special designs for salt water, practically all the freshwater designs for bugs have been brought to the sea, the only alteration being that they are tied on heavier hooks to combat the crushing power of saltwater gangsters' hard-mouthed jaws. In the early days of saltwater fishing, because of the rust problem, all these flies were tied on Z-nickel hooks, but rust proofing has now made many of the lighter hooks suitable, too.

As with freshwater flies, color is always a point of argument. It seems that the color which is good one day may be totally ignored the next. And saltwater fish being the obstreperous hitters they are, will sock almost anything that is offered them, at one time or another, further confusing the issue.

But in general, the same color combinations which have proven fish getters in fresh water are emerging as the standbys for salt. Barred rock wings are good in streamers, as are red and yellow, red and white, yellow and white, and brown and white. Plain yellow and plain white in the bucktails are universally good. And so are small white bucktails in any of a number of variations of trim, from a few hairs of blue on top to a few of brown.

Orange has come on strong as a saltwater color, and the combination of red and orange, as in the Strawberry Blonde fly, has proven to be great for many saltwater fish, including the spotted sea trout, ladyfish, snook, redfish, jacks, and both baby and big tarpon.

Chumming and Offshore Fly Fishing

When you fly fish the salt there are many fish that ordinarily would not come within reach but which can be coaxed up to hit a fly by the use of chum. Chumming is the process of throwing out on the surface some food which the fish might like and thus attracting them to or near the surface where the fly can be presented to them.

In the Chesapeake Bay and many other places, striped bass fishermen have long chummed with shrimp, pouring them overboard until a heavy slick is formed, into which the stripers eventually work. In many of the bays where there are crab canning plants, there is a more or less constant flow of natural chum in the waste that is dumped, and fishing is frequently very good in those areas. Another natural chum that attracts fish is spread out in the water when oyster tongers stir the bottom, and the fly caster who anchors downtide from them and casts his fly in the general direction of the oysterman has a good chance of coming up with stripers that are there feeding on the tidbits pushed up by the tongs.

In Bermuda, where chumming is common because of the deep water around the island, one of the favorite chums is hog-mouthed fry, an inch-long, silvery minnow that is all head and mouth, as his name implies. A handful of these fry thrown on the surface will usually bring a concentration of gray snapper and yellowtail and other reef dwellers to feed, and once they start to feed, a well-placed bucktail tied to match the fry will usually get hits.

Fly casting into a chum line doesn't call for any particular skill because the fish are not usually far away and will stay in the one area. It does, however, demand extreme care with equipment. Everything must be right, from the knots in the leader to the mechanics of the drag on the reel. Even hook points should be thoroughly sharpened. Some terrific fish come to the chum line, strong fish and fast fish and long-running fish, and to be prepared for their maneuvers everything must be in the angler's favor when he fights these ocean roustabouts.

In almost all chum fishing, and especially when fishing for snappers, no motion is given to the fly, as these canny and sharp eyed "sea lawyers" are seldom taken in by a trick. The fly must be allowed to float along with the fry, looking just like it, at the mercy of the tide. The slightest movement, and a snapper will spot it as a phony. He may tear right up to it in his wild feeding, and then, at the last second he will slam on the brakes and give it the old cold eye. But let it float "dead" with the rest of the fry, and the angler is in for some fun. Gray snappers are very strong fish and usually they dive straight for the bottom and cut the leader on the rocks.

After the chum line has been out a while, it will extend far downtide and cruising fish, crossing it, will turn and follow it to the boat, feeding as they come, grabbing the hog-mouthed fry avidly and moving in fast on the source of supply.

The first time I chum-fished in Bermuda, we anchored the big Aquarium boat, the *Iridio*, about 10 miles offshore, over 60 feet of water. In no time, our chum line pulled in a large school of yellowtails, so many that the water around them appeared yellow. They were big for the species, 5- and 6-pound fish that worked through the chum, sucking it in as if they had magnets in their bellies.

A fry fly did the trick. We dropped them into the floating chum and whammie, a big yellowtail would smash into them like a blow from a hammer. Yet even so, once is a while those sharp-eyed babies would give us a fit, dashing headlong at the fly, then turning off at the last second, coming so close to taking that we would often strike.

Then far out on the chum line we saw other fish breaking.

"Mackerel!" shouted Brose Gosling.

These were the same fish as the Florida false albacore or little tuna, fish strangely built by nature so that they always have to keep swimming. The gill structure is such that if they stayed still they would die. Now we saw them slipping through the chum within 30 feet of the boat. They didn't hesitate, but seemed to grab the floating fry at top speed. When they turned, they went far out, then getting a bearing they charged back into the fry. This time we were ready.

Both Brose and I dropped flies in front of them. Fish took both flies at the same time and the two reels went into high gear. I thought these fish had been travelling at top speed before, but now they really turned it on. They ran 500 feet before we finally stopped them, and it was 20 minutes before we could finally boat that pair. They weighed 7 pounds apiece, as nice an example of what the fly-rodder may expect from the chum line as anything I could name.

Bread is also widely used as chum in Bermuda. There, along the beautiful pink beaches, the gaff topsail pompano often come inshore and can be seen swimming through the curl of the breakers.

These tough bits of fish flesh, also called palometa, have a top weight of 4 pounds and average just under a pound. But they're as strong as little bulls. A 2-pounder can snake out a fly line and a hundred feet of backing before he stops. They feed extensively on sand fleas and nature has equipped them with amazingly sturdy ribs that are built to take a beating as the fish dash ashore in the wake of a receding wave and grab a flea before it can bury itself in the sand. Sometimes the game little pompano are left almost high and dry, flapping their bodies hard to get back to the water. They then will come in again, their long, black dorsal and anal fins showing dark in the clear green water, just under the crest of the breakers.

They will hit a very small fly and spinner combination as well as an inch-long white or yellow bucktail, and will take almost any of the small spoon-type lures that fit a fly rod. Because of the clearness of the Bermuda water, these all have to ride on the end of a fine tippet, one that tapers down to at most 4-pound test.

When the gaff topsail pompano are first spotted, they can often be taken without chum, but as they are fished they grow a little scary and move into deeper water, and then the bread is crumbled into little balls and thrown out to coax them back within wading and casting distance.

It used to be that the light-tackle angler was not very welcome on charter boats, largely because when he hooked a big fish it took him so long to land it that the other fishermen sharing the charter became disgruntled. However, in the past few years, more and more light-tackle anglers are using charter boats to go after unusual and sporty catches in the deeps, and when several pool their funds and go together, the charter men are only too glad to have them.

Casting from a charter boat has its hazards because of the superstructure, but usually the backcast can be managed without snagging a mate, an outrigger, or a fellow fisherman, as almost all casts in this kind of fishing are short, seldom more than 50 feet. And since the fish sought by this method are usually close to the boat, feeding on chum, or are school fish like dolphin and are following an already hooked fish, there is no need to hurry the cast.

There are other hazards of fishing the deeper water, too. Sometimes a hooked fish is lost to sharks, and sometimes a fish will dive to the bottom and cut the leader. Or the anglers may tie into such a big, seagoing speedster that it just won't stop at all and ends by either snapping the leader or breaking the backing where it is tied to the reel core. But these are pleasant risks to take, with the ever-pleasant chance of coming up with something really unusual.

A lot of this kind of fishing is done on the Florida Keys, where charter boat captains are all "light-tackle minded." Captain Howard Victor took us out on his boat, *The Cadet*, to look for school dolphin in the line of driftage along the Gulf Stream just off Islamorada. Pete Perinchief of Bermuda was with me, making his first go for dolphin.

"Let's try these big red and yellow streamers," I suggested. "But first, let Vic get the fish in here where we can reach them."

Vic put out a trolling outfit and handed Pete the rod.

"Get one on," he instructed him. "And hold it. Bring it in to about 20 feet from the boat and just keep it there. The whole school will follow and stay with it, and then Joe can cast to them with his fly rod."

Ten minutes later Pete's rod bounced down and he held on while something tore line from the reel, then came out in a beautiful jump—a leaping, rainbow-hued dolphin, about 7 pounds.

He slipped back in and Pete fought him hard for five minutes, then he began to get him. We could see him out there in the water, and right in back of him were the brilliant yellow, golden and green streaks that told us the rest of the school was zipping around him, staying with the hooked fish.

I false-cast line out, dropped the big streamer near Pete's fish. It looked as if the entire school rushed it at once. One socked it hard, and I set the hook and leaned back on the rod. Out he came in a really high jump, a dolphin that could have been the twin of the one Pete had on. It took me fifteen minutes to land him.

Pete was still holding his hooked fish out there.

"Here," he said, shoving the rod at me and grabbing his own fly rod. "I gotta get in on this."

The school was still there and Pete was into a fish on his first cast, a leaping, jumping powerhouse that looked like flames from a wind-driven fire. He was in and out of the water like something was after him, but he finally tired and Pete got him in. As he released his catch, I brought the decoy in.

"We'll release him, too," I said. "He deserves it."

We hit two more schools in short order and each time we had the same fast action. Then a bit after, as we cruised along a heavy mat of sargasso weed, we saw something dash out from it, right along the top. It hit the bait like a ton of bricks. This was no school dolphin. This was a good big bull.

"He'll go 30 pounds," said Captain Vic.

I had the bait rod at the moment, and that fish kept me tied to it for half an hour. It was touch and go the whole time. Then he began to tire. He surfaced, away out, and right back of him we spotted another shape, something long and brown looking.

"That's another big dolphin," shouted Vic. "Get your fish in closer, Joe, so Pete can put a fly to the other one."

I pulled harder on my now tired fish, and brought him closer. The brown shape followed like a shadow. They were both at 35 feet. Pete shot the fly out, a perfect cast that dropped the fly two feet in front of that shadow. The dolphin took at once and came out in the most tremendous leap I've ever seen, an arching jump that took him 10 feet in the air and carried him 30 feet across the ocean waves before he lit.

Pete's mouth was open, his eyes gleaming with a mixture of delight and disbelief. I probably had exactly the same look on my face. Never was there such a wonderful sight as that beautiful fish jumping across the ocean. Then I looked to the rear where my fish had been dogging it during all this wild excitement. Suddenly, as if jealous of the show his pal was putting on, he rushed to the top and came out, too, in a straight up jump, and threw the hook. I heaved a sigh and started reeling in, and suddenly, right where my hook was, Pete's fish came up, busted into the sunlight and threw Pete's fly. We reeled in a couple of empty lines.

Pete took three 7-pounders on his fly from the next school that hopped onto the trolled bait. They really punched holes in the ocean, like fast moving sewing machine needles.

"Catching 'em or losing 'em," said Pete, "if there's any better kind of fishing than this, I've yet to see it."

I thought of Pete that winter when I was using a popping bug for dolphin, down in Panama Bay. There are all kinds of strikes to a popping bug, fast ones, slow, majestic ones, sloppy tries, and pinpoint aiming. For pinpointing, the dolphin probably takes the diploma. They like poppers, and when one of those flossy looking numbers comes from under seaweed or a floating log to bop down on a lure, he does it with mathematical precision.

Dolphin are very curious about the noise made by a popper, and on this trip out in Panama Bay I coaxed a whole school of about a dozen 20-pounders out of some driftage to see what was going on. They bore down on that popper like a cavalry charge. The smallest one got there first, but even so the hit was so strong that it pulled the fly line out of my left hand and I had no control over the line until it hit the reel with a bang, and the leader snapped like a strand of spider web. The rest of the school followed that brilliantly hued dolphin as he leaped and leaped, trying to throw the fly, and every now and then another dolphin would jump clear to see what was happening. Then the whole bunch faded under the line of driftage and didn't come out again until we popped the next bug.

Dolphin will hit just about any feathered lure or popper that is tossed to them. But after a couple of fish have been taken from one school with the same fly, they will often stop hitting, as if getting wise to the lure. Then a change of color or pattern will usually stir them up again and put the angler back in business.

In the Florida Keys area, the hot time for this kind of fishing is from about May 25 to the end of the first week in July. There are some school dolphin around all the time, of course, but they are spotty, and you may lose a lot of time hunting for them before ever getting a cast. But in the spring months they appear in numbers, following the line of sargasso weed, hanging around it and hiding under it, using it for a salty umbrella.

In July these Florida fish work northwards and during the summer they furnish great sport off the North Carolina coast. In Panama Bay, on the other hand, the dolphin continue on into October, following the fallen trees and driftage that float out into the Bay from the rain-swollen rivers.

Salty Grab Bag

Whether we fished beach, reef, or ocean, Bermuda kept us guessing. But—with bonefish, mackerel, wahoo, and many more—we really struck it rich.

Bobby Ray was throwing handfuls of chum over the side of the *Iridio*, the 40-foot collection boat belonging to the Bermuda Aquarium. The chum, consisting of inch-long, hog-mouthed fry, floated along with the tide, sinking slowly in the clear blue water.

I stood on the left side of the cockpit, fly rod in hand, and Tom Mc-Nally was on the stern deck, similarly armed. We were waiting for the bottom to roll up, as it often does when you chum the Bermuda coral heads for gray snapper or any other ocean fish that might cruise by.

"Mackerel!" cried Louis Mowbray, from up forward. "Get ready. Quick."

We saw them at the extreme end of the chum, bluish-colored, torpedo-shaped fish with a multitude of spikelike finlets. These babies are built for speed. And they can't ever get a finhold on a rock and sleep, or bask on top of the water like the great, lazy ocean sunfish, for their gills are so constructed that they must keep moving or die.

Now there were into the chum, gulping up the floating *hors d'oeuvres* with lightning changes of pace. They traveled so fast that one would hit the chum unexpectedly and go into a 15-foot skid as he slammed on the brakes.

I chose one to cast a fly to, and my bucktail dropped three feet in front of him. He made the merest swerve, snatched up the fly, and then I was into the fastest thing on fins. The end of the ocean was his goal. Line left the reel in a single leap and all at once the backing was almost gone.

"Stop, fish!" I yelled. "Slow down."

Tom and Bobby looked back to see how much line I had left.

"He's taken 650 feet already," I said. "Only 50 feet left. Stop!" I yelled again.

And presto he came to an abrupt stop. I reeled fast. He came my way for a second or two, then roared away again so fast that the reel click went back into a shriek. He started to sashay from right to left, but he was on a tack now where I could get line back. I reeled like mad, but then let go of the handle once more as he reversed and took off again to the right.

He stopped sooner this time, and then I kept at him, beginning to pull him my way. In he came, foot by foot. Then he pawed the water hard and away he went, taking 100 feet of line before he slowed. But when he stopped this time, I kept him coming, and when he was close to the boat I saw the long-handled net go out. I raised the top tip and dragged that spent fish into the net.

Bobby lifted him aboard. He weighed 7¾ pounds.

"What a fish!" I gasped.

"It's the same fish they call false albacore or little tuna," said Louie, who's Curator of the Bermuda Aquarium. "Mostly he's taken on trolling gear."

"He's a whiz-bang on a fly rod," I commended. "Where are the others?"

"Gone," said Bobby. "These fish are fast travellers. They probably picked up the scent of our chum a quarter of a mile away and followed it in. Now they've gone somewhere else."

Five minutes after the mackerel fight subsided, the snappers down below decided that all was clear. Then it really did look as if the bottom were rolling up, as a school of snappers showed, at first indistinct, then clearer as it broke the surface, feeding fast and without caution. A dark line extending backwards a couple of inches over each eye of the fish grew blacker and blacker, registering their excitement over the feast as a thermometer registers fever.

"Wait till these lines are really black," said Louie, "then cast. But be sure to let the fly float free. Don't move it at all. The snappers want it dead, like chum."

I dropped the same inch-long white bucktail I'd used for the mackerel and watched it float slowly along. A four-pound snapper raced for it but turned away at the last second. I was so sure he had it that I struck and my line flew high in the air. I dropped the fly again. A snapper hit it right off and was cellar-bound. He didn't stop until he'd wrapped my leader around a rock and cut me off.

The commotion scared the other fish and they all headed down. But Bobby tossed out another handful of chum and in a few minutes they were topside again and in there pitching, their black lines throbbing with greed.

I heard Tom shout as he was into one. His snapper dived, then levelled off, halfway down and darted away for 100 feet. Soon it turned, got sideways to the boat, and pulled a healthy bend into Tom's rod. But Tom didn't back up, and as the pressure told, the fish came slowly up and into the net.

"Not an ounce over three pounds," said Tom. "And I thought he was seven or eight."

The gray or mangrove snapper is one of the strongest fish of the ocean. So far as is known, a 16-pounder is the largest ever taken on fly or spinning tackle. They have the strength to go into a terrific power dive and cut you off on the rocks. Besides brawn they have brains. They have eyes like an eagle, and their ability to spot a phony is one of the reasons they're dubbed sea lawyers.

"Did you ever notice that fish in the live well?" Louie asked us. "Of all the fish we put in there, when we're collecting for the aquarium, only the snappers try to escape. They stick their heads above the water, looking for a way out."

"They're smart, all right," we all agreed.

"If they weren't such gluttons, they'd never get caught," said Louie.

"Do any other fish have that feeding line?" I asked

"Quite a few," he answered. "Amberjacks, bonito, and in a different way the wahoos and marlin, which have vertical bars that show more plainly when they're feeding."

This Bermuda fishing was like dipping into a salty grab bag. You never knew what might come out. It might be a five-pound yellowtail, a 10-pound bonito, or a great amberfish. Or it might be a school of ocean robins (related to the jacks), or some specimen never before recorded by icthyologists. This was the middle of June. I wondered how long this kind of fishing could hold up.

As if reading my mind, Brose Gosling spoke. "April to the end of October is when we get the biggest variety," he said. "But you can catch something here all year."

On our way in that day we stopped to fish a deep coral head that we'd picked up with the echo finder. Again we tossed chum overboard and cast into it. A large, whitish fish came slowly up and took my fly. I struck, but too late. That fish had discovered something wrong and spit the fly right out. More chum brought him up once more, this time with a friend. One of them took the fly and again I struck and missed.

Next time he showed I outfoxed him. As soon as he was within half an inch of the bucktail, I struck and caught him with the fly in his mouth. Then he turned it on. He was a terrific fighter for a two-pounder.

"That's a triggerfish," said Louis, when at last I led it into the net. "Pirates of the sea, they are. During the war when sailors were shipwrecked and floating on rafts, a triggerfish would ease up to the raft and take a nip out of a leg or arm dangling in the water."

"They don't stop at a nip, either," said Bobby.

"No," agreed Louis. "They're like the piranha. They'd take all of your flesh off you, bite by bite, if you fell into a school of them."

Bermuda is a 22-mile strip of islands shaped like a fishhook, as if to point out that there's some wonderful fishing around the islands which in the past have owed their fame mostly to honeymooners. Even the beautiful pink beaches have their share of unique fishing, notably the flashy gaff-topsail pompano that swim within easy reach of a cast lure.

As I stepped off the plane on my first trip to Bermuda, Jimmy Williams met me, with a loaf of bread tucked under one arm.

"No time to waste," he said. "We'll leave your luggage here till later and go right out to the beach."

"Dry bread for lunch at a beach party?" I asked.

Jimmy grinned. "This bread is for the pompano," he explained. "For chum. You throw bits of bread out and they start feeding on it, then you bait your hook with another bit, and cast."

Maybe they'll hit a fly, I suggested.

They did, and we also caught pompano on small fly-rod size spoons. First they hit well inshore. Then as they grew cautious and moved further out, we moved out too, until we were shoulder-deep in the water, beyond the crash of the breakers.

Those fish reached up to four pounds, and any gaff-topsail pompano over a pound will give you a scrappy fight on either fly or spinning tackle.

That day we used bread. On later occasions we chummed with hog-mouthed fry and took two bonefish, a four-pound bonito, and some pompano.

Some of the biggest bonefish in the world have been taken from Bermuda's inshore waters, and at one time three world records were posted for the island. One of them, a 14-pounder caught in Shelley Bay by Dr. H.R. Becker of York, Pa., still holds lead position in the 20-pound line-test class of the International Game Fish Association.

It's a tough job to take most Bermuda fish on straight away casting without use of chum, because the water is so clear. But the bonefish is one which inshore anglers can reach by wading or by skiff. And Bermuda bonefish present a special challenge. They seem particularly strong, they're found in deeper, clearer water than most other places—hence are more difficult to spot and cast to before they see you and swim away—and there's always a chance of a record fish.

On a trip to Whale Harbor with Pete Perinchief and George Morris, I noticed that they were constantly making quick, jerky movements with their heads as they waded along, so as to get a better view through the water with their Polaroid glasses.

Suddenly Pete stopped and stood there, snapping his head from side to side. "Shadows," he reported.

"Are you nuts?" asked George. "There can't be; there isn't a cloud in the sky."

"Bonefish shadows," said Pete.

And then I remembered. Pete and I had fished here a few years ago on a day when we couldn't spot the fish but could see their shadows against the sandy bottom. Even while I was remembering, Pete made his cast and was into a fish.

A second later George yelled, "There's another." And he was fast to a speedster that was on his way to Cuba. George knew it was useless to try to stop that run.

"He'll clean me," he said. "He's gone 200 yards already."

But that big saltwater reel had plenty of line. George got the bonefish coming back our way, though he fought all the way in and then went off again on a 150-foot run before George finally towed him in for keeps.

"Ten pounds," he said, as he put him back. "What a runner."

Besides bonefish, gaff-topsail pompano, and gray snapper, anglers fishing the beaches, shallow bays, and coral heads of Bermuda can take barracuda, gwelly, chub, and occasionally a yellowtail or a prowling bonito. Farther out, over 25 fathoms, they can connect with yellowtails, bonito, mackerel (false albacore), ocean robins, and many other surface cruising fish. Also, deep-sea charter boats troll for Allison tuna, Bermuda tuna, dolphin, wahoo, white marlin, blue marlin, and mako. Occasional visitors to Bermuda waters are tarpon, bluefish, horse-eye jacks, jack crevalle, and blue-fin tuna.

But one of the greatest thrills of deep-water fishing is that you may come up with just about anything. Louis Mowbray has done many kinds of fishing in his search, but one of the most interesting is his "deep-line" work at night.

"That's when the deep dwellers come to or near the top," he explained. "They don't like the light rays and so only move up when it's dark."

By deep-line fishing, after dark, he's collected the terrible-tempered tapioca or oilfish and the rare Bermuda ocean catfish. He's landed great tuna and albacore at night, and just recently made one of the great icthyological finds of the century when he caught a lancet fish. Only three of these creatures are known to have been caught on hook and line, and none of them reached scientific hands, so all previous information about them came from specimens washed ashore in a decomposed state.

The lancet is an elongated, scaleless, and almost boneless fish with a high, sail-like dorsal fin. Mowbray's specimen was 41 inches long, four inches wide. It took a garfish bait at 30 fathoms.

With things like this to intrigue the curious, more and more anglers are sure to go deep trolling and drifting in Bermuda waters, and I for one would like to be in on it when some new, strange, and terrible-looking monster comes protestingly up from the depths.

One of my own strangest catches there, to date, has been a flying fish. That day the water was so rough that we couldn't see if any fish were coming to our chum line.

"I'll fix that," said Louie, who has a remedy for every piscatorial ailment.

He ducked into the cabin for a small bottle of dark-colored liquid which he started sprinkling overboard. The drops spread quickly and a film began to cover the water downtide from us.

"Shark oil," said Louis. "It calms rough seas. It's a weather gauge, too. If bad weather is coming, the fluid will cloud up."

Through the water, now flattened, and cleared by the shark oil, we could see flying fish, close to the boat. I got a hook—baited with fry—out there fast, and saw one of those little seagoing butterflies take. We landed several that day and found that they're just about the tastiest morsel in the ocean.

Next day we went for Bermuda chub.

"I'll bet you can't land one over four pounds on either fly or spinning gear," said Louie on the way out to the reef. "They'll dive to the bottom and cut you off on a rock."

"They get as heavy as 18 pounds," added Pete Perinchief. "But even on heavy tackle the average landed is four pounds."

That day we were chumming with chunks of lobster.

"You'd better bait with lobster, too," suggested Louie. "They hit bait better than flies or lures."

But I wanted to try my own choice of lures. I started with a fly, and the chunky fish hit that fine, but they were hard to hook. Finally I managed to hook two but lost both of them in a hurry.

I changed to spinning gear and lost two more. They went down under some rocks and cut me off, just as Louie had said. Seeing the writing on the wall, I picked up a big trolling outfit with 20-pound-test line and finally brought in a two-pounder. Then I fought it out with a 2½-pounder that acted more like a whale.

The third one to hit was a monster who all but tore the rod from my hands. He ripped line from the reel in spite of the heavy drag.

"You may only have seen them up to 18 pounds," I told Pete. "But I'll bet this one's over 20."

When I finally got him in, he weighed 4½ pounds. I took my hat off to the chub.

All the while we had been fishing, Capt. Roy Taylor had been in touch with other charter boats around Bermuda. We'd hear him give the call letters of his boat, the *Wally III*, then when some other boat came in, he'd ask, "How's fishing?"

Capt. Lewis Martin of the *Sea Wolf* reported a 128-pound white marlin just landed. Capt. Charlie Christianson chimed in to tell us there were wahoo in his neighbourhood.

"Better get over here," he advised. "There are some good ones."

We wasted no time heading that way. The record for wahoo in Bermuda waters is 110 pounds, while the average taken there ranges from 35 to 45 pounds.

The wahoo probably got his name from the excited shout of the first angler who ever hooked one. He's a streamlined, vertical-barred powerhouse that makes fanatics out of those who connect with him. I've met anglers who will go for no other fish, period. And the wahoo is the fish most often named by charter-boat captains who have told me their favorite catch.

"That bait is a tantalizing thing," I thought, as I sat in the fighting chair, watching the one-pound garfish bait dance along the surface. It jumped from wave to wave. Once it disappeared and I sat bolt upright, ready and hopeful. But it reappeared, skipping along, throwing up splashes of water.

The sun was bright, the waves were a couple of feet high, providing just the right action and oxygen, at the surface, for a cruising wahoo. My eyes dropped and I shook my head. This was the way many a guy had lost a good fish. I shook my head again and looked at the bait. Nothing back of it, and only the waves and the deep blue of the ocean around it. I glanced up at the outrigger. The 10-pound-test line was fast in the clothespin up there. The captain had advised a heavier line, but I wanted to go light.

"This could go on all day," I thought to myself, as we churned along. My head drooped again. For how long, I don't know.

"Fish!" shouted Roy Taylor. "Fish! Fish! Wahoo! Back of your bait!"

My eyes popped open a foot and I saw the brown shape right under the bait. I took one quick look at the outrigger, to see that everything was O.K. up there, then yanked my eyes back to the skipping bait just in time to see it taken.

Barrels of water flew upward and again I looked to the outrigger. This time the line came out of the clothespin and was suddenly tight between the fish and my rod. I struck hard twice. Then, as I felt that bozo, I braced myself and watched one of angling's greatest sights—a wahoo churning the ocean into lines of bursting bubbles as he surged on top, getting up speed with every swipe of his crescent-shaped tail. This fish was faster than I thought. His surges covered 50 feet, and then he slipped into high and struck a pace that made those surges seem like pygmy efforts. He charged across the ocean just under the surface for 1,000 feet.

Then the line went slack, and every drop of blood in my veins ran to my feet. I'd wanted that fish so badly.

"He's not off," the captain observed. "He's reversed, that's all. He just showed out there."

The line came tight again, and I felt him. I tightened the drag and began to pump him. He was slower now, tired after that terrific burst of speed. Soon we could see his outline lying broadside to the boat. Slowly I worked him in.

"A 40-pounder," said Captain Roy. "A nice fish."

Then, "Shark! Shark!"

The wahoo saw the shark at the same moment we did. He accelerated even faster than he had the first time. But we knew it couldn't last. The fish was too tired, and pulling against the drag of the reel didn't help any.

I looked at Roy, then pointed the big rod right at the wahoo. I felt the 10-pound-test monofilament line come up in the water, saw it straighten out, and then heard the crack of the line as it parted.

"I couldn't sit here and watch that shark get him," I said.

"You and me both," said Roy. "I'd have done the same thing."

Out there we saw the shark give up the chase. He turned and came back toward us, as if he'd like to get even with us for letting his meal get away. Then, as he got closer, he sank from view.

We were thinking just as nasty things about him. That was a fish we had wanted. But after a while we began to feel better. That wahoo would live to fight another battle, to give some other anglers, or maybe even me, another thrill, the great feel of being tied to a seagoing comet.

Panama

I had just landed my first black marlin and skipper Ospina Newball was grunting and groaning as he stretched the fish out on the cockpit.

"I'll measure him for weight," said Jack Mahony.

"You mean measure him for length, don't you?" I asked.

"For weight," Jack repeated, taking a tape measure from his pocket. "Get a pencil and paper and I'll show you. You can figure it to within a couple of pounds."

"Write this down," he said, as he applied the tape to the fish. "Girth, 52 inches. "Square that," he said.

I dug into my very vague memory of elementary arithmetic and finally remembered that to square a number you multiply it by itself.

"52 x 52," I mumbled as I put the pen to work. "That's 2704."

"Multiply that by the length from lower jaw to the crotch of the tail," Jack said. "That's 95 inches."

Some fancy figuring got me 256,880.

"O.K." said Jack. "Divide that by 800 and you have the weight of your marlin."

"321 pounds," I came up with.

"That's the method we use to check big fish entered with the International Game Fish Association for world record listing," said Jack, who was a representative of that organization. "It seldom varies more than three pounds either way. I'll give you even money your fish weighs within a couple of pounds of 321."

"Does that work only on marlin?" Lee Cuddy asked.

"No," said Jack. "It works for all big fish."

We never were able to confirm his figure on a scale because it was early in the day—10.30 a.m. to be exact—and the sun was hot and we still had plenty of fishing ahead of us. So we cut the marlin up and put the pieces in the ice box to keep fresh, to give to the Girls' Orphan Home in Panama City when we got back. Those tiny tots would dine well on it, for black marlin is one of the best eating fish, a rare treat even for a gourmet.

We were at remote Piñas Bay on the Pacific side of Panama, only 20 miles north of the Colombian line. This trip to Piñas Bay was something I had dreamed about for a long time, ever since Frank Violette of Balboa, in the Canal Zone, had made a pioneering trip there the previous January and had found marlin and Pacific sailfish all over the place. He wrote us in Miami and invited us to join him, and so, on January 9th, 1958, almost a year later to the day, Jack Mahony, Lee Cuddy, and I were winging our way down to Panama. It took us just 4½ hours by plane to reach Tocumen Airport from Miami. Frank met us there and early next morning we were aboard his boat, the *Seri*, steaming out of the Balboa Yacht Club. On board were Jack, Lee, Frank, and I, plus skipper Ospina Newball, who has fished with Frank for 17 years, and the mate, Clarke, who was on his second trip to Piñas Bay.

We made the run across Panama Bay to Cocos in the Perlas Islands in seven hours, and there found a quiet anchorage for the night. Next day we were under way again before dawn and another seven hours brought us to the Moros, two small, round islands about a half a mile apart, that stand sentinel just outside the entrance to Piñas Bay. We went on in and found an anchorage as sheltered as a bath tub.

"This is headquarters," said Frank. "From here we can fish straight for 40 miles, or alongshore in either direction for as many miles as we want. We should find marlin anywhere along the run and there will be sails, too. We'll be on the northern fringe of the Humboldt Current."

We knew that meant fish, because the Humboldt is famous as one of the greatest feed bags of the Seven Seas.

We steamed out the next morning rigged like an old frigate, but instead of sails galore we were loaded with fishing lines, seven of them trailing in our wake, baited with assorted come-ons for some of the gamest fish in the ocean. There were two outrigger lines baited with 5 pound bonito; two handlines tied to cleats on the transom trolled feathers 40 feet astern trying to pick up some more bonito for marlin bait; and two flat lines offered strip bait to sailfish. Still another sailfish rig ran from a clothes pin fastened on the mast and this one trolled a Panama bait back 80 feet, in between the outrigger lines.

One of the outriggers was fitted with 39 thread line, and other with 80 pound test dacron. For the sails we were using 10 and 15 pound test monofilament, thus bringing any catch made on those two lines into the 12 and 20 pound line test classes of the International Game Fish Association. On the line going to the mast we used 50 pound test dacron, hoping that a big marlin would take that, because it was baited with a big Panama bait.

This day we were expecting any of three kinds of marlin— black, striped, or Pacific blue—plus sailfish and dolphin.

"Besides those," said Frank, "you may tie into bonito, rainbow runners, yellowfin tuna, wahoo, amberjack, and any number of others. You can be sure you'll be busier than you've ever been in your life, regardless of where you've fished."

It sounded great to me. We had a fine boat, an excellent crew, and the right fishing companions. To top everything else, my companions had insisted that since I had never caught a marlin, I should have complete charge of both marlin rigs.

"You catch the first one," they said. "Then we'll try it."

After a few feeble protests I gave in and agreed that if a marlin hit one of the baits I was to fly into action. But having no idea which way to fly, I called Frank into conference.

"It's simple," said that veteran marlin man. "If a marlin takes, you free spool. Then, when he stops to swallow the bait you wait half a minute or so, then start to reel as fast as you can, and when you feel him, strike and keep striking, eight or nine times, with all you have. Lay back on it, drive the hook home, good.

"But," he went on, "if you have a hit and the fish starts jumping right away, then you must start reeling for a tight line, and start striking at once. That's the only chance you have in a case like that. Probably he has hit the leader wire or found something else that scared him, so he doesn't try to swallow the bait. So try to hook him right away."

I settled down in the fighting chair, first watching one bait, then the other, until my eyes felt as though they were watching tennis balls being batted back and forth across a net.

"Relax," said Lee. "If a fish hits, you'll see it first, or hear the line come from the outrigger."

Then, even before I could start to relax, he yelled "Strike!" so loud he made me jump a foot in the air.

He had been reaching up to test the line in the pin on the mast when something struck his bait on the 10 pound test flat line. Without looking to see what fish had hit he stuck the rod butt in the gimbal of the belt he was wearing, and put the reel in free spool. Line leaped from the spool as Frank threw the gears out and slowed the *Seri* to a stop.

"It's a sail," said Clarke, "I saw him take."

Lee waited a bit, then struck with a sharp lift of the rod tip. The rod bent down and then he lifted again and again in a series of short, firm strikes. He didn't dare hit too hard with 10 pound test line.

The fish felt the hook and slammed off a mile a minute for a hundred yards, then got on top and started to tailwalk, churning the water, wiggling its long, lean body for another hundred feet, a beautiful sight, a bragging show of great power.

"A beauty!" shouted Jack Mahony. "Get him in close and make him jump, Lee, so I can take a picture."

"Photographers!" snorted Lee. "I suppose you want me to make him jump exactly 10 feet away, with the sun over your left shoulder."

Fifteen minutes later and exactly 10 feet astern and with the sun where it should have been, the sail did stick his long, thin spear out, then his head, and with a last desperate try for freedom, came straight up, stood on his tail, broadside to us, and fell back in.

"Nice fish," said Ospina. "He'll go 115 pounds."

"Did you get your picture, Jack?" shouted Lee.

"You jumped in front of me just as I clicked the shutter, and all I got was a good view of your back," said Jack in disgust.

We all forgot about pictures then, as Lee tightened down on the drag and finally wound the double line in and when the leader wire came up Ospina grabbed it, got a good grip on the bill of the fish, took the hook from the corner of its mouth, and let it go. The tired sail sank slowly from view, unharmed, but probably wondering what kind of lightning had hit him.

Lee put on another Panama bait, dropped it back and got ready to relax a bit. But he didn't have time for relaxing. We saw another fish back there, sail up, bill out—wham!

"Strike!" shouted Lee.

It proved to be a hundred pounder that tore the ocean wide open, a jumping jack from away back, a fighter to the end. Lee released that one, too.

"Those Panama baits are dynamite," Lee said.

Anyone who plans to fish in Panama should certainly learn to make the Panama bait. For sailfish Lee uses either the belly of a dolphin, or a bonito. The bait fish is cut down either side from the throat to the anal fin, tapering in as it is cut down. The hook is laid in near the top or throat part, and then the whole thing is folded over and sewed, so that the entire bend of the hook sticks out of the throat or top section. When put out, the bait skips along the surface, occasionally kicking up its tail, making a most attractive lure for a hungry fish. From the results we got I think it is probably one of the most enticing baits ever devised. Everything that came our way powdered it without hesitation, with forthright strikes. Even with Ospina and Clarke busily making baits in their spare time, we were always in short supply.

"I notice that you use nothing but whole bonito for marlin," I said.

"Barracuda, mackerel—practically anything in the 2 to 5 pound class will do," said Frank. "Dolphin, too. Even houndfish. But I like to use bonito because they are so hard headed. They ride well on the surface, stand up much longer than other fish under the pounding they take. They are the toughest, there are plenty of them, and they're also easy to catch."

So on the outriggers we used whole bonito ranging from 2½ to 5 pounds, rigged in what is called "the New Zealand way." The mouth of the bait is sewn shut with a piece of twine, the twine tied to the bend of the hook, which is about 1½ to 2 inches ahead of the fish. This free-showing hook does not scare the striking fish in the least and certainly allows for cleaner and more positive penetration.

Sails and marlin often "bill-wrap" the leaders, making spirals in them and kinks that may break easily. Frank makes his wire leaders with three swivels, each length of wire being about 4 feet long, thus keeping the whole thing within the 15 foot leader length allowed by International Game Fish Association rules. And because most leaders are damaged near the terminal point, Frank's technique saves both time and leader wire. When a leader is damaged it is usually only necessary to add a terminal wire to the rest of the leader. The swivels also help the mate when he grabs the wire to bring the sail in so he can bill it, or to haul a marlin within gaffing range.

It was only a few minutes after Lee landed that second sailfish that I saw a long shape in the water back of the bait on the port outriggers. I rushed over and grabbed the rod from the gimbal on the gunwale, slammed down in the fighting chair, put the rod in the gimbel there, and was ready for the hit.

And there it was! A bill came stabbing out. A great dark body swung sideways, the fish hit and yanked the line from the outrigger. I sat there as per instructions, free-spooling line out as the mighty fish ran off, and praying that he'd follow the rules, too. But instead of going down, the line was coming topside and the fish exploded in one of the most spectacular leaps I've ever seen. That long, silvery marlin, with his body shining brightly in the sun, jumped 25 feet across the water, fins extended, as though he were going to run on them when he lit. He cleared the water by 7 feet. The beauty, the grace, the seeming slow motion of it all, sort of suspended in space, reminded me of a bird dog roading, his muscles flowing like oil, up on tip toe, every nerve tense.

I was so busy striking that I didn't get more than a glance, but it was forever photographed in my mind. It was a wonderful feeling to be tied to that seagoing powerhouse, to have him on the end of the slender line that suddenly seemed far too light for such a terrific task.

And he was putting it all over me. He ran 100 feet and came out again, in a broaching leap this time, and while he had his head out we all saw the bait soar through the air, away from him. He had thrown the hook.

I felt terrible. I had muffed a marlin.

"It wasn't your fault," they said. "He wasn't well hooked. You'll get the next one."

The *Seri* was under way again, nosing out into the deep blue. We were 30 miles offshore now and looking in we could see the tops of the 9000 foot Choco Mountains that parallel the Panamanian coast and continue down into Colombia.

Things dropped off a bit. We turned and headed in.

Jack took time out from his camera to land a 120 pound sailfish. Lee caught another just under that weight. Those Pacific sails were tremendous battlers, game to the core. They jumped up fits and gave our expert anglers fits, too. And all the while I sat there and watched the marlin baits skip along, vowing to myself that I'd do this and that to the next marlin that had the temerity to test my tackle.

Then something slapped the bonito bait on the 80 pound test line. I grabbed the reel and dropped back to the fish. This one performed according to Hoyle and so did I. He had the bait for 10 seconds and then I struck, good and hard, several times. I felt him and knew I was into him.

Right away I knew it was a sail instead of a marlin. He came bursting through the surface, ramming it with his spike, jumped high and wide, and tied himself in barrel knots. I weathered that outburst, stayed with him and finally brought him in. As we released him, Ospina estimated the fish at 100 pounds, by far the biggest sailfish I had ever caught.

This seemed to be the home of Pacific sailfish. It was at this very spot that one of the all-time great catches of sailfish had been made. It happened in July, 1957, when Tracy Haverfield and Jack Russell told their fishing partners, Frank Baxter and Frank Violette, that they could have the trolling to themselves that day. Tracy and Jack were going to skiff fish the shores of the Moros, the two islands at the mouth of Piñas Bay. They spent a few hours casting along the shores of the first island, then decided to move across to the other, and since it was quite a long haul, Tracy put overboard a 20 pound test trolling outfit with a rubber squid for bait.

They hadn't gone 100 yards when two sails suddenly appeared in back of the skipping bait and began to fight for it. One took. Tracy gave a quick, foot-long dropback by dipping down with the rod and then struck. The fish was hooked. He came out, looking as long as the skiff, and with blood in his eye, and jumped six times in a row, in a terrific exhibition of power and grace and wildness. Tracy weathered the jumps and then just held on when the fish settled down to a long, steady boring away. This was really the beginning of the fight. And it was a long bout! That sailfish towed the skiff 20 miles out to sea before it began to weaken and even then it was still another hour before Tracy could work it in close to the skiff.

Then the problems really began. They were not organized to land a fish of that size in a 14 foot skiff and this fish was far from worn out. He was still plenty green. They weren't a bit anxious to share the boat with him. Finally Jack got in the bow and when Tracy brought the fish in, he grabbed the bill in both ungloved hands. Then that stubborn fish went right up in the air, his whole body out.

"Don't let him fall in the boat!" Tracy yelled.

Somehow Jack managed to keep his grip, the fish fell back into the water and quickly Tracy jabbed the short gaff and got it through the head. The point pinned the fish to the side of the skiff. So there they were 20 miles at sea, in a cockleshell of a 14 foot skiff, with a 9 foot sailfish pinned to their small craft.

"It gave me sort of a funny feeling," Tracy said. "We finally decided the only thing to do was to bring him aboard, so he hit him over the head with a club, inched him on board, and ran on in to anchorage."

The sailfish weighed 120 pounds. And when the *Seri* steamed in, Frank Baxter had a 159 pounder, a new world record on 10 pound test line.

"A wonderful day," said Tracy. "But not too much to expect at Piñas Bay."

A second story every angler is almost sure to hear on every trip he makes out of Balboa deals with a great fight with a marlin, a fight which, although it happened many years ago, still goes the rounds whenever anglers meet in Panama. Bob Walker and Jack Mahony were fishing off San Jose, on their way back from Piñas Bay to Balboa. Jack, who was with us on the current trip, remembered it as clearly as if the incident had happened only yesterday.

"Bob was using a 16/0 reel and 39 thread line," he said. "But we knew from the first that he had an extra big fish and that even with such equipment he was in for a long fight."

They were right. The first three hours were rough, with the mighty fish pulling against the drag while the doughty angler used every trick he knew to beat this salty, big-finned Firpo.

Then it jumped, and everyone on board gasped.

"An elephant with fins," Jack described it. "This was the grandfather of the species. This marlin was 12 feet long, at least, and had a tremendous girth around the shoulders. His bill was like a baseball bat."

It was one of the all-time great battles between man and beast. The marlin broached at least 30 times, surging forward on the surface, half way out. He never stopped fighting. By nightfall Bob had got the double line in four times but that brute was still too green to handle. As night fell so did the hopes of the fishermen. They used a flashlight to follow the line as Bob went on fighting. After 5½ hours it seemed to him that the fish was weakening and again he started to bring it in closer.

"He's rubbing against something!" he shouted suddenly.

Out there in the darkness it could be anything. He eased off on the drag, away off, and the marlin took line slowly from the reel. When Bob tightened down again the scraping feeling was not there. Then came that awful moment that every fisherman knows, but is so hard to believe—and harder to take. The line parted. Bob reeled in the 35 feet of line left him and the great fight was over.

"Scraped against a wooden plant or floating log, I guess," he said. And that was all.

"I wonder if anyone will ever hook that monster again," I said to Jack when he had finished telling the story.

"Can't say," he replied. "But you can be sure that plenty of us have tried that same area, in hopes."

Even with two stories like those ringing in our ears, we had better luck than we could have dreamed of. The sailfish were really on the prowl. They took everything we offered and turned on some fancy fin work, running the gamut of jumps, leaps, broaches, and soundings, laying down a pattern of runs, dashes, and dives that left us hanging on the ropes. It was fantastic fishing. We came in that night without a marlin, but between them Jack and Lee had landed 8 sailfish, probably lost that many more, and I had added two to the score. Besides that, we were in dolphin up to our ears, dolphin that were dashing streaks of yellow and green lightning, that ranged from 20 to 50 pounds, the biggest dolphin we had ever encountered.

Generally you expect dolphin to powder the cut baits, but these blunt-nosed blankety blanks thought a 5 pound bonito rigged carefully for marlin was the kind of chowder they craved. They tore up the small baits first, then turned their venom on the bonito. They jumped slam bang, helter skelter around the boat as if trying to outdo the acrobatics of the sails and marlin. They kept us busy as much as an hour on a single 40 or 50 pound fish. It was wonderful.

We kept a few of the dolphin to eat, using the bellies for Panama baits, and carried a few more in to our anchorage. There was a small village ashore and every evening the Spanish-speaking natives, descended from long-ago canal workers, plus a crew of colorful Choco Indians, would appear. In a session of high-speed bargaining we would trade them fish hooks, fishing lines and fish for the wonderful bananas, oranges, coconuts, and corn they brought with them. Then they would stay for hours, just sitting there in their cayucas looking at us, talking a little now and then. All the time every one of them had a handline overboard, baited with a bit of fish, and constantly they were pulling in small ones, spiced now and again with a 3 pound snapper or a 4 pound Pacific barracuda.

The Choco Indians were dignified, gentle, and quiet, and very friendly, but we learned that only a few miles inland the mountain-dwelling Indians are dangerous. It was in this general area that five American missionaries were killed by hostile Indians.

The next day things went as the first—lots of sails and dolphin, but no marlin came near my outrigger lines. Then in the late afternoon fate played a mean trick on me.

"Watch my outrigger baits for a few minutes," I told Frank. "I've got to reload color film and I want to go below where it's dark."

No sooner was I below than I heard a yell.

"Strike!" shouted Frank.

I felt the boat stopping and I dropped everything on the bunk and rushed on deck. Frank had the port outrigger outfit in the fighting chair and I saw line running off the reel.

"A marlin," said Lee. "We saw him."

Finally the fish stopped, sat down and chewed on the bonito bait. Frank reeled in the slack, felt the fish, and starting striking. He struck a dozen times. He kept reeling and striking and each one of those hard strikes must have befuddled the thinking apparatus of that fish. He came half way out, a small black marlin, pectoral fins rigid. When he fell back, Frank kept at him, kept him coming in. Then the fish dashed off and went down a hundred feet or so, but again he stopped and again Frank went to work on him. The double line showed and the fish must have seen the boat because he dashed off once more. This time he didn't go far and Frank was pumping and pumping and gaining line, and again the double line showed. Then came the wire leader and Ospina had it and sent the gaff home.

"Four and one-half minutes," said Jack. "And that fish will go about 218 pounds."

"A fine way to treat a friend," I said. "Wouldn't even let me get a roll of film in my camera without snatching a marlin while my back was turned."

"Too bad," said Frank with a grin. "But I always say, if you want to fish you should fish, and if you want to take pictures you should take pictures."

Camera or no, I finally did get my marlin that day, the 321 pounder that Jack showed me how to weigh by measurement. It turned out to be the heaviest marlin of the trip.

In all, during the nine days we fished at Piñas, we took 2 black marlin, 31 Pacific sailfish, 96 dolphin and uncounted other species such as amberjack, bonito, grouper, mackerel, jacks, African pompano, rainbow runner, sharks, tuna, and snapper. Even as we headed home, the fish would give us no respite. The morning we started north, Lee and I were sitting in the fighting chairs, ready. Jack was filling in the daily log. Frank was running the boat. Twelve foot waves built up and came rolling in on us from behind.

"Look!" said Lee suddenly. "There's a dolphin in that wave."

"It's not a dolphin," I said. "It's a sail and he's standing on his head."

"It's a dolphin," Lee stared. "Oh, I see the sail, too. But the dolphin is 20 feet to the right of him."

I switched my eyes, and I saw him, too! The dolphin was just under the curl of the big wave and all I could see was his two evenly spaced, bright blue pectoral fins. I looked back at the sail. He was 30 feet back, riding in on a great wave, head down at the base of it, his entire length showing clear.

"Strike!" I heard Lee shout.

Then I saw the sail head for my skipping bait. He took.

"Strike!" I shouted, in my turn.

My sail ran out and I hooked him. It was a great fight for perhaps 30 seconds. Then he came up and out, stood on his tail, shook his head and threw the hook.

"I have the big dolphin on," grunted Lee as he pumped for line.

The beautiful, chopped-faced acrobat came out in a startling leap in a try for escape that carried him 30 feet across the water. He twisted his long body, seemed to be swimming in the air. Lee held on. Thirty minutes later he was still holding on. This was the largest dolphin I had ever seen and he fought harder than any I had every watched. He ran a series of 100 yard dashes, going so fast he seemed to bat the waves down. He jumped a dozen times, each jump a masterpiece of flowing motion and grace. His yellow and green body glinted in the sun. He was everything a game fish should be and he fought like the champion he was.

Because he had hit an outrigger bait, Lee was using 80 pound test line, but even so it took 40 minutes to get the fighting dolphin in. He weighed 55½ pounds, a new Club Record for the Miami Beach Rod and Reel Club books, and a wonderful catch to write *finis* to the trip. We made the Perlas Islands that night and nosed into a quiet cove. Next day we ran across to Balboa.

Fishing so far from any centers of population, on the edge of the South American continental wilderness, you'd expect to be beyond contact with anyone but the members of your own party. But it's surprising how those Panama boats get around. All the way from Cocos to Piñas, on the way out, we had the *Skipjack* for company, with Sam Moody and Bob Daniel of the Canal Zone aboard, along with Colonel and Mrs. R.W. Glock. Colonel Glock had been stationed in the Zone at one time and they were back for a vacation visit. Their boat swung in right beside us the first night at Piñas Bay and we threw lines and tied the boats together, stern to stern, and all had dinner together while the fishing talk flew in all directions.

Frank told us about a reef that lies 7 miles north of Piñas Bay, perhaps 5 miles offshore and which, since its discovery only a few years ago, has been the arena for some strange happenings, fish-wise. This reef is a mountain peak that rises up to within 300 feet of the surface. The number, size, and variety of fish around it is so fantastic that it must be seen to be believed. A few years ago the *Caiman II*, out of Balboa, pulled over the reef and the boys aboard spotted a great marlin as he came out of the water with a bonito crosswise in his mouth. They knew he would drop down and swallow the fish and come up for more so they put our four buoys to mark the spot and began to troll the area, waiting and hoping. He had looked like a thousand pound fish and these veterans were ready for him with 39 thread line which tests out at 117 pounds breaking strength.

In the meantime, the *Chi Chi*, also out of Balboa on its way to Piñas bay, came up on the markers. Aboard the *Chi Chi*, George Nickel was trolling a two day old bonito on 39 thread line. He was ready for anything too, but what he really needed was some new bait and when he saw the buoys and the *Caiman* circling around he was sure they were into bonito, catching them for marlin bait. So he headed for those same markers. And there, right in front of those hard-working fishermen on the *Caiman*, that great black beast came up and took George Nickel's old and ragged bonito!

George recovered from his amazement in time to grab the rod, go through the motions and hook the fish. The marlin, estimated at 1000 pounds by men who had seen plenty of them, started to jump. He jumped and he jumped and he ran every bit of line off the big reel and snapped the line like a thread. Then he jumped a few more times, just to rub it in, and kept on jumping till he looked like a minnow in the distance.

"Another time," said Frank. "We did land a 755 pound marlin there. It was a big silver,[3] a new world record. We took it ashore to weigh it, then went right out again and 10 minutes after we started to fish we were into another. This one was a black and he weighed 777 pounds."

Fishing over this fabulous reef is by no means limited to bill fish. It was here that Frank Baxter and Ed Corlett of Miami, both using spinning outfits and casting heavy jigs, had simultaneous hits and were into a pair of extra heavy fish. An hour later each of them landed a world record amberjack in their respective line test classes. Ed took over the 30 pound line test class on the International Game Fish Association charts with a 93½ pounder, while Frank won in the 20 pound line test class with a 63 pounder.

When the *Skipjack* headed home, another boat, the *Caiman II*, which had figured in the story Frank told us that night, but now skippered by Ted Schmidt, had already started picking us up on the ship-to-shore phone. They had just cleared the Perlas Islands and were fishing their way over to us. On our first contact they were fighting a 180 pound marlin and the next time we heard from them, one of their fishermen, Colonel Post, had just landed a 250 pounder. That night the *Caiman* was tied up at our stern and again we had dinner with the people on board and again the fishing stories that went the rounds were enough to scare you. Ted Schmidt

---

[3] Silver marlin have now been re-classified by the International Game Fish Association as black marlin, and the "silver marlin" classification removed from the lists.

told us the one to top them all, with his own brother Louis as the main actor in a real hard-luck drama.

In June, 1949, Louis, who as a boy, had lost an arm and a leg in a railway accident, tied into a great black marlin off San Jose. He fought it for four hours, until one arm of the fighting chair broke off under the pressure. This may sound far-fetched to anyone who isn't familiar with marlin fishing, but it is a fairly frequent occurrence for a chair to come apart under the terrific strain. Sometimes the arm does come off, as happened in this case. It can be rugged.

Louis survived the broken chair but soon the harness broke, too. Although all hands agreed that at this stage he had the fish licked, Louis was out of business, hampered as he was by his physical disabilities. So he passed the rod over to his brother John. John fought the marlin for another 48 minutes before he finally brought it in and landed it. That fish went 1006 pounds, the first over 1000 pounds to be landed anywhere. But, of course, because of the change of fishermen handling the rod, the catch could not be regarded as "legal."

It's too bad the breaks were against Louis on that one. Everyone who fishes with him credits him with as much know-how on marlin as anyone they've met—a statement strongly substantiated by the number of fish brought into his boat, the *Caiman II*, originally built for Zane Grey. In late January and early February of 1963, my friends Mr. and Mrs. Ross Walker of Richmond, Virginia, went out with Louis and in 12 days of incredible fishing around the reef 10 miles from Piñas Point they landed a total of 47 marlin. Ross's largest going 723 pounds, and Mrs. Walker's weighing 655. All but 11 were released, those 11 being retained for butchering as food for the natives, and for hospitals in Balboa. The Walkers' take on that trip was undoubtedly the greatest black marlin catch of all time.

It will be a long time before their record is equalled.

On my own first few trips to Panama waters we were always too busy with bill fish and other oceanic swimmers to put our minds to the casting possibilities of the inshore area. But in 1962 we made a trip that was pointed specifically at trying for some of the monsters we knew were around and could be reached by casters. We were using heavy, 5 ounce plug rods, 6 feet 2 inches long, and stout bait casting reels mounted with cub drags and loaded with 15 pound test monofilament line. To foil the tricks of some of the crafty deep dwellers that head straight for the rocks when hooked, we added 2-foot lengths of number 5 wire as leaders, and these were fastened to the line with a swivel in order to prevent twisting.

Our lures ranged through an impressive battery of offerings, from 1½ to 3 ounce Creek Chub popping plugs, some of them 6 inches long, to 1½ and even 3½ ounce Upperman Big Ben under-water bucktails with 3/0 and 5/0 hooks. We had selected lures that had good strong hooks because some of these heavyweights can completely demolish a lure with their crushing jaws. Some of the big plugs come from the manufacturer with hooks already wired together, while others, which had two or three sets of tre-ble hooks, we had wired ourselves by fastening number 5 wire from the eye of one hook to the eye of the other, so if these strong-mouthed fish pulled one set out they would still be held by the second set.

To the fresh water plug caster this may sound a little on the fan-tastic side, but this heavy plug casting outfit fills a need in the salt water and is becoming increasingly popular with those who like to cast rather than troll and who enjoy the thrill of probing the depths to see what monsters they can find "down under." You can lift and land a heavy fish much more quickly with this outfit than is possi-ble with the more pliable spinning rod or lighter plug rod.

Best of all, it allows you to reach fish you might not get to with other tackle. For deep water jigging, where the lure must go down 100 feet or even 200 feet, the heavy plug rod is unbeatable, having the power to bring the lures up smartly through the water in 2-foot hops, an action that is irresistible to those deep-dwelling fish. And the big, heavy jigs have the weight to go down fast, and, once down, to withstand the current rather than be swept away by it.

The short, stout rod also allows you to give more action to any bucktail or plug, than, say, spinning tackle. You can make a surface plug stand up and talk fish talk, give it the zip to bring strikes. You can give it the force to make underwater lures jump forward or upward, as the case may be—action that is needed to tease the fish into striking. You can cast heavy lures long distances, as much as 150 feet, with accuracy. And you can strike harder and faster and drive the hook home with more authority with the stiff plug rod than you can with a pliable plug or spinning rod.

Because of all this, the heavy plug casting outfit can be used in many types of water. You can throw a lure against the banks of an island, under an overhanging limb where you suspect a fish may lie, or drop it alongside the rocks that jut up from a reef. It's a thoroughly adjustable instrument.

"You've got to be tough when you go after these babies," said Luke Gorham of Miami, who was with us on the 1962 trip.

We were at Isla Pacheca, close inshore, casting big bucktail jigs, letting them sink, then jigging them up. Luke leaned back on his rod, putting it to the fish he was fighting.

"I've been in training for this trip. I knew what we would be up against."

Just then his fish surfaced, some 20 feet out.

"Broomtail grouper," I said, as I saw its tail stick out.

Luke had been fighting the fish for half an hour then. It was another 30 minutes before he landed the 30 pounder. Once it was aboard, Moses Nunnally and I picked up our rods, cast our jigs overboard, let them sink down to the bottom and started jigging.

"Got 'im!" Moses yelled almost immediately.

He struck one, twice, three times, and kept on striking, so hard that he came up on his toes each time. Then when he figured the hook was set in the mouth of whatever was down there, he moved in to the rail and tried to lift. Instead of the fish coming up, the rod tip went down to the water.

"A regular Panama horse," growled Moses. "I've got the drag set as tight as it will go, yet he's taking line."

His battle lasted even longer than Luke's. It was 20 minutes before he started the fish moving at all, and another 10 minutes before it showed, deep down.

"It's another broomtail," said Luke, peering over the side. "It's coming fast now."

But it was a long time before it finally reached the surface and lay there on its side.

"39 pounds," said Moses a few minutes later when we weighed it. "Imagine getting a fish like that on a plug casting outfit."

It's particularly good fun casting a big popper with the plugging gear, trying not for the surface swimmers but for the deep dwellers that often come up to feed on them. One day at Isla Gallera we spotted an acre of finning rainbow runners. As we watched, it looked as if a mine field exploded as some other kind of fish attacked them from below. Two pound rainbow runners were rammed into the air. The water boiled up and popped. Petrels gathered noisily to pick up leftovers from the feast of the marauders.

I cast a 7-inch popping plug into the maelstrom and gave it a short pop. It blurped good and deep, sounding like the cut-short bellow of a bull. Suddenly there was a reddish tinge to the water around it and I knew it was a big snapper. When I struck, it felt like chopping into a locomotive with an axe. Shivers ran up my arms. I struck again, then held the reel handle tight and let the cub drag do the work. The fish dove for the bottom, yanking yards of line from the spool, making the reel handle shake in its moorings. He didn't stop until he had taken out 150 feet of line. Then he settled down to some plain and fancy head shaking. When he finished that he took off again, slowly this time, but with plenty of power.

It was a long time before I got him coming our way but at last I did and finally got him in. He weighed 33 pounds even, a great, fighting, dog-toothed snapper that I'll remember for a long time for his fight, but mostly for the strength of his strike to the big surface popper.

There's a very definite technique to casting with the big plug outfit. You don't cast with a snap of the wrist with these heavy lures; and rather than starting with the lure tight against or only a few inches from the rod tip (which can be done, but makes for erratic casting), the lure is allowed to hang down about 12 to 18 inches from the tip. The throw is then made sidearm and slightly under-arm, as a sort of lob, up and out. Using 15 pound test line and thumbing the line lightly as it goes out, you can get off a good cast.

This tackle is widely used in Panama waters by those who like to intersperse their trolling for marlin and sails and dolphin with casting, either from a skiff, which they carry on the cruiser, or from the stern of the cruiser itself, which is feasible in many places such as the Piñas Bay and Perlas Island. Old hands will try it on anything. One of the greatest catches ever made on such tackle was an 80 pound Pacific sailfish taken by Luis de Hoyos of Monticello, N.Y., who has fished Panama for many years.

Luis was fishing off Piñas Bay one day when he spotted several tailing sailfish lolling on the surface. He cast out a feathery jig to them and had a hit at once. That sail came right out in a straight up leap, showing all his length. It was an awesome sight to Luis, stand-ing there with a plug casting outfit in his hands. Sailfish are tough on any tackle. What could he do with this?

He hung on and then ensued one of the most grueling and thrilling battles in plug casting history. It was an hour and a half before he got the sail within 50 feet of the boat. Then he saw that closely following it were 12 other sails, all watching the action. After another half hour all but four of them departed but the quartette came in and swam like a convoy, only 20 feet out and 20 feet down, escorting his fish through all its maneuvers. They stayed with it till the bitter end when, at long last, after 2½ hours from the moment it hit, he brought the fish in.

Those Freedom-Loving Sickletails

The permit of southern waters is fast, powerful and shrewd, and he doesn't want publicity. That's why the all-tackle record has never exceeded a mere 42 pounds, 4 ounces.

"Permit!" shouted Captain Floyd Majors.

Fred Pabst, Jr., of Manchester, Vermont, cast the blue crab two feet in front of the black, sickle-shaped caudal fin the guide had sighted. He held his breath as he waited, then saw the entire tail as the feeding fish stood on his head to suck in the bait. He waited to be sure that the fish had it deep, then, as the tail slipped under and line started to go through his fingers, he braced and struck. The spinning reel shook to the core as the hook went home and that permit bolted and shot down the shoreline.

"He's a big one!" cried Floyd Majors. "You'll never stop him. I'm going to crank up and follow."

"Make it fast," gasped Fred. "He's taking line by the handful."

The outboard buzzed into action and they took off after the charging fish, Fred reeling desperately, trying to get line back, and Majors just as busy dodging jutting coral rock in the shallow water.

"He's running as fast as we are!" cried Fred. "And I can't give him any more butt on account of the line."

"You and your five-pound test," groaned Majors.

Then with a snort of relief, he gunned the motor as at last the skiff cleared the shallows. The fish was running steadily down the shore. A mile and a half from where he hit, he turned toward the Gulf Stream. The chase moved seaward perhaps another mile and a half, only to reverse itself when the permit turned back, quartering a bit, toward where the fight had begun.

He had weakened some, now, from the long, hard pull, and Fred was putting the line back on the reel. On the flat again, at Craig Key where they had started, Majors killed the motor. But somehow that permit didn't seem so tired. He circled, using his big, flat body broadside to the boat. He was good at in-fighting.

"He's pulling my arms right out at the shoulders," moaned Fred.

"Pump him," said the captain.

"Pump!" replied Fred. "What do you think I'm doing? This fish is killing me."

But bit by bit he was gaining in that tug of war and at last he steered the permit alongside and Majors netted the fish, which weighed an even 36 pounds and was posted by the International Game Fish Association as the world record permit caught on line testing under 12 pounds.

Found throughout the Caribbean area and up the Florida coast, with a few strays going north in the Gulf Stream, the permit is strictly a warm water fish. They are seen in tempting numbers from Miami southward, and farther down the Keys they are fairly numerous, particularly at remote Content, Harbor, Sawyer and Johnson Key on the outer fringes as you look to the Gulf of Mexico. Still further out, they frequent exotic places with euphonious names like the Marquesas and the Dry Tortugas Islands, favorite permit spots, where the angler really has a chance because there are usually enough permit that he may muff a few casts and still try again.

At Content is perhaps the hottest permit fishing of the entire Keys. There you see great schools flittering along over the white sandy bottom in unbelievably clear water, a perfect mark but a hard target to hit. They feed on the shallow banks sometimes, in water from 12 inches to six or seven feet deep. Schools numbering from a few to 20 fish move smartly along in military formation, snatching food as they go. When they flash suddenly into a sandy spot, their dorsal and caudal fins are waving black streamers, marking their course. No bottom-feeding fish moves faster.

As is the case with every species that anglers seek, fishermen tell stories of monstrous permit seen, but the biggest one on the books of the IGFA is the all-tackle world-record catch made on Sept. 11, 1953, when R.H. Martin took a 42 pound 4 ouncer while fishing at Boca Grande, Florida. The only report of a larger member of the species taken on rod and reel was a 62-pound fish sent to Al Pflueger from Bimini in the Bahamas 20 years ago for mounting. But that tremendous catch apparently went unheralded among anglers generally. Anyone catching a 62-pound permit today would be famous.

The old saying that there are bigger fish in the ocean than ever were caught certainly applied to the permit. Dixie and Bill Knowles, well-known Keys guides, found that out first hand, as they fished the reefs off Tavernier. They were commercially fishing for mutton-fish and grouper in 60 feet of water and were using handlines that tested 72-pounds, strong enough to pull down a B-49. Their sturdy 8/0 hooks were baited with crawfish. Dixie had a strike and feeling perfectly secure with that stout line, heaved back and started hauling. Imagine his surprise when the haul went into reverse and he found the line slipping through his heavily gloved hands. He braced his feet and tugged back and fifteen minutes later hauled over the side a permit that they both knew was no teenager.

Hardly had that one flopped aboard when something almost yanked Bill out of the boat. He tightened, and yelled as 200 yards of line zipped out. Finally he stopped the run and the fight was on. That fish gave Bill a fit. It ran and sounded and tore things wide open until he despaired of ever landing it. Neither fisherman could guess what it was until, 25 minutes after the strike, Bill raised it to the surface and they saw that he, too, had connected with a big permit. By the time he had that one in the boat his calloused hands had deep grooves in them, his gloves hung on by shreds and his fingers were sore and bleeding. It was a bigger fish than the one Dixie had landed.

When they reached shore and weighed those permit, they were 45 pounds 4 ounces, and 48 pounds 8 ounces, both heavier by far than the existing IGFA world record.

While it may only be due to the fact that more anglers fish the Keys than cover other waters where the permit is found, it does seem that big permit like that area. A quick survey of IGFA records bears this out. Two of the listed world records were established on the Keys—E.J. Arnold's 41 pounder, a 20 pound test record; and the woman's all-tackle record, 38 pounds, both taken at Islamorada.

Yet while the above are world records, reports continue to pour in about great hulks of permit roaming far waters and scaring the pants off timid anglers. I talked to a native of the Isle of Pines, Cuba, and he told me about catching 80-pound permit on handlines off the south coast of the island. He claimed to have seen some that would weigh 100 pounds. At Bimini, an anglerette guided by Captain John Cass tied into a permit that weighed 42 pounds. But just before it was landed, the line wrapped around the tip of the rod and broke it, thus spoiling the unhappy lady's chance at both the men's and women's all-tackle record of the time.

Before light-tackle angling for permit came to the front, a scattered few went for them with the lighter thread lines and with plug and fly casting outfits. In 1950 Bob MacChristian of Miami cast a spinning lure in front of a feeding permit, had a hit and an hour later boated a 23-pounder, an outstanding catch on 5-pound line. That, as far as can be learned, was the first record of a permit caught on an artificial lure cast and retrieved in regulation spinning manner on regulation spinning gear. (Fred Pabst set his world record with a spinning outfit, but he used bait.) But since that time many other casters have taken permit on small, lead jigs on 1/0 hooks.

There are also a number of reports of permit being taken by plug casters. Miamian Howard Clark leads the field with two, a 26½-pound fish caught in 1949 and a 31¾ pounder taken in 1950. He took both at the same spot, plug casting from Long Key Bridge on the famed Overseas Highway to Key West. With suitable modesty, the author claims the only two permit ever recorded as taken on fly-fishing equipment, one 5 pounds 10½ ounces, and another that went 11 pounds 8 ounces. Both were taken at Content Key.

From the moment of my first encounter with him, the shy and elusive permit has been the fish I dream about. They may not be too numerous and they are difficult to get to, but they put a fever in a fisherman's blood.

Permit are bottom feeders, the majority of the items on their diet being found on, and in some cases under, the ocean floor. Even those who are familiar with the rising blood pressure occasioned by the discovery of a bonefish tail sticking straight out of the water will admit that there is extra punch to the sight of the black sickle of the permit cutting up into the air, disappearing, and slashing up again 10 feet further along his course. They feed fast, darting along peering into holes in the coral, looking under rocks, digging into grassy beds for tasty shrimps and crabs, and, as they feed head down, their bodies tilt upward and in shallow water their tails break the surface and flash in the sunlight. The sight of a permit tailing is one of angling's greatest thrills. It does things to the knees.

The flat-bodied permit is designed for the tough, flashing life he leads, with a framework of ribs that can take a terrific pounding. I have seen the little gaff-topsail pompano and the common pompano feed on the surf on sand flees in the midst of tumbling breakers that knocked them to the sandy bottom and slammed them on the beach. And recognizing the similarity of the permit in form and feeding habits, one would naturally expect them to have stout ribs. But my first view of a permit rib was an eye opener. Taken from a 22-

pound permit, that rib, just below where it joined the backbone, was 2 inches across and almost an inch thick. The composition was as hard and dense as ivory. There are four ribs of this nature, then they taper rapidly towards the tail, where the ribs are again mere fish bones.

Permit have a habit of sunning themselves, lying on the surface with the tips of their dorsal and caudal fins sticking out, head down, dozing it seems. In such a position they look as if they were on the flats feeding and tailing, but they must either be asleep or very intent on scanning the bottom because when they behave in that manner it is possible to get much closer without frightening them.

While I have never had a hit from one at such a time, once at Content Key when we were fishing for baby tarpon in 10 feet of water I watched a more or less accidental encounter with one. We were into tarpon up to our ears. I cast to what I thought was one of that species and had a hit but didn't connect. Then Bill Smith, my companion, yelled he had a permit on. It put a permanent screech in Bill's reel and the hook pulled out when he had run 200 yards in 9½ seconds flat. After that we looked more closely when we went for baby tarpon, and sure enough, we began to find permit feeding and staying right with them as they moved along.

For three years I had the good fortune to be one of a party that took off on a sort of busman's holiday every spring. The personnel was made up of several well-known Keys guides—Captains Bill and Bonnie Smith, Captain Leo Johnson and his mate Steve, my wife and myself, with transportation supplied by Captain Leo's charter boat the *Islamorada*. The jaunt was strictly "Operation Permit" with equipment limited to fly tackle, and with only occasional sorties for snapper for the table. Our first trip will always be a sad memory of endless, fruitless casting to hundreds of permit. School after school swept by without even a side glance at our offerings. Now and then a single would deign to follow a fly for a few feet, then fade away. Day after day we cried in our coffee and figured ways to make a permit take a fly. We knew they could be taken on feathers, trolling, because it had been done. They should hit a fly.

On the last afternoon of that first trip, I finally had a hit. He took a white streamer fly and departed with both fly and leader. I'll never know whether the leader was not attached to the fly line properly, or if the line had been rubbed across some coral rock till it had become weakened. I do know that that was, and still remains, the blackest spot in my fishing memories.

The next year we went back loaded for bear with every kind of fly, feather, spoon, and lure that could be cast with a fly rod. This trip we had three hits and I landed a 5 pound 10½ ounce permit that hit a Johnson Golden Minnow Spoon, fly rod size. Things seemed better, but even then, being purists all, we did not feel that we had really proved a permit would take a fly.

Meantime, we heard reports of this and that angler tangling with a permit on fly equipment—how so-and-so almost landed one that hit a yellow bucktail or a red and white streamer. Dick Splaine of Key West had had several hits from permit and Hagen Sands of Islamorada had tangled with four that were bigger than average. The first, and largest, Sands estimated at 50 pounds and this baby hit and started for Europe and never did stop. He took everything Sands had in the line department whisking it from the reel a mile a minute, the fly line, 200 yards of backing—then zing! exit Mr. Permit. Three others around the 30 pound class put up terrific fights, one of them taking Sands a mile out to sea before breaking off. Another got away in a hurry, and the fourth supplied the real heartbreak. Sands had his hand on the fish when it gave a last desperate wiggle and snapped the leader.

But in spite of our own past grief and that of others we knew, we set out on our third annual trip more pepped up than ever. This was going to be the payoff.

The first day out it blew 20 miles an hour and things were plenty tough for fly casting. The wind even blew our retrieved line out of the bottom of the skiff and finally Bill Smith and I, who were partners that day, decided that we should go overboard and wade the flats. We pushed along, about 30 feet apart, peering at the bottom for the shadowy forms and scanning the surface for the sickle-shaped tails. Suddenly I saw Bill stop and cast directly upwind. The fly dropped and the dorsal of a permit cut the water as the fish went for it. There was a big swirl as he took. And then, as Bill struck, that permit made a comet seem slow. He went across the flat so fast he seemed to knock the waves down in front of him, like a bowler making a strike in every frame.

I turned and looked at Bill. His face was all happiness.

Then he came back to earth. "He's taking me!" he yelled. "My backing is nearly gone!"

"Maybe he'll turn!" I yelled back.

"He's going too fast for that!" Bill cried.

A minute later I saw the rod tip bend down almost to the water then spring back up. The line jumped back, too. The fish had run the line out to the reel core and then snapped the tippet.

Later that same day, Leo had his share of being pushed around by a permit. One fish hit his fly so hard that it knocked the rod right out of his hand. It fell into the water and as he groped for it with his right hand, he forgot that he still kept a grip on the line with his left hand. That galloping ghost went out of there like chain lightning, and almost cut his fingers off before he snapped the leader tippet.

"Why, that little round-nosed rascal!" said Leo. "Look what he did to me."

The next day Bonnie Smith dropped a fly right in the teeth of a school of tailing fish and three of them bumped pectorals as they rushed for it. She put home the steel and held the rod high as a 20-pounder reached out for Brownsville, Texas, and never stopped. If he kept his course and his speed, he made the 900 miles in 36 hours. But perhaps he found a patch of sand somewhere out in the Gulf of Mexico, and just rubbed that fly out and forgot about it. Bonnie was still shaking an hour later.

The same day, my wife, the only other feminine member of the party, also joined the ranks of those who have hooked and lost permit on a fly. With Bill poling her, she spotted a tailing fish in deep water. She cast the fly, felt the fish and set the hook. He had just got warmed up in a 100-yard dash, a mere trial run, when the fly dropped out of his mouth.

The last day, Bonnie and I went out together and I started right off with a strike from a fish that fought like a 40-pounder. While I had him on, I could see Bill overboard, casting and chasing after a fast-moving school that had come in on a particularly nice bit of sand beach. He hooked one and suddenly I saw it slant over toward where mine was making like a bucking bronco.

"Get that minnow out of here!" I shouted. "He'll cut off my permit."

"Minnow!" screamed Bill. "It's a 30-pound permit. Look out or he'll sink you."

Then both fish got off within seconds and Bill and I glared at each other across the barren water as if each had caused the other's misfortune.

"Well, anyway, that's eight permit we've had hit flies this trip," I said to Bonnie when my temperature had gone back to normal. "At least I feel sure now that they'll make a fly rod fish."

"Well, don't waste your time talking about it," she said shortly. "Get a fly to one of that school over there and we'll be back in business."

Sure enough, there came a school of probably 50 fish, showing black above the light bottom. As we watched, several of them turned sideways, their silvery bodies signalling like a battery of heliographs.

"Try one of those three!" Bonnie said tensely, and I saw where three were swimming along, single file, coming our way. "Cast and pray," she added.

I dropped the fly in front of the first one. The prayer came double from both of us. "Take it. Take it. Take it." I muttered in time with the strip of my retrieve.

And he didn't hesitate, just moved forward a little faster, slanting upward, opened his mouth and swallowed that fly. I struck.

That permit went out of there faster than the reel could click, as if every porpoise in the ocean were after him. He made a straight-away dash, then curved to the left in a looping run that made the line slash through the water. And he held that wild curve till my backing was almost gone. He had close to 700 feet of line out. I was going through mental convulsions trying to hold onto that backing just by wishing. And then, just as if the wishing worked, he turned and came charging at us, a mile a minute, so that he got ahead of the line and I had to reel and reel like mad to try to keep up with him. A couple of times he had so much slack that it seemed to me he could have reached up a fin and pushed that fly right out of his mouth. That was when I began to call him mine. I knew he was thoroughly hooked.

I finally got the line tight between us again. And he was slow-ing. But it was just to try a new trick. He flipped his tail and rubbed his round little nose in the sand till the rod shook and so did I. No matter how firmly that hook was in there, those were tough tactics. Desperately I pulled harder and turned him completely over. That hurt him and he staggered some, while I kept horsing him as hard as I dared on the 8-pound test nylon leader. Then he got his nose down and rocked the rod tip again until I thought he would pull the top section off. I held on with both hands. If anyone ever wanted a fish, I wanted that one.

Once more he headed straight out, still showing plenty of power. But this run was a mere hundred feet and then he went into a series of short dashes, off tackle to the right, then reversed his field and slashed back the other way.

"He's tiring," said Bonnie. "Stick with him."

"Uh," was all I could reply.

He came close in then and I turned him over as he tried to rub his nose again. I kept him coming, with rod held high and managed to lift him away from the bottom as he circled the skiff once, twice, three times. Standing on the seat, then, I turned to Bonnie.

"Ready?" I asked.

"Uh-yes." She answered in a small voice. "I have no landing net but—"

"No net!" I cried in anguish.

"We forgot it," she stated in a firmer tone. "So I'll just pick him out of the water by his tail. That's why permit have those handle-shaped tails, you know."

Silently I swung him around, while Bonnie kneeled in the bottom of the skiff, arms out over the water. I pulled the tired fish in, raising him to the surface. Bonnie reached out as if she landed permit by the tail any old day. She groped, her body between me and the permit. There was a splash and I closed my eyes.

"You can look now," she said calmly. "Here he is."

She was holding a shiny, silvery permit on the bottom of the skiff. He weighed 11 pounds 8 ounces.

Editor's note—since this story was written the author has landed a 19 pound 8 ounce permit while fly fishing at the Isle of Pines, Cuba, with Captain Vic Barothy. Three other permit have also been taken on flies by other anglers.

The Bahamas

The sea off Bimini was as slick as a bowling alley. Two balao baits skipped quietly along behind our cruiser, the *Susie IV.* I had the whole boat to myself because my fishing partner had to stay ashore that afternoon to wait for a business call from stateside. I wondered what I would do if I had a double strike.

"Marlin!" shouted Captain Bob Moody. "On the port bait!"

I saw it at the same time, a fish that seemed to be creeping along on his fins, just back of the balao. Then he sank down and I lost him. There he was at the other bait! I rushed over to the starboard reel, yanked it from the boat gimbel and was ready to strike. Again the fish disappeared without taking and again I saw that big brown spot in the water that meant a fish back of the port bait.

"Wish he'd make up his mind which one he wants," I thought as I frantically shoved the starboard rod back in its gimbel, plunged across the cockpit and grabbed the port rod.

Right then that fish stuck his bill out and took. I was in free spool and let him have some line before I threw the reel into gear, waited till the line came tight, then struck, once, twice, three times, four, five.

Out he came, a long, lean white marlin that looked about 70 pounds. He shot four feet into the air, fell in, came out again, dropped back and streaked for the horizon over Palm Beach way. When he was 200 yards out he jumped again, a sliver of a fish in the distance. Then he went off on another arching run and ended that with another leap.

"You almost had a double header," the Captain shouted.

"Wasn't it the same fish at both baits?" I panted.

"There were two of them—one at each bait," he said. "You'd have been right busy if both had taken."

That was the understatement of the day, I thought as I fought that marlin. It took me 30 minutes to beat him on the 20 pound test line I was using. He weighed close to our guess—65 pounds.

An hour later a big hulk of a blue crashed my bait and took off in a smother of flying spray. He ran a fast hundred yards, jumped and threw the hook.

"300 pounds," said the Captain. "Too bad you didn't get him. Two fish like that in a couple of hours would have been good fishing."

I knew it could happen. Don McCarthy, who heads the Fishing Information Bureau for the Bahamas, at Nassau, had told me about an experience he once had. A friend of his, Bill Berri of Miami, had chartered a boat, the *Neptune,* captained by Harold Schmitt, the "Crunch" of Phillip Wylie's Des and Crunch stores. He had fished for a full two weeks without a strike. Finally, in disgust, he decided to give up and go back to Miami. That was the afternoon that Don showed up.

"The boat's there at the dock," Bill told him. "Why don't you give it a try?"

At 3 o'clock, with only two hours to fish, and armed with only a couple of very old, soggy bonefish for bait, Don started out from the Bimini Docks. In 15 minutes there was a double header strike. Both those soggy baits simply disintegrated. The two marlin, not hooked, sank down in the water. There was no more bait on board.

Then Don spotted two old rubber strip baits, one about 12 inches long, the other about 16, hanging in the cabin.

"Better than nothing," he and Captain Schmitt decided.

They put out the smaller rubber strip on the 9 thread line, the larger one on the 39 thread outfit. Almost immediately there was a terrific strike to the smaller bait and Don had a nice white marlin jumping all over the ocean. Half an hour later he landed it.

Off they started again and the first thing he knew, Don was into a big blue that exploded all over the larger bait. In less than two hours from starting time he was back at the dock with a white that weighed 60 pounds and a blue that went 285, as nice a brace of marlin as you could ask for.

"I hated to face Bill after all those days he fished without a strike," said Don. "But that's the luck of the game."

There are some blue marlin around the Bahamas all year but the best time is in May, June, and July. White marlin are also taken year round, with the biggest showing from January through May. Sailfish seem to follow the same pattern as the white marlin, but for some reason sails are not as plentiful here on the eastern edge of the Gulf Stream as they are on its western borders along the Florida coast. Your chances are much better to come up with a white marlin than a sailfish.

Bimini and its twin island of Cat Cay have long been the center of big game fishing in the Bahamas, with special emphasis on the big tuna run that comes through there in late April and May. At this time great schools of migrating bluefin tuna, 300, 400, and 500 pounders, come rollicking up "tuna alley" between Bimini and Cat Cay, in water so shallow and so clear that from the tuna tower on a boat the fish can easily be seen 200 to 300 yards away. From a plane they look like giant tadpoles, silhouetted again the white sand bottom in singles, pairs, threes, and schools of up to 50 fish.

When the annual tuna tournament is on, a beehive is a rest home compared to Bimini and Cat Cay. Anglers dash around making last-minute arrangements with charter boat men, captains swarm all over their craft checking gear, and mates flex their muscles, thinking of boating those big blimps of tuna. All day long streamlined boats come tearing across the Gulf Stream from Palm Beach, Fort Lauderdale, and other south Florida fishing ports. These are the most beautiful craft of any sport fishing fleet in the world, top-equipped and fast. They have to be fast to get a bait in front of the travelling tuna that have nothing on their minds but these schools of baitfish up north in New England, Nova Scotia and Newfoundland.

Tuna fishing calls for an athlete in the fighting chair but it is undoubtedly one of angling's greatest thrills to join in the chase. The big fish are sighted, you roar along, cut them off so the bait can be dropped back to them, see the water foam in a tremendous boil and then feel the shock of a thudding strike and be tied to a fish that may weigh from 300 to 600 pounds.

Those who seek smaller swimmers of the ocean also find great sport in the waters around these two nearest-to-the-U.S.A. islands of the Bahamas group. Some of the biggest bonefish taken any-where have come from the flats around Bimini. One of the most exciting episodes in all my years of bonefishing took place right on those flats in 1962. I was fishing with Bonefish Sam Ellis, who has guided out of Bimini for 25 years. He took us first to a slough of rel-atively deep water—4 feet is deep for bonefish—where we could see a vast mud put up by a school of bonefish as they nudged the bottom in search of food. Every now and then a flash of silver con-firmed that our prey was there, in that great cloud. For an hour we cast wiggle jigs and artificial "shrimp flies" and took fish after fish, both spinning and fly casting. They were all small, not more than 4 pounds, but even at that they gave a good account of themselves. Then Sam suggested that we go to another flat where he thought we would find some bigger fish.

I knew that big fish are often solitary swimmers, and Sam said that at the flat he had in mind these loners travelled with stingrays, picking up bits of food left by their host.

Several different species of fish have this habit of moseying along with the feeding rays. I've seen them accompanied by redfish, pompano and jacks, as well as bonefish.

"The bonefish that go with stingrays are usually big," Sam was assuring me, as we eased onto the flat. "They're hard to catch, but it's fun to try."

"There!" he said sharply. "To the right. A nice bonefish with a ray over there."

I saw them at once, silhouetted against the bottom, the bonefish swimming over the top of the ray. As I watched, it darted out to the left to grab some bit of food, then went back to the ray, staying right with it as it moved nearer and nearer.

I got ready, and when they were in casting distance I dropped my pink shrimp fly a foot in front of them. There was a streak as the bonefish went for it. I felt him and struck. He left the ray then like Ty Cobb taking off to beat out a bunt. Water jumped from the speeding line and the noise scared the ray and he took off with a loud plop.

The bonefish ran 150 yards at breakneck speed before he stopped. Then when I pulled back on the rod he took off to the right again, then turned and went back to the left. This time when he stopped I put on the pressure, turned him and he came my way. I kept at him, began to get line back, and soon the fly line showed. But about 35 feet out he began to circle and for five minutes he went round and round the boat, beating the water with his strong tail, fighting every inch of the way. At last I got his head up and led him in over the landing net.

Sam took the fly out of his mouth and we let him go. He was at least 10 pounds. Sam had been right when he said the bonefish with those rays were big ones.

Later that day on another flat, as we slipped slowly along looking for fish, Sam scared me half to death.

"Permit," he whispered. "Over there."

About 80 feet away a big black tail waved in the air. It was a permit all right, one of the rarest and most exciting fish of the flats. He

317

was feeding hungrily, head down as he dug in the sand and among the coral, and every time he found a tasty morsel he wiggled his tail like a signal.

My first cast put the fly a foot in front of him, but he was so busy he didn't even see it. I brought the fly in and cast again. This time it lit three feet in front of him just as he brought his head up from where he'd been nosing. He spotted the fly, rushed, and took, and the battle was on. Three-quarters of an hour later I landed him, a fine 23 pounder, only my fourth on a fly in many years of fishing, and the biggest I'd ever taken. That was a good day, on the flats at Bimini.

Originally Cat Cay, Bimini, and a few of the islands near the Bahaman capital of Nassau were the only ones which could readily be reached by anglers. Later the horizon was extended. Soon Bahama Airways, Cat Cay Airways, Mackay Airlines and several charter plane companies were running services from Miami, Fort Lauderdale, and West Palm Beach to various distant islands.

There's a sort of natural geographic division in travelling the islands. The western Bahamas include Bimini, Cat Cay and Grand Bahama; the central Bahamas encompass Andros Island, Joulters Cay and the Berry Islands; the northern Bahamas are the Abaco Cays and Green Turtle Cay; while the eastern islands are Eleuthera and the Exumas. Throughout all of them the bonefish is the staple fish for the light tackle man.

From tiny Walker's Cay, the northernmost island of the Bahamas, all the way down the 660 mile chain to the little known Mayaguana Island, wherever there is a shallow bank the hordes of bonefish pour in with the tide to feed on the minnows, worms, crabs, and shrimp they find along the sandy or marly bottom. On some banks, such as Joulters Cay, I've seen thousands of them, their tails glinting in the sun as they nosed down to root out their food. Wherever there are cuts and rivers among the mangroves you can often find them finning on the surface as they wait for the tide to rise so they can move back among the mangroves to feed. And in deeper water you can spot the great clouds of mud set up as the feeding fish nose along the bottom.

Once I had a week of fabulous bonefishing at Club Peace and Plenty, Georgetown, Exuma, where a long string of cays, all with wide, sandy flats, reach out for miles of almost untouched fishing. As Edroy Rollie, one of the guides, told me, most anglers seldom go as much as a mile from the dock. There's no need to. Edroy himself said he had never gone more than four miles from Georgetown in all his years of guiding. It just hadn't been necessary because fish come at you practically the moment you cross the deep water channel where the skiffs come in.

Edroy proved his point on my second day out. That morning we fished a large muck-bottomed bay that was backed by endless wastes of mangroves. In here you felt almost as if you were in a river, as the tide swirled in and out. Apparently the bonefish liked the water movement, for Edroy soon spotted something.

"Big mud," he said. "Straight ahead."

I looked, and what I saw made my eyeballs come out on sticks. I've seen big schools of bonefish and I've seen big schools of them finning, but never anything like this. The water was discolored as far as we could see, and sticking up, wiggling and swaying as the fish fed or just floating still, were a million bonefish fins. I stood there with my mouth open till at last Edroy couldn't endure it any longer.

"Cast!" he said. "Cast!"

I came to, made the throw and dropped the fly right on the edge of the vast school, where I could see one particularly big tail waving back and forth. That big fish was too busy eating to see the fly but the fellow right behind him must have thought he'd spotted an unearned dividend. He made for it with a splash and a surge that put up a bow wave big enough to spread out over the flat. Wham! He had it, and then he knew he had it. He went into high gear and took off along the edge of the school with a series of explosions that shattered the nerves of everything for miles. The whole school busted out of there in every direction, and by the time I could slow my fish down and finally get him headed our way, there wasn't a tail in sight where seconds before there had been thousands.

"We find them again," Edroy promised. "Just down there a way."

And we did. Half a mile down the flat, there they were again, innocently finning in the sun.

"They may be a little scared now," said Edroy. "We have to be careful."

He pushed us gently in closer and once more I made ready to drop the fly. Again a bonefish rushed it, and again the whole school was spooked. But again, after I had landed him, we found them farther down the flat. And that kept up all morning.

During the rest of the week we saw many more schools like that, huge muds stretching over an acre and more of water. Occasionally there would be a shark with them but after losing a couple fish to the sharks, I learned how to deal with them. Instead of hooking a bonefish, which was then helpless against the attack of the shark, I would cast the fly to the shark and get in some extra fun. A 5 to 10 pound bottlenose or blacktip will make long runs and put up a good, scrappy fight and the blacktip also makes some sensational jumps. More times than not, they cut my leader either with their teeth or by fraying it against their tough, rough hides, but by that time they were usually upset by the whole affair and went away to nurse their wounds and so left the bonefish alone, at least temporarily. Occasionally I used spinning tackle on them, with a wire trace, and for a lure a small wiggle jig or a surface lure such as the Old Joe or Big Boy, and it was a cinch to land them on this gear.

The Phillips wiggle jig is ideal for spinning on many Bahamas flats because the lead head is so shaped that it rides nicely through the water and the hook being set upright, rather than down, allows the lure to bounce across the bottom without getting hung up. Either the deerhair or the feather tail is good. For shallow water the ⅛ ounce is best, while for deeper water the ¼ ounce suits better. Similarly, in fly fishing I use the Phillips pink shrimp fly in size 6 for the very shallow flats but go to the size 4 in the deeper water and occasionally even to size 1.

Certain flats get a reputation for fish of a certain size, but it has been my experience that wherever there are lots of little ones there are also some big ones. Once when I was fishing at Gilbert Drake's Deep Water Cay Club, off the east end of Grand Bahama, I spotted two unusually big bonefish tailing in a school of smaller ones. Those big fellows looked like 15 pounders.

"Big ones!" said Gil. "Really big ones!"

I knew by his voice that he was as excited as I was. We started a quiet approach, leaving the skiff and going overboard to wade. The closer we got the bigger they looked. At 80 feet I figured they might go to 16 pounds apiece, and at 60 feet I had upped that to 18 pounds. That's when I made my throw, a single false cast to get line out, then the forward cast. The small artificial shrimp fly fell four feet in front of the two fish. One of them spotted it, turned and charged. I felt the strike and I struck back and off went the fish.

But somehow his strength didn't come through to me. He didn't make the long run he should. The drag on the reel pulled him to a stop only 50 yards out and when I reeled, he came in fairly easily.

"A little fish got there first," Gil said.

That's the way it goes sometimes. But the little ones don't always get there first, and even in areas where you hear that the fish run small, remember, there can always be a big one.

The best time for bonefish throughout the Bahamas is in November and December, and the season picks up again in April, May, June, and July. However, there are plenty of fish around all year.

Another swimmer of the shallow waters that anglers can usually count on finding around almost any rocky point or in the guts through the flats is the barracuda. Cuda are particularly fond of a plug, especially if it makes a good pop. Once while fishing near Georgetown, Exuma Island, I watched Curt Gowdy, famous Boston Red Sox radio and TV announcer, tangle with a good sized cuda we had spotted at the entrance to a beautiful sandy bay where we had pulled in for lunch. When Curt eased out toward the fish and made his first cast, the plug fell practically on its long snout. It bolted, leaving a big round hole in the water.

"Throw back to him," said Joe Rollie, our guide. "He stopped out there."

This time Curt put the plug 20 feet on our side of the big fish. When he gave it a good hard pop, the cuda moved slowly closer, the way only a cuda can move, without apparently wiggling a fin. Another pop, and he turned away again. Curt pulled the lure in fast, then threw again, and this time it landed five feet beyond the cuda. That seemed to make him mad. He didn't like to be annoyed by that noisy thing. He seemed to set his fins and bare his teeth and then he came at that popper and chomped down hard and when he felt something bite back at him the fight was really on. He sprinted away on a 100 yard dash and came out five feet into the air, rocketing 25 feet across the surface before he hit the water again. I could hear Curt's breath blast out and I heard it again each time that fish jumped, which was again and again. But he finally got him in and Joe reached with the net and scooped. The cuda was so long it hung over the net. Joe reached down, grabbed the leader with one hand and clamped the fingers of the other hand over the back of the fish's neck.

"Watch out for those teeth!" both Curt and I shouted.

But Joe just grinned. He'd handled plenty of cudas and he knew enough to keep his fingers out of reach of the many and sharp teeth that rim the vicious jaws of a 15 pound barracuda—or any size cuda for that matter.

Almost anyone who has flown over the Bahamas has noticed the big, dark blue spots in the water. Fishermen call these "the blue holes." They can be full of big mutton snappers and the jacks that you would expect to find in any deep pocket amidst rocks or flats. But they have their share of surprises, too. Once at Andros Island, Don McCarthy and I fished one of those blue holes that we found set like a lake amid the green water of the shallows. It was about 50 feet in diameter. I dropped my fly into the middle of it and started to retrieve.

"Swwooosshh!" There was a toss of water, a violent wrench at my rod, and automatically I pulled back in a strike. A 40 pound tarpon came sailing out. As he reached the top of his twisting leap he threw the streamer fly far up into space.

There aren't too many tarpon in the Bahamas but every once in a while you'll find them in these blue holes and in the cuts between the keys. They seem to cruise back and forth in the channels and sometimes, unexpectedly, they'll explode all over a cast plug. I'll never forget one such fish. Sam Rolle, a guide at Peace and Plenty, the resort where I was staying at Georgetown, Exuma, had just poled me to the edge of the channel to look for big snappers.

"Tarpon in here, too," he said casually.

I had a fly rod popping bug all ready, so when Sam staked out on the edge of the channel I cast the big red, white and blue popper out to the other side. I gave it a good hard pop and at the same time pulled back a couple of feet. It set up a cascade of bubbles that could be seen a long way. Then I let it sit there motionless.

"Another boat coming," said Sam. "Just turned into the channel."

I looked around and thought: that's the way it always happens. You just start to fish and someone comes along to disturb the water—and just then something hit the bug so hard it almost yanked the big fly rod from my hands. I struck and the next second and a 50 pound tarpon was in the air. Then he was back in the water with a crash and he headed down the channel straight for the boat that was still coming on. Out he came again, half way between us and the other skiff, which now stopped and then began to turn away. Out came the tarpon once more and this time he almost jumped into that skiff. He certainly splashed a bucket of water over the occupants.

"He's going to jump in that boat!" Sam shouted.

Again the tarpon came out right in back of the boat and this time he threw my bug a mile. At the same time the man at the motor in the other skiff opened her up wide. They cleared out of there as if some monster was after them. When Sam and I could finally stop laughing we went back to fishing for snapper or tarpon again, or whatever might happen to stick its head out from under the channel banks. Nothing could surprise us now.

The reefs out in the islands can deal you an unexpected hand, too. At West End on Grand Bahama Island, there's a reef about five miles out where we took amberjack from 4 to 8 pounds on light spinning gear and fly tackle, getting a real eye-opener when the amberjack went for a fly rod popper. We had such terrific reef fishing that day that we couldn't pull ourselves away to try some nearby trolling, as we had planned. When we docked that night we met a charter boat party coming in from the trolling grounds. They had been out exactly two hours, only 200 yards from the western end of the island, and they heaved out onto the dock six big wahoo, from 36 to 47 pounds.

So you never know just what you may come up with when you fish Bahama waters. But it will take some experience to equal that of Dr. Curt Mendelsohn, formerly of New York, who owns a house on Green Turtle Cay. Dr. Mendelsohn, Mrs. Mendelsohn, and a local guide named Arnold went out in their skiff for an afternoon's fishing. Half a mile out they started to troll, using a small bonefish for bait.

"Nothin' goin' t' hit that bait," said Arnold. "It's too old and it smells."

He hardly had the words out of his mouth when there was a crashing hit. Out into the air came a blue marlin that looked longer than the skiff. He fell back in with a splash that sprayed water in all directions and then he took off on a run that made line melt from the big reel spool.

The next two hours were rugged. That big fish turned in a stellar blue marlin performance, while on the other end of the fight Dr. Mendelsohn battled from the tiny skiff against a cacophony of cries of "Don't bring that big thing into this boat!" from Mrs.

Mendelsohn, and mutters of "We'll never land him in this skiff!" from Arnold.

Dr. Mendelsohn ignored them both. He was not about to give up, and at last his fine angling and the capable tackle began to tell. The big marlin was weakening. He was in close. Fifteen feet from the boat he made a last tremendous effort. Out he came, first the great bill, then the heavy shoulders, then the lashing tail, driving him into the air. He all but swamped the boat.

But that was his last effort and Dr. Mendelsohn knew it.

"Get the flying gaff, Arnold!" he yelled.

He reeled in the double line, then the wire leader. Arnold grabbed the wire and pulled the big fish in close, picked up the gaff and drove it home. That's when Dr. Mendelsohn got the shock of his life. Out of the corner of his eye he got a look at Arnold and something was wrong.

"Arnold!" he yelled. "Take that line from around your waist."

This was Arnold's first encounter with a flying gaff and he had tied the line around his waist. If the marlin had made another run or a lunge, with the gaff in him, it would have taken Arnold right along with it and drowned him for sure.

Fortunately there wasn't an ounce of fight left in the fish and after administering a couple of good solid thumps on the head to assure a lasting quiet, Arnold and the doctor managed to slide the marlin across the skiff broadside. Thus laden, they chugged slowly and majestically toward Green Turtle Cay. Someone on the island spotted them from afar and soon other boats put out to meet them and by the time they reached the harbor an armada was on hand to escort them to the scales. That marlin weighed 498 pounds, a whale of a catch for any skiff fisherman, a real Bahama adventure.

British Honduras

"Have found new fishing spot," Vic Barothy cabled me. "Join me at Belize to sample some of the best angling you ever saw. Bring Lou Klewer."

Vic had been in the British colony of British Honduras in Central America about a month when I received that telegram. I knew Vic of old, knew his love of pioneering outpost fishing, where things were a bit on the rough side but the fishing was wonderful. If he said it was good, I believed him. So it wasn't many days later that Lou, who was Outdoor Editor of the *Toledo Blade*, my wife Mary, and I were on a non-stop flight from Miami to Belize, the capital city of British Honduras.

Vic met us at Stanley Field, about 20 minutes out of Belize.

"We're going right to the *Vickey*," Vice said. "She's a 40 foot houseboat and we'll live on her for the next 10 days while we explore the coast from Belize south."

We boarded the *Vickey*, stowed our gear, waved goodbye to Vic's wife and son, and within the hour we were headed out.

British Honduras is on the eastern seaboard of the Central American Isthmus. On the north is the Mexican Province of Quintana

Roo and on the west and south lies Guatemala. Running the entire length of the coastline, about 5 miles out, is the second longest coral reef in the world, surpassed only by the Great Barrier Reef of Australia. It's a natural setup for 200 miles of the best fishing you ever saw.

Vic told us that just outside the reef there were great numbers of sailfish and that while there is no organized angling for the deeper water species, sometimes fisherman troll feathers from skiffs and catch sails. They have also caught marlin and those who know the waters are convinced that, if charter boats were available, this British Honduran sail and marlin fishing would be great. There are also big schools of kingfish and tremendous concentrations of wahoo, called queenfish in British Honduras. They are big ones, too, some that go to 80, 90 and even 100 pounds. And there are lots of 8 to 12 pound blackfin tuna. Besides these glamour fish there are oceanic bonito, mackerel, and huge jack crevalle.

Inside the reef, where we would be fishing, Vic promised mighty groupers, big mouthed and big bellied, barracuda by the bushel, mutton snapper, and the mangrove and dog-toothed snapper, huge, hard fighting fish that would tip the scales to 50 and 60 pounds. Inshore, in the shallows along the keys, in the bays and the rivers, we would find tarpon and ladyfish; along the flats the flashy, elusive bonefish and permit, two of the greatest light tackle fish that swim. In the rivers that pour down the Mayan Mountains would be tarpon and snook and jacks. This was a fish grab bag, loaded with the finest finny fighters we could wish for—running fish, diving fish, jumping fish. Most of them had never been fished by rod and reel before.

"We'll tie up at Calabash Cay tonight," Vic said. "It's part of the Turneffe Island group. You'll see something you never saw before—pigs that feed on the bonefish flats.

"There's no soil on the island, just sand," he went on. "The pigs have no place to root, so they discovered that they can dig up sea worms, sea cucumbers and vegetation on the flats."

We pulled into the copra dock at Calabash Cay exactly four hours out of Belize.

"Look!" said Mary. "There they are!"

Sure enough, on the bonefish flats on the outer side of the island we saw the seagoing pigs, snouts down in the salt. Just beyond them we saw bonefish tails flashing in the setting sun.

We didn't waste any time getting to that flat. I went down the shore a good hundred yards beyond the pigs, then moved out beyond the level at which they were feeding. The fish were still there, slowly easing along, nosing out bits of food as they went. When I was within 60 feet of them, I dropped a fly in front of the lead fish. He saw it and grabbed it and went out of there like a bullet, followed by all the others, making a series of pops that echoed all around the island. But instead of running out towards the deeper water as bonefish usually do, this wild-eyed fish dashed towards me and passed not 30 feet away, headed on a dead run for the pigs.

They saw him and heard him coming, bristled up their hackles and squared off, but refused to budge. The bonefish thought better of trying to buck the line of big black porkers and turned and slanted seawards. The pigs settled back to their rooting. We caught five bonefish there in about an hour and the pigs never stopped their digging.

While we had been fishing, John Eley, the Captain of the *Vickey*, who also doubled as a guide, had gone off on a jaunt of his own. When we returned to the boat he was just climbing aboard with half a dozen huge crawfish that he had got from a local fisherman.

"The people on these islands are Carib Indians," he said. "You'll hear their drums tonight because they are celebrating their Independence Day. They came from the Cayman Islands originally. They were driven from their homes by the Spaniards, driven from island to island, till, many years ago they were at last given asylum in British Honduras. Each year they celebrate the day of the arrival of their ancestors in this country."

We dined well on the luscious lobsters that night and then the beat of the distant drums lulled us to sleep. Next morning we ran in to the main island and saw the natives working on the copra, shucking the big green coconuts to remove the inner meat from which the copra is made, eventually to produce coconut oil. Nothing is wasted, even the shell being used for the fires in the drying sheds.

One of the residents, Virginia Menendez, called us over to take a picture of her baby, sitting on the doorstep of her small frame house. In front of the door we saw a table spread with a pink seaweed that she was drying. It is apparently a well known edible seaweed there and when dried and mixed with a little canned milk provides a very palatable and healthy food for babies, judging from the healthy looking youngsters we saw around.

That noon found us heading southward along the coast, aiming for Tarpon Cay, about 10 miles farther on. "It's on the charts as 'Tarpum Cay'," Vic said. "People here call tarpon 'tarpum.'

"You might as well troll as we go," Vic said. "See if you can pick up a barracuda or two."

Trolling from the high top deck of a houseboat is a far cry from the fighting chair in the cockpit of a proper fishing boat, but we had not gone 200 yards before Vic had a hit and landed a 35 pound wahoo.

"Wahoo steaks tonight," said Vic. "Nothing better."

We trolled on. Then all three of us had hits at once. My fish threw the hook. Vic and Lou fought it out with two battlers that waged their fight flashily, just under the surface. As they came in close we saw that they, too, were wahoo. Vic's went 40 pounds; Lou's was a substantial 47. It was my turn next: half a mile farther on our way I connected and this time it was a wahoo that weighed 40 pounds. We had trolled less than two miles and had landed four better than average-sized wahoo.

"Tarpum Cay just ahead," John called soon after, using the local name for the island.

"Pull in your lines," yelled Vic. "We're turning inshore here."

Tarpum Cay is a crescent-shaped island perhaps half a mile long and a quarter of a mile wide. We dropped anchor just outside the top of the crescent so we wouldn't run off any fish which might be in the bay. Then we all piled into skiffs and headed in. We cut the outboard motors while we were still far out and poled the rest of the way, in water from 2 to 10 feet deep. All over the shallows we could see great dark shadows that we knew were tremendous schools of small bait fish. In the midst of one shadow, right along the mangroves, onshore, there was a sudden explosion, like a string of land mines going off. But it wasn't land mines—we could see the silvery bodies of tarpon as they flung themselves out of the water, chasing bait fish. They fell back in with a crash like the sound of surf on a distant shore. Then all was quiet again, only drifting bubbles and foam to show us what was going on, and where.

As we eased toward that spot we could see the black masses of minnows everywhere, ahead of us, beneath us. Then I spotted about 30 tarpon just under the surface, cruising slowly along toward our skiff. I was using a fly rod and a popping bug on a 3/0 hook. I started false casting to get line out and then shot the bug out and dropped it a good 5 feet in front of the tarpon. I gave it a slight pop. The tarpon seemed to come closer to the surface. I gave it another, harder pop. As one, those fish charged the bug, shouldering each other aside as they went for it. One of them butted the feathery fooler into the air, another was waiting with open mouth to grab it as it fell. He turned and dove and I set the hook and had him.

That is, I had him for three of the most electric, bombastic, eye-jolting jumps I've ever witnessed. Then he threw the hook a mile. It hit the water and another tarpon busted it before I could even say shucks, and off he went on a slashing run. When I set the hook the leader parted. No wonder. When I brought it in, the tippet was frayed throughout its two foot length where the rough cheeks and lips of the fish had sawed on it.

Vic was at the other end of the bay and we could hear him talking to John. Then we heard the thunderous uprising of feeding tarpon as they slugged the bait fish over there. A moment later Vic's shout told us that he was into one. We looked around and saw a tarpon in the air. It looked big!

"Over there," suddenly said Jim, our guide, calling me back to the business at hand.

I jerked my head around, saw where Jim was pointing and there was another school of silver kings coming our way. I dropped the bug a couple of feet in front of the leader, popped it once and he ran up to it, hesitated, then used a head-shaking, one-two punch to grab it, like a bulldog shaking a rat. I struck, hoping to get the 3/0 hook into his concrete mouth. Evidently it did go in because I survived five fast jumps, several spurts and one long run and another leap. Then he began to tire and I could move him my way. At the boat, as we released him, we figured him at about 30 pounds. He was so well hooked it took a pair of pliers to get the hook out.

We caught those tarpon on fly rods using 12 pound test leader tippets and balsa wood popping bugs tied on 3/0 hooks. We took them on the breather type multiwing streamer flies in red and white and red and yellow, and we took them on 3/0 platinum and Honey Blonde bucktails. We caught them on medium spinning outfits with both bucktail jigs and surface plugs. It seemed as if they were ready to take anything we offered and come back for more.

We finished the day beaten down and bedraggled but happy. Our tackle was standing up well considering the onslaughts of those hard-mouthed thunderbolts but we lost a lot of streamers, bugs, and plugs, one way or another. A lot more that some of the tarpon returned to us needed new hooks after the mashing they had taken. They looked as if someone had hit them with a hammer. It was hard to leave Tarpum Cay, but our schedule called for a try for barracuda at Long Cocoa Cay.

"Lots of barries there," said John who had fished commercially through this whole area.

"Sounds good to me," I said. "Barracuda are great fish on light tackle. They're underestimated by too many anglers."

"You're right," said Vic. "I've seen them hit a top water bug and jump 30 feet across the water. Terrific jumpers, and as fast as all get out."

John was right about Long Cocoa. Barracuda were everywhere, going from 4 to 24 pounds, ready for anything we offered them, either under water, or on top, hitting with a vengeance.

It spite of its name, Long Cocoa Cay was not very long, so Vic headed one way while I went the other, planning to circle the island, fishing the shoreline as we went. When we met on the opposite side a couple of hours later we each had landed a goodly number of cudas, releasing most of them, just keeping a couple of the smaller ones that the boys wanted to eat. Small barracuda are tasty eating, though the larger ones are often too gamey for most tastes.

The very name of the next spot that Vic had his sights trained on was enough to set a fisherman dreaming.

"Our next stop is the Golden Stream," he told us that night at dinner. "That's a river that comes down out of the mountains, across the jungles, and pours into the sea only five miles north of the Guatemala line. They say there are tarpon all over the place and something big and heavy and hard hitting that I suspect is snook."

"Let's go!" we all exclaimed.

We went past sandy beaches on the mainland, framed with coconut trees and with the Coxcomb Mountains, part of the Mayan Range, where the great Mayan Indian civilization flourished 700 years ago and where today they are still finding the remains of cities that were not even known to have been in existence. It is said that at one time there were 750,000 native Indians living in what is now British Honduras.

We passed Columbus Cay, visited by the discoverer of America after he had found San Salvador. We went past Laughing Bird Cay, with coconut trees 95 feet high, and Mosquito Cay, named not for the insect but for the Mosquito Indians from the mainland south of here, one of the friendliest of the Indian tribes, wiped out long ago by the Spaniards. At last we came to the river we were looking for.

The Golden Stream comes coursing through the mangrove stands some five miles north of Punta Gorda. It runs fresh from the Mayan Mountains, clear and sparkling, through the jungle growth. Along its path you see the jaguar, el tigre of the jungles, the tapir, and the peccary and deer. Macaws, hummingbirds, and parrots by the hundreds flit and cry among the orchid-hung trees, and in the lower reaches the turkey-like currasow, quail, doves and pigeons haunt the pine-topped ridges. In spring the howler monkeys scare you half to death as they burst into a scream right above your head along some shore where you're seeking tarpon and snook.

Vic hooked his first tarpon only 200 yards up stream from the mouth of the river.

"Watch out!" yelled Vic. "He's coming right at you!"

Our skiffs were only 100 feet apart and the big silver king came roaring out right beside us, Vic's surface lure flapping from his big jaws, his whole 100 pounds shining like a silver thunderbolt. He went back into the water with a splash that threw water all over us.

He headed for a long narrow arm of the sea that cut through the mangrove roots, a thoroughfare scarcely 30 feet wide, with the mangrove fingers coming out on either side. Jimmy, who was guiding Vic that day, began paddling after the fish. We trailed along to watch the fight.

"He's going to go through into the ocean," we heard Vic shout.

As if to make Vic eat his words the silver king jumped, down in that narrow track, then turned and shot back towards us. He went past the other skiff, and I could see Vic cranking the reel handle a mile a minute, working for a tight line. When it finally came tight, the tarpon tried to jump. It was a half-hearted lunge this time and he didn't clear the water—but he ended up across a mangrove root in the narrow channel. The line popped.

After all that commotion we didn't really expect to get any more action. Nevertheless, John got me into position and I dropped my plug a foot from a sunken tree along the shore. A dim outline appeared just below the surface; then something took in a big splash of water. I set the hook and out he came, a 10 pound snook with fire in his eyes.

Right away he acted as though he had attended a school that had a course on infighting. He dove for the mangrove roots. He tried to wrap the line around a sunken tree. He tried to cut it with his sharp gill covers. He tried everything in the books. But luck was with me. I brought him in and John netted him. That fight, on top of the battle with the tarpon, had really stirred things up.

"We should rest them a bit here," I said. "Let's run up river a way and try it there."

We ran for 15 minutes, cut the motors and began to drift, letting the current take us back towards the sea. John kept the boat out a good 50 feet and I cast a spinning lure in to the pockets in the mangroves. I took three jack crevalles, averaging 10 pounds, two snook that looked like 8 pound brothers, and three tarpon going an estimated 10, 12, and 16 pounds. We passed several holes where I was sure there would be great snappers and maybe groupers. But the drift casting was so good that we just went with the river, taking what came—and what came was mighty fine.

Time was running out. Back aboard the *Vickey* that evening Vic announced we would have to turn northward again and head back for Belize. As we skirted the coast next day, our first stop was at Placentia. John Eley had two teenaged nieces there who informed us in no uncertain terms that "Placentia is the most beautiful place in the world." Certainly it was lovely, with its long spit of white sand beach, tall, feathery palms, the little houses on their stilts, all surrounded with lush-flowering hibiscus and bougainvillea, and the sea air as soft as down and as sweet as wine. On a little point beside the dock the two Romero sisters, last remnants of one of the earliest families who settled here, grew cashew trees, and from the fruit made a wine they claim is comparable to the best Spanish sherry.

It was hard to leave that charming spot but next morning early we were on our way, past Devil's Point, where John told us that in

January there is a tremendous run of big snook, thousands of them. We moved on, looking for the Mullins River which was to be our landfall that night.

"One day we'll have at Mullins," Vic said. "And the last day at Sapadilla, and then it's a short run back to Belize."

We passed many other river mouths as we ploughed on up the shore, but we couldn't stop. And Mullins made it worthwhile, with tarpon and snook by the score. We fished there half a day, then ran for Sapadilla, and were settled there before dark, so we would have the next day to fish.

That morning Mary and I went out in one skiff, Lou and Vic in the other. As we had done on the Golden Stream, we ran far upstream, cut the motors and started to drift. We didn't have much luck, just two small jacks and one 10 pound tarpon in the first hour. We amused ourselves watching the birds and trying to identify some of the lush vegetation. Once we saw two iguanas and once we heard the hollow rasping cough that could only have been made by a jaguar.

Then, carried swiftly along by the strong current, we were down to the mangroves, a sure sign that we were back to salty water. There had been never a sign of tarpon or snook.

"The tide has almost turned now," said John. "Perhaps—"

That was as far as he got

"Tarpoon!" yelled Vic from the other boat.

We looked where he was pointing and saw the tail of a tarpon as it completed its roll. Then there was another and another. Across the river and downstream we saw more, and turning to look upstream we saw another dozen. It made you want to cast in six different directions at once.

Mary and I dropped our plugs a foot apart. Two tarpon came up like a team of horses and took our respective offerings. We had a pair of 15 pound jumping jacks on our lines. We landed them both, and then released them. Across the river we could hear Vic shouting that he too was into them. And for the next hour that was a busy river, as we fought tarpon from 3 to 50 pounds, as fast as we could land one and hook another.

Then along shore I heard the slushing *bruuummppp* of a striking snook. Looking towards the sound, I saw the white water and the bubbles his rise had put up. The tarpon had been in the middle of the river, and that's were we had been casting. Now I turned and put one over among the bubbles close to shore, where the fish had shown. He hit and when I struck he took off as if a thousand devils were after him.

And there was one devil after him! We saw a big dorsal fin come up, and beneath it the dim outline of a great shark. He was gaining on the snook. I held my rod straight out toward the speeding fish, let the line come tight and broke him off.

"He'll make it," I said. "That shark will never catch him now."

Things slowed then. The tarpon had become wary. Then we saw Vic out in the middle of the river and he had one on.

"They're too scared to hit on top now," he said. "But they're down there. I'm catching them right near the bottom on a spin jig. Let the lure sink. Then bring it back very slowly, hardly moving it, letting it bounce along the bottom"

We tried that technique and soon everyone was tied to a tarpon . . . everyone but Lou, that is, and the only reason he wasn't was that he was making movies. But he could only stand it so long. He put his camera down, grabbed his rod and made a cast.

"I've got one!" he shouted, almost right away. "El grande!"

It was a big one, all right. It busted through the surface with its gill covers flared out, gill rakers rattling, a long, heavy fish that looked to be 100 pounds. He fell back in, rushed past our boat, right across my line and cut my fish off, then went on to do the same thing to Mary and continued his attack by slicing across Vic's line, too, as he went past the other boat. Then he came out in a straight up leap, wiggled his great, silver clad body and threw the hook.

We looked at each other and grinned.

"Time to head for home," said Vic. "It's almost dark. And besides, they're starting to get the best of us."

Mexico

The fish looked long. He was tailing a hundred yards away on our starboard. The captain speeded up and ran in front of him and when the bait drew near, the tail sank out of sight.

"Watch now!" shouted the Captain.

I was ready. I knew that when a tailing sailfish sights a bait he goes down and comes at it from below. Suddenly there was the bill right in back of the six inch long mullet, cutting back and forth as he pushed forward with quick beats of his tail. His head came out. He opened his mouth. I dropped the bait back and when the fish turned and took off I let him go, holding the rod pointed straight at him, finger tipping the speeding line, the reel in free spool, waiting, waiting for him to swallow the bait.

"Strike!" shouted the mate.

I still waited another 10 seconds, then threw the brake on, watched the line come tight, the rod tip start to bend. Then I struck, hard, several times, with swift uplifts of the rod. The fish was hooked. He came out, stood on his tail and with side to side swipes of his long, lithe body began swaying across the surface, like a sea-going Ray Charles. He was a beautiful fish, fighting with everything

339

he had to escape this hampering thing that kept pulling at him.

He fell in with a splash, surged forward just under the surface and out he came again in a going-away, greyhounding leap. Then he made the mistake of circling and when he jumped again I pulled back on the rod, got him coming and kept him coming, all the way in to the boat. The mate grabbed the leader, snipped the number 8 wire off at the hook where it was sunk in the scissors of the fish's mouth, and we watched that great fighter sink slowly down in the waters of the Gulf of California. He gave a flip of his tail, as if to say "Thank you" and slowly swam away.

A Pacific sailfish is a great game fish, a wonderful acrobatic performer, and they grow to substantially greater size than do the Atlantic sails. This 100 pounder was the average for Pacific sails.

I was fishing the Gulf of California, often called "The World's Greatest Fishtrap" because the 710 mile strip of water, between Mexico's mainland and the long, thin peninsula of Baja California, "catches" millions of fish as they move northward each year on their migrations. The bay is saturated with plankton, as thick as bubbles in a foamy sea. There are vast schools of baitfish, herring, sardines, anchovies, and mullet. Pouring into the bay to feed on all this plenty come the billfish, black marlin, striped marlin, and sails. A myriad other species follow—there are dolphin, amberjack, yellowfin tuna, and the mighty roosterfish, called pappagallo here; and inshore are the corbinas, jacks, snappers, groupers and pompano, permit, and innumerable smaller species.

We had reached these waters by driving south from Nogales, 269 miles down through Sonora Province to the town of Guaymas, about half way down the Gulf. It was a different kind of country than I'd ever fished before. Mountains came down to the sea but they were strange looking, desert mountains, brick red in color, as if heat-scorched. Here and there we could see the congealed streams of ancient lava flows, hardened now, but back in the dimness of time they must have poured down molten from the boiling volcano into the waters of the Gulf of Mexico.

We arrived at the Playa de Cortes Hotel about four in the afternoon, got settled, and then hurried over to talk to Tommy Jamison, Director of Sport Fishing at Guaymas. Tommy had his office at the Miramar, the resort right next to the Playa where we were staying, and from his office window we could see the boats of the fine sport fishing fleet tied up at the dock.

"It's too late to go out on a boat today," Tommy said. "Why don't you take your casting tackle and try along the shore this afternoon and I'll set you up for a charter boat trip in the morning.

"Work along the shoreline south of the hotel, there," he said, pointing to where the shore cut out below the Playa de Cortes and some rocks had been dumped overboard to hold back erosion.

"You might pick up some small stuff."

I rigged up a spin casting outfit and headed for the spot he had indicated. My first cast with a wiggle jig got me a 2 pound pompano. I tried a big white bucktail. That got me a 4 pound pargo, a member of the snapper family. Then I took a 6 pound corbina.

It was getting dark and in the quiet evening air I heard the dinner gong ring, back at the hotel. I gave myself 10 minutes more to fish. And exactly 10 minutes later there was a big swirl in back of my lure. I kept it coming, and in the halflight I saw a flash and then he had it and I struck. This was a strong fish. He went deep, then came up and tore the surface water apart and whisked it into such a lather that I couldn't see what he was or how big. I could only guess from the way he fought that he was the best one yet.

He headed out on a long run, then came back at me. By the time I got a tight line to him again I sensed he was tired so I started working down the rocks toward a bit of beach. Once there I reeled fast and this time he came. I skidded him up on the sand. He was a 12 pound corbina, well worth waiting dinner for!

The next morning at nine we pulled out of the Miramar dock on the *Sail-O*, with Captain Gabe Aldrete. He told us that this was not the peak of the fishing season for these waters.

"But I'll get you something," he assured us. "There've been a few sailfish around and we'll go out and try those first."

We were lucky, and that's how I had got into that hundred pounder we had found tailing. But after that things were very quiet. The water was glassy calm. There were no baitfish showing anywhere. That one lone sailfish seemed to have been the only thing moving out there. Gabe suggested that we go inshore and see if anything was stirring closer to home.

As we came in, we had a fine view of the burnt-looking mountains and the town spread out along the bay shore.

"That's Bacochibampo Bay," Gabe said, waving his hand over the half-moon bay where the town of Guaymas and the two resort hotels, Playa de Cortes and Miramar, stood out against the beach.

"Bacochibampo is Yaqui Indian for 'The place of the underwater snakes,'" he added. "But I never see any snakes."

I didn't see any snakes or any fish either. Everything looked as somnolent as a Mexican peon taking his siesta. The water was slick calm with a long, lazy roll that made me want to close my eyes and sleep, too. Then, vaguely, through drooping lids I saw half a dozen queer looking objects poking up through the surface, a couple of feet into the air.

"What's that?" I asked Gabe.

"Sea lions, sleeping with their flippers sticking out," he said.

"Everybody and everything takes a siesta here," I thought.

When we were about 35 feet away from the sea lions they suddenly dove. I went to the rail and looked down. The water was full of sea nettles. I looked up and the sky was filled with birds. Everything was not asleep after all!

"Sea lions, sea nettles, sea gulls," I thought. "Next thing on the program should be fish."

"Baitfish!" yelled Gabe. "Baitfish coming!"

We saw the closely packed baitfish pushing up a ripple as they moved. Suddenly everything in the bay came awake with a vengeance. Something down under those baitfish, some great marauder roared up open-mouthed and ravenning, and in a mighty splash of water fed avidly on the bait. You could see the small fish tossed into the air and the flash of fins as the feeders slashed this way and that, gobbling up their prey, putting mighty swirls in the water as they fed.

"The fish are sierras," said Gabe, easing the *Sail-O* towards the commotion. "Mackerel."

I picked up my spinning rod and when we were close enough I threw a quarter ounce Phillips Wiggle Jig, a brown and white bucktail, into the milling mass. I didn't even get the lure started back. Something slapped into it so hard I thought the rod was broken.

He hit on the run, too, and before I knew it he was 100 feet away and still getting up speed. He dove, came back near the top and made another dash that took 50 feet more line. He was fighting the way sierras do—hard, fast, with everything he had. I finally turned him and got him headed my way. As he came closer I could see the silvery flash of his long body as he switched ends and made several more short, fast runs. When I finally boated him he turned out to be a 4 pounder, a spunky fighter for his weight.

During the fight we had drifted away from the school and now Gabe gunned the motors and we ran back to casting range. Another cast, another sierra. Another, and another—then the baitfish went down, and with them the sierras.

"We'd better look for something else," said Gabe. "These fish are scared now."

"Where shall we look?" I asked. For the surface of Bacochibampo Bay was dead again, as still as a desert at high noon.

Gabe just grinned. "I find," he said.

We ran out past a rocky point near the mouth of the bay. Gabe slowed, then threw the motors into neutral and let the boat drift.

"Let's give it a whirl here," he said.

I could see the bottom, some 25 feet down. I tied on a half ounce white jig and dropped it down to grouper water, on the bottom. One was there and when he hit I couldn't budge him. He just stood there and balked for a few minutes, then took off and ran under a rock. I couldn't do a thing to make him come out so I gave him slack, pulling several yards of line off the reel, then waited.

"Maybe he'll think he's free and swim out of there," I said.

I waited about three minutes, then tightened and pulled up hard. He was out, all right, about 10 feet away from the rock. I gave him everything the line and rod would take and kept him from getting back into cover. I kept yanking at him, pulling, pumping, and reeling. He came up by inches, a slow pull, but suddenly his fins lost their grip on the water and I had him beside the boat.

"Rock bass," said Gabe. "About 10 pounds."

I started casting again. This time I had a hit from a running fish.

"That's a mackerel," said Gabe.

He turned it on for 10 minutes and I had all I could do to hold him. But then he tired and finally came in, a good 7 pound fish.

I hardly had him off the hook when Gabe was pointing out to the middle of the bay and starting the motor.

"Skipjack out there," he said. "Bonito."

I rigged up a surface lure as we ran over. My first cast brought a hard hit, the fish throwing so much water that I couldn't see him. But I surely felt him. He took off on a dead run and never stopped. He cleaned the spool of 300 yards of spinning line in nothing flat, and pop went the line.

Luckily I had two spools for that reel, each loaded with 8 pound test line. It didn't take long to change spools, re-rig and cast again.

Wham! The rod twisted in my hands. Somehow I managed to hold on. The fish hooked himself and then ripped line off the spool as though he would strip this one, too. But he changed his mind, slowed, then dove. I stopped him at last, turned him and got him started my way. He fought all the way in but I finally brought him to gaff, a fine 10 pounder.

"Now we will catch a few sierras for bait," suggested Gabe. "Then we can troll and see what happens."

Davis, the mate, put a feathered jig out on one of the big trolling rods while I picked up my spinning outfit again. A sierra hit the feather right away and another took my spinning lure almost before it was in the water. By the time I had survived his first run, then horsed him in, Davis had one in the boat and was tied to another. In short order we had a dozen fish in the live well.

"Now we make your arms sore," Gabe promised.

Davis baited up with one of the sierras, using three hooks and 80 pound test line. I didn't want to use such a big outfit but Gabe and Davis both insisted that nothing lighter would do the job for the fish they had in mind.

We ran past White Island, so named because of its covering of guano left by the thousands of birds that roost there every night. About 100 feet past the end of the island I had a hit, struck, and felt that I was towing the world. The rod tip bounced up and down. Then the fish took off. He ran 200 feet and stopped. I couldn't budge him.

"He's under a rock," I said.

"No rocks here," Gabe told me. "Fight him."

I heaved back and did some pumping and moved the fish a couple of feet. He sat there a minute, then with relentless force went back where he had been. I put the pressure on again and up he came again. Then back down he went as if I weren't even on the other end of the gear. It went on like that for 20 minutes. I'd gain, he'd take it away; I'd gain, he'd take it away. But finally the tackle began to tell. I edged him up a bit, inch by inch, and at last got him coming steadily, and there he was.

"A big grouper," said Gabe, as he and Davis hauled it aboard.

"What will he weigh?" I asked.

"About 85 pounds," said Gabe. "Not bad."

"We'll take it in for the hospital," he added. "These big groupers make mighty fine eating. You want to catch another one?" he asked.

I clenched and unclenched my fingers to get the cramps out of them.

"I've had enough tug-of-war fishing for today," I said. "Let's try something else."

"How about some red snapper, then?" he suggested. "They come into the shallow water here—that is, shallow for snappers. They're in 25 to 30 feet of water."

We headed across the bay where we could see a fleet of commercial boats working the snappers. I knew there must be plenty or these commercial men wouldn't be there. When we had anchored, the mate handed me a boat rod with cut bait on the hook.

"I'm going to use my spinning outfit," I said. "I'll let the jig down to the bottom, then work it up and down."

"You'll never catch one, señor," said Gabe. "You need bait."

"Let's try it anyway, and see what happens," I said, as I let the jig out and down till I felt it hit bottom.

I reeled it up a couple of feet, then started making upward jerks with the rod tip. Down near the bottom the jig would be hopping up and down a couple of feet with each movement.

Wham! The tip of the rod slapped down so fast that it went straight into the water. It was a good thing I was leaning over the side of the *Sail-O* or the rod would have hit the gunwale and been broken. About 30 feet down a snapper was trying to turn himself inside out as he twisted and turned and yanked his head in his effort to get rid of the hook.

The rod tip was only an inch from the surface. Then suddenly it jumped up. The fish had got off. Bang! Another one was there to take over! I was hanging on again. This time I brought him in, a bright red snapper that weighed 6 pounds. And I took seven more like that, all from 6 to 9 pounds.

Gabe and the mate were goggle-eyed. By the time we left those eager snappers even the commercial fishermen were beginning to be interested in artificial bait!

This Mexican fishing was something to be in on—the willing sierras, the rambunctious skipjacks, the groupers I ran away from, and now the deep dwelling snappers. The waters of Bacochibampo Bay were teeming with game fish in spite of the fact that this was October, supposedly the "off" season for fishing.

On our third day at Guaymas we joined forces with Seymour and Eleanor Margules of New York, who were also staying at the Playa, and walked through the town to the beach on the north side of the bay. It was pleasant wading there and we moved up and down the shore casting out to deeper water. Tommy had told us that there might be some bonefish in here and we were anxious to catch one. The bonefish on this coast are apparently a sub-species of the Atlantic bonefish. They are so plentiful in numbers that we heard reports of a single angler taking as many as 200 on bait in one day, but they are considerably smaller in size than those usually found in other places. A single 8½ pounder reported there must have been a stray because other than that one fish, the top weight seems to have been 2½ pounds.

Seymour was the first one to connect.

"I've got something," he said. "It's small, but fast! Look at it run!"

He was using a light, fresh water spinning outfit and the fish really tore line off it. When at last Seymour got his catch in we found that it was a bonefish, the smallest I have ever seen, not quite 2 pounds. We learned later that this was, as far as anyone knew, the first bonefish ever taken at Guaymas on an artificial lure.

That afternoon we decided to try some more onshore fishing we had heard about. Hank Hodorosky, at the small boat livery at Guaymas, had told us that if you hit the tide right, at the start of the ebb, you can get some good fishing for small inshore species from the railroad bridge that connects Guaymas and the neighboring town of Empalme.

"You won't find anything big there," he said. "But with light spinner gear you can have lots of fun. There'll be snappers, and maybe a pompano or two. I'll go with you any time you want."

So we picked him up after lunch and headed for the bridge. We parked the car at one end and walked out on the ties till we were over the middle span, where the tide was already pouring out from the inner bay.

"If you hear a train whistle, head for shore," Hank said. "There aren't many trains come across here, and they always give a warning."

Very accommodating of the railroaders, I thought to myself. But only what a fisherman deserves!

I made my first cast into the current where the tide poured out through the struts of the bridge. Right away I had a 4 pound snapper, a "pargo," as Hank called it. It must have been waiting down there with its mouth open. Mary was into a fish almost as quickly, a pompano. Hank got a larger pargo. And we kept on that way for an hour, alternating pompano and pargo, sometimes all with fish on at once, and half the time fighting to keep our lines from crossing as the fish fought us back and forth across the swift current.

Then the tide fell away to nothing. Everything went dead. A train whistled, over at Empalme, as if it had just been waiting till our fishing began to decline. Politely we beat it out of there, just ahead of the engine.

At lunch next day we met Ray Chapin, a photographer from Long Beach, California. Ray had fished Guaymas waters for many years.

"Let's drive out to Cruz de Piedra Beach," he said. "It's about 16 miles. There might be some good fish that we could get casting from shore and wading."

We took off across country, through typical desert land, with giant cactus trees everywhere, and big, rough, thorny bushes, these two providing the only growth of any kind on the landscape. Here and there we passed a little shack where some Mexican farmer managed to eke out a living. Everywhere we looked it was sandy, dusty, as if there were no water for a thousand miles in any direction. Every time we stopped to open and close a gate, as we did several times, the dust we had raised would catch up to us, overflow us, and settle on us as we overtook it again.

Then suddenly we drove up a little ridge, paused on top, and before the dust closed in on us we saw spread out ahead of us as lovely a bay as you'll ever find in any ocean.

"Cruz de Piedra," said Ray. "Step on it and get out of this dust."

We did. And the minute I pulled the car to a stop at the beach everyone piled out and headed for water. It felt clean and cool and looked so fishy we forgot all about the dust. We started to cast.

We hadn't even got our lures out when we all saw the splashing break of feeding fish, not far out. Then another, throwing water high. There was a school of them out there, swimming parallel to the beach as they fed.

"They must be yellowfin corbina," Ray called to me. "They look big! Maybe 35 pounds!"

They were crossing right ahead of me. I cast a jig several feet in front of where a fish had just showed. I started it back. It didn't go far. One of those yellow-finned, orange-mouthed fish hit it. He yanked the rod tip down and went away in a long, steady run, parallel to the beach. He took out a couple of hundred feet of line. I started after him. Eventually I caught up to him and began to get line back and then I put the pressure on the rod. Confident that the drag was set just right for this fish, I fought him to the hilt.

I finally turned him, but off he went back along the beach, back where we had started. Once he surfaced and showed his long length. He came out of that and headed for the beach, getting so much slack that I thought I'd never catch up with him and he'd drop the hook. But he turned away again and the line came tight. Ten minutes later I skidded him up on the beach. He was a good 20 pounds.

Meantime, the school had moved on and we had to hurry down the beach to where an occasional splashing strike marked their progress. Mary had the next one, a 6 pounder. Then Ray got one, 10 pounds. Those three were the largest of the day, but we took fish all afternoon and finally had to leave that school there still patrolling the beach, in order to get back to the hotel and clean up for dinner. We didn't want to miss a special Saturday night feature at the Playa de Cortes—the ceremony of the "flaming swords."

We just made it to the dining room in time. As we sat waiting to be served, the lights suddenly were dimmed and at the far end of the dining room eight waiters appeared, each carrying a long sword on which were impaled a dozen or so huge barbecued shrimp, all aflame. In single file formation the waiters marched down the room between the tables, while the flames flared high. As they gradually died down, the waiters tilted the swords down at each table so the diners could pull the savory, hot shrimp from the blade and eat them, as fine an hors d'oeuvre as I've encountered anywhere.

"I wish you could come here to fish in the summer when the tortuava are running," Ray told us, as we ate dinner. "The tortuava is the biggest member of the croaker family. They migrate into these waters in the summer. They run as high as 100 pounds and its quite a feat to catch one.

"It's a strange thing," he went on. "The only other place I have ever heard of them being caught is in China. The Chinese value them so highly for the vitamins in the bladder that they used to come here all the way from China to fish for them."

Ray told us that August is the month to be at Guaymas if you really want to get into another migratory species, the roosterfish. And the corbina, present in smaller numbers all year, really builds up in population during the winter months.

After dinner we went over to Miramar to say goodbye to Tommy Jamison, as we were leaving for home the next morning. Tommy and his pretty wife, Dinah, were just finishing a meal of barbecued chicken cooked in the fireplace of their Mexican style home on the beach. Even after the feed I'd just had at the Playa, it made my mouth water. I told Tommy that Ray had been getting me all excited about the migration of roosterfish. He laughed.

"You should be here in the billfish season!" he said. "May, June, July and August are the months. The fish come in in droves then. We land 600 marlin a season here, and 1500 sailfish. That's a lot of billfish and if you figure the ones that get away—at least three times as many as are caught—then you have some idea of the tremendous schools of billfish that come along this coast."

The biggest Pacific blue marlin ever taken at Guaymas weighed 596 pounds, the largest striped marlin was 420, and the largest Pacific sailfish weighed 165 pounds. Those are big fish!

The great number of these species that are found around Guaymas in season brings out the sporting instincts in the local anglers and stirs them to some fantastic efforts. Dinah, for instance, will not fish with anything but a barbless hook. For trout, yes, you may think, but marlin and sailfish—that's another matter. Yet using a barbless hook Dinah boated a sailfish that weighed 88 pounds 6 ounces, on 10 pound test line. Then she went on to show them that it wasn't a one night stand by landing a big striped marlin.

"I was sitting here in the office one afternoon," said Tommy. "One of the charter boats came in early. The captain told me that Dinah was out on the *Delphino*, hooked to a real big fish. 'She's had it on for an hour, now,' he told me. 'She must be using a regular hook today.' Well, I was sure she wasn't, because Dinah just won't go for anything but barbless hooks any more. But I was also sure from what he told me of the size of the fish, that she had probably lost it by now."

"That was some fish," said Dinah, taking up the story. "I was trolling a 6 inch mullet. We hadn't seen a thing for half an hour. And then, there was that crazy marlin running on top of the water on his tail. He flopped in, came half way out again and charged the teaser. You could hear him hit. Then he rushed the left outrigger bait good and hard, yanking the line from the clothes pin. When the line came tight I struck and struck and struck.

"He started off on top in a smother of spray and then suddenly he was greyhounding. He was a wild, fierce fish and I was glad he wasn't headed towards us. He'd probably have come aboard and chewed us all up. He slowed after a bit and I started to pump. That only made him mad and he went tailwalking again. What a sight!"

Dinah sighed, remembering every moment of that battle.

"Well, to make a long story short, I fought him for three hours while the crew fed me bottles of coke and drinks of water. Half a dozen times I thought I'd lose him. but after the first hour, when I still had him, I figured he was well hooked, and I just kept plugging."

"She landed him, all right," said Tommy proudly. "It was a striped marlin and it weighed 187 pounds—and on a barbless hook."

"I was using 27 pound test line that day," said Dinah modestly, as if to minimize her feat.

The Angler in Action

Possibly the fish most sought by offshore trollers is the wahoo, a surface cruiser, a wanderer of many seas, a great game powerhouse that hits and runs like lightning. Technically the wahoo bears the pedantic name of *Acanthocybium solandri*, for the early explorer Solander, who first identified the species. But wahoo he is to sportsmen, and wahoo he will remain. As I suggested earlier, many an angler firmly believes that the name was spontaneously born when the first fisherman to hook one felt the jolting power of that sensational strike.

The wahoo belongs to the mackerel family, resembling the king mackerel and in some places even being known as the queen mackerel. The fish has a pointed, beak-like head, streamlined body that reaches as much as six feet in length, and is dark blue gray with vertically barred sides. Mostly it is a solitary prowler, although occasionally a couple will appear together. But this is the exception.

There seem to be more wahoo in Bermuda waters than elsewhere, and bigger ones; and they put up such a good fight that they are the number-one fish in the book with most charter-boat captains.

The average size of wahoo taken in Bermuda waters increased by ten pounds in fifteen years, from an average of 35 pounds to a hefty 45 pounds. The largest ever caught there on rod and reel weighed 110 pounds, one of the heaviest ever taken anywhere. And there is a substantial list of wahoo caught in Bermuda and weighing between 70 and 90 pounds, none of which were regarded as unusual catches. Above that weight, even a Bermudian of many years' wahoo-fishing experience will admit the catch merits a little attention. Ambrose Gosling ranks among the lucky few who can boast of having landed such a fish. Brose was fishing offshore and after one of the most memorable fights of his fishing career, landed a wahoo that went 91 pounds 8 ounces.

"He had stripes like a tiger," said Brose. "And he fought like one, too."

There are some wahoo around Bermuda all year, but they reach their peak in May, August, and September, when they are frequently found in very great numbers. On one phenomenal fishing trip, a party of three commercial fishermen took 27 wahoo in a single day. Their total catch weighed better than 1,000 pounds, with a 91-pounder the heavyweight of the lot.

Wahoo will hit almost any bait, from small sennet to small gar (the balao of Florida), or strip bait as used on light tackle, and consisting of strips cut from the bellies of 'cuda, wahoo or tuna. Since the wahoo is a big-mouthed fish, a large 7/0 hook is used on heavier tackle, while with 20- or 10-pound-test line, a 6/0 is used, well sharpened, because the angler's strike cannot be too hard for fear of breaking the light line.

Baits are trolled from outriggers, usually about 100 to 115 feet back. If there is no action, sometimes just a slight variation of the distance seems to be all that's necessary. Or again a 12-inch white teaser may be trolled 35 feet astern. The teaser attracts the wahoo and brings them in for a look-see, and then they will usually leave that come-on device and dash over and take one of the outrigger baits. Occasionally one of them will hit the teaser, a thrilling sight, and a tip-off to the angler to be ready when that fish rushes out and grabs a bait.

When a wahoo hits, he throws water all over the place and rips the line out of the clothespin on the outrigger as he takes off on a run that may cover 1,000 feet. Then everything must be right, tacklewise and anglingwise. It is important to withhold the strike until the line becomes tight between fish and rod, and then as the rod bends down, strike hard. But the strike should never be made on slack line.

Once the line is tight, the barb sinks home, and then the angler sees a wonderful sight as the wahoo gets up speed. The force of the powerful swipes of his tail churns the water into a million bursting bubbles. Each sideways thrust of his tail sends him rocketing forward at a greater speed, until the tailbeats are like the roll of a drum and off he charges across the ocean like a gone-wild torpedo.

Even when finally brought boat-side, a wahoo can think up schemes to outwit the angler, and may move his fight to the bow of the boat, so that the angler has to leave the fighting chair and conduct his battle up forward; and it may take the combined efforts of mate and captain to gaff the fish.

Because of the size of the wahoo and the precision timing of the peak runs, Bermuda waters offer great world-record potential for competitive-minded anglers. On May 19, 1957, Pete Perinchief and I went out with Harry Dunkley on his private boat, the *Barracuda*, with Buck Stubbs at the controls. On board with us was cameraman Jerry Hollis, because the trip was planned primarily to get some action shots for a movie on Bermuda fishing.

Off the northeast breaker-light we saw five or six boats trolling in close formation. As we came up to them we saw that one boat was fighting a fish, the angler bending forward, pulling up and back as he tried to pump the fish surfacewards. Ship-to-ship radio talks told us that it was a good wahoo and had been fighting back for 20 minutes—but it was the only fish hooked that morning.

We trolled on, feeling disconsolately that we were probably going to get no fish and therefore no pictures. We passed Charlie Christensen on the *Troubador* and Roy Taylor on the *Wally III*. Roy raised his arm in a lazy salute, and just as lazily I waved back. Then a terrific commotion at the skipping bait back of our boat brought me suddenly to life. The line was yanked out of the outrigger as if by some giant fist. I grabbed the rod in both hands, watched the line slam forward and come tight between the rod and the fish. The rod tip bowed down, and then I struck, a good firm, upward flip of the rod. The hook went home.

Then we saw him, a long, bullet-like shape running on top of the waves it seemed, his long body bridging the hollows between the crests, a great wahoo that slammed off so fast, back and dorsal out, that he seemed to be swimming on spindrift. I clenched my teeth, praying that the terminal tackle was in good order. I knew that everything would have to be right to stay with this barred ocean speed demon. He was a big fish, and the 10-pound-test line I was using seemed like a spider strand when I thought of it now.

That fish ran 600 feet in 2½ seconds. It was unbelievable. It was fantastic. Line just up and evaporated from the reel spool; and as I looked at the diminishing supply I wondered if he would ever stop, or if he would clean me and keep right on going, towing all that line behind him, away out there in the ocean.

Then abruptly the tempo changed. He dove deep, 600 feet out, and slowed, then stopped. I reeled so fast that line came back on the reel almost as fast as it had melted off. This was the danger spot, when he stopped like that. It would give him a chance to wag and shake his great head and maybe throw the hook. But the fast retrieve saved the day, and I weathered that tight spot and kept on reeling fast as he swam back our way, off to the right, coming fast now. But as he surfaced 100 feet off, he must have seen us; and he didn't like our looks because once again he tore off, 500 feet this time, a half second slower than the first run, maybe, this time slanting to the left and racing along just under the surface.

Again he sounded, going down 300 feet this time and aiming that dive back at us instead of away. Down he went. Closer he came, and now the line went down right under the boat. But there he stopped and I began to pump. I pumped for ten minutes and moved him a little, and fortunately he moved away from us again. He came up only 50 feet out from us, took a breath and dived again. This time I thought he would never stop. Down and down he went. Line once again melted from the reel and I hoped we were over the 1,000-fathom deep, so he wouldn't hit the bottom and cut himself off.

Finally he stopped and I pumped some more. He began to come up, faster. But he put on the brakes and hung there, half way up, and no matter how hard I worked I only gained on him by inches. I'd get a foot ahead of him and then he would take two feet. It was a see-saw affair with the fish on the heavy end.

But tackle told, and finally I got him coming topside.

"Get the gaff, Pete!" I yelled. "He's coming fast."

The line was coming in fast now, and I was reeling hard to keep a tight line. Then I could see the fish, the great length of his body, as he surfaced 15 feet away from the boat, his back out, hardly a flap left in his fins. Pete moved in, gaff ready. I reeled some more, until the leader came to the rod tip.

Pete reached up, grabbed the leader and pulled in. Then the gaff went down and was home, and Pete lifted the wahoo aboard.

"I got it!" yelled Pete, meaning the fish.

"I got it, too!" yelled Jerry Hollis, meaning the picture. "A good shot. A beautiful shot."

"He's a big fish on 10-pound line," said Harry. "We'll weigh him at the dock. He might be a record."

At the dock that wahoo tipped the scales at 55 pounds 8 ounces, a potential world record in the 12-pound-test line class of the International Game Fish Association, beating the 49-pound wahoo caught by Mrs. George Bass at Walker Cay, Bahamas, in 1954.

As we stood around waiting for Jerry to set up his camera for more pictures, Charlie Christensen brought his *Troubador* in to the dock and Nancy Conyers stepped off. Captain Christensen leaned down and picked up a wahoo that looked almost a twin to mine. He put in on the scale.

"54 pounds," he said to Mrs. Conyers. "You've missed the women's 20-pound test line class world record by a pound. Never mind," he added. "There'll be plenty more fishing days. And there'll be plenty more wahoo, too, you can bet. They're out there just waiting to be caught."

Bonefish Bonanza

A voyage of discovery to the Isle of Pines, Cuba—Robert Louis Stevenson's "Treasure Island."

"Bonefish," I said. "Bonefish."

I imitated the swishing noise of a jet plane going by, then waggled my fingers, trying to make like a bonefish tailing.

"No comprendo," Obilio, the taxi driver, said.

"Like a comet! Agua! Bubbles!" chimed in Vic, and he and Jean joined me in producing a hullabaloo of noises and hand wiggles designed to suggest a bonefish taking off across a flat.

"Momento!" exclaimed Obilio as he dove into the pocket of his shirt, produced a stubby pencil, and then with deft fingers lifted the envelope containing my plane ticket from my own pocket and handed the two to me. No further words were necessary. Quickly I drew a rough sketch of a bonefish and shoved it in front of Obilio.

"Ah! Ah-ha!" he exclaimed in a tone of great discovery. "Macabi! Si, si! Macabi!" He spread his arms to embrace the whole island in a magnanimous gesture. "Mucho macabi!"

Vic Barothy, well-known Florida Keys resort operator, Jean Crooks, veteran Miami fly caster, and I had just landed in the land of the Latins, flying in from Key West to Havana and then hopping southward again via Aerovias "Q" to Cuba's picturesque little Isle of Pines, believed by many to be the inspiration for Stevenson's "Treasure Island." We had been hearing rumors about great numbers of bonefish in Cuban waters and we wanted to check these reports.

Obilio had met us at the airport, as if by appointment, gravely handing us a card which stated "English spoken." And without further ado he escorted us to his taxi cab which stood waiting on the very doorstep of the airport office.

Obilio's taxi, a Model A Ford, painted a bright yellow, was quickly christened "The Yellow Peril," but it was the best available method of getting around. From our headquarters at the Isle of Pines Hotel, at Nueva Gerona, we went with Obilio to many parts of the island during our stay and discovered beaches where probably no one but ourselves had ever fished.

Our first trip was to the west coast of the island, a 25-mile ride through rolling country, with views of the 1,500-foot mountains which are the outstanding scenic feature. Along the roads grew the tallest Royal Palms I have ever seen. In addition there was stand after stand of bottle palms, from the swollen midsection of which dugout canoes were often made. All the way across to our fishing grounds we saw paired quail and white crowned pigeons and doves galore.

At last we came out on a long, sandy bay that looked plenty fishy. The three of us hit the beach simultaneously, almost before the Yellow Peril had settled its shakes. We broke all records getting our fly tackle together. Vic headed up the beach to the right, I hustled down to the left, and Jean went straight out from where we had stopped. Before I had gone a hundred feet I heard Jean shout. I turned and saw his rod bent almost double. Probably the first Isle of Pines bonefish ever to swat a fly was racing for the deep.

"Macabi!" shouted Jean.

"Macabi!" I yelled back.

And from far down the beach, like an echo, we heard Vic's cry, "Macabi!"

On the running board of the Yellow Peril, Obilio stood with one hand fondly placed on the yellow hood, and the other, palm up, as if conferring a blessing.

"Ha!" he said. "Macabi! Mucho, mucho macabi!"

In the course of my fishing days I've seen lots of bonefish. On the Florida Keys I've seen a thousand of them on one bank at one time. Schools of a hundred are not an every day sight, but certainly not unusual. That one day on the Isle of Pines, however, I saw more bonefish than I had ever seen in a week's time before. They were everywhere. Singles, doubles, quartettes, schools of twenty, fifty, a hundred and more went by in formation. One great mass of them that passed me must had held 500 fish in its ranks.

Where I had started to fish, the bottom was sandy and you could see fish for a long way. The sun was at my back and the first thing that caught my eye was a huge, shadowy blotch on the bottom. It seemed to be moving slowly my way and for a moment I thought that it must be a manatee or a great manta ray. I adjusted my Polaroid glasses and looked again. And then I realized that it was a tremendous school of bonefish. So I didn't take to the woods and climb the nearest tree. Instead I dropped a fly right in front of the oncoming horde.

A dozen fish saw that fly and all of them wanted it. They bumped into each other going for it. I struck as I felt one connect, and I was fast to my first Cuban macabi. That Spanish version of the fish that makes like a comet acted as if he didn't know he was hooked. He stayed right with the school and the school kept coming straight at me.

I stood there frozen for a minute. Then I came to, tightened up enough to let him know that everything was not as serene as he seemed to think. The feel of that hook turned him wild. He started off for the deep, striking other fish in the school, spreading panic as he went, until at last the whole kit and kaboodle of them was racing for the deep, throwing water high and charging across that flat like a herd of wild horses.

I managed to extract my fish from that surging, sea-going school and finally brought him in. He looked to weigh about four pounds as I took the hook out of the corner of his mouth and put him back in the water.

As I turned and looked down the flat again, I spotted more fish coming, several tails already flashing in the sun. Then, off by itself I saw a big, dark shape, a hundred feet away, slowly moving in my direction. It looked longer than a bonefish should, but at that distance I couldn't be sure. I strained my eyes in their sockets and edged a couple of steps closer. The fish turned broadside and I was pretty sure it was a permit. But suddenly he swam my way, nosing the bottom and sending up little puffs of mud as he searched for prey in the sand and grass.

"Smokin'!" I said aloud. "A-smokin' and a-puffin'—not a permit but a really big bonefish! Maybe the biggest macabi on the whole Isle of Pines, and I'm the guy that's going to trade punches with him."

But then I lost him again and though I popped my eyes out, I couldn't locate him. And just as I was about ready to give up and forget him, that macabi stood on his head twenty feet in front of me, did a hula with his caudal and like to scared me out of my boots. Somehow I got a fly I front of him, saw him charge. I set the hook and held the rod high as he steamed out of there, heading for the rim of keys five miles off shore. After about 200 feet he broke his headlong sprint and slanted down the shoreline as if to dash himself to pieces on the rocks. But he didn't do that. Instead, he cut the 8-pound test tippet on something sharp and the slack line let my rod snap back into shape.

"Hasta la vista!" I shouted after him, and I was very sincere in that parting wish.

The next day we left from the Jucaro River in a skiff powered by an outboard which we had toted all the way from Key West. We went two miles downstream until we came to the ocean. Here, on the east side of the island we found somewhat deeper water, but at high tide the fish seemed to be in and we could spot them as they cruised across sandy patches.

When the tide ebbed, we decided to drop Jean on a half mile stretch of sandy shoreline while Vic and I went farther down the beach to similar spots. At my appointed place, the sand reached out 150 feet from the shore and the water deepened gradually until it was about knee deep at the outside edge of the bar.

I slipped into ankle-depth water and looked for tailers. And it didn't take long to spot a regular procession of them, going in a circle, tails a-wagging, feeding avidly. I had on a small white bucktail, tied on a number 2 hook. On the whole, these macabi seemed small and having found that they were hitting short on the longer streamers, I turned to the smallest fly I had. I cast to the tailers only forty feet away and so intent were they that I pulled my fly back without them seeing it. My next cast dropped in the middle of the circle and this time they all seemed to see it at once. Out of the wild scramble, one got there first and gobbled it up entirely. I set the hook and watched the sand fly as the whole school followed the hooked fish.

He headed right down the middle of the sandy patch, flushing bonefish right and left, then doubled back a way, slashed off toward the deep, and dropped the hook. By the time I reached the end of that sandy patch, I had landed and released six bonefish and lost five. A total of eleven fish hooked in a half mile stretch and in an hour of fishing is worth going a long way for. And it is not unusual on the Isle of Pines.

As I neared the end of my sandy spot I noticed Vic standing off a point ahead of me so I scrambled ashore and walked on down. He was fighting a fish, and released it as I watched him.

"It's been like this ever since I got here," he shouted at me. "I just stand here on this spot and wait for them to come to me. Boy, what fishing!"

That afternoon was like all the rest of the trip. Bonefish were everywhere and we had strikes and fights most of the time. The third day was the same. Once again we fished out of the Jucaro, but this time we headed north when we reached the ocean, and as before we left the boat at strategic points, fished out a stretch of beach, then gathered together at lunch time to swap experiences. When we figured it out, we found that the first day the three of us had landed 31 bonefish up to six pounds and had lost almost as many. The second day we had almost matched that and the third was just as good.

It was almost dark when we headed into the dock that third day, but when we saw tarpon rolling on the other side of the river, we couldn't resist them. Vic steered that way and cut the motors. Jean started casting. He was using only an 8-pound-test leader and those rolling silver kings, called "sabalo" here, looked to be hundred pound fish, but even so, when one rolled up right in front of the boat, Jean dropped his fly practically in its mouth. It hit, and came roaring up, 35 pounds of silver dynamite, and for half an hour fought like mad. Then it tired and Jean brought the tarpon to boat and Vic grasped the leader and took the fly out. We watched the tarpon swim away.

"Sabalo too!" mused Jean, running his fingers along the leader where the tarpon's gill covers had roughed it. "Sabalo and macabi both . . . !"

As we headed in, we heard a soft, inquisitive chattering coming out of the dusk. We looked up and sweeping across the mangroves came a flight of tree ducks. They flew off into the darkness across the river, their piping and whistling fading off to a whisper. Night had fallen and it was good to be alive under Cuban stars.

When we pulled up to the dock, Obilio was waiting.

"Macabi?" he asked anxiously.

"Macabi," we nodded. "Mucho, mucho macabi!"

Afterword: Trout in the Sky

Having gone as far as we could, laterally, in Montana, we decided to try "up."

It was six a.m. and we were sitting in a restaurant at Silver Gate, Montana, 7000 feet high on the Red Lodge Pass. A moose and her calf were ambling down the main street. Our pack string was tied across the road at Elmer Larson's Switchback Lodge, and in the still morning air we could hear the horses restlessly stamping their feet, occasionally neighing. Moose and calf paid no attention, wandered on and disappeared behind a log cabin. From across the road, Johnny Linderman signalled us that he was ready to go.

There were just the three outfitters, Elmer Larsen, Gene Wade, and Johnny Linderman, and five of us dudes—Grace and Walt Weber, Bill Browning, and myself and wife. Walt was after pictures and sketches of alpine wildlife; Bill was after pictures, and I was just there for the fishing, to get some of those big brookies that were rumored to reside in well-named Aero Lake.

"Elmer and I have seen them in there up to five pounds," said Gene. "The best looking fish I've ever caught, fat and bright and full of pep."

"I've never been in to Aero Lake before," said Johnny. "But I have been over it. I helped stock it from an airplane, back in 1937. I've been as far as timberline on horseback since, but never up those last 2000 feet. But this string can make it," he added.

We looked at the horses with a mixture of dread and confidence. We knew that a Linderman, member of one of America's best known cowboy families, would produce a good string of horses. What we didn't know was our own ability to stay on a good horse on such a ride as we were about to start.

It was a lung-busting climb. Aero Lake lies 11,500 feet high in the remote Upper Beartooth Range of Southern Montana. Twenty-five miles south as the crow flies, we could often spot Pilot and Index Peaks, famous landmarks for every traveller through this Montana-Wyoming border country. And about the same distance to our north the Grasshopper Glacier put a nip in the wind that could still be felt even at this distance. Close to Grasshopper was Granite peak, the highest point in Montana, rising 12,850 feet into the sky.

The first part of the ride was through foothill country, if it can be called foothill when you are working up from 7000 to 8000 feet. But that was what the horses apparently considered it, and an old wagon road provided a good trail, so we ambled right along. But at 9000 feet the trail petered out into a narrow path through lodge pole pine. Almost at the same minute the temperature seemed to drop. We put on leather jackets over wool sweaters, donned gloves, and then really began to climb. We worked up through the timber on switchback trails, crossing sudden glades where there were deer and elk sign, and spooky clumps of pine where the horses shied at the scent of bear. Then suddenly we were out above the timber line and riding through shale and jagged rock that kept both horse and rider tense. It was practically straight up climbing, with the horses digging in with all fours and the riders hanging on the same way. We found out what saddle horns were for.

At last we came to what looked like a perpendicular wall, only a few chipped rocks showing where at some time a horse had gone up there, scrambling and plunging.

"Get a good grip and hang on," said Elmer. "This is pretty steep."

That was the understatement of the day. Even though the climb was short to the ledge we could see above us, it was the longest, hardest part of the trip. The grade was so steep that a horse could only make a couple of plunging steps before he had to stop to breathe and brace himself for the next lunge. Every movement sent sparks flying as iron-clad hooves scraped the rock. Only the fact that I had heard about the law of gravity convinced me that we were not actually climbing on an outward incline.

But at last, one by one, our horses scrambled over the top, and onto a narrow ledge which ran along the side of the mountain. We dismounted and threw ourselves down to rest, as winded from that rocky ride as if we had climbed every step of the way on foot.

Above us rose a gigantic mass of rock, forming a ragged skyline.

"The lake lies behind that," said Gene.

"We're on foot from here," said John Linderman. "Horses can't get over that divide."

He spoke with the heartfelt sadness of the cowboy who has no use for walking. As we looked up to the divide, we shared his sadness. From here there was not even a hint of a path, only great, rounded boulders that must have been piled there by some ancient glacier. It might be duck soup to a mountain goat, but it was no place for a tenderfoot.

"John will take the horses back down to pasture," said Elmer. "The rest of us will each pack what we can over the divide."

"Take a light load," instructed Gene. "Don't forget, you're at 11,000 feet right now, and carrying will be tough."

Gene and Elmer each heaved a deflated rubber boat on their shoulders while the rest of us picked up loads from the welter of sleeping bags, air mattresses, cooking gear, and fishing tackle that Johnny was unloading from the pack horses.

Elmer looked at what we had chosen and grinned.

"Take about half that much," he advised.

Then he and Gene started away, climbing slowly but steadily. We followed but within seconds were puffing and blowing, discarding part of our loads and finally collapsing on the boulders every two minutes to get our wind again. Elmer and Gene passed us on their way back for a second load before we had even reached the summit. They were beside us again with their second pack when we came over the top.

"Right pretty, isn't it?" said Elmer, as we stood spellbound.

Before us lay Aero lake, a glittering gem of blue set in the midst of one of the bleakest Arctic scenes I have every seen. The lake was almost circular, with two long arms running off into the distance and two little islands half way across. They had told us we would camp on the far island, and now we saw why. The mainland on which we stood was a solid mass of boulders, similar to the pass which we had just traversed. There was not a single square foot of land anywhere in which to sink a tent peg, just rocks, rocks, some as big as houses. Here and there the remains of a glacier running down to the shore afforded the easiest means of approach to the lake. All around us jagged peaks rose to poke at the sky, all bare and brown, without any vegetation at all, while lower down on our own level were only a few dwarfed bushes. It was as desolate as tundra country, bleak and forbidding, but lovely.

We stepped out onto the nearest snow field, following Elmer's and Gene's tracks toward the shore.

Suddenly Walt stopped and pointed down. I looked.

"Hey, Elmer!" I yelled. "What's this? The snow is bleeding!"

Elmer came back to see what we meant. Everywhere he and Gene had stepped, the snow glowed red in their foot prints. "Insects," he said. "Thousands of tiny insects that live in the snow and only show up when you step where they are."

"They certainly must be small," I said.

"Look at those stunted cedars and willows," he replied. "And the only animals you'll see are the cony and a small ground squirrel. Everything is undersize up here."

"Everything but the fish," he added. "You don't need to worry about them being undersized."

In the lake, which lay 25 feet below us, the water was so clear that you could have seen a penny on the bottom. The rocks shelved out quickly to a drop-off with here and there wide ledges running out just under the surface, ideal hiding spots for trout.

"You go ahead and fish," said Elmer. "We'll set up camp on the island and then pick you up wherever you are along the shore."

Walt started around the lake to the right, while I went to the left. It was rough going, a constant scramble over boulders, and once I had to circle a 200 foot snow bank which dropped off sheer into the water like the edge of a glacier. I was afraid to try to cross it for fear it would crumble away beneath me and I would be plunged into water so icy that a man couldn't last in it for five minutes.

The fishing was rough, too, and though I tried streamers, bucktails, nymphs, wet flies, and dry flies, I didn't raise the first fish. By late afternoon I was better than a mile away from the pass, on the far shore of the lake. And there, at last, in a long, narrow bay marking the inlet of a small stream that splashed down from Upper Aero Lake, still higher above us, I found the fish.

I was working my way over the high cliff along the inlet when I looked down and there they were, several good sized trout feeding along the drop-off, turning as they fed, so that their bodies flashed silver and red.

I was too high above them to fish from the cliff but further along I spotted a four foot wide ledge just three feet above the water, and somehow I scrambled down to that.

I dropped a black ant near those fish and it hadn't sunk three inches before there was a flash and the line and leader jumped forward. I lifted the rod tip and watched it bend down as that husky trout hit and headed out. When he stopped, he began to wag his head from side to side and I couldn't budge him with the light leader I was using. I just stood there, holding my own and watching the beautiful red glow that shone all around him in the water.

"He's a big one," I thought. "And a beautiful one. He gives out like a Christmas tree light."

He kept rocking the rod for a while, then switched back down the inlet and scared me when it appeared that he would go under a rock and cut me off. Then he headed out again, and pretty soon I had him coming my way. When I finally did land him, he was the deepest, fattest, prettiest Eastern Brook trout I have every seen, a bit over two pounds.

A few minutes later I had two more just like him and an almost equally beautiful pair of cutthroats that went about two and one-half pounds apiece. Their sides were crimson, and their bellies too, with a liberal sprinkling of big black spots, light towards the front, and heavy towards the tail.

Just as I got my knife out to clean the fish Walt came up behind me.

"I didn't raise a thing around the other shore," he said. "I tried everything in the book, too. I even dug around in the water to see what they might be feeding on, but couldn't find a thing."

Then he saw the fish.

"Where'd you get them?" he asked.

"Right here," I answered.

Walt grabbed the knife out of my hand.

"Let me clean them," he said. "I want to see what's in them."

He kneeled at the water's edge and slit up the belly of a brookie and laid the flesh back. It was deep red, darker than salmon.

"Did you ever see such beautiful messenaries?" said Walt with awe in his voice.

I looked around hurriedly. Nothing unusual appeared near us or on the horizon.

"Where?" I asked. "What?"

"The messenaries," said Walt, ever the scientist, pointing with his knife tip. "Those magenta colored sacs, there."

He meant the cellophane-like case which contained the guts of the fish.

"The fish with the beautiful guts," I grinned. "First time I ever heard anyone call a fish's guts beautiful."

Walt, meantime, had slit the stomach sac and now he came up with a mess of black, spotted here and there with what looked like bits of red pepper. He held the mass in his cupped hands and put them into the water. The mass separated into small pieces, some black, some red.

"It's like Elmer told us," Walt said. "Everything is on the small scale up here. Those are daphnia—water fleas. The red ones are some kind of tiny fresh water shrimp that I've never seen before. I'll send a few in to the lab and find out what they are."

Next he pried open the mouth of the fish and we both peered in. A sprinkling of small black dots adhered to the roof, and a few showed in the gills.

"That must be the way they feed," said Walt. "They get into a school of those little fleas and swim through with their mouths open. They're too small to take individually."

He took out his pocket handkerchief and wrapped the wet mass of fleas and shrimp he had collected and stuck it in his pocket.

"Well, let's go feed them something larger," I suggested, and we both grabbed our rods and started off.

But though we fished for another half hour, we didn't find any more fish. Then Gene showed up in one of the rubber boats and we started back to the island, picking Bill up en route, from further along the shore.

"I've got two in the ice box," he said, pointing to the snow bank behind him.

There in the gleaming snow he had carved out the words HIGH LAKE TROUT, and close by lay two nice trout, a native and a brookie. We had fish for dinner and besides being the most beautiful fish we had ever seen, they were the best eating.

The next day was a terrible letdown. We fished the whole morning without a strike. We fished from boats and from shore. We went out to the reefs that showed here and there beneath the clear water. But not the first strike and never a sign of a fish. Gene and Elmer were shaking their heads gloomily.

"There's weather coming," suggested Elmer. "That will put high altitude fish down."

But the sky was clear and bright, the lake placid. And there were no fish. By three o'clock we were all spread along the arm of the cove where I had taken those few trout on the previous afternoon. The two rubber boats were pulled up on the shore, one in the cove, the other at the mouth of the cove. We were all fishing from shore, trying, but our hearts were not in it.

And suddenly Elmer's weather prophecy came all too true. We heard a far off, rushing sound, and instantaneously the lake began to build up waves, big ones, like breakers on the sea. Before we could get back to the boats a blast of wind roared down on us loaded with the chill of the Grasshopper Glacier, 25 miles to the north. It created havoc.

Grace Weber was only a few feet from the edge of the cliff on one side of the cove. I saw her sway in the wind and grabbed her just in time. Hanging on to each other, we managed to withstand the buffeting of that mighty blast. Across the cove we saw Mary throw herself down on the ground for safety. Then everyone was looking up.

A big yellow boat was soaring over our heads, fifty feet high, closely followed by a cowboy hat. It was seconds before it dawned on us that it was one of our lifeboats. Everyone started to run, forgetting wind, forgetting altitude and rough terrain.

We staggered over the rim of a little dip in time to see the lifeboat crash to the ground and grind into tatters on three big jagged rocks. The cowboy hat floated down beside it, in the now dying wind.

Bill Browning came puffing up.

"My hat," he said inanely, picking it up and jamming it on his head. "I tried to hold it—the boat, I mean. But I couldn't. The wind lifted it right out of the water and carried it away."

"The other boat!" Gene and Elmer both yelled at once.

We all had the same thought. If the other boat was done for, too, we were stranded here, in bleak, forbidding country, without food or extra clothing. All our supplies were on the island, with half a mile of ice cold water between.

Just then we spotted the second boat. Floating down the inlet toward us. One oar still in it, the other floating a few yards away. The onshore wind was driving it towards us. We all rushed down to meet it.

It, too, had several bad gashes, but at least it was still afloat. Elmer looked it over carefully.

"That just about fixes our trip," he said. "We have eight people, we're camped on an island, and we have one badly damaged five man boat. We'll have to try to patch it and start ferrying back to the island, two or three at a time. We'll break camp first thing in the morning and ferry over to the pass the same way. It means cutting the trip two days short, but there's no other way to do it. You can't take risks in this kind of country."

He started to work on the boat, then took a look at our glum faces.

"You might as well fish while you can," he said. "I'll take the women back to camp first, then pick you up on the second trip."

We didn't need any further invitation.

"I have an idea that storm may have wakened the fish up," said Walt.

And how right he was. Fish were everywhere. We had hits right and left. We caught them spinning and fly fishing, on streamers, ants, nymphs, spoons, and jig type lures. They liked everything. We caught plenty of 2-pounders, a few 3-pounders, and a couple of 4-pounders. We kept six for dinner and threw the rest back with the admonition to grow even bigger. They were still hitting hard when Elmer came back for us to take us to camp.

"I shouldn't take the time," he said. "That boat is in pretty tough shape and I want to get us out of here. But I just have to catch me one of those beauties."

He grabbed Bill's rod and made a cast and in minutes had landed as bright and beautiful a brookie as I've ever seen.

"One more," he said. "One for the road. Let me try one on a fly, Joe."

I gave him my outfit, and he made a couple of nice casts. Suddenly the big one we'd all been hoping for socked that fly. We all saw him flash up and hit, illuminating the water around him with his brilliant color. He busted that leader point like it had been a cobweb. He was a good 6 pounds.

"Well," said Elmer, trying to look unconcerned. "I knew there were some big ones in here."

"It'll give me something to come back for," he said, quite a few minutes later, as he rowed us back to the island.

And we all agreed, "Me, too."

SOURCES

"Preface" appeared in *The Complete Book of Fly Fishing,*
   Outdoor Life, 1958.

"The Trout We Fish For" appeared in *Trout Fishing, Revised
   Edition,* Outdoor Life Books, 1972.

"Dry Fly Fishing for Trout" appeared in *The Complete Book of
   Fly Fishing.*

"Terrestrials" appeared in *The Complete Book of Fly Fishing.*

"Fishing the Wet Fly" appeared in *The Complete Book of Fly
   Fishing.*

"Nymph Fishing" appeared in *Trout Fishing, Revised Edition.*

"Fishing Streamers & Bucktails for Trout" appeared in *The
   Complete Book of Fly Fishing.*

"Landing Bass on the Fly" appeared in *The Complete Book of
   Fly Fishing.*

"Boca Fever" appeared in *Greatest Fishing,* The Stackpole
   Company, 1957.

"Argentina" appeared in *A World of Fishing,* D. Van Nostrand
   Company, 1964.

"New Zealand" appeared in *A World of Fishing.*

"Scotland" appeared in *A World of Fishing.*

"Iceland" appeared in *A World of Fishing.*

"Tumble Rocks!" appeared in *Greatest Fishing.*

"Add a Little Salt" appeared in *Greatest Fishing.*

"Northern Lights Fish" appeared in *Greatest Fishing.*

Sources

"Montana" appeared in *Complete Guide to Fishing Across North America,* Outdoor Life, Harper & Row, 1966.

"Inshore Saltwater Fly Fishing" appeared in *The Complete Book of Fly Fishing.*

"Chumming and Offshore Fly Fishing" appeared in *The Complete Book of Fly Fishing.*

"Salty Grab Bag" appeared in *Greatest Fishing.*

"Panama" appeared in *A World of Fishing.*

"Those Freedom-Loving Sickletails" appeared in *Greatest Fishing.*

"The Bahamas" appeared in *A World of Fishing.*

"British Honduras" appeared in *A World of Fishing.*

"Mexico" appeared in *A World of Fishing.*

"The Angler in Action" appeared in *Bermuda Fishing,* The Stackpole Company, 1957.

"Bonefish Bonanza" appeared in *Greatest Fishing.*

"Trout in the Sky" appeared in *Greatest Fishing.*

799.12   Brooks, Joe
B
         Joe Brooks on fishing

	DATE DUE	

12-04